Cinéma Divinité

Cinéma Divinité

Religion, Theology and the Bible in Film

Edited by
Eric S. Christianson,
Peter Francis
and
William R. Telford

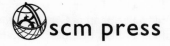

scm press

© Eric S. Christianson, Peter Francis and William R. Telford 2005

British Library Cataloguing in Publication data

A catalogue record for this book is available
from the British Library

0 334 02988 0

First published in 2005 by SCM Press
9–17 St Albans Place, London N1 0NX

www.scm-canterburypress.co.uk

SCM Press is a division of
SCM-Canterbury Press Ltd

Typeset by Regent Typesetting
Printed and bound in Great Britain by
William Clowes Ltd, Beccles, Suffolk

Contents

For Andrena, Helen and Sonya

Preface

The Context

The chapters of this book were originally lectures delivered at the annual colloquium on film and theology (1998–2004) held at St Deiniol's Library in Hawarden near the cathedral city of Chester. St Deiniol's Library is a unique theological resource. It was founded by William Ewart Gladstone 'for the pursuit of divine learning' and is Britain's only Prime Ministerial Library. Its renowned collection of 250,000 books is housed in a Grade 1 listed building.

Gladstone was a devout Anglican throughout his life and he set up his library to help keep theology in dialogue with other intellectual currents. He feared that the growing tide of secularism would push his beloved Anglicanism into a sect, cut off from the woof and warp of contemporary intellectual debate. Dialogue between academic disciplines had always been important to Gladstone. From boyhood he had prized Dante, Aristotle, Homer, Augustine and Butler over and above the four Gospels. These authors (his favourites) together with great works of literature, the movements of history and the beauty of mathematics were for him repositories of truth just as surely as Scripture.

> The negative movement of the age aims at establishing a severance between the Christian system and the general thought of the time; . . . but no enlightened Christian will ever admit that our Christianity was intended to be an isolated thing standing apart from all other conditions of our life . . . we assert the right for the Gospel to associate with every just influence over the whole sphere of our nature and its functions.[1]

It is, therefore, completely in keeping with Gladstone's vision for St Deiniol's that religion and theology should be in dialogue with film especially as film has become such a popular and potent force in contemporary Western culture.

1. The Importance of Film

Cinema-going is increasing in the UK with 78% of the population going to the cinema at least once a year. Statistics tell us that 25% of the population go to the cinema at least once a month (up from 5% in 1984), while 46% of Generation 'X' go to the cinema at least once a month (only 10% in 1984). The proportion of children going to the cinema once a month has risen from 10% in 1984 to 37% in 1999 and the percentage of older people has also increased from 1% to 12%.[2] If you add to this the 90 million DVDs purchased in 2002 (only 4.1 million in 1999) and the 79 million videos purchased, not to mention the 57 million DVD rentals and 119 million video rentals in 2002 – it is possible to see the renewed pervasive power of film in the UK.[3]

Popular film provides Generation 'X',[4] and even baby boomers, with shared common texts and myths. These are the things we talk about over drinks and meals. The value of film to theology is that it helps the process of inculturation and of contextualization of a now largely pagan Western world.

Film enables theology, as Clive Marsh has pointed out, 'to work out what it is going to be possible to say in our contemporary climate about any of theology's major themes'.[5] It also gives a strong indication of how it can be said, and of the values and assumptions that it must engage with. Film provides a language and images that can enable theology to be expressed in a way that is readily understandable in today's cultural climate.

2. The St Deiniol's Colloquia

If that gives the official *raison d'être* of the colloquia and this volume, there remains a more accurate, less worthy, genesis to the process. Frankly, the colloquia were instigated because we liked watching films. The idea for the first colloquium was mooted at the book launch for *Explorations in Film and Theology* during the 1998 Leeds Film Festival. The colloquia, lectures and subsequently this volume are an attempt to build upon the work of that volume.

Since its inception in 1998, interest in the annual colloquium has pleasantly taken the organizers by surprise (each has been 'sold out' with long waiting lists). Over 250 people have now attended the colloquia in which film buffs, clergy, laity, academics and students (not all categories are exclusive) have felt a keen desire to reflect on the various relationships emerging between religion, theology, the Bible and film.

3. Religion, Theology and The Bible in Film

The title of this volume accurately reflects not only the content but also the make-up and interests of those who attended the colloquia as well as the perspectives and expertise of the contributors. Together the contributors embrace the academic disciplines of religious studies, Christian theology, biblical studies and film studies/film criticism. Because we come from different backgrounds and disciplines, it is inevitable that we offer an array of critical approaches to the study of film such as formalism, expressionism, realism, textual analysis, contextual analysis, postmodern eclecticism, narrative criticism and cultural studies.

The various relationships between religion, theology, Bible and film represent a growing area of study and academic interest. Film is a potent force in Western culture and cannot be dismissed as mere entertainment or as being popular (as opposed to high-brow) culture. Margaret Miles rightly comments that 'popular film provides an index of the anxieties and longings of a large audience'[6] and as such it compels our attention and serious study.

4. Acknowledgements

The editors wish to thank the staff of St Deiniol's Library for hosting seven excellent colloquia. All the contributors would like to thank the participants in the colloquia for their enthusiasm about film and the insights they offered on these lectures, all of which has helped to shape these pages. We would especially like to thank Patsy Williams, the St Deiniol's Librarian, for carefully building an excellent collection of literature on the subject. We thank Kate Sury for deciphering and typing the transcript of *The Passion of The Christ* discussion, Victor Morales for his work on the bibliography and Jo Wilkinson for her work on the indexes. Barbara Laing of SCM Press has been a patient, tolerant and perceptive editor. We only hope that you enjoy the book as much as we have enjoyed writing the lectures, attending the colloquia, and, above all, watching the films.

Eric S. Christianson
Peter Francis
William R. Telford

Notes

1 W. E. Gladstone, Gladstone Private Papers, Undated Manuscript, Hawarden: St Deiniol's Library, 1893.

2 Peter Brierley (ed.), *UK Christian Handbook Religious Trends 3*, London: Christian Research, 2001, Part 2, p. 21.

3 Eddie Dyja (ed.), *BFI Film and Television Handbook 2004*, London: British Film Institute, 2003, pp. 52–7.

4 The age range 19–37 (the so-called Generation 'X') makes up 25% of the population (14.6 million out of a population of 59.2 million).

5 Clive Marsh and Gaye Ortiz (eds), *Explorations in Theology and Film*, Oxford: Blackwell, 1997, p. 32.

6 Margaret Miles, *Seeing and Believing*, Boston: Beacon Press, 1996, p. x.

The Contributors

George Aichele is Professor in the Department of Philosophy and Religion at Adrian College, Adrian, Michigan. As part of the Bible and Culture Collective, he was a co-writer of *The Postmodern Bible*. More recently he has written *The Control of Biblical Meaning: Canon as Semiotic Mechanism* and co-edited (with Richard Walsh) *Screening Scripture: Intertextual Connections Between Scripture and Film*.

Tom Aitken became a freelance writer in the early 1980s. Since that time he has contributed general articles and book and theatre reviews to numerous publications, including, among others, *The Times*, *The Times Literary Supplement*, *The Guardian*, *Lumen Vitae*, *The Charleston Magazine*, *The New Zealand Woman's Weekly* and *The Morning Star*. He must be one of relatively few writers to be (at different times) a regular contributor to *The War Cry* and *The Tablet*, of which he was cinema critic from 1994 to 2002. He has served on ecumenical and Catholic juries at film festivals in Berlin, Venice and Portugal.

Brian Baker is Senior Lecturer in Literature and Film in the English department of University College Chester. He currently has three books in the process of completion: with John Cartwright he has recently completed *Science and Literature* for ABC-Clio's 'Science and Society' series; he is writing a book-length study of the contemporary British novelist Iain Sinclair for the Manchester University Press's 'Contemporary British Novelists' series; and also completing a book-length project on screen masculinities, entitled *Masculinities in Fiction and Film: Representing men in popular genres 1945–2000*.

Eric S. Christianson is Senior Lecturer in Biblical Studies, University College Chester. Since publishing his *A Time to Tell: Narrative Strategies in Ecclesiastes* (Sheffield Academic Press) he has continued publishing on Ecclesiastes and is writing a commentary that focuses on the Bible's *Wirkungsgeschichte* (cultural 'impact history'). He teaches, researches and publishes in film and Bible, and reviews films for *Third Way* magazine. He is currently working on a monograph developing a rigorous comparative approach to Bible and film.

Peter Francis is Warden of St Deiniol's Library. He was ordained into the Anglican Church in 1978, his ministry has included rural and urban congregations, in addition he has been a chaplain at the University of London and Provost of St Mary's Cathedral, Glasgow. At St Deiniol's Library he has edited two collections of essays on Gladstone: *The Grand Old Man* and *The Gladstone Umbrella*, as well as a book of essays on rural ministry and theology, *Changing Rural Life*. He is currently writing a book on film, mission and ministry.

Jeffrey F. Keuss is Visiting Professor of Theology and Ethics at Seattle Pacific University, Fuller Theological Seminary and Northwest Graduate School. An ordained minister in the Presbyterian Church (USA) having served in churches both in the USA and Scotland, he currently teaches in the areas of theology and ethics, Christian spirituality and mysticism, and theology and contemporary culture. He has published articles and reviews on theology and contemporary culture and is a contributing editor to *Literature and Theology* (Oxford University Press) and *Reviews in Religion and Theology* (Blackwells). He is the author of *A Poetics of Jesus: The Search for Christ through Writing in the Nineteenth Century* and *The Sacred and the Profane: Contemporary Issues in Hermeneutics* (both with Ashgate Publishing).

Gerard Loughlin studied at both the University of Wales, Lampeter, and at Cambridge University, where he wrote his doctorate in philosophical theology. He is Senior Lecturer in Theology and Religion at the University of Durham. Gerard Loughlin is the author of *Telling God's Story: Bible, Church and Narrative Theology* and *Alien Sex: The Body and Desire in Cinema and Theology*, and editor of *Queer Theology: Rethinking the Western Body*.

Robert Pope is Senior Lecturer in Contemporary and Applied Theology in the University of Wales, Bangor. He is the author of *Building Jerusalem: Nonconformity, Labour and the Social Question in Wales, 1906–1939* and *Seeking God's Kingdom: the Nonconformist Social Gospel in Wales, 1906–1939.*

William R. Telford studied at the Universities of Edinburgh, Glasgow and Cambridge, as well as at Union Theological Seminary, New York. After a period of research and teaching at the University of Oxford, and a number of years as Senior Lecturer in Religious Studies (Christian Origins and the New Testament) at the University of Newcastle, he is currently Senior Lecturer in the Department of Theology and Religion at the University of Durham. His research interests include the historical Jesus, the canonical Gospels and especially the Gospel of Mark, methods of interpretation, and the Bible in literature and film, and he has published on these subjects in a number of books, journals and edited works. His books on the New Testament and the Gospel of Mark include *The Barren Temple and the Withered Tree*, (ed.) *The Interpretation of Mark*, *The Theology of the Gospel of Mark*, *The New Testament: A Short Introduction* and (with others) *The Synoptic Gospels*.

Melanie J. Wright is Academic Director at the Centre for the Study of Jewish–Christian Relations and a Member of the Faculty of Divinity, University of Cambridge. She is the author of *Moses in America: The Cultural Uses of Biblical Narrative* and *Understanding Judaism*, and is currently writing a book on religion and film.

Cinéma Divinité:
A Theological Introduction

GERARD LOUGHLIN

At the end of *Explorations in Theology and Film* (1997) – an earlier collection of essays on cinema and religion edited by Clive Marsh and Gaye
Ortiz – David Jasper offered a chastening reflection on the possibilities of
film for theology. While Jasper allowed that 'popular cinema' was not 'all
bad', he doubted that it could provide the means for a challenging and
liberatory theology, deconstructive of the West's self-righteousness and
healing of its spiritual malaise.[1] Hollywood is in the business of entertainment rather than edification. It favours cultural conformity rather than
critical analysis. Hollywood wants us to go on consuming its products,
and to believe in the benignity of the economic system that allows us to do
so. All will be well, and all manner of material consumption will be well,
in the best of all possible worlds, in the land of the free and its dominions.

While Jasper did not doubt that biblical stories and theological themes
can be found in modern cinema, and not least in its many 'Christ-figures',[2]
he questioned whether these allusions and resonances amounted to much
more than narrative traits, borrowings that both repeated and occluded
their prototypes, neutralizing the story of Christ through its secular repe-
titions. Jasper did admit that some film directors are theologically literate,
and come close to producing genuine and 'stimulating theological
reflection' in their films. But they are exceptions, and Jasper named only
Martin Scorsese.[3]

Jasper's analysis is accurate regarding much that Hollywood produces.
Most films, but especially the most popular and successful, demand little
more of their audiences than that they sit back and gawp at the spectacle,
while consuming the fruits of the concession stand. Audiences feast on
highly calorific but nutrionally null food. They are satiated with a void,
and so hunger again once the credits have finished rolling – but who waits
for the credits? Yet Jasper's brief discussion of Martin Scorsese reminds us
that Hollywood is not 'all bad', that it can produce fare that demands
more of its viewers than is at first apparent. Jasper is too quick and too
generalizing when he tells us that cinema, unlike theatre, is a 'solitary and
finally undemanding medium', 'effective in as much as, demanding nothing of the viewer, it seems to offer the viewer the power to understand

without the need seriously to think or change'.[4] It may be that before we ask more of film-makers and the systems within which they work, we should ask more of ourselves as viewers, demand more of the films we watch. For when we ask more, we may find that the films have more to give, that their writers and directors have given us more than we first think.

Jasper's complaint about cinema is not new. Andrei Tarkovsky – for one – distinguished between those who, like himself, strove to turn film into art, and those who produced mere entertainment. 'As soon as one begins to cater expressly for the auditorium, then we're talking of the entertainment industry, show business, the masses, or what have you, but certainly not of art which necessarily obeys its own immanent laws of development whether we like it or not.'[5] One might think that there is nothing much wrong with producing mere entertainment, unless one also thinks that entertainment can be ideology, the projection of a partial view as universal, and one that dulls the wits and turns viewers away from what they should be seeing: the spiritual emptiness of modern life and its possible redemption.

These, then, are the stakes for the encounter of theology with film. Can cinema be more than entertainment, more than ideology? Can it show us what we would rather not view but need to see, if we are to find grace in our lives; if we are to be saved? Theology is an old discipline, even if newly thought each day. It is answerable to both past and present communities, to deeds done – both lauded and repented – and still to do, and it treads a difficult path, having to continually renounce the pictures of God by which it tries to hide from the divine gaze. Film, on the other hand, is new; barely a hundred years old at the start of the twenty-first century, and changing rapidly, developing new technologies and languages, new modes of illumination. It too must answer to a community: of bankers and financiers; and only secondly to wider social concerns and traditions of artistic achievement and, on occasion, religious yearning. Theology on film – as a mode of academic discourse – is newer yet, but the interrelation of film and religion is as old as cinema can be, since religion took an interest in what cinema could show from the first, and from the first cinema was interested in showing religion.[6] Both are concerned with the showings of the other.

1. Dialoguing with Movies

While the interest of most film studies has been to think *about* film in its various aspects – aesthetic and technical, sociological and philosophical – the interest of theology is often presented as a wish to enter into a *dialogue* or *conversation* with film, as if theology hesitated to speak about its subject before its subject had first spoken. (Which is not to deny a proper hesitancy, a willingness to wait upon the other's speaking.) The 'preferred critical approach' to theology and film, as Terry Lindvall notes, is 'tidily labelled the dialogic'.[7] There is nothing very wrong with thinking that theology's interest in cinema should be framed as a kind of dialogue or conversation, akin to that long practised within theology – when honest – and between different religionists. Conversation is an oft-repeated figure for interdisciplinary discourse, and the dialogic is a venerable theological form, as most famously evidenced in Thomas Aquinas's *Summa Theologiæ*, with its questions, objections and responses. But except when discourses on theology and film are reports of actual conversations between film-makers and theologians, such dialogues are nearly always acts of ventriloquism, since film itself is a cultural product about which we may talk, but which is not itself a conversing partner.

It would be unusual for an art critic to seek conversation with an art work, a sculpture or painting, as it would be for the literary critic to enter into dialogue with a novel or poem, since the responses of the latter must be but further acts of the critical imagination, of the reader's discernment and discretion, or engagement with the readings of other critics. When theology or religious studies turn to consider film they must do so as responsible critics, who bring their own interests and critical tools to bear on the films they seek to illuminate with their own particular lights. Of course we may want to see this as the having of some kind of interchange, a mutual interrogation, since in asking we often receive an answer in the very form of our questioning, in being made to think what the other would say if it could but speak. But academic theology does not enter into some kind of interdisciplinary discourse with film, since film is not itself an academic discipline, but entertainment and possibly art, and possibly a venture upon the religious. Film is not conversational, but epiphanic.

The danger with thinking the relationship between theology and film properly dialogical is that we may be led to forget that theology, in all its conversations, is ultimately seeking to understand that which – in some sense – it is already given to know. It seeks to bring to light, for itself and its conversation partners, that by which it has already been encountered, and thereby given something to think and to say – to proclaim – as its own proper speaking. Theology can never really reduce or denigrate its conversation partners, since it must seek to understand them in the same light as it understands itself. But by the same token it cannot treat them disinterestedly or neutrally, but must seek in them – with them – for that truth which has already called theology forth. This is why theology can really only be undertaken in faith, in the communities and cultures of those who understand themselves to stand in relation to a transcendent source, and recognize and seek to understand such a relationship. Theology

undertaken otherwise – outside such a relationship – has no real object of
learning, and is a kind of vacuity. At best it is knowledge of discourses
about God, and so not theology but history of ideas.[8]

Since theology is 'faith seeking understanding', it is always first and
foremost a relationship of knowledge, since one cannot understand that
to which one is unrelated. In some sense one must already know what one
would seek to understand; and since that which theology knows and seeks
to understand is the mystery of the world – its infinite 'cause' – there is a
sense in which theology must seek to understand everything so as to better understand the source of all things.[9] And this limitless pursuit includes
the practice of cinema, the making and watching of films. The same can
hardly be said of other academic disciplines – such as film and religious
studies – except in so far as they recognize their participation in the
theological quest.

Unlike theology, religious studies has no proper object of study nor
methods of studying. It is now widely recognized that 'religion' – understood as a determinate thing, as a unified tradition of beliefs and practices
– is very much a conception of Western modernity, used first as a synonym
for Protestant Christianity, and then, when pluralized, for such alien
forms as Catholicism.[10] It was this already polemical category that was
then employed to constitute the forms of cultural piety discovered by
Christian missionaries in the non-European world. Thus it was that
the West gave birth to such 'world-views' as Hinduism and Buddhism,
which are now so natural as to be used by those whom they characterize
and so in part constitute. But while vexed, the problem of 'religion' as a
disciplinary construct is no more acute than in other disciplines, which
also construct their objects of study through their study of them. There is
no need to abandon the category of 'religion' so long as we recognize its
contingency as a term of art.[11]

Likewise, it is no great problem that religious studies works with borrowed tools, from sociology and anthropology, philosophy and theology.
For this – and the elusiveness of its object – has led to the emergence of
an eclectic, postmodern religious studies. This embraces both anthropological approaches to religion and a relatively new formation that is more
philosophical, influenced by 'continental philosophy' rather than Anglo-
American analytic philosophy of religion. It is a peculiarly academic mode
of 'religious thought', which is neither theological nor anthropological,
but liminal. '*Religion* and *religious studies* have . . . become interstitial
terms that refer to forms of thought that occur *between* theological
thought and thought "about religion."'[12] Borrowing from Alasdair
MacIntyre, Gavin Hyman names this new religious studies 'a community
of contested discourses',[13] and it is within this community that religious
and film studies can meet, along with theology, in mutually enriching conversations about what and how they seek to know. But only theology as

such will avow its quest to know the unknowable; to guard the grammar of the world's unassailable mystery.[14]

We will read a theology of film because it has something interesting to say about film, about the making and watching of films and of particular films watched. And in this process we will discover a return from film to theology, a questioning of theology through its cinematic encounters. But this will not be different in kind from the return that other arts make to theology, when theology is open to seeing itself as it looks from elsewhere, from different theological locations, from different construals of the world.

What I have elsewhere called 'cinematic theology' is that kind of looking that seeks to enter into the world of a film before speaking about it, and then using film – the language of cinema – to speak theologically.[15] Such looking is of course an exercise of the theological imagination, but one that seeks knowledge through habitation, through dwelling in another place, from where theological critique must become a kind of self-critique. But except on those occasions when such theology is the fruit of conversations between different interests – the record of real dialogues – all such discourses are forms of ventriloquism, albeit the ventriloquy of an empathetic vocalist, who has sought to learn the language of another.

2. Passionate Conversations

At the beginning of the third Christian millennium, the *succès de scandale* that was Mel Gibson's *The Passion of the Christ* (USA 2004) proved a timely reminder that the relationship between theology and film is both intimate and powerful. While many questioned the religious and aesthetic aspects of the film – the means and morality of its storytelling – none could question its box-office returns. By the end of 2004 it was reported to have earned upwards of $370 million at the US box office alone. While benefiting from extensive and astute publicity, it was amazing that an independent film – made by Gibson's own company, ICON Productions, and reportedly with $25 million of his own money – and one that was also in effect a 'foreign language' film (Latin and Aramaic), was so successful. Liberal critics were aghast.

It is for these reasons that *The Passion of the Christ* receives an extended discussion at the end of this book. The story of the film's making and reception demonstrates the necessity of religious studies and theology for fully understanding film, for understanding the practice and possibility of cinema. For as the round-table discussion between the contributors to this book circles around questions of authenticity (to the biblical text and the historical past), antisemitism (the film's intervention in the still fraught relationships between Jews and Gentiles[16]) and theology (the film's near-pornographic portrayal of Christ's death as a sadomasochistic transaction between Father and Son), it becomes clear that understanding the film and its reception requires multiple considerations of its making and seeing. The film's contexts and intertexts require lively conversation between film studies, religious studies and theology, and the disciplines on which all of these must draw in order to sustain their engagements (art history, sociology, psychology). To understand a film we have to understand the cultures of its showing and seeing.

Handsomely staged and beautifully lit by cinematographer Caleb Deschanel, Gibson's movie is something of a curiosity: a two-hour film of a man being tortured to death. As Mark Kermode noted, *The Passion of the Christ* is a horror film, a 'gore fest'.[17] It opens with clouds shrouding a full moon, and closes with a newly resurrected Christ, who – with his thigh visible through the CGI hole in his right hand – looks like nothing so much as the newly arrived Schwarzenegger at the beginning of the *Terminator* films, I and II.[18] Back from hell, Christ exits screen right, marching off – one might think – toward *The Passion of the Christ II: The Return*. As if alluding to Martin Scorsese's *The Last Temptation of Christ* (USA 1988), Gibson's Jesus (Jim Caviezel) undergoes a last temptation by Satan in the garden of Gethsemane. Rosalinda Celentano's Satan bears a striking resemblance to a fleeting image of the demon in William Friedkins's *The Exorcist* (USA 1973).[19] Thus Gibson's film translates not only the story of the canonical Gospels but of previous cinematic encounters with Christian demonology. At the same time, early Hollywood biblical epics – such as those of Cecil B. DeMille – are recalled in the use of costume and make-up, most especially in the scene of King Herod's heavily mascaraed court, which also recalls its twentieth-century rendition in Norman Jewison's *Jesus Christ Superstar* (USA 1973).[20] All of these filmic phantoms and more, not to mention images from the Western tradition of Christian piety, are skilfully melded together within the film's design by Francesco Frigeri.

The Passion of the Christ is a translation of the Gospels – not least in translating their original Greek into the film's Latin and Aramaic[21] – but it is more nearly a film of the 'gothic novel', *The Dolorous Passion of Our Lord Jesus Christ* (1833). This is attributed to the German stigmatic and 'visionary', Anne Catherine Emmerich (1777–1824), but is more properly the work – forgery – of her devoted amanuensis, the Romantic novelist and poet Clemens Brentano (1778–1842). The first of a projected three-volume work on the life of Christ, *The Dolorous Passion* was the only one to be published in Brentano's lifetime, and not the first work in which he had improved on his source material. Between 1806 and 1809, Brentano and Ludwig Achim von Arnim published three volumes of collected German folk songs, *Des Knaben Wunderhorn*, with many of the songs actually written by their 'collectors'. It is from the Emmerich/Brentano

Dolorous Passion that Gibson and his co-screenwriter, Benedict Fitz-gerald, took most of the non-canonical incidents in their telling of Christ's arrest, trial and execution: the near constant beating of Christ from the moment of his arrest, the near constant presence of his mother and the equally constant presence of a snarling Caiaphas and other priests.[22] This last aspect reflects the antisemitic culture of nineteenth-century Europe, and Brentano's avowed aversion to Jews. In 1811, Brentano and several of his friends founded the Christian-German Table Society (Christlich-deutsche Tischgesellschaft), which explicitly excluded Jews, women and 'Philistines'.

'Christianity really is a blood cult and a death cult; as much as they say otherwise and talk about the God of love, it really does focus on the Passion and the bleeding, and those are the images that hit a child.'[23] This is Paul Schrader, the writer of Scorsese's *The Last Temptation of Christ*, and while one might wish to demur from his estimate of Christianity, it certainly finds support in Gibson's *Passion*, which is drenched in Christ's blood. But, as others have noted, the modern focus on the suffering and death of Christ derives from the late medieval period, and is not that of the early or patristic church. Thus *The Passion of the Christ* may be understood as a motion picture of Matthias Grünewald's 'Crucifixion' for the Isenheim altarpiece (1515), but filtered through the mawkish senti-mentality and antisemitism of a certain German Romanticism. To under-stand this film we need a theology well versed in the history of modern pieties, and to which it can bring a sure sense of what makes for spiritual sustenance, for what makes for good news in the telling of Christ's story. Needless to say, this will be a theology of passionate conversations.

3. Video Divina

Cinéma vérité named both a style and an aspiration, both the desire to picture reality and a means of doing so. The development in the 1950s of relatively small, mobile cameras with synchronized sound recording, enabled documentarists like Jean Rouch and Edgar Morin to develop a more impromptu style of film-making than had previously been possible. Adopting an ethnographic approach to their subjects, these directors fore-grounded the effect that their film-making had on the persons and events filmed. Their cameras saw with a subjective eye, an avowed presence, and it was the combination of immediacy with knowingness – a self-conscious 'detachment' – that caught the imagination of those film-makers who would become the Nouvelle Vague: Claude Chabrol, Jean-Luc Godard, Jacques Rivette, Eric Rohmer, François Truffaut. The new technology and sensibility allowed them to flee the constraints of the studio, filming by available light, on the streets and in the apartments of Paris, creating a

new realism and truthfulness, a cinema suited to the emerging freedoms of
the 1960s. However, the return of such techniques – in the films of *Dogme
95*[24] and, more pertinently, in the work of such an established director as
Steven Soderberg – indicates how the style of truth has become a signifier
for the artifice of *cinéma vérité* itself. In one scene in Soderberg's *Ocean's
12* (USA 2004), the use of a handheld camera and apparently natural or
found light signifies a kind of truth, but it is the truth of the film's manufacture, since, as it were, we are seeing the video that one of the characters
is filming in the scene, to be spotted in the background of one of the shots.
The film becomes a replica of itself: a recurring conceit throughout the
movie, which is about – plays with – all manner of doubles and fakes,
and above all the fakery of cinema itself, of Hollywood, and, of course,
documentary.

Naming a collection of essays *Cinéma Divinité* obviously plays on the
idea of *cinéma vérité* and the possibility of making truthful films in which
reality appears, films in which the 'religious' will be honestly displayed
and ventured. The naming of the book signals its authors' concern with
both the means by which cinema presents the pursuit of divinity – in the
stories and practices of 'religious' people – and the possibility of divinity's
appearing in the darkness of the cinema itself, in the flickering of celluloid
shadows. The wager of *Cinéma Divinité* is that film can be theology.

Carl Dreyer, Robert Bresson and Andrei Tarkovsky – to name but three
of the most illustrious director-theologians – have produced profound
and subtle pieces of cinematic theology, exploring in their stories what it
might mean to live by the two commandments which rule salvation
(Matthew 22.39–40).[25] These are directors for whom the challenge of the
twentieth century was to show how the mess that is modern life might
still disclose grounds for hope and so once more become meaningful. In
the work of these directors – in, say, Dreyer's *Ordet* (Denmark 1954),
Bresson's *Pickpocket* (France 1959) and Tarkovsky's *Andrei Rublev*
(USSR 1966) – cinema inherits the aspirations and achievements, the
narrative traditions, of Western art. At a time when the arts had generally
become more concerned with questions of aesthetic form than with
human transfiguration, cinema remained true to the West's dual inheri-
tance of biblical and classical narratives, to *storytelling* as the means by
which the tribulations of human life can be borne and its tendernesses
rendered significant. In the films of Bresson, Dreyer and Tarkovsky, the
world is shown to give unto more than just itself.

Away from Europe, in the North American films of Paul Schrader and
Martin Scorsese, but also in those of directors like David Fincher and
Quentin Tarantino, we find a willingness to use and cite biblical texts,
employ theological motifs, and even venture upon moments of transcendent hope. At the end of *American Gigolo* (USA 1980), Schrader has his
imprisoned protagonist, the narcissistic gigolo of the title, Julian (Richard

Gere), reprise the end of Bresson's *Pickpocket*, as he finally accepts the relationship, the love, into which he has fallen with Michelle (Lauren Hutton), who sacrifices her reputation in his defence. 'It's the acceptance of unconditional goodness, which is the same as spiritual grace.'[26] Grace is similarly found and accepted at the end of Scorsese's *Bringing Out the Dead* (USA 1999). But we can also find stories of grace in any number of other, less mannered, films: in, say, Isabel Coixet's *My Life Without Me* (Canada/Spain 2002) or Nicholas Philibert's touching documentary about a small country school, *Être et avoir* (France 2002). Elsewhere we can find more equivocal examples of cinematic theology, in the work of directors who disavow religious intent but remain haunted by theological themes. For these directors the disparities of life still call for spiritual consolations, even if those proffered by religion are found wanting. Ingmar Bergman and Luis Buñuel might be named in this connection. Buñuel was an atheist, but a devout one, who cleaved to the God he denied.[27]

Any number of film writers and directors, and their films, can be shown to use, negotiate and display religious and spiritual concerns, to produce, if not cinematic theology itself, then a cinema that engages the theological. Several of these directors and their films are engaged in this book: Joel and Ethan Coen, Francis Ford Coppola, Robert Duvall, Clint Eastwood, Stanley Kubrick, Charles Laughton, Carol Reed, Ridley Scott; Spaghetti Westerns, animation films and *film noir*.[28] These directors and film genres are already the concern of film studies, on which cinematic theology must always be dependent (and more than it has been). But a truly cinematic theology – as performed by theologians rather than film-makers (who of course can be theologians) – must go beyond technical and aesthetic concerns, beyond historical, philosophical and sociological enquiries, and engage with film as theology engages with any other text that may display the source for which all theology seeks. Cinematic theology must engage with film as theology engages with Scripture. It must practise its own form of *lectio divina*, which, while it seeks to understand Scripture in all the contexts of its formation, transmission and interpretation, seeks also to enter into the text in such a way as to find there – to be found there by – that which is alone worth the finding.[29] Ultimately, those who practise *lectio divina* seek to be read *by* Scripture, or, better, by that which Scripture discloses to those who read *in love*; the love by which they have been read into being. Cinematic theology must risk a similar *video divina*, in which viewers enter into the world of a film so as to find there the very same truth by which they are encountered, when in love, in Scripture. It is a *risk* because some films deflect or even defeat the finding of that which would be sought.[30] They can endanger their viewers' moral sense.[31] But to practise *video divina* is to watch films in the belief – common to all theological engagement with the arts – that they may not only disclose a 'world,' an interpretation of the world, but that which most fundamentally sustains our world. It is to watch films with love, in love; in the love that makes them to be, to show. This is the venture of cinematic theology, of *cinéma divinité*.

Notes

1 David Jasper, 'On Systematizing the Unsystematic', in Clive Marsh and Gaye Ortiz (eds), *Explorations in Theology and Film: Movies and Meaning*, Oxford: Blackwell, 1997, pp. 235–44 (238).
2 See Lloyd Baugh, *Imaging the Divine: Jesus and Christ-Figures in Film*, Kansas City: Sheed & Ward, 1997.
3 Jasper, 'On Systematizing the Unsystematic', p. 240.
4 Jasper, 'On Systematizing the Unsystematic', pp. 242–3. Jasper forgets that in many cultures cinema is more social than solitary. Even when people can watch films alone (on video or DVD) they often choose to watch them with other people in the movie theatre, and talk together about the films afterwards.
5 Andrei Tarkovsky, *Sculpting in Time: Reflections on the Cinema*, trans. Kitty Hunter-Blair, Austin: University of Texas Press, 1996 [1986], p. 170.
6 See, for example, Terry Lindvall, *The Silents of God: Selected Issues and Documents in Silent American Film and Religion, 1908–1925*, Lanham, MD: Scarecrow Press, 2001.
7 Terry Lindvall, 'Religion and Film Part I: History and Cinema', *Communication Research Trends*, 23/4 (2004): 1–44 (p. 15).
8 The history of ideas is vastly important for theology, not least for its self-understanding. But the history of ideas is ingredient in, not constitutive of, theology.
9 For something on the grammar of 'first cause' see Nicholas Lash, *Holiness, Speech and Silence: Reflections on the Question of God*, Aldershot: Ashgate, 2004, especially ch.4 (pp. 75–95).
10 See Wilfred Cantwell Smith, *The Meaning and End of Religion*, London: SPCK, 1978, and Peter Harrison, *'Religion' and the Religions of the English Enlightenment*, Cambridge: Cambridge University Press, 1990. '"Religions" existed first in the minds of Western thinkers who thought that the lives of other peoples were governed by the kinds of concerns which were really only character-istic of one episode of Western history. The "world religions" were thus generated largely through the projection of Christian disunity onto the world' (Harrison, p. 174).
11 See Will Sweetman, '"Hinduism" and the History of "Religion": Protestant Presuppositions in the Critique of the Concept of Hinduism', *Method and Theory in the Study of Religion*, 15 (2003): 329–53.
12 Gavin Hyman, 'The Study of Religion and the Return of Theology', *Journal of the American Academy of Religion*, 72/1 (2004): 195–219 (p. 213).
13 Alasdair MacIntyre, *Three Rival Versions of Moral Enquiry: Encyclopaedia, Genealogy and Tradition*, London: Duckworth, 1990; cited in Hyman, 'Study of Religion', p. 216.
14 For more on the practice of theology and religious studies in the university, see Gerard Loughlin, 'The University Without Question: John Henry Newman

and Jacques Derrida on Faith in the University', in Jeff Astley, Peter Francis, John Sullivan and Andrew Walker (eds), *The Idea of a Christian University: Essays in Theology and Higher Education*, Carlisle: Paternoster Press, 2005.

15 See further Gerard Loughlin, *Alien Sex: The Body and Desire in Cinema and Theology*, Oxford: Blackwell, 2004.

16 For more on antisemitism in film, see Chapter 16 ('His blood be upon us, and our children': The Treatment of Jews and Judaism in the Christ Film), and with particular reference to Mel Gibson's *Passion* see the round-table discussion at the end of the book. See also J. Shawn Landres and Michael Berenbaum (eds), *After the Passion is Gone: American Religious Consequences*, Lanham, MD: AltaMira Press, 2004, Part 3.

17 Mark Kermode, 'Drenched in the Blood of Christ', *The Observer*, 29 February 2004. See further Kermode's more detailed and highly perceptive review in *Sight & Sound*, 14/4 (April 2004): 62–3. In the same issue see also Nick James, 'Hell in Jerusalem', pp. 15–18.

18 Melanie Wright also sees the Terminator in Gibson's resurrected Christ. See the round-table discussion at the end of the book.

19 The demon face was that of Linda Blair's stand-in, Eileen Dietz, in an early make-up test for the possessed Regan. See Mark Kermode, quoting William Friedkin, in *The Exorcist*, 2nd edition, London: BFI, 1998 [1997], pp. 45–6.

20 This allusion is also noted by Peter Francis. One might also detect a nod to Terry Jones's *Life of Brian* (UK 1979), in the scene where the young Jesus builds a 'tall' table and demonstrates to his mother how one might sit at it, in 'tall' chairs, though he has yet to make these. 'It will never catch on,' Mary replies. The scene, however, reminds William Telford of a similar piece of carpentry in Nicholas Ray's *King of Kings* (US 1961), and Peter Francis of Jesus's carpentry shop in Scorsese's *Last Temptation of Christ*.

21 The effect of translating the story into virtually unspoken tongues returns to it the power of the *written* word, through the film's vernacular subtitles, as in silent film; but not, unfortunately, the power of a distinguished script. As the discussion in the Epilogue makes clear, the use of ancient languages is not for historical but aesthetic reasons; an alienating technique that renders the film 'foreign' to all audiences.

22 John Dominic Crossan is probably right when he estimates that 80% of the film is based on *The Dolorous Passion*, 5% on the canonical Gospels, and 15% on Gibson and Fitzgerald's imaginations. See John Dominic Crossan, 'Hymn to a Savage God', in Kathleen E. Corley and Robert L. Webb (eds), *Jesus and Mel Gibson's* The Passion of The Christ: *The Film, the Gospels and the Claims of History*, London: Continuum, 2004, pp. 8–27 (12). See also in the same book, Robert L. Webb, '*The Passion* and the Influence of Emmerich's *The Dolorous Passion of Our Lord Jesus Christ*', pp. 160–72.

23 Paul Schrader in Kevin Jackson (ed.), *Schrader on Schrader and Other Writings*, revised edition, London: Faber & Faber, 2004 [1990], p. 5.

24 Examples of *Dogme 95* films are Lars Von Trier's *The Idiots* (Denmark 1998) and Thomas Vinterberg's *Festen* (Denmark 1998). See further Richard Kelly, *The Name of this Book is Dogme 95*, London: Faber & Faber, 2000.

25 For more on Carl Dreyer see Melanie Wright's essay below; and on Dreyer and Robert Bresson see Paul Schrader, *Transcendental Style in Film: Ozu,*

Bresson, Dreyer, New York: Da Capo Press, 1988 [1972]. On Tarkovsky see his own inestimable *Sculpting in Time*; and Vida T. Johnson and Graham Petrie, *The Films of Andrei Tarkovsky: A Visual Fugue*, Bloomington, IN: Indiana University Press, 1994, and Robert Bird, *Andrei Rublev*, London: BFI, 2004.

26 Schrader in *Schrader on Schrader*, p. 166.

27 See further Tom Aitken's essay on Buñuel's *Viridiana* (Mexico/Spain 1961) below. When Paul Schrader was a student at Calvin College (Grand Rapids, Michigan) he taunted the authorities by showing ever more challenging films in the College's film club, reviewing them in the student newspaper, and organizing seminars about the films with the 'more liberal members of the faculty, particularly the theology faculty'. But it was the showing of Buñuel's *Viridiana* that 'broke the camel's back'. See *Schrader on Schrader*, pp. 9–10.

28 See further below the essays by Jeffrey Keuss, Eric Christianson, Peter Francis, Robert Pope and George Aichele.

29 I owe this use of *lectio divina* to conversations with Robert K. Johnston, who rightly suggested that it provided an appropriate model for what I had been trying to say in talking about *entering into* the world of the film. For his own approach to theology and film see *Reel Spirituality: Theology and Film in Dialogue*, Grand Rapids, MI: Baker Academic, 2000.

30 *The Passion of the Christ* might be – is – such a film. It would require an extended discussion to suggest how its dramatic choices compound its theological shortcomings, but one point would be to note how the final shot of the resurrected Christ alone inside the tomb eschews the reticence of the Gospels, and thus refuses their insistence that the resurrection is an eminently social event – constitutive of community. Christ will not tarry with Mary Magdalene in the garden because he – and she – must go on ahead to meet with the other disciples (John 20.17–18). The film continually refuses the Gospels' stress on communion in favour of an individualized spirituality.

31 See further Gerard Loughlin, 'Looking: The Ethics of Seeing in Church and Cinema', in Mark Thiessen Nation and Samuel Wells (eds), *Faithfulness and Fortitude: In Conversation with the Theological Ethics of Stanley Hauerwas*, Edinburgh: T. & T. Clark, 2000, pp. 257–85.

Part 1
Key Concepts

1. Through a Lens Darkly:
Critical Approaches to Theology and Film

WILLIAM R. TELFORD

1. Introduction

The Aims of the Chapter

The title of this chapter is 'Through a Lens Darkly: Critical Approaches to Theology and Film'. Those readers with intertextual expertise, or, simply, with a knowledge of the Bible, will spot that the title is an echo of the words of the apostle Paul in 1 Corinthians 13.12, 'Now we see through a glass [or 'mirror', RSV] darkly; but then face to face. Now I know in part; but then shall I know [or 'understand fully', RSV], even as also I am known [or 'have been fully understood', RSV]' (AV). Snatched out of its context, this verse could well describe the feelings that many of us have in approaching the topic of this essay, namely, cinema spectatorship and the nature and application of film theory, or film criticism, to theology. Most of us have only a partial knowledge of film theory or film criticism, and to that extent 'see through a lens darkly'. Viewing film in a systematic, critical and insightful way is not an easy exercise, yet film theorists and film critics have engaged in this process for a century now, and offer us the promise of a clearer vision, a purer gaze, of 'seeing face to face'. The interdiscipline of theology and film requires, indeed, that we (i.e. students and teachers of theology, biblical studies or religious studies) engage responsibly with film studies, and so this, then, is the task before us.[1]

My aims in this chapter are as follows. In the first part of the chapter, I want to review briefly some of the critical approaches that have been taken to film over the last century, thereafter focusing on two that have a particular relevance for the interdiscipline of theology and film (narrative criticism and cultural studies). In the second part of the chapter, I want to suggest a number of ways that film may be approached critically within our interdisciplinary field of theology and film. In the course of these two discussions, I want, thirdly, to mention some of the key books and articles that have been published recently on the subject. Finally, at the end of the chapter, I shall offer an exercise involving some selected films and film clips that may be watched and commented upon in light of the approaches that have been reviewed.

Approaching Film Critically

Before we proceed to a review of film theory and criticism, let me just say a general word about the notion of 'approaching film critically'. Many people think of films as entertainment, as a means of escape or recreation, even as ephemeral cultural products on which it is not worth expending any great mental effort or critical reflection. Even so, one observes, films are one of the commonest points of discussion among people today. Everyone likes to give their views on the films that they have seen. Analysis, however superficial, is something we do almost naturally, and to that extent, there ought to be no real conflict between treating films as entertainment and treating them as a subject for reflection.

There is no need to make the case, therefore, for treating films as a subject for reflection, especially to the readership of a book like this. Most of us would share the view, I am sure, that film is not only a source of entertainment or escapism, but also, as one critic has expressed it 'a representation of universal human values, of the truths of human experience, of insights that will help us to understand better the complexity of human life and human society'.[2] If we reflect on films naturally, then, it is simply one further step for us to learn to do it better. Sharpening our analytical tools can actually enhance our enjoyment of films. As Timothy Corrigan points out in *A Short Guide to Writing about Film* (1997):

> Every discipline has it own special language or use of words, which allows it to discuss its subject with precision and subtlety . . . With film, too, a critical vocabulary allows you to view a movie more accurately and to formulate your perceptions more easily.[3]

'Cleaning the lens', as it were, can improve the vision. Moreover, reflecting on the lenses through which we personally view films can also be valuable, and this is one of the objectives of this essay.

But what are these lenses? In 2003, in a 'Theology and Film' conference discussion group at St Deiniol's Library, Hawarden, I noted down some of the common 'lenses', the 'wide-angle' lenses, one might say, that people who reflect on films, and who have been regular participants at these conferences, tend to employ.

- One popular lens is the *moral* lens, where a response to the film is given in relation to the moral issues it raises, or the contemporary values it reflects.
- A second lens is the *theological* lens, where the film is engaged with respect to what it has to say about Christian teaching or doctrine.
- A third lens is the *textual* lens, where the film has interest because of its relation to literature, and especially the Bible.

- A fourth lens is the *cultural* lens, the film being discussed in relation to what it communicates about contemporary world-views, ideology or practice.
- A related lens is the *sociological* one, a perspective that views the film in light of its social context or what it says about contemporary society.
- A sixth lens is the *psychoanalytic* lens that approaches the film with a view to what it discloses about the human psyche.

In common with some of the contributors to this book, I have given a number of presentations over the seven years that the St Deiniol's conferences have been running (1998–2004). One such presentation reviewed the very rich harvest of films appearing between 1993 and 1999 that engage to a greater or lesser extent with religion, the Bible or theology, or offer scope for religious, biblical or theological reflection.[4] Four others treated the biblical epic or the Christ film from the point of view of their representation of women,[5] of Jewish and Christian ritual, of Jews and Judaism, and of the characters of Peter and Judas.[6] The most recent, 'Searching for Jesus: Recognizing or Imagining Christ-Figures in the Movies' (yet to be published) reviewed the Christ-figures claimed to have been recognized in films (a list of these appears as Appendix 2 in this volume) and explored the question of what constitutes genuine 'recognition' and what constitutes mere 'imagination' in the alleged detection of such figures.

My own characteristic approach to films, therefore, as a biblical scholar, has been to view them in terms of their form and style, their narrative content (plot, settings, characterization), their relation to the biblical text, and their relation to contemporary culture. My own filmic 'lenses', in other words, (to use the jargon) have been those of aesthetics, textual analysis, narrative criticism, intertextuality, social context and ideology, including such contemporary issues as gender and ethnicity.[7] This essay, however, has given me the opportunity to reflect further on how films can be approached, to extend my knowledge of film theory and film criticism, and to share with the reader something of what I have learned. With these few introductory remarks, let us begin our review.

2. Through a Lens Darkly: Critical Approaches to Film

The Critics' Lenses: Some Traditional Theoretical Frameworks

Let me start with a review of the traditional theoretical frameworks that have been adopted in film studies. There isn't space to do more than briefly summarize these, but those readers who wish to delve further will find useful discussions in the books and articles listed in the notes at the end of the chapter,[8] and additional reading in the bibliography at the end of the book.

Film Theory, Film Criticism and Approaches to Film

Up until now I have used expressions such as 'film *theory*', 'film *criticism*,' and '*approaches* to film'. How are these different? According to Ephraim Katz:

> A theory of film attempts to explain the nature of cinema and analyze how films produce emotional and cognitive effects. Often, film theories place cinema in a broader context (social, political, philosophical) and provide a framework for evaluating artistic merit. Unlike practical criticism, film theory seeks to establish principles applicable to all films.[9]

James Monaco puts it more succinctly: 'In general, theory is the abstraction; criticism is the practice.'[10] Film 'criticism' (the practical exercise) can be distinguished in turn from an 'approach to film' in that 'criticism' often involves distinct procedures, steps or operations which are performed on the subject matter for investigation in pursuance of specific aims, whereas an 'approach' is often characterized more by the particular concerns, perspectives or point of view that it adopts towards the cinematic text (or the spectator).

The first hurdle that the amateur must face is the nature and diversity of the theories, criticisms and approaches encountered in film studies. In Text Box 1.1, you will find a small representative list, and you might like to use this in conjunction with the further reading, to learn more about each.

1.1 Some Theories, Criticisms and Approaches

Aesthetics
Auteur Theory
Cognitive Film Theory
Cultural Criticism
Eclecticism
Expressionism
Feminist Criticism
Formalism
Genre Criticism
Historical Criticism
Marxist Criticism
Narrative Criticism
Postmodernism
Psychoanalytic Theory
Queer Theory
Realism
Semiotics and Structuralism
Thematic Criticism

1.2 Some Theorists

Louis Althusser
Rudolf Arnheim
Béla Balázs
André Bazin
David Bordwell
Gilles Deleuze
Ferdinand de Saussure
Boris Eikhenbaum
Sergei Eisenstein
Sigmund Freud
Siegfried Kracauer
Jacques Lacan
F. R. Leavis
Claude Lévi-Strauss
Vachel Lindsay
Christian Metz
Laura Mulvey
Hugo Münsterberg
V. I. Pudovkin
Andrew Sarris
Peter Wollen

Within the film studies Hall of Fame is a panoply of distinguished or influential theorists. Again consider the list in Text Box 1.2.

As with any academic discipline or field, one has also to run a gamut of technical concepts and specialized vocabulary. Text Box 1.3 gives some of them.

All of this can be very confusing until one realizes that the various theories, criticisms and approaches provide in their own way different understandings of the impact of films upon us, various questions with

---

1.3 Some Concepts and Vocabulary

The Cinematic 'Gaze'
Diegesis
Ideology
Mise-en-Scène
Montage
Spectatorship
Syntagmatic and Paradigmatic Structure
Voyeurism

which we may interrogate them, and alternative perspectives from which to view them.

There is no space in an essay of this kind to summarize the history of film theory, but the books and articles mentioned in note 8 (p. 40), and in the bibliography, offer very good treatments of this fascinating subject, and will introduce you to many of the theories, theorists and concepts listed above.

But how do we make sense of this very confusing array of theories, criticisms and approaches. In analysing how meaning is constructed from literary texts, literary critics focus on a threefold model of communication represented by *the author, the text and the reader*. In film studies, a similar model can be invoked, namely *the film-maker, the visual images that make up the cinematic text or film, and the spectator*. Film theories can be seen to differentiate themselves, therefore, in terms of the relative weight given to each member of this triad. Earlier theory, for example, focused on how film created meaning from its raw material (visual images). More recent film theory has turned much more to the relationship between films and audiences, from what can be termed generative theories to theories of reception, from how a film is made to how it affects our lives. In attempting to make sense for myself of all these theories, criticisms and approaches, to develop a 'taxonomy of approaches', to employ the jargon, it seems to me that they can be divided more or less into three main categories.

First, there are text-based theories or criticisms, that is, those theories or criticisms that focus on the film text itself, its genre, its author (or auteur, to use the French term beloved by film critics – the director, in other words), its narrative structure (plot, characters, settings, point of view), its surface themes and its deeper structures of meaning.

Second, there are context-based theories or criticisms, that is, those theories or criticisms that focus not on the filmic text but on the film's social, historical, political or cultural *context*, and claim that the meaning of a film can be found by examining these.

Third, there are spectator-based theories or criticisms, that is, those theories or criticisms that claim the meaning of a film is constructed by the viewer or the viewing audience in line with social, cultural, educational, racial or political factors.

Two words beloved of literary and cinematic theorists are 'diachronic' and 'synchronic', the one designating, as its Greek roots imply, an approach to a literary or cinematic text that focuses on the process that brought it into being in the first place (lit. 'through time'), the second an approach that focuses on the world conjured up or imaginatively projected by the book or film (lit. 'together with time'). Most of us, when we watch films, approach them 'synchronically', that is, we become caught up in the story, the plot, the characters, the acting, the settings, etc. Some of us, however, view films 'diachronically', that is, we are interested in the production process, the filming, the composition, the framing of shots, the editing, the subsequent distribution, etc. Both of these dimensions, then, are further useful ways in which to differentiate film theories, criticisms and approaches.

Historical Criticism

One major diachronic, and contextual approach, for example, and indeed one of the most popular in film criticism, as in other fields, is historical criticism, the organization and investigation of films 'according to their place within a historical context and in light of historical developments'.[11]

Formalism/Expressionism and Realism

A key issue or debate within the early history of film theory was that between formalism, or the closely related expressionism, on the one hand, and realism on the other. Formalism and expressionism are what I have called text-based approaches in that they are little interested in a film's social, political or cultural context. Formalism is interested in the structure and style of a film, and expressionism in the power of the film-maker to manipulate images. Here Katz is again helpful: '[M]eaning in cinema', according to formalism, 'is constructed from the juxtaposition of shots' while 'realist theories', on the other hand, 'locate the power of film in its ability to capture objective material reality'.[12] Formalism, and its sister approach, expressionism, are associated with the names of V. I. Pudovkin and Sergei Eisenstein, among others, and both dominated the film criticism of the 1920s and the 1930s. Realism, on the other hand, linked with theorists such as Siegfried Kracauer and André Bazin, was the prevailing influence in the 1940s and 1950s. Each employed different styles and techniques. Formalism and expressionism, with their emphasis on cinematic artifice, preferred close-ups, stylized sets, rapid editing and montage (the rapid juxtaposition of images) for their effects. Realism, with its emphasis on the representation of reality, preferred long takes, sequence-shots and deep focus photography (where foreground and background are both in focus) and it privileged *mise-en-scène* (literally 'that which is put into the scene', or before the camera, with its composite elements of setting, acting style, costumes, lighting) over montage (the succession of images).

Textual Analysis

I have suggested that theories, criticisms and approaches can be divided into three categories depending on whether they focus on the film text itself (textual analysis), the film's context (contextual analysis) or the observer (spectatorship and audience research).

Genres and Genre Criticism – One form of textual analysis (though it also has a contextual element) is genre criticism.[13] Genre criticism encourages us to seek understanding of a film through the recognition of its genre. Films come in a variety of genres depending on their form and content (Westerns, sci-fi films, thrillers, comedies, musicals, biblical epics, disaster movies, film noir, road movies, melodramas, holocaust movies, costume dramas, etc.). Genres have a particular world-view, and their common themes and conventions give us clues as to how to interpret them. A good film-maker will make a creative use of genre by developing, reinterpreting or subverting these conventions.

Auteur Theory/Criticism – Auteur theory or criticism focuses not on the genre but on the film-maker where that film-maker, usually the director, has created a body of work that expresses a very distinctive vision of the world. (Further, see 'What is Auteur Theory?', p. 82.)[14]

Thematic Criticism – Thematic criticism, on the other hand, focuses on the main ideas explored by a film, isolating and analysing its key themes, and often treating these intertextually, that is, comparing them with other films or literary texts in which similar themes are found.[15]

Semiotics and Structuralism – Semiotics and structuralism move to an entirely different level of textual analysis, analysing not the ideas and themes to be found at the surface of a cinematic text but exploring its deeper structures of meaning. Associated with Christian Metz and derived from the work of Ferdinand de Saussure, semiotics and structuralism investigate the fundamental questions of how film communicates its message, what is the nature of film language, how images and their manipulation convey meaning, what codes are embedded in the cinematic process and how we may unlock these codes to find understanding.[16] To examine the meaning conveyed by camera shots and angles, for example, is a 'semiotic exercise' (the word 'semiotic' itself derives from the Greek 'semeion', a sign). It is an investigation on what structuralists call 'a system of signification'.

Cognitive Film Theory – Allied to semiotics and structuralism but more recent is cognitive film theory which seeks to explain the way we, the individual spectators or the audience, actually come to understand film, how we unpack the various codes that the cinematic experience confronts us with.[17]

Contextual Analysis

Social Science Approaches – If various forms of textual analysis (genre criticism, auteur criticism, thematic criticism, and semiotics and structuralism) tend to focus on the cinematic text itself (although not exclusively), others engage in contextual analysis, invoking external factors to explain the significance of the film and the viewing experience. Prominent among these are the social science approaches that seek to interpret films within their social and psychological contexts. In Eichenberger's words:

> [T]he critics of this 'school' are interested more than others, in studying the effects of films on the viewers' behavior, emotions and attitudes. The critics want to know if and how a movie is affecting the conscious or the unconscious dimension of an individual moviegoer or of a collective audience.[18]

Marxism – With its distinctive understanding of capitalist society, Marxist criticism, for example, in the hands of influential theorists like Louis Althusser, has contributed, among other things, the notion of 'ideology' to film criticism. Ideology relates to the fundamental ideas, beliefs or values that govern our lives, and it is now common to approach films with a view to establishing the particular visions of the world, the specific world-views, which they reflect.[19]

Psychoanalysis – Another prominent approach has been the application of psychoanalytic tools and concepts to the mental or psychological processes whereby film audiences draw meaning and significance from projected film images. Here the theories of Sigmund Freud – on dreams and the unconscious, on the suppression of emotions like desire, aggression, guilt, on the Oedipus complex and other neuroses, fetishism ('the pathological attachment of sexual interest to an inanimate object'), scopophilia ('the practice of obtaining sexual pleasure from things seen, as e.g. naked bodies') and voyeurism ('[the derivation of] gratification from surreptitiously watching sexual acts or objects')[20] – and Jacques Lacan (the theory of the mirror stage in infant development when personal identity is first experienced) have proved particularly influential.[21]

Cultural Studies – Marxist criticism and psychoanalytic theory have been around for a long time, and have to an extent been absorbed by the more recent cultural studies approach which like them examines film with respect to its social and psychological contexts. In R. K. Johnston's words: 'It studies the life cycle of a film from production to distribution to reception.'[22]

Spectatorship and Audience Research

Sociology and Ethnography – Cultural studies or cultural criticism is hence a bridge to the currently popular interest in reception or audience research, an approach to film in which the third dimension of film communication is addressed, namely, the effect films have on spectators and all the social, economic, political, racial, physical or psychological conditions that influence our interpretation of films, or which lead us to accept, resist or modify the ideological messages that films impart.[23] Research on cinema audiences has borrowed extensively, therefore, from the social sciences, especially from sociology and ethnography.[24] Two factors in particular that influence audiences' perceptions of films are gender and ethnicity.

Feminist Film Criticism and Queer Theory – Where the former is concerned, film studies have been greatly enriched by feminist film criticism, and latterly, to some extent, by the gay or lesbian perspectives of so-called 'queer theory'. Employing some of the analytical tools hitherto reviewed, like psychoanalysis, feminist criticism has drawn attention to the cinema's propensity for cultural stereotyping, highlighted and challenged the cinema's representation of masculinity and femininity, and even exposed the extent to which the camera itself in its cinematic treatment of women has tended to reproduce the 'male gaze'.[25]

Postmodern Eclecticism – Given the plethora of theories, criticisms and approaches that I have attempted to summarize, it is instructive to ask where we are today. The position that film studies finds itself in is one that could well be described as 'postmodern eclecticism'. No longer can the cinematic experience be explained by one totalizing theory. No longer is film criticism dominated by any one approach. Like the golfer searching in his bag for the appropriate club to play a particular shot, so the film critic selects the cinematic tools best suited to the analytical task. And this, I suggest, is what we ourselves must do in seeking to develop a theological approach to film.

The Lens of Narrative Criticism: Films approached as Texts

Narrative Theory/Narrative Criticism

Before I go on to do this, in the second part of this chapter, let me briefly highlight two particular approaches to film that I personally think are particularly appropriate for a theological perspective. The first is the lens of narrative theory or narrative criticism. Narrative theory attempts to analyse and explain the mechanics of storytelling, and narrative criticism provides its practical application. Though a prominent method for interpreting literary texts, it is being increasingly extended to films.[26]

Narrative and Film: Films as 'Texts'

'A narrative presents a chain of events which is situated in time and space',[27] and to that extent films can be considered to be 'texts', albeit 'filmic texts' or 'cinematic texts'. Treating them as such, of course, has given them a certain respectability, which in small measure accounts for the popularity of this approach among the critics.[28] Narrative theory supplies models and narrative criticism offers procedures for analysing the 'filmic' or 'cinematic text' through concentration, for example, on characters and characterization, plot, settings and point of view.[29]

Films as More than 'Texts'

A film is, of course, more than a text, or at least different from a literary text like a novel. The cinematic experience, being visual, is not the same as the reading experience. Images are presented to the moviegoer not constructed by the imagination, and these images are manipulated by the film-maker by means of editing, sound, lighting, music and so on. Novels describe characters, film presents them. Every novel has a narrator but the cinematic equivalent is more difficult to discern.[30] Film has a language but that language is communicated not only through the dialogue spoken by the actors but by the camera positions, by montage (the framing and linking of images), by *mise-en-scène*, costumes, lighting, colour, sound, music, etc.[31] In the words of Cook and Bernink:

> A fiction film's narration involves the discursive process of telling the story via various narrating systems such as the selection and ordering of story elements, the narrative voice and point of view, musical interventions, *mis-en-scène*, sound to image relations, and editing strategies. The textual analysis of any individual film or group of stories involves precisely the investigation of which narration devices are at work for which effects.[32]

For this reason, although narrative theory and narrative criticism have much to offer us, film must still be respected as film, and film criticism treated not simply as another form of literary analysis.

The Lens of Cultural Studies: Films approached in Context

The second approach to film that I think is particularly relevant for a theological perspective is the lens of cultural studies. This approach, as I have said, views film in its cultural context, and has been applied fruitfully by some recent authors of books on theology and film.

Among the useful recent interdisciplinary treatments is the volume of conference papers edited by J. C. Exum and S. D. Moore, entitled *Biblical Studies/Cultural Studies* and published in 1998.[33] Another is Margaret Miles's *Seeing and Believing. Religion and Values in the Movies* (1996), which (according to its cover blurb) 'refocuses attention from the film as a text to the social, political, and cultural matrix in which the film was produced and distributed'.[34] Using cultural studies, Miles focuses on the way religion is presented in modern film, as well as on the values that are 'imaged' in film, especially with regard to race, gender and class. A third recent book employing the cultural studies approach is *Imag(in)ing Otherness. Filmic Visions of Living Together* edited by S. B. Plate and David Jasper and published in 1999. The essays in this intelligent book 'examine the particular problems of "living together" when faced with the tensions brought out through the otherness of differing sexualities, ethnicities, genders, religions, cultures, and families'.[35]

3. Through a Lens even more Darkly: Critical Approaches to Theology and Film

Defining Theology and the Theological Approach to Film

If after the first part of this essay, on film theory and film criticism, the reader still 'sees through a lens darkly', then I am afraid in the second part we may 'see through a lens even more darkly'! We turn now to theology and film, and to the critical approaches that *currently* distinguish this interdiscipline. Let me begin with some definitions. What do I mean by 'theology'? The word 'theology' can be used in three major ways, depending on how widely or narrowly one defines it. At its narrowest, it is used to refer to systematic reflection on the nature and work of God. A slightly wider definition would see it as systematic reflection on Christian doctrine, embracing in addition the traditional categories of Christology (the person of Christ), soteriology (the work of Christ), pneumatology (the Spirit), cosmology (the nature of the world), eschatology (the end of the world), ecclesiology (the Church) and ethics. At its widest, it would embrace other religions and be understood as reflection upon what various religious traditions might regard as the ultimate reality (the sacred, the holy, the eternal).

It can also be understood in two ways. First, as an intellectual or academic discipline which can be engaged upon by believer and non-believer alike (study *about* God, *about* religion, *about* the Bible), or, second, as a spiritual exercise on the part of the believer (the study *of* God, *of* one's religion, *of* one's sacred text, the Bible). I myself would approach theology in its widest sense (though with a particular emphasis on Christianity), and understand it in its first sense, that is, as an academic or intellectual discipline capable of being practised irrespective of one's faith.[36] The appropriate subject of enquiry for theology, then, is first, religion(s), their sacred texts, their beliefs and practices, and, second, Christianity, the Bible and Christian doctrine and practice.

How should the two academic disciplines of theology and film relate to each other? And, within the circle of faith, how should the Church relate to the cinema? There has been a lot of discussion in recent books on theology and film on this very issue,[37] and the consensus that appears to be being reached is that theology, or the Church, and film studies, or the cinema, should treat each other as 'conversation' or 'dialogue partners', neither seeking to denigrate the other, neither seeking to judge the other, neither seeking to dilute the integrity of the other by reductionism or misguided attempts at appropriation.

What are the critical tools available to those who wish to participate in this dialogue? From the side of theology, there is a very wide arsenal of analytical methods and procedures, and a very rich technical vocabulary with which to interrogate films theologically. The traditional divisions of Christian doctrine just mentioned (Christology, soteriology, pneumatology, cosmology, eschatology, ecclesiology, ethics) are a case in point. From the side of film studies, as I hope to have shown, there is an equally wide armoury of critical approaches that can be employed, a number of them of particular relevance to theology: genre criticism, auteur criticism, thematic criticism, narrative criticism and intertextuality, cultural studies.

Religious Studies Approaches, or 'Screening the Sacred'

Theorizing the Relation between Religion and Film

In line with my wider definition of 'theology' as embracing the study of religion, the study of sacred texts like the Bible as well as the study of theology in its narrower sense, let me now briefly review some of the ways that film has been approached recently within the three academic areas of religious studies, biblical studies and theology. Within the field of religious studies, a key recent book is that by J. W. Martin and C. E. Ostwalt, *Screening the Sacred* (1995).[38] One major contribution of this book is to offer its readers three distinct ways in which to theorize the relation between religion and film: the theological, the mythological, and the ideological. Of the first way, they assert:

> The basic assumption behind theological criticism is that certain films can be properly understood, or can be best understood, as an elaboration on or the questioning of a particular religious tradition, text, or theme. Thus, underlying certain films there must be some basic moral, ethical, or theological position upon which the meaning of the film depends.[39]

What distinguishes the mythological approach is that those who practise it

> see religion as a universal and ubiquitous human activity; they assert that religion manifests itself through cross-cultural forms, including myth, ritual, systems of purity, and gods. Myth consists of stories that provide human communities with grounding prototypes, models for life, reports of foundational realities, and dramatic presentations of fundamental values: Myth reveals a culture's bedrock assumptions and aspirations.[40]

With reference to the ideological approach, they make the following statement:

> In contrast to theologians and myth critics, still other scholars interpret religion in relation to what is not religion; for example, the social structure, the unconscious, gender, and power relations. Although not reducing religion to something nonreligious, they think it is important to situate religion in its historical, social, and political contexts. They focus especially upon how religion legitimates or challenges dominant visions of the social order. In other words, they study the relation of religion and ideology.[41]

'Looking at' or 'for Religion' in the Movies

So how do we look for religion in the movies? The literature I have reviewed suggests different routes using different methods. A classic in the field, Paul Schrader's *Transcendental Style in Film: Ozu, Bresson, Dreyer* (1972) employs a mixture of *formalism* and *auteur criticism* to claim that we can recognize religious transcendence or 'the Holy' in film by means of its common cinematic *style*, as exemplified in three very different directors (Yasujiro Ozu, Robert Bresson and Carl Dreyer) working in three very different cultural milieux (Japan, France and Denmark). What Schrader calls transcendental style is characterized by an 'aesthetic of sparseness' and this is achieved by such formal devices as 'austere camerawork, acting devoid of self-consciousness and editing that avoids editorial comment'.[42] A much more recent book, R. A. Blake's *Afterimage: The Indelible Catholic Imagination of Six American Filmmakers* (2000) also employs *auteur criticism* to claim that we can observe the religious *worldview*, in this case, that of Roman Catholicism, in the work of six prominent film-makers (Martin Scorsese, Alfred Hitchcock, Frank Capra, John Ford, Francis Ford Coppola and Brian De Palma).[43] Also approaching film via the concept of *world-view*, but employing the *mythological approach* is B. B. Scott's *Hollywood Dreams and Biblical Stories* (1994).

Instead of propagating its myths round the fireside, as it were, modern society does it through the movies. Drawing on Claude Lévi-Strauss in order to expose these myths, Scott brings the Bible into conversation with aspects of American culture and its values: 'wealth and poverty, race relations, moral aloneness, the superhero and the solo redeemer, violence and war, the mythical West, relations of the sexes, and fears of the future'.[44]

One very popular route to explore religion and film is to do so by way of religious themes. M. Alsford in *What If? Religious Themes in Science Fiction* (2000) uses a combination of *genre* and *thematic criticism* to explore the religious *themes* that are reflected in one of the most popular movie genres, science fiction.[45] Using cultural criticism, Plate and Jasper in the aforementioned *Imag(in)ing Otherness. Filmic Visions of Living Together* (1999) cast their net wide over religious traditions like Chan Buddhism, Hinduism, Native American religions, Christianity and Judaism to explore the single theme of 'otherness' in film and its implications for 'living together' or community. T. Sanders, on the other hand, in the recently published *Celluloid Saints. Images of Sanctity in Film* (2002) confines herself to Christianity, and largely the Catholic Church, and explores the depiction of saints in the movies.[46]

So in answer to our question, how do we look for religion in the movies, the classic and current literature seems to suggest that we can do it using different methods, by focusing on transcendental style, on religious auteurs, or on myths and world-views and religious themes.

Biblical Studies Approaches, or 'Screening Scripture'

Bringing the Bible and Film into Dialogue

A number of books have appeared recently in my own field, biblical studies, that have also reiterated the notion of bringing the Bible and film 'into dialogue with one another', or treating them as 'conversation partners'. 'Intertextuality' is the buzzword, and it is exemplified in the work of two scholars, to whom I wish to draw attention, Larry Kreitzer and Robert Jewett, and in a collection of newly published essays entitled *Screening Scripture. Intertextual Connections Between Scripture and Film* (2002), and edited by George Aichele and Richard Walsh. The essays discuss a variety of films that 'screen', 'project', 'quote' or 'rewrite' Scripture in the sense that they make a cultural appropriation of the sacred text and present it to contemporary audiences within a different narrative setting and within a more vivid medium, namely film. What distinguishes the volume is its 'postmodern world-view', the contributors (academics all, from established scholars to doctoral candidates) reflecting a variety of multidisciplinary approaches and concerns (some theoretical, some merely personal), whether intertextual, sociocultural, psychoanalytic, gender or sexuality-oriented, or narrative-critical.[47] Aichele edited in 1997, along with Tina Pippin, a similar intertextual compilation entitled *The Monstrous and the Unspeakable. The Bible as Fantastic Literature* (1997).[48]

If *Screening Scripture* focuses on the Bible's relation to its many filmic 'tributaries', then Larry Kreitzer's book, *Gospel Images in Fiction and Film. On Reversing the Hermeneutical Flow* (2002), as its subtitle suggests, 'reverses the hermeneutical flow' by concentrating on the way that an intertextual study of literature and film can enrich our understanding of the sacred 'source'.[49] Kreitzer, Tutor of New Testament at Regent's Park College, Oxford, has published three previous volumes with this cross-disciplinary approach in the Biblical Seminar Series: *The New Testament in Fiction and Film* (1993), *The Old Testament in Fiction and Film* (1994) and *Pauline Images in Fiction and Film* (1999).[50]

While also adopting intertextuality (as well as cultural criticism) as an analytical tool, Jewett's approach to the dialogue is different. In his *Saint Paul at the Movies. The Apostle's Dialogue with American Culture* (1993) and his *Saint Paul Returns to the Movies. Triumph over Shame* (1999), he proposes the model of the 'interpretive arch', at one end of which is the biblical text in its ancient cultural context, at the other the contemporary film in its modern cultural context. In a process that he describes as 'prophetic', the task of the interdisciplinary interpreter is to exchange insights between the two while offering each its due respect.[51]

Intertextuality, then, is an important tool in the arsenal of those who would bring the Bible into relation with contemporary culture, but it is not the only one. As with modern day film studies, many interpreters are eclectic or multidisciplinary in their choice of analytical tools, and in some cases, 'postmodern' in their attitudes to the enterprise. I have already referred to B. B. Scott and his combined use of mythological criticism and thematic criticism in *Hollywood Dreams and Biblical Stories* (1994). My own work, as I've indicated, uses a mixture of aesthetics, textual analysis, narrative criticism, intertextuality, social context and ideology, and includes a focus on such contemporary issues as gender and ethnicity.[52] R. C. Stern, C. N. Jefford and G. Debona's *Savior on the Silver Screen* (1999) employs historical criticism, aesthetics and contextual analysis as the three lenses through which they view the Christ film.[53] In *Biblical Epics. Sacred Narrative in the Hollywood Cinema* (1993), Bruce Babington and Peter Evans employ genre criticism, narrative criticism and cultural criticism in their treatment of the biblical epic, focus on themes of ethnicity, sexuality, gender and religion, and, in their words, 'deliberately stop short of totalistic theorising, as part of a strategy aimed against reductionism'.[54] Finally, sophisticated literary analysis combined with cultural criticism combine in Melanie Wright's recently published *Moses in America. The Cultural Uses of Biblical Narrative* (2002).[55]

'Looking at' or 'for Jesus' in the Movies

Just as religious studies approaches to film investigate the 'Screening of the Sacred' and 'look at' or 'look for religion' in the movies, so a major preoccupation in biblical studies approaches is 'looking at' and especially 'looking for Jesus' in the movies.

This is a subject I have treated more extensively elsewhere,[56] but here let me briefly comment on the literature. I have already mentioned R. C. Stern, C. N. Jefford and G. Debona's *Savior on the Silver Screen* (1999). To this may be added W. B. Tatum's *Jesus at the Movies: A Guide to the First Hundred Years* (1997), one of the most comprehensive recent guides to the story of Jesus on film.[57] I myself published an essay on 'Jesus Christ Movie-Star: The Depiction of Jesus in the Cinema' in C. Marsh and G. Ortiz (eds), *Explorations in Theology and Film. Movies and Meaning* (1997),[58] and there I treated not only the classic Christ films (where Jesus is the central character) but also referred to the more elusive Christ-figures that have made various cinematic appearances. Lloyd Baugh's book, *Imaging the Divine. Jesus and Christ-Figures in Film* (1997) is the most comprehensive recent contribution to the subject.[59] Among other things, Baugh identifies eight manifestations of the Christ-figure in film: as saint, as priest, as woman, as an extreme figure such as a clown, or fool, or mad-man, as outlaw, as child, in a dramatic role, and as popular adventure hero.

In my *Epworth Review* article of 2000, which was based on a presentation I gave in 1999 at the St Deiniol's Theology and Film conference, I added to the number of Christ-figures that have been or could be detected in the films appearing between 1993 and 1999,[60] and in my most recent paper, given at the conference in 2004, this list was further updated (see Appendix 2). Christ-figures in film continue to be spotted and proposed in the current literature. Three candidates nominated (with qualifications) by Christopher Deacy, for example, in his *Screen Christologies. Redemption and the Medium of Film* (2001) are Travis Bickle in *Taxi Driver* (1976), Jake La Motta in *Raging Bull* (1980) and Max Cady in *Cape Fear* (1991), all films by Martin Scorsese.[61] A further candidate, the mentally challenged Karl Childers (played by Billy Bob Thornton) in *Sling Blade* (1996) has been suggested by Mark Roncace in an essay appearing in Aichele and Walsh's *Screening Scripture* (2002).[62] This whole area opens up a series of related issues, raising not only the question of how we establish the Christ-figure in film, but even how we read films and how theology and film should relate responsibly to one another.

Theological Approaches or 'Looking for Mr Good(bar)'/ 'Waiting for God(ot)?'

Theorizing the Relation of Theology and Film

Let me turn finally to the subject of theological approaches to film, and review some of the literature that is appearing on the subject. Theological approaches to film may be concerned to understand the relation between film and theology, or simply interested in the uses of film for theology. They can be 'cognitive' or 'actualizing', or, to put it another way, academic or practical. And this reveals itself in the literature. Mention has already been made of the valuable essay by David Graham on 'The Uses of Film in Theology' in C. Marsh and G. W. Ortiz (eds), *Explorations in Theology and Film. Movies and Meaning* (1997) and of the perceptive discussion of 'Film and Theologies of Culture' by Clive Marsh in that same volume. A miscellany of essays on the relationship between religion and film is also to be found in J. R. May (ed.), *New Image of Religious Film* (1997).

What are the approaches that current writers are taking to the relationship between theology and film? I have identified four approaches, each of which works with a different model, and each of which implies a different understanding of the relationship. Some are cognitive in orientation, others actualizing. You might spot your own characteristic approach among these, or, if not, you might like to consider how you might describe or theorize your own personal approach.

Approaching Films Evangelistically – One observed strategy is 'approaching films evangelistically'. This is the approach taken in Ian Maher's, *Faith and Film. Close Encounters of an Evangelistic Kind* (2002), a book that, 'after addressing some key issues . . . looks at the ways in which discussing films can open surprising opportunities to build bridges and share faith. It concludes by setting out practical ways to use film in the local church and suggests some useful further resources'.[63] While seeking to encourage Christian appreciation of the cinema, Brian Godawa's *Hollywood Worldviews. Watching Films with Wisdom and Discernment* (2002) is a somewhat more aggressive book. Written by a Christian screenwriter, it aims to educate the believer on how to recognize the myths, world-views and (existentialist and postmodern) ideologies promoted by contemporary film, often with a view to resisting or countering them.[64] A similarly exclusivist position is taken in P. Fraser, N. Fraser and V. Edwin's *ReViewing the Movies. A Christian Response to Contemporary Film* (2000) as the cover blurb indicates:

> With film being one of the most powerful cultural influences in America, we Christians cheat ourselves and limit our opportunities to

witness to the culture when we label all movies as either 'completely corrupt' or as 'harmless entertainment.' The one stance thoroughly excludes a possible source of greater understanding; the other allows ungodly values to freely enter our hearts. What we need is the balance that discernment provides.

A film not made solely by or about Christians can still be uplifting and connect with us spiritually – as long as it conveys truth with cinematic excellence. Yet many of us are unequipped to determine which movies meet that qualification. That's why we need the right tools. With them we can shift to the offensive and intentionally evaluate and discuss how a movie illustrates God's truth.[65]

Approaching Films Spiritually – 'A film not made solely by or about Christians can still be uplifting and connect with us spiritually.' This last statement illustrates a second observed strategy among those who wish to relate theology to film and that is 'approaching films spiritually'. The approach was discussed in a special edition of *Image. The Journal of Arts & Religion* in 1998 entitled *Screening Mystery. The Religious Imagination in Contemporary Film*, and is one popular among those who take an 'actualizing' rather than a 'cognitive' view of the relation between film and theology, who welcome the cinema's treatment of human values, but who are not necessarily supporters of institutionalized religion.[66] On the other hand, some recent books are unashamedly devotional in tenor, 'connect[ing] movies with the spiritual life of moviegoers' like E. McNulty's *Praying the Movies. Daily Meditations from Classic Films* (2001)[67] or, like B. P. Stone's *Faith and Film. Theological Themes at the Cinema* (2000) using 'movies and phrases of the Apostles' Creed to illustrate basic themes of theology and how they manifest themselves in popular culture'.[68]

Approaching Films Sacramentally – A third observed strategy, and here we move on to more academic or intellectual ground is 'approaching films sacramentally'. The concept is introduced in Peter Fraser's *Images of the Passion. The Sacramental Mode in Film* (1998). In a manner reminiscent of Paul Schrader but emphasizing content as much as style, Fraser 'analyses "sacramental" films, where the narrative has been disrupted and redeemed by a divine presence, in an analogy to Christian liturgical and devotional patterns. This presence transforms the film's narrative into the most recognizable of all Christian narrative patterns: the Passion.'[69] Fraser describes the 'sacramental mode', in respect of characterization, as follows:

Characters who undergo a Passion experience in a film narrative will first take on a representational role as bearers of the desires of a community . . . The redemptive figure in many films will typically undergo a lonely purgative ritual in the course of the narrative. This ritual includes either physical, emotional or spiritual suffering, and it concludes as the character resigns to the forces compelling this trek and accepts whatever consequences the narrative movements decree.[70]

Approaching Films Redemptively – A fourth but closely related strategy is 'approaching films 'redemptively'. This approach is impressively illustrated in Christopher Deacy's aforementioned *Screen Christologies. Redemption and the Medium of Film* (2001), a book that is arguably the most consistently theological reading of film that we have seen recently. Using genre criticism on film noir and auteur criticism on the films of Martin Scorsese, Deacy explores the Christian notion of redemption in relation to the medium of film. In its treatment of the human condition and in its treatment of the film noir protagonist (a functionally equivalent Christ-figure) film noir can become, he argues, a 'site of redemptive activity' for the spectator.

'Looking at' or 'for God' in the Movies

'The religious imagination is alive and well in the movies.' This is the conclusion of A. Bergesen and A. M. Greeley's recent *God in the Movies: A Sociological Investigation* (2000), a book that employs sociology, cultural criticism and narrative criticism to explore the images of God and angels in the cinema.[71] A similar conclusion was reached by J. R. May in *New Image of Religious Film* (1997), as well as now more than a decade ago in *Image and Likeness: Religious Visions in American Film Classics* (1992), a collection of essays using ideological criticism to trace 'America's religious vision in thirty-five classic American films, from *City Lights* to *Hannah and Her Sisters*'.[72]

Conclusion

Film studies and the academic trinity of religious studies, biblical studies and theology are not only established but vibrant disciplines, and it is to be hoped that the relatively recent interdiscipline of theology and film will lead to new and fruitful insights and results. If they are to have a productive dialogue and to function as suitable 'conversation partners' then they will need to learn from each other, and this learning process must include an understanding of their respective critical methodologies. I trust that this chapter has contributed to that understanding, and that, even if you still see through a lens darkly, then I can claim to have provided you with more than one lens to do so.

4. Face to Face: Critical Approaches to Theology and Film – Some Selected Films and Clips

In this section of the chapter, you are encouraged to follow up what has been said by watching three selected films or film clips and commenting upon them in light of the approaches that have been reviewed. To help you do this, I have supplied three further text boxes.

The first text box (1.4), *Notes on the Films/Clips Selected*, specifies the films selected, and some key descriptors (genre, cast, plot). The brief plot descriptions are taken from a useful tool, J. Walker (ed.), *Halliwell's Film and Video Guide* (London: HarperCollins, 2000), as are the short selected reviews. A specific clip, or sequence (together with its approximate time location within the film) is suggested for each film, as is some select reading on it. The second text box (1.5), *Critical Methods and Approaches*, is a summation of the various theories and criticisms reviewed, together with some of the key questions that they put to films, or by means of which they interrogate them. They are arranged in the form of six lenses, three from each of the two disciplines of Film and Theology: Aesthetics, Textual Analysis, Contextual Analysis, Religious Studies Approaches, Biblical Studies Approaches and Theological Approaches. The third text box (1.6) is a *Comment Sheet* on which you may wish to note your comments.

1.4 Notes on the Films/Clips Selected

Apocalypse Now (Francis Ford Coppola, 1979)

Genre: War Film; Literary Adaptation from a novella by Joseph Conrad, *Heart of Darkness*

Cast: Martin Sheen, Robert Duvall, Frederic Forrest, Marlon Brando, Sam Bottoms, Dennis Hopper

Plot: 'A Vietnam captain is instructed to eliminate a colonel who has retired to the hills and is fighting his own war.'

Review: 'Pretentious war movie, made even more hollow-sounding by the incomprehensible performance of Brando as the mad martinet. Some vivid scenes along the way, and some interesting parallels with Conrad's *Heart of Darkness*, but these hardly atone for the director's delusion that prodigal expenditure of time and money will result in great art. (The movie took so long to complete that it was dubbed *Apocalypse Later*.)' (J. Walker (ed.), *Halliwell's Film and Video Guide*, London: HarperCollins, 2000, p. 36).

Clip: 'The Horror! The Horror' (Kurtz's Death): *c*.02.29.08–02.31.58

Read: L. J. Kreitzer, *Gospel Images in Fiction and Film. On Reversing the Hermeneutical Flow*, The Biblical Seminar, 84, Sheffield: Sheffield Academic Press, 2002, pp. 45–104; C. E. Ostwalt, 'Hollywood and Armageddon: Apocalyptic Themes in Recent Cinematic Presentation', in J. W. Martin and C. E. Ostwalt (eds), *Screening the Sacred. Religion, Myth, and Ideology in Popular American Film*, Boulder, CO: Westview, 1995, pp. 55–63.

Babette's Feast (Gabriel Axel, 1987)

Genre: 'Foodie Movie'; Literary Adaptation from a story by Isak Dinesen (Karen Blixen)

Cast: Stéphane Audran, Jean-Philippe Lafont, Jarl Kulle, Bibi Andersson, Bodil Kjer, Birgitte Federspiel

Plot: 'A French refugee in nineteenth-century Norway wins 10,000 francs in a lottery and spends it all on preparing a sumptuous banquet for her Lutheran employers and their friends.'

Review: 'Ironic and elegant fable juxtaposing bacchanalian extravagance with narrow piety' (Walker, *Halliwell's Guide*, p. 50).

Clip: 'An Artist is never Poor' (Babette's Verdict on the Feast): *c*.01.40.32–01.43.43

Read: A. M. Greeley, 'Babette's Feast of Love: Symbols Subtle but Patent', in A. Bergesen and A. M. Greeley (eds), *God in the Movies: A Sociological Investigation*, New Brunswick, NJ: Transaction Publishers, 2000, pp. 49–53; R. Jewett, *Saint Paul Returns to the Movies. Triumph over Shame*, Grand Rapids, MI and Cambridge, UK: Eerdmans, 1999, pp. 38–51; M. C. Maisto, 'Cinematic Communion? *Babette's Feast*, Transcendental Style, and Interdisciplinarity', in S. B.

Plate and D. Jasper (eds), *Imag(in)ing Otherness. Filmic Visions of Living Together*, 1999, Atlanta, GA: Scholars Press, pp. 83–98; P. Fraser, *Images of the Passion. The Sacramental Mode in Film*, Trowbridge, Wilts: Flicks Books, 1998, pp. 107–16; C. Marsh, 'Did You Say "Grace"?: Eating in Community in *Babette's Feast*', in C. Marsh and G. W. Ortiz (eds), *Explorations in Theology and Film. Movies and Meaning*, Oxford: Blackwell, 1997, pp. 207–18.

Bram Stoker's Dracula (Francis Ford Coppola, 1992)

Genre: Horror Film; Vampire Movie

Cast: Gary Oldman, Anthony Hopkins, Winona Ryder, Keanu Reeves

Plot: 'In the 1480s Dracula curses God and becomes a vampire after his wife, thinking that he has died in battle, commits suicide; 400 or so years later in London he falls in love with a woman who seems to be her reincarnation.'

Review: 'A lush, over-dressed Gothic romance that plays down the menace and dread of the original, with performances that range from the inadequate to the over-ripe' (Walker, *Halliwell's Guide*, p. 109).

Clip: 'Where is my God? He has forsaken me. It is finished!' (The Death of Dracula): *c.*01.40.32–01.43.43

Read: T. Pippin, 'Of Gods and Demons. Blood Sacrifice and Eternal Life in *Dracula* and the Apocalypse of John', in G. Aichele and R. Walsh (eds), *Screening Scripture. Intertextual Connections Between Scripture and Film*, Harrisburg, PA: Trinity Press International, 2002, pp. 24–41; L. J. Kreitzer, *Pauline Images in Fiction and Film. On Reversing the Hermeneutical Flow*, The Biblical Seminar, 61, Sheffield: Sheffield Academic Press, 1999, pp. 113–42.

1.5 Critical Methods and Approaches

A. Lens 1: Aesthetics (Formalism/Expressionism/Realism)
Comment on the mise-en-scène (setting, acting, costumes, lighting, sound, etc.) and montage (camerawork, editing, etc.)

B. Lens 2: Textual Analysis.
1. *Genre Criticism*
What is the film's genre and how are the genric conventions treated?

2. *Auteur Criticism*
Does knowledge of the director's other work illumine the film/clip?

3. *Narrative Criticism*
Comment on the plot, characterization (acting), settings, etc.

4. *Thematic Criticism*
What themes are treated?

C. Lens 3: Contextual Analysis
1. *Historical Criticism*
What relation does the film bear to history?

2. *Marxist Interpretation*
What ideology or world-view is presented and how does it relate to notions of alienation, class conflict, capitalist production, etc?

3. *Psychoanalysis*
What light is furnished by psychoanalytic or psychological categories (desire, aggression, guilt, sexual interest, the Oedipus complex and other neuroses, personal identity, etc.)?

4. *Cultural Studies*
What light is shed by cultural factors as well as by matters relating to production, distribution and reception?

5. *Sociology and Ethnography*
What social or ethnic issues are raised?

6. *Feminist Film Criticism and Queer Theory*
How is gender configured in the clip under review (masculinity and femininity)?

D. Lens 4: Religious Studies Approaches
1. *Mythological Approach*
How is religion presented in the film in terms of cross-cultural forms, including myth, ritual, systems of purity, and gods, etc.?

2. *Ideological Approach*
How does the film/clip challenge or legitimate dominant visions, world-views, etc. of the social order?

E. Lens 5: Biblical Studies Approaches
1. *Intertextuality*
How is the Bible treated in the film/clip?

F. Lens 6: Theological Approaches
Does the film/clip have evangelistic, spiritual, sacramental or redemptive significance for you?

1.6 Comments on Films/Clips

Apocalypse Now (Francis Ford Coppola, 1979): 'The Horror! The Horror' (Kurtz's Death)

Babette's Feast (Gabriel Axel, 1987): 'An Artist is never Poor' (Babette's Verdict on the Feast)

Bram Stoker's Dracula (Francis Ford Coppola, 1992): 'Where is my God? He has forsaken me. It is finished!'(The Death of Dracula).

Notes

1 For an example of one New Testament scholar's critical reflection on his interpretative approach to religion and film, see R. Jewett, *Saint Paul at the Movies. The Apostle's Dialogue with American Culture*, Louisville, KY: Westminster John Knox, 1993, pp. 7–12.

2 A. Eichenberger, 'Approaches to Film Criticism', in J. R. May (ed.), *New Image of Religious Film*, Kansas City, MO: Sheed & Ward, 1997, pp. 6–7.

3 T. Corrigan, *A Short Guide to Writing about Film*, The Short Guide Series, New York: HarperCollins College, 1994, p. 33.

4 See W. R. Telford, 'Religion, the Bible and Theology in Recent Films (1993–99)', *Epworth Review*, 27 (2000): 31–40 for a popular version of this presentation, and the Appendix of this book for a list of the films reviewed (now updated to 2004).

5 This was published in an expanded form as 'Jesus and Women in Fiction and Film', in I. R. Kitzberger (ed.), *Transformative Encounters. Jesus and Women Reviewed*, Leiden: Brill, 2000, pp. 353–91.

6 These last three presentations are published here.

7 This approach was articulated in W. R. Telford, 'The New Testament in Fiction and Film: A Biblical Scholar's Perspective', in J. G. Davies, G. Harvey and W. Watson (eds), *Words Remembered, Texts Renewed. Essays in Honour of J. F. A. Sawyer*, Sheffield: Sheffield Academic Press, 1995, pp. 360–94.

8 See, for example, P. Cook and M. Bernink, 'Part 7: Theoretical Frameworks', in P. Cook and M. Bernink (eds), *The Cinema Book*, London: British Film Institute, 1999, pp. 319–73; R. K. Johnston, *Reel Spirituality. Theology and Film in Dialogue*, Engaging Culture, Grand Rapids: Baker Academic, 2000, esp. chap. 7; R. Stam, *Film Theory. An Introduction*, Oxford: Blackwell, 2000; Eichenberger, 'Film Criticism', in May (ed.), *New Image*, pp. 3–16; D. Browne, 'Film, Movies, Meanings', in C. Marsh and G. W. Ortiz (eds), *Explorations in Theology and Film. Movies and Meaning*, Oxford: Blackwell, 1997, pp. 9–19; Corrigan, *Writing about Film*; E. Katz, 'Theory, Film', in E. Katz (ed.), *The Macmillan International Film Encyclopedia*, London: HarperCollins, 1994, pp. 1348–9; J. Monaco, *How to Read a Film. The Art, Technology, Language, History, and Theory of Film and Media*, Oxford and New York: Oxford University Press, 1981.

9 Katz, 'Theory, Film', in Katz, *Macmillan Encyclopedia*, p. 1348.

10 Monaco, *How to Read a Film*, p. 389.

11 Corrigan, *Writing about Film*, p. 78.

12 Katz, 'Theory, Film', p. 1348. See also Monaco, *How to Read a Film*, pp. 394–416; Corrigan, *Writing about Film*, p. 85.

13 See, for example, Johnston, *Reel Spirituality*, pp. 126–32.

14 See Johnston, *Reel Spirituality*, pp. 132–9; Eichenberger, 'Film Criticism', pp. 7–8; Corrigan, *Writing about Film*, p. 83; Katz, 'Theory, Film', p. 1348.

15 See Johnston, *Reel Spirituality*, pp. 139–46; Corrigan, *Writing about Film*, p. 34.

16 See Browne, 'Film, Movies, Meanings', *Explorations*, pp. 12–13, 17–18; Katz, 'Theory, Film', p. 1349; Monaco, *How to Read a Film*, pp. 417–24; Cook and Bernink, 'Theoretical Frameworks', pp. 319–32.

17 See Monaco, *How to Read a Film*, p. 424.

18 Eichenberger, 'Film Criticism', p. 8.

19 See Browne, 'Film, Movies, Meanings', p. 18; Corrigan, *Writing about Film*, pp. 86–7; Katz, 'Theory, Film', p. 1349.

20 C. Schwarz, G. Davidson, A. Seaton and V. Tebbit (eds), *Chambers English Dictionary*, Cambridge: Chambers, 1988, pp. 526, 1318, 1656.

21 Cook and Bernink, 'Theoretical Frameworks', pp. 335–7, 341–52; Browne, 'Film, Movies, Meanings', pp. 18–19; Katz, 'Theory, Film', p. 1349.

22 See Johnston, *Reel Spirituality*, pp. 146–50, and esp. p. 147.

23 See Cook and Bernink, 'Theoretical Frameworks', pp. 323, 332–3, 366–73.

24 Browne, 'Film, Movies, Meanings', p. 19.

25 See Cook and Bernink, 'Theoretical Frameworks', pp. 353–65; Katz, 'Theory, Film', p. 1349.

26 See J. Lothe, *Narrative in Fiction and Film. An Introduction*, Oxford: Oxford University Press, 2000, esp. p. viii: 'Another characteristic of recent developments is that, partly as a result of the decreased differentiation between fiction and history, narrative theory is being used to a greater extent in research which is not primarily (or not only) concerned with literature. The link between narrative theory and film studies has also been strengthened.'

27 Lothe, *Narrative*, p. 3; cf. also pp. 8–9; Corrigan, *Writing about Film*, pp. 36–7; Browne, 'Film, Movies, Meanings', pp. 16–17.

28 See Stam, *Film Theory*, p. 186.

29 'Like narrative, *point of view* is a term that film shares with the literary and visual arts. In the broadest sense it refers to the position from which something is seen and, by implication, how that point of view determines what you see. . . . Point of view is central to writing about films because films are basically about seeing the world in a certain way' (Corrigan, *Writing about Film*, p. 42).

30 For discussion of the differences, as well as the similarities, between literature and film, see Lothe, *Narrative*, esp. pp. 8, 11–13 (on film communication), 27–31 (on the film narrator), 62–3 (on narrative time in film), 85–91 (on events, characters and characterization in film adaptation). On the difficulties in extending literary models to film, see also Stam, *Film Theory*, pp. 185–92. On film and the novel, see Monaco, *How to Read a Film*, pp. 44–8.

31 For discussion of these various elements, see Cook and Bernink, 'Theoretical Frameworks', pp. 320–2 and Corrigan, *Writing about Film*, pp. 47–68.

32 Cook and Bernink, 'Theoretical Frameworks', p. 322.

33 J. C. Exum and S. D. Moore (eds), *Biblical Studies/Cultural Studies. The Third Sheffield Colloquium*, Journal for the Study of the Old Testament Supplement Series 266, Gender, Culture, Theory 7, Sheffield: Sheffield Academic Press, 1998.

34 M. R. Miles, *Seeing and Believing. Religion and Values in the Movies*, Boston, MA: Beacon, 1996.

35 See S. B. Plate and D. Jasper (eds), *Imag(in)ing Otherness. Filmic Visions of Living Together*, American Academy of Religion Cultural Criticism Series, 7, Atlanta, GA: Scholars Press, 1999, cover blurb.

36 For other views, see, for example, Johnston, *Reel Spirituality*, pp. 16–17.

37 See, for example, Johnston, *Reel Spirituality*, esp. pp. 41–62, 151–72; C. Marsh, 'Film and Theologies of Culture', pp. 21–34; D. J. Graham, 'The Uses

of Film in Theology', pp. 35–43; T. M. Martin, *Images and the Imageless. A Study in Religious Consciousness and Film*, Lewisburg, London and Toronto: Bucknell University Press; Associated University Presses, 1991.

38 J. W. Martin and C. E. Ostwalt (eds), *Screening the Sacred. Religion, Myth, and Ideology in Popular American Film*, Boulder, CO: Westview, 1995.

39 Martin and Ostwalt (eds), *Screening*, pp. 13–14.

40 Martin and Ostwalt (eds), *Screening*, p. 6.

41 Martin and Ostwalt (eds), *Screening*, p. 7.

42 P. Schrader, *Transcendental Style in Film: Ozu, Bresson, Dreyer*, Berkeley, Los Angeles and London: University of California Press, 1972, cover blurb.

43 R. Blake, *Afterimage: The Indelible Catholic Imagination of Six American Filmmakers*, Chicago: Loyola, 2000.

44 B. B. Scott, *Hollywood Dreams and Biblical Stories*, Minneapolis, MN: Augsburg Fortress, 1994, cover blurb.

45 M. Alsford, *What If? Religious Themes in Science Fiction*, London: Darton, Longman & Todd, 2000.

46 T. Sanders, *Celluloid Saints. Images of Sanctity in Film*, Macon, GA: Mercer University Press, 2002.

47 G. Aichele and R. Walsh (eds), *Screening Scripture. Intertextual Connections Between Scripture and Film*, Harrisburg, PA: Trinity Press International, 2002.

48 G. Aichele and T. Pippin (eds), *The Monstrous and the Unspeakable. The Bible as Fantastic Literature*, Playing the Texts, 1, Sheffield: Sheffield Academic Press, 1997.

49 L. J. Kreitzer, *Gospel Images in Fiction and Film. On Reversing the Hermeneutical Flow*, The Biblical Seminar, 84, Sheffield: Sheffield Academic Press, 2002.

50 L. J. Kreitzer, *The New Testament in Fiction and Film. On Reversing the Hermeneutical Flow*, The Biblical Seminar, 17, Sheffield: Sheffield Academic Press, 1993; L. J. Kreitzer, *The Old Testament in Fiction and Film. On Reversing the Hermeneutical Flow*, The Biblical Seminar, 24, Sheffield: Sheffield Academic Press, 1994; L. J. Kreitzer, *Pauline Images in Fiction and Film. On Reversing the Hermeneutical Flow*, The Biblical Seminar, 61, Sheffield: Sheffield Academic Press, 1999.

51 R. Jewett, *Saint Paul at the Movies. The Apostle's Dialogue with American Culture*. Louisville, KY: Westminster John Knox, 1993; R. Jewett, *Saint Paul Returns to the Movies. Triumph over Shame*, Grand Rapids, MI and Cambridge, UK: Eerdmans, 1999.

52 See, for example, Telford, 'Fiction and Film' and 'Jesus and Women'.

53 R. C. Stern, C. N. Jefford and G. Debona, *Savior on the Silver Screen*, New York and Mahwah, NJ: Paulist, 1999.

54 B. Babington and P. W. Evans, *Biblical Epics. Sacred Narrative in the Hollywood Cinema*, Manchester: Manchester University Press, 1993, p. 22.

55 M. J. Wright, *Moses in America. The Cultural Uses of Biblical Narrative*, AAR Cultural Criticism Series, Oxford: Oxford University Press, 2002.

56 W. R. Telford, 'Searching for Jesus: Recognizing or Imagining Christ-Figures in the Movies' (unpublished paper given at the St Deiniol's Theology and Film conference, April, 2004).

57 W. B. Tatum, *Jesus at the Movies: A Guide to the First Hundred Years*, Santa Rosa, CA: Polebridge, 1997.

58 W. R. Telford, 'Jesus Christ Movie-Star: The Depiction of Jesus in the Cinema', in Marsh and Ortiz (eds), *Explorations*, pp. 115–39.

59 L. Baugh, *Imaging the Divine. Jesus and Christ-Figures in Film*, Kansas City, MO: Sheed & Ward, 1997.

60 Telford, 'Recent Films (1993–99)', pp. 31–40.

61 C. Deacy, *Screen Christologies. Redemption and the Medium of Film*, Religion, Culture and Society, Cardiff: University of Wales Press, 2001, esp. pp. 123, 128.

62 M. Roncace, 'Paradoxical Protagonists: *Sling Blade*'s Karl and Jesus Christ', in Aichele and Walsh (eds), *Screening Scripture*, pp. 279–300.

63 I. Maher, *Faith and Film. Close Encounters of an Evangelistic Kind*, Cambridge: Grove Books Ltd, 2002, cover blurb.

64 B. Godawa, *Hollywood Worldviews. Watching Films with Wisdom and Discernment*, Downers Grove, IL: InterVarsity, 2002.

65 P. Fraser, N. Fraser and V. Edwin, *ReViewing the Movies. A Christian Response to Contemporary Film*, Wheaton: Crossway Books, 2000.

66 G. Wolfe, 'Screening Mystery. The Religious Imagination in Contemporary Film', *Image. A Journal of the Arts & Religion*, 20 (1998).

67 E. McNulty, *Praying the Movies. Daily Meditations from Classic Films*, Louisville, KY: Geneva, 2001.

68 B. P. Stone, *Faith and Film. Theological Themes at the Cinema*, St Louis, MI: Chalice, 2000, cover blurb.

69 P. Fraser, *Images of the Passion. The Sacramental Mode in Film*, Trowbridge, Wilts: Flicks Books, 1998, cover blurb.

70 Fraser, *Images*, pp. 9, 10; see also Eichenberger, 'Film Criticism', pp. 14–15 for another application of the 'sacramental' approach to films.

71 A. Bergesen and A. M. Greeley, *God in the Movies: A Sociological Investigation*, New Brunswick, NJ: Transaction Publishers, 2000, cover blurb.

72 J. R. May (ed.), *Image and Likeness: Religious Visions in American Film Classics*, Isaac Hecker Studies in Religion and American Culture, New York: Paulist, 1992, cover blurb.

2. Key Concepts in Film Studies

BRIAN BAKER

This chapter will offer a basic introduction to some of the key concepts used to analyse film, and will treat Cecil B. DeMille's 1956 film *The Ten Commandments* as a case study to illustrate ways of 'reading' a film. Films make meaning not in one way, but in a plurality of ways. By using one film, and analysing it through a variety of critical approaches, this chapter will hopefully provide a mini-casebook with concrete examples.

1. *Mise-en-scène* and Narrative

Mise-en-scène is from the French, literally meaning 'the fact of putting into the scene'; a term derived from the theatre. It means how the filmed event is staged, in terms of the film frame: physical space, objects, décor, costume, movement and expression of actors, focus and lighting. Reading the *mise-en-scène* of a film sequence is a kind of visual close reading, paying attention to the way in which the actual composition of the film frame is organized to create meaning.

In *The Ten Commandments* (1956), the composition of the film frame tends to be fairly static. The film begins with a sequence of static shots: first, sunlight illuminating a dark, cloudy sky; second, a blue-coloured, cloudy sky at dawn; third, a line of slaves pulling on a rope leading to a giant Egyptian statue, the frame dominated by red and orange; fourth, a slow zoom onto a baby being laid in a crib, which fades into an interior scene, with low light levels. Although the camera zooms slowly back during this shot (the fifth), the actors stay in the positions we first see them in. In the centre of the frame is the old Pharaoh Rameses I, lit against a dark background. To the left are soldiers; to the right, the high priest. The *mise-en-scène* here expresses the static, hierarchical power and caste structures of ancient Egypt: Pharaoh is in a position of unassailable authority, and though his subordinates offer advice, his central position in the frame signifies his dominance. Throughout the film, De Mille moves the camera very little. The compositions tend to be static, approaching the status of 'melodramatic and painterly tableaus',[1] or of the religious paintings the film attempts to bring to mind. This is clearest perhaps in the scene of the first Passover, where Moses, Miriam, Aaron and their family gather around a table, a scene that has the rich, brown tones of ancient varnish. These painterly compositions are not coincidental to the content of *The Ten Commandments*, of course; not only do they signify that the film self-consciously places itself in the Western visual tradition of religious art, but also attempts to take on the authority of that art. Curiously, although the film goes on to expose the power and authority of Pharaoh through explicit comparison with Moses, *The Ten Commandments* assumes a position of authority with regard to its audience. What you watch is not only a spectacular film, it asserts, it is religious art. Its message, therefore, should be accepted without question. We will consider some of the implications of this didacticism later in this chapter.

Another scene that opens itself to close analysis is Moses' banishment from Egypt. The scene begins with an establishing shot of Rameses (Yul Brynner) standing on a chariot in the background, while soldiers minister to the prisoner Moses (Charlton Heston) who stands in the foreground. The scene is clearly shot in the studio, with a pyramid seen behind through use of 'blue-screen' technology. (This process, which films action in front of a blue screen, allows what is filmed to be superimposed on another image, which takes the place of the photographed blue.) High-key lighting plays off the gold that adorns Rameses's body, but the effect is not of richness or opulence, rather a tinsel-like artificiality. Moses, by contrast, is adorned in the ochre-red Levite cloth, visually echoing the surrounding desert. This sequence is shot using the shot/reverse shot style, which means that if two people are interacting on screen, one faces one way, one the other. It mimics the way we would look from one person to another as they spoke to each other. This is how dialogue is depicted in classical Hollywood style editing. (See Text Box 2.1 for more.) After Heston has been given his robe, and the axle from a chariot as a staff – both of which, and Rameses's dialogue, indicate that this is a parodic coronation – Heston exits, unusually, forward past the camera, a shadow passing across his face. The film then cuts back to Brynner's face, and then the next shot is of Heston, standing in a real desert, next to a monumental boundary marker. Moses has walked from the artificiality of Egypt into the reality of the spiritual wilderness. Marc Vernet, in his article 'Wings of the Desert', suggests that this is entirely deliberate: 'The result is parallelism and opposition since De Mille cannot resist contrasting the men aesthetically . . . Nature versus artifice, simplicity versus pride, truth versus trickery, movement versus stasis.'[2] Whether this is intended or not, the *mise-en-scène* of this scene reinforces the symbolic and moral opposition of Egypt and the Hebrews, Rameses and Moses, that the film certainly encodes.

Mise-en-scène analysis has often been used in combination with 'auteurism' (a form of criticism which places the film director at the centre

---

2.1 Summary of Classical Hollywood Style

- The use of the '180° line': an imaginary line drawn through a set. The actors stay on one side, the cameras on the other. This ensures that the background remains constant. (It also hides the fact that on film sets, the room is fabricated and open: there is no 'fourth wall'.)
- There is continuity of direction: if a character walks left to right across the screen, in the next shot s/he will enter from the left and move to the right.
- Individual characters and their personal actions and choices determine the narrative.
- Motivation for action is as clear and as complete as possible.
- Time is subordinate to these events of personal importance. The plot will order the story to present the character-driven causes and effects most clearly.
- There is a strong tendency to avoid subjective effects, and to maintain the illusion of 'objective' reality.
- There will be strong closure and resolution to a narrative. Avoidance (wherever possible) of 'loose ends'.

---

of film meaning, suggesting that s/he imposes her or his 'signature' on films, resulting in a recurrent use of motifs or themes across the director's work). In this way, as Pam Cook has suggested, *mise-en-scène* analysis, 'whereby detailed description of films is seen to be the basis for criticism', can become rather untheoretical and subjective, treating auteurist films as 'great art' and relying on concepts such as 'style' and 'personal vision'.[3] Where *mise-en-scène* analysis concentrates on the visual and relies on close reading of the visual, analysis of narrative tends to be global and structural. Martin Barker's recent *From Antz to Titanic: Reinventing Film Analysis* is an accessible re-evaluation of methods of film analysis, which stems from his reading of a book on film theory in his university library, in which a bored undergrad had written 'this is pants'![4] Barker's emphasis is narratological, drawing on the work of David Bordwell, film historian and author of the canonical film text *Film Art: An Introduction*. Bordwell is what Barker describes as a 'Formalist' critic. That is, he is primarily concerned with the way in which films are constructed, and the ways in which the viewer makes sense of the film narrative.

Essentially, Barker follows Bordwell in imagining a film viewer who makes sense of the film largely through narrative, and the success or otherwise of the film experience for the viewer is based on her or his competence in assembling meaning from the film's chosen materials. Some types of film will assume a far greater knowledge of, or engagement with, film history or film styles as a way of creating meaning (the use of intertextuality, for instance). For a viewer without this competence the film will inevitably be a less rewarding experience. Barker argues about the relationship between film and viewer: the film creates a role (which Barker calls the 'implied audience'), which is 'made up of the sequence and the sum-total of cued responses necessary for participation in the world of the story',[5] and the viewer has to agree to that role and be able to perform it. The 'cued responses' include: guessing ahead, forming opinions about characters and events ahead; taking sides, and recognizing the moral codings of certain characters; being puzzled and not trusting the information given; revisiting and reassessing previous moments in the film; responding physically, sensually, emotionally, aesthetically, intellectually; to create a possible shape of the film as a whole, and ask the question, 'what is this film about?'

The narrative of *The Ten Commandments* is, of course, 'about' the biblical story of Moses and the deliverance of the Hebrews from slavery in Egypt. Therefore, there is a predetermined structure to which the film must adhere. However, as DeMille's introduction to the film suggests (which we shall look at in more detail later), the story of Moses' life is incomplete in the Bible itself: therefore, the film-makers turned to 'ancient texts' (of varying provenance) by Josephus, Eusebius, Philo and the Midrash, and also to contemporary historical novels. What transpires in the film is a narrative organized around a central conflict between Moses (Charlton Heston) and Rameses (Yul Brynner), the two 'brothers', over succession to power, which in ancient Egypt was determined by marriage to the 'throne princess' Nefretiri (Anne Baxter). Moses, as a prince of Egypt, Rameses, and Nefretiri are then in a Hollywood 'love triangle', encouraging the viewer to understand conflict through personal motivation (see Text Box 2.1 for more details on the classical Hollywood style). *The Ten Commandments* depicts the events in a personalized, emotive manner to encourage audience empathy and identification. However, in the form of Nefretiri, who can only conceptualize Moses' actions in terms of love or hatred – thinking he can spare her son from the death of Egypt's firstborn – understanding the grand spiritual narrative in terms of emotion is revealed as limited and self-deceiving. Where, for Rameses, the gods are the inventions of humankind, and his conflict with Moses understood merely in terms of power and conquest, for Nefretiri God is in one man: Moses. It is only Moses who understands the true forces at work. Therefore, although the film organizes its narratives around archetypal (and romantic) personal conflicts, it seeks to disavow those conflicts in the end in the name of a true understanding of the religious import of the story.

The film has a three-part narrative structure: the times of ignorance, testing and enlightenment for Moses. The first is in Egypt, and can be considered as Moses' time of unknowing, of his own identity, and of his race and religion (which are the same thing in *The Ten Commandments*). This is inaugurated by the seventh shot of the film, where Moses' Hebrew mother Yoshabel (Martha Scott) places Moses in the basket and casts him upon the Nile. He is found by Bithia (Nina Foch), the recently widowed princess of Egypt, who was introduced in the film with a gaggle of young women who talk like sorority girls from 1956. This is Moses' first 'deliverance' (he who will be the 'deliverer'), the first scene of birth or rebirth. Each scene of 'rebirth' leads to a different Moses, and a different section of the film. There are, in fact, three versions of Moses in the film, each identity corresponding to the structural needs of the film. The remainder of the first section leaps over childhood entirely, and concentrates on the love triangle between Moses (Heston), Rameses (Brynner) and Nefretiri (Anne Baxter). When Moses' Hebrew identity is finally revealed to him, he goes to join the Hebrew slaves, understanding domination and oppression from below, as he had tried to soften it from above as a prince. Finally cast out of Egypt, Moses then wanders in the wilderness, a place of testing: having been intellectually enlightened, he is now 'purged'. This leads to his second 'rebirth'. Staggering to an oasis, he passes out; the film cuts to another gaggle of young women, this time Sephora (Yvonne de Carlo), his future wife, and her sisters, watering their flocks by the well. They, like the young women of the palace, also talk like bobbysoxers, wanting a 'man'. As Bithia 'prayed for a son', and was given one, they desire a husband, and one emerges from the undergrowth to drive away the brutish Amalekites who threaten the well: Moses.

This announces the second section of the film, where Moses marries, becomes successful, yet is consumed by religious doubt: why does the God of Abraham turn away from the cries of the Hebrew slaves? Once again, this spiritual or religious journey is read in personal terms: Moses desires a direct conversation with God in order for his faith to be proved. When Moses sees the burning bush, the third scene of deliverance or rebirth (this one from fire rather than water), he hears the voice of God, which is, in fact Heston's own, slowed down and deepened. He becomes not a man, but Moses the Prophet, 'more than a man' as Joshua (John Derek) rightly declares. In this third section, Moses acts as an instrument of God's will, and is in fact largely effaced as a character in his own right. Heston, never the most expressive of screen actors in any case (a fact that suits him to the epic form), becomes increasingly declamatory in his performance, particularly after his encounter with God at the burning bush. To effect this suppression of Moses 'the man' and bring forth Moses 'more than man', Heston deploys a rather stiff body posture, and his sight-lines disappear well into the middle distance. As the film progresses, Heston downplays Moses' humanity. Somewhat like the trajectory of Heston's own star persona, he turns from man to monument.

2. Stardom and Gender

Gender came to the fore as a central focus of film studies in the 1970s. Laura Mulvey's 'Visual Pleasure and Narrative Cinema' (1975) changed the field of film studies when it was published, and was the entry of psychoanalytical models into a theorization of what we do when we watch films, using Freud's model of voyeurism. It was a model that would dominate cutting-edge film theory for the next ten years, largely played out on the pages of the British film journal, *Screen*. Mulvey's main point was that there is no space for female pleasure when watching a 'Classical Hollywood' film. Her thinking is in binaries, but the central one to remember is in who *looks*: active = male, passive = female. The male looks, and the female is looked at. The male is the subject, the female is the object. Film spectatorship is gendered, repeating the power positions of patriarchal culture. The female body, under this theoretical model, came to be theorized as being objectified, made into a commodity. Mulvey states: 'In a world ordered by sexual imbalance, pleasure in looking has been split between active/male and passive/female. The determining male gaze projects its phantasy on to the female figure which is styled

---

2.2 Laura Mulvey's Theory of the Gaze

Mulvey suggests that there are three 'looks':
- that of the camera towards that which is being filmed (called the pro-filmic event);
- that of the audience towards the screen when watching the film;
- that of the characters within the film towards each other.

In each of these, the male position is dominant. The 'gaze' is about power relations as much as it is about desire.

The look or 'gaze' of the camera stages and films the event to emphasize the pleasure of the masculine spectator (by shooting the male and female in certain ways).

1. The 'male' spectator then identifies with the 'point-of-view' offered by the film, which is a masculine one, and is complicit in finding pleasure in what is shown on film (e.g. the image of a woman).
2. The gaze confers power, and the characters within the film world also correspond to this regime: the men look, the women avert their gaze and are looked at.

The power of the masculine position is constantly reinforced. In fact, there is nothing outside it: because the gendered gaze means the female body is displayed to be looked at, female spectators derive no pleasure. To do so, they have to adopt the 'masculine' position, and (masochistically) embrace the painful as pleasurable.

accordingly.'[6] The female figure, Mulvey argues, is styled, signifying patriarchal/consumer society's destructive control over female body image. The female body therefore becomes the object, the commodity or spectacle which is then consumed.

In *The Ten Commandments*, clearly Anne Baxter is the medium of exchange, through which the conflict between Rameses and Moses can be expressed. Although the body of Nefretiri controls succession, she herself cannot succeed: her role is to produce (or deliver) the next Pharaoh through marriage. She is a token of exchange in a game of power, and the way Anne Baxter is presented in the film, 'mediated by all the stereotypes of the Hollywood *femme fatale*' as Cohan puts it, indicates her status as object rather than desiring subject.[7] Either she is dressed in gold, the high-key lighting signifying her body as an object of display; or she is sometimes robed in diaphanous silks, again indicating eroticism and desire: the desire of others rather than simply her own. It is instructive that Nefretiri's seduction of Moses fails, not once but twice, in repeated scenes on her barge: once when she takes Moses from the mud-pit, then later when Moses returns to Egypt as God's instrument. The principle of female desire, coding non-patriarchal succession, must be overcome by Moses and his patriarchal will. Cohan notes that Egypt is 'a "feminized" state in contrast to the federation of patriarchal Hebrew tribes', because of Nefretiri's key role in the succession (who she marries will be Pharaoh). However, the film also seeks to contain the historical fact of non-paternal succession by making her 'the victor's reward, handed over from father to son to define generational continuity as a homosocial exchange'.[8] 'Homosocial' is a term that has achieved some currency in the field of gender studies, and particularly studies of masculinity, to describe bonds and relationships between men, which disavow homosexuality but contain a disruptive, if repressed, element of homoeroticism.

Steve Neale's 'Masculinity as Spectacle' (1983), also published in *Screen*, also discovers the homoerotic within the homosocial. It explored the psychoanalytical model of the Mulvey article to discuss screen masculinities. He wrote that

in a heterosexual and patriarchal society, the male body cannot be marked explicitly as the erotic object of another male look: that look must be motivated in some other way, its erotic component repressed. . . . We see male bodies stylized and fragmented by close-ups, but our look is not direct, it is heavily mediated by the looks of the characters involved. And those looks are marked not by desire, but rather fear, or hatred, or aggression.[9]

In both Mulvey's and Neale's articles, the model of gendered spectatorship (the male looks), has, as its result, a gendering of the object of desire.

Because the look is masculine, in a patriarchal (and homophobic) culture, the possibility for the male look supporting desire for a male body is cancelled. Any (male) desiring gaze is represented as wounding the male body; desire is repressed and channelled into competition, violence and wounds.

Kenneth MacKinnon reworked Mulvey's article to rethink images of male beauty. He notes that Mulvey's article 'also has its uses in impassioned debate well beyond Film or Media Studies', a project that he is involved in himself.[10] He explains Mulvey's concept of the fetishization of the female body as follows: 'the female star is "overvalued", made into a breathtakingly beautiful sight by means of an armoury of effects, such as lighting, gauzes, make-up'.[11] Where MacKinnon distances himself from Mulvey's argument is in Mulvey's insistence that because the male is reluctant to gaze upon the male figure, it does not happen. He argues:

> What is surprising is that the male object could seem to be of such recent invention. He has been there throughout the history of Classical sculpture, of fine art. How can a male be an object if he is so clearly a subject?, it could be counterposed. This is essentially what Laura Mulvey asks rhetorically about the male on the cinema screen. He has the power to initiate action, to create the narrative on which dominant cinema depends. He is clearly, unequivocally, a subject. In diegetic terms, yes, but every character on screen is also an object of the cinema spectator's gaze.[12]

MacKinnon suggests that the theorization of 'disavowal' of the male gaze, which displaces homoerotic looking at the male figure onto culturally sanctioned behaviour (like sport or combat), still holds in contemporary culture.

This combat is symbolic in *The Ten Commandments*, but still, like the gladiatorial combat in other epics, sanctions the display of male bodies seemingly without the disturbing element of homoeroticism. In his book *Masked Men*, Steven Cohan draws upon the work of gender-oriented theorists of film such as Mulvey and Neale, and also the work of Richard Dyer, whose book *Stars* helped focus upon the ways in which stars and stardom are constructed in film.[13] In his reading of *The Ten Commandments*, Cohan suggests that the star personae of Heston and Brynner are key to an understanding of the film's binary oppositions, between freedom and tyranny, the Hebrews and Egypt, patriarch and tyrant. Cohan goes further, to insist that it is in the very bodies of the two stars that this difference is played out: 'Heston and Brynner objectify the American/ alien opposition which ideologically governs the film's attitudes toward "Hebrew" and "Egyptian."'[14] Cohan suggests that Brynner's overt sexuality is bound up with the 'Orientalist' codings of his persona: his baldness, his 'mysterious' origins (Russian, Gypsy, Swiss), and the way in which his body is displayed in *The Ten Commandments* and in *The King and I*, which was released the same year, 1956. While not necessarily feminized, as Mulvey's theory would suggest, Brynner's body is sexualized, made available as an erotic object. By contrast, Charlton Heston's 'monumental' physique is made much of in the film, and becomes synonymous with the epic genre itself. His is a powerful and patriarchal, rather than a sexual, body, however. (Heston also notably starred in *Ben-Hur* (1959), which opened as the long run of *The Ten Commandments* began to wind down.) 'Heston's close identification with the epic genre,' notes Cohan, 'solidified his emerging star image as a patriarchal male.'[15] The conflict between Moses and Rameses, noted above, is in part played out through the gazes of the two men, and in the display of their own bodies. One is sexual, hairless, dangerous, Oriental; the other patriarchal, bearded, monumental, Western. In other films of the epic genre, such as *Spartacus* (1960), Neale's 'wounding' thesis is much more apparent, but even in *The Ten Commandments*, Heston must undergo his ordeal of purging and bodily punishment before he can emerge as the instrument of God.

3. Hollywood and the Cinema of the Spectacle

Tom Gunning, a noted film historian, has recently complicated what has been regarded as the 'history' of cinema. In the classical conception, early cinema (what Gunning called the 'cinema of attractions') is a primitive cinema, one which has yet to develop the narrative strategies of later filmmaking. In the films of Edison and the Lumiere brothers, the spectacle of the cinema (cinema as an experience or event, the primacy of wonder at what the spectator is seeing) was central to its early development. However, the emphasis in film history on the narrative elements of film developed later has led to a downgrading of the spectacular elements, particularly in film criticism and theory.

In her book *Cecil B. DeMille and American Culture: The Silent Era*, Sumiko Higashi argues that DeMille, and the role of spectacle, plays a key role in the 'legitimating' of cinema for a middle-class audience in America. DeMille, Higashi argues, used the 'genteel' form of the domestic stage melodrama to bridge the gap between cinema and theatre; and in his determination to make film successful, exploited the elements of spectacle already present in American popular culture: World's Fair, department stores, museums and civic pageantry such as parades. DeMille's films, she argues, have an investment in spectacle that goes beyond mere 'entertainment', or cinema as an event in itself. Spectacles such as DeMille's original (1923) *The Ten Commandments*, which were enormously expensive undertakings, 'contributed to the evolution of filmmaking as commodification in an Orientalist form, that is, the exercise of hypnotic power through the sheer accumulation of objects displayed as spectacle'.[16] DeMille's biblical epics, according to Higashi, are both expressions of American capitalism's conspicuous consumption – the high cost of a DeMille epic was widely known, and part of its 'event' status – and a quasi-imperialist display of 'exotic', therefore titillating, objects and action.

By the time DeMille came to remake his own film in 1956, for Paramount, the Hollywood studio system was in a time of change, if not quite – yet – crisis. The biggest challenges to studio dominance came from two directions: first, the anti-trust legislation that, in 1948, had forced the studios to divest themselves of their movie-theatre chains, depriving them of their major revenue stream; and second, the increasing popularity of television. Technological developments in the 1950s have often been seen in the light of the latter. To differentiate its product from television, it is argued, Hollywood emphasized the spectacular nature of its product, through Technicolor (television still largely being black-and-white in the fifties); through widescreen processes such as Panavision, CinemaScope, Todd-AO and the process used to shoot *The Ten Commandments*, Vista-Vision; and later, improvements in sound, such as stereo and Dolby sound. As Pam Cook has pointed out, however, Paramount was also at the forefront of exploiting other media to complement its film-making operation. It invested in the CBS radio network in the late 1920s, for which DeMille himself hosted and directed the 'Lux Radio Theater', it bought television stations in Chicago and Los Angeles, and involved itself in video production, to the extent of planning theatrical video projection.[17] The release of *The Ten Commandments* in 1956 highlights the kind of efforts the studios made to maximize its profits. It was originally released in New York and Los Angeles on a 'roadshow' basis, a travelling event in itself, before being shown across the country. (The massive 'opening weekends' of contemporary blockbuster releases, where a film opens at a thousand screens or more, were an invention of the 1970s, particularly with *The Godfather* and *Jaws*.) By the first anniversary of its release, *The Ten Commandments* had been seen by over 22 million people in the United States; by the end of the decade, when the film had been in continuous release for over three years, it had been seen by 98 million people.[18] Pam Cook states that the film grossed an 'astounding' $34.2 million.[19]

For DeMille, spectacle and narrative are not in opposition: cinematic narrative is spectacle. Brooks Landon has written:

[Gunning] reminds us that the classical style codified by Bordwell, Staiger and Thompson in *The Classical Hollywood Cinema* was not just the development of primitive cinema, a refinement of its crude attempts at narrative, but the development of one kind of primitive cinema, while the non-narrative focus of what Gunning calls the 'cinema of attractions' represents another kind of primitive cinema, whose traditions continued even after the codification of the classical style.[20]

Landon suggests that this emphasis on spectacle, on wonder, has been inherited by the science fiction film, and particularly in science fiction films special effects sequences. The same argument can be made for the 'epic'. The effects sequences in the 1956 *The Ten Commandments* are an integral part of its self-presentation as an object of awe, a monumental spectacle. Geoff King, in his book *New Hollywood Cinema: an introduction*, suggests that the use of spectacle sequences has changed in contemporary cinema. In classical Hollywood narratives, the action flows 'a curve, rising gradually, the rate at which it rises accelerating in the latter stages as the film moves towards a climax'.[21] In contemporary cinema, however, 'spectacular moments . . . are both larger and more frequent, fragmenting the narrative'.[22] If we look at the spectacle sequences in *The Ten Commandments*, we can see that they are quite regularly spaced. The first occurs when Moses arrives at court, where tributes from Ethiopia are displayed, just as in Higashi's argument, for the audience's visual consumption. The second comes when Moses builds the treasure-city for Sethi: a huge obelisk is spectacularly set in place. These are both in the first part of the narrative. At the end of what we saw earlier was the second part of the narrative, Moses encounters the burning bush and hears the voice of God. The third part does indeed show a 'rising curve': there are the plagues of Egypt, notably the burning hail and the death of the first-born, then the spectacular parting of the Red Sea, then, finally, the writing of the tablets, intercut with DeMille's signature 'orgy' spectacle surrounding the Golden Calf and its destruction. The function of these spectacle scenes is, as in other films, to cause excitement in the viewer, but particularly in the Red Sea and Mount Sinai sequences, to instil a sense of wonder. The 'cinema of attractions' here is deployed in the service of quasi-religious feeling. As Cohan has suggested, *The Ten Commandments* offers itself as an 'ersatz religious event'.[23] This is pointed out to the viewer right at the beginning of the film, in the titles: 'Those who see this Motion Picture – Produced and Directed by CECIL B. DEMILLE – will make a pilgrimage over the very ground that Moses trod more than 3,000 years ago.' To experience the film is to go on a pilgrimage, with Moses and the Hebrews, a rather grandiose, but significant, claim.

The shape of the film is worthy of further comment. We have seen that the narrative falls into three significant parts. However, the film was actually shown in two halves, with an intermission, as its running length is three hours and thirty-nine minutes. Unusually, the film also has a formal musical structure that announces its 'epic' status: it opens with an

'Overture', has an 'Entr'acte' after the intermission, and closes with 'Exit Music'. The only other contemporary film to use the same devices was David Lean's similarly 'epic' *Lawrence of Arabia* (1962), the overture to which was played in the darkened movie theatre before the film began, as was the entr'acte after the intermission. Such overt demonstrations of 'high-culture' influence indicate to the audience that *The Ten Commandments* was certainly not television, though, as Sumiko Higashi points out, it is the continued showing of the film on television, at Easter and Passover in the USA, which dominates its contemporary consumption as a spectacle.[24]

4. The Cold War Context

The Ten Commandments was released in 1956, the era of the Cold War between the United States and the Soviet Union, three years after the end of the war in Korea, the same year as Third World nationalism began to make itself felt, the same year as the Suez crisis. (As Cohan notes, the location shooting for the film was originally negotiated with King Farouk, then had to be negotiated with his successor President Naguib (who deposed the king in a coup), then finally President Nasser, who only allowed filming to continue as Egypt needed the money. The film was in post-production when President Nasser nationalized the Suez Canal and precipitated the unsuccessful Franco-British invasion.)[25] Although *The Ten Commandments* is not 'about' conflict in the Middle East – though its focus upon the Hebrews/Israel as God's chosen people, and the destruction of its Egyptian/Arabic foes, provided convenient propaganda – it most certainly is a political film. This is clearly signified by the short filmed introduction that was shown before the beginning of *The Ten Commandments*. This introduction features DeMille himself, who stands on a stage, in front of silvery curtains, gripping the microphone stand in the same way that Moses will grip his staff – rather than like that other sensation of 1956, Elvis Presley. DeMille speaks directly to camera, assuming a position of authority, one granted by his own status in Hollywood, and as the 'Producer and Director' of the film. DeMille's own voice is also used to 'narrate' the film proper, conferring more authority to the film's narrative. The didacticism of the film as a whole is revealed in DeMille's address; and the terms in which the audience should understand the film are set out explicitly. DeMille says:

> The theme of this picture is whether man ought to be ruled by God's Law, or whether they are to be ruled by the whims of a dictator like Rameses. Are men the property of the state, or free souls under God? The same battle continues throughout the world today.

Here, then we find binary oppositions, between freedom and tyranny, between God's Law and dictatorship, between the 'free soul' (or individual) and the state. In 1956, the message could hardly have been clearer: Moses is a proto-American who enjoins Joshua to 'Go, proclaim liberty' in his last words at the end of the film. The mission of biblical Israel is paralleled in the American mission of spreading liberty and combating dictatorship. For Rameses, read Stalin or Khrushchev. This is the overt 'message' of the film, at least. If we look at the narrative in more detail, however, this rhetoric of 'liberty' is somewhat disrupted by the depiction of the 'people'. On the journey out of Israel, although Moses has delivered them from slavery, when Rameses's chariots seem to pin them against the Red Sea, Dathan almost manages to get the Hebrews to stone Moses to death. 'Ten times have you seen the miracles of the Lord,' declaims Moses, 'but still you have no faith.' Again, when Moses is absent on the mountain, receiving the tablets, Dathan (Edward G. Robinson) rouses the Hebrews to 'sin a great sin' by orgiastic behaviour and worshipping the Golden Calf. DeMille's voice-over characterizes the Hebrews as 'children'. In the rhetoric of the film, what they are missing is a strong father. Although the 'theme' of the film is the conflict between liberty and tyranny, according to DeMille's introduction, the film actually displays great anxiety about the 'people': they quickly turn into the 'mob', prey to a demagogue like Dathan or weak when left to their own devices. *The Ten Commandments* is profoundly undemocratic, even anti-democratic: it valorizes the patriarch, Moses, without whom the Hebrews would be in chains. While seeming to critique the 'dictatorial' power of Pharaoh, its alternative is a patriarchal authoritarianism.

5. Genre

Genre is at once a seemingly simple means of categorizing and analysing films – the musical, the film noir, Western, the 'epic' – and also an area fraught with difficulty, for genres are not fixed, and neither are their boundaries impermeable. Genres tend to have their own productive histories, and some can be understood through the deployment of certain imagery or iconography – particularly in genres such as the Western or the gangster film – or in the recurrence of certain preoccupations or themes. Some genres, such as melodrama, shift their meaning over time: in the first decades of the twentieth century, for example, 'melodrama' in Hollywood was today's term 'drama', without the connotations of excessive emotionalism or stereotyping associated with it now; 'comedy' seems to have little in the way of commonly identifiable structures, motifs or themes. Genres also transform over time, and seem to gain a kind of productive dominance in some periods while almost disappearing in others (the fate

of the Hollywood musical, once accounting for a quarter of all Hollywood films, is instructive). Genres are not timeless, and recent genre
criticism tends to historicize films rather than create rigid templates for
categorizing them. There is enough diversity within the 'epic' form,
for instance, to problematize any preconceptions about their narratives or
their thematic preoccupations.

The Ten Commandments is only one of many 'epics', on biblical or
Roman themes, that were made between the end of World War Two and
the decline of the studio system in the 1960s. From DeMille's own *Samson
and Delilah* (1949), to *The Robe* (1953, the first film released in
CinemaScope), *The Ten Commandments* (1956), *Ben-Hur* (1959), *King
of Kings* (1961) and the studio-crippling *Cleopatra* (1963), lavishly
expensive spectacles were made by studios to try to keep the audiences in
the movie theatres, in a spiralling game of escalating production costs and
(hopefully) escalating profits. DeMille himself died in 1959, and the studio
system that had borne the weight of his extravagance perished soon after.
In a sense, DeMille created his own genre, the 'sin and sanctimony' spectacles that put some religious varnish on scenes of monumental production
and orgiastic (and exoticized) sexuality. DeMille was careful to promote
himself as an 'auteur', the director as originator and controller of the film,
but most other 'epic' films tend to erase the marks of auteurship, even with
such noted film-makers as Stanley Kubrick for *Spartacus* (1960) and
Anthony Mann for *The Fall of the Roman Empire* (1964). The form has
been recently revived with *Gladiator* (2000), directed by Ridley Scott, and
2004's *Troy*. In later films in the 'epic' mode, religion tends to be sidelined
in favour of politics or simply personal narratives of romance or revenge.
Between the end of the studio system, and the rise of CGI (Computer
Generated Imagery) technologies, 'epic' spectacles were also prohibitively
expensive. Now the Colosseum in Rome can be generated on computer,
rather than a facsimile built on the studio backlot or elsewhere, 'epic'
cinema once more becomes a productive reality, and sits well in contemporary Hollywood's economic reliance on the summer blockbuster and
the 'event' or spectacle film (see 'What is Genre?', p. 152).

6. Conclusion

This chapter has outlined some key concepts that have informed the study
of film over the last four decades. In the practice of studying film, though,
critical approaches now tend to be hybrid rather than discrete. Theories
of the gaze can be used in star studies, genre can be analysed with *mise-en-
scène*. As titles of film essay collections like *Reinventing Film Studies* and
From Antz to Titanic: Reniventing Film Analysis might suggest, the field
has become less one of theoretical or ideological contestation and more

one of plurality. There is now a strong historicist bent to the study of film, whether it is national or institutional film histories, star studies, audience studies, or the reclamation of 'lost' films or directors, or revisions of genre histories. This is not to argue, however, that film studies is in a state of moribund consensus. As this collection of essays demonstrates, new avenues of enquiry may be opened to illuminate 'art' or classic cinema from Europe, as well as popular film from Hollywood and elsewhere.

Further Reading

The Ten Commandments – *Hollywood Biblical Epics and Genre*

Steven Cohan, *Masked Men: Masculinity and the movies in the Fifties*, Bloomington and Indianapolis: Indiana University Press, 1997.

Jared Gardner, 'Covered Wagons and Decalogues: Paramounts's Myth of Origins', *Yale Journal of Criticism*, Fall 2000,13(2): 361–89.

Sumiko Higashi, *Cecil B. DeMille and American Culture: The Silent Era*, Berkeley, Los Angeles and London: University of California Press, 1994.

Alan Nadel, 'God's Law and the Widescreen: *The Ten Commandments* as Cold War Epic', *PMLA*, May 1993, 108(3): 415–30.

Steve Neale, *Genre and Hollywood*, London: Routledge, 2000.

Erica Sheen, '*The Ten Commandments* meets *The Prince of Egypt*: Biblical Adaptations and Globals Politics in the 1990s', *Polygraph*, 2000, 12: 85–99.

Andrew G. Tooze, 'Moses and Reel Exodus', *Journal of Religion and Film*, April 2003, 7(1), 51 pars.

Marc Vernet, 'Wings of the Desert; or, The Invisible Superimpositions', *Velvet Light Trap*, Fall 1991, 28: 65–72.

Mise-en-scène *and Narrative*

Martin Barker, *From Antz to Titanic: Reinventing Film Analysis*, London: Pluto, 2000.

David Bordwell and Kristin Thompson, *Film Art: An Introduction*. 7th International edn, New York: McGraw-Hill, 2003.

Pam Cook, *The Cinema Book*, 2nd edn, London: BFI, 1999.

James Monaco, *How to Read a Film*, 3rd edn, Oxford and New York: Oxford University Press, 2000.

Spectacle and Special Effects

Scott Bukatman, *Matters of Gravity: Special Effects and Supermen in the 20th century*, Durham, NC: Duke University Press, 2003.

Geoff King, *New Hollywood Cinema: An introduction*, London: I.B. Tauris, 2002.

Annette Kuhn (ed.), *Alien Zone II: The Spaces of Science Fiction Cinema*, London: Routledge, 2000.

Brooks Landon, 'Diegetic or Digital? The Convergence of Science Fiction litera-ture and Science-fiction film in Hypermedia', in Annette Kuhn (ed.), *Alien Zone II: The Spaces of Science Fiction Cinema*, London: Routledge, 2000, pp. 31–49.

Christine Gledhill and Linda Williams (eds), *Reinventing Film Studies*, London: Arnold, 2000.

Tom Gunning, '"Animated Pictures": tales of cinema's forgotten future, after 100 years of film', in Christine Gledhill and Linda Williams (eds), *Reinventing Film Studies*, London: Arnold, 2000, pp. 316–31.

Stars and Gender

Richard Dyer, *Stars*, London: BFI, 1998.

Paul MacDonald, *The Star System*, London: Wallflower, 2000.

Kenneth MacKinnon, 'After Mulvey: Male Erotic Objectification', in Michelle Aaron (ed.), *The Body's Perilous Pleasures: Dangerous Desires and Contem-porary Culture*, Edinburgh: Edinburgh University Press, 1999, pp. 13–29.

Laura Mulvey, 'Visual Pleasure and Narrative Cinema', *Screen*, 16, 3 (1975): 6–18. Reprinted in Mandy Merck (ed.), *The Sexual Subject: A Screen Reader in Sexuality*, London and New York: Routledge, 1992, pp. 22–34.

Steve Neale, 'Masculinity as Spectacle: reflections on men and mainstream cin-ema', *Screen* 24, 6 (1983). Reprinted in Steven Cohan and Ina Rae Hark (eds), *Screening the Male: Exploring Masculinities in Hollywood Cinema*, London and New York: Routledge, 1993, pp. 9–20.

Notes

1 Steven Cohan, *Masked Men: Masculinity and the movies in the Fifties*, Bloomington and Indianapolis: Indiana University Press, 1997, p. 148.

2 Marc Vernet, 'Wings of the Desert; or, The Invisible Superimpositions', *Velvet Light Trap* 28, Fall 1991, pp. 65–72. (67).

3 Pam Cook, *The Cinema Book*, London: BFI, 1999, p. 269.

4 Martin Barker, *From Antz to Titanic: Reinventing Film Analysis*, London: Pluto, 2000.

5 Barker, *From Antz to Titanic*, p. 48.

6 Laura Mulvey, 'Visual Pleasure and Narrative Cinema', *Screen*, 16, 3 (1975); reprinted in *The Sexual Subject: A Screen Reader in Sexuality*, London and New York: Routledge, 1992, pp. 22–34 (27).

7 Cohan, *Masked Men*, pp. 143–4.

8 Cohan, *Masked Men*, pp. 142, 143.

9 Steve Neale, 'Masculinity as Spectacle: reflections on men and mainstream cinema', *Screen* 24, 6 (1983). Reprinted in Steven Cohan and Ina Rae Hark (eds), *Screening the Male: Exploring Masculinities in Hollywood Cinema*, London and New York: Routledge, 1993, pp. 9–20 (14, 18)

10 Kenneth MacKinnon, 'After Mulvey: Male Erotic Objectification', in Michelle Aaron (ed.), *The Body's Perilous Pleasures: Dangerous Desires and Con-temporary Culture*, Edinburgh: Edinburgh University Press, 1999, pp. 13–29 (13).

11 MacKinnon, 'After Mulvey', p. 28.

12 MacKinnon, 'After Mulvey', p. 23.

13 Dyer, Richard, *Stars*, London: BFI, 1998.

14 Cohan, *Masked Men*, p. 150.

15 Cohan, *Masked Men*, p. 156.

16 Sumiko Higashi, *Cecil B. DeMille and American Culture: The Silent Era*, Berkeley, Los Angeles and London: University of California Press, 1994, p. 201.

17 Cook, *The Cinema Book*, p. 15.

18 Cohan, *Masked Men*, pp. 122–4.

19 Cook, *The Cinema Book*, p. 16.

20 Brooks Landon, 'Diegetic or Digital? The Convergence of Science Fiction literature and Science-fiction film in Hypermedia', in Annette Kuhn (ed.), *Alien Zone II: the spaces of science fiction cinema*, London: Routledge, 2000, pp. 31–49, p. 33.

21 Geoff King, *New Hollywood Cinema: An introduction*, London: I.B. Tauris, 2002, p. 185.

22 King, *New Hollywood Cinema*, p. 187.

23 Cohan, *Masked Men*, p. 129.

24 Higashi, *Cecil B. DeMille and American Culture*, pp. 202–3.

25 Cohan, *Masked Men*, p. 138.

Part 2

Case Studies – Films and Film-makers

3. Shot, Burned, Restored:

Dreyer's *La Passion de Jeanne d'Arc*

MELANIE J. WRIGHT

1. Introduction

This essay comments on Carl Theodor Dreyer's *La Passion de Jeanne d'Arc* (*The Passion of Joan of Arc,* 1928) and more generally on religion and film (for a short biography of Dreyer, see Text Box 3.1). I have chosen Dreyer's *Jeanne* for several reasons. Its subject matter is the ecclesiastical trial and death of Jeanne d'Arc (1412–31) who believed that she had been divinely commissioned to save France, fought the English and their

---

3.1 Carl Theodor Dreyer

Carl Th. Dreyer (1889–1968) was born in Copenhagen. After a brief career as a journalist, he became a writer and director of films.

As a director, Dreyer has a reputation for experimental visual style: while *La Passion de Jeanne d'Arc* (1928) is characterized by repeated cuts, the later *Ordet* ([The Word] 1955) uses long panning shots that extend over several minutes. Also running through Dreyer's work is a preoccupation with religion. In such films as *Vredens Dag* ([Day of Wrath] 1943), *Vampyr* (1932) and *Prästänkan* ([The Parson's Widow] 1920) he explores themes including individual faith versus communal intolerance, miracles, martyrdom and witchcraft. In the aftermath of the Holocaust, Dreyer also planned (but did not make) a Jesus film, which he hoped would portray Jesus as an observant Jew and thereby help combat antisemitism.

Some critics regard Dreyer's interest in the socio-political aspects of religion as reductionist. However, it is essentially an argument for the unity of the natural and the supernatural (rather than a demythologizing of the latter). Thus *Ordet* portrays with sympathy the lived faith of loving wife and mother Inger – preferring her Christianity to the abstract theological debates that divide her family and have driven her brother-in-law insane, and strikingly depicting her resurrection from the coffin in realistic terms.

Donald Skoller (ed.), *Dreyer in Double Reflection* (New York: E.P. Dutton, 1973) is a helpful anthology of Dreyer's writings about cinema, and several of his films are available on DVD from the British Film Institute.

Burgundian allies, and was burnt as a heretic-witch; but was subsequently rehabilitated, and ultimately canonized in 1920. Moreover, *Jeanne* was
made by a director who used words like 'spirit' and 'soul' when talking
about film and whose style is often characterized as 'transcendental' or
'purified'.[1]

There are comparatively few detailed studies of *Jeanne*. This is partly
due to the mythology surrounding Dreyer, 'whose work everyone reveres
and no one bothers to see'.[2] But there are other reasons for the film's neglect. Notoriously, its fate has been almost as remarkable as that of the war-
rior-peasant herself. Not long after the Copenhagen premier in April
1928, fire destroyed the film's negative. A replacement was also lost. For
many years the most widely available version of *Jeanne* was one based on
a poor print of the second negative, which (to Dreyer's chagrin) had been
augmented with medieval iconography and music in the 1950s. There
were more reputable, but differing, versions in archives in Paris, New York
and London. In the 1980s, the Danish Film Museum constructed another
print, using material from the other versions. In simple terms, then, studying *Jeanne* has been difficult, because of the 'instability' of the film text
itself. Which version – if any – was the 'original' or 'authentic' film?[3]

This situation altered in 1984, when the Norwegian Film Institute
opened some canisters that had been discovered by a cleaner in an Oslo
psychiatric hospital some three years earlier. In a discovery paralleling
Joan of Arc's resurrection as French national heroine, they revealed a
print of Dreyer's first negative, in its original wrapping, and bearing the
1928 censor's seal of approval.[4] Just how the print found its way to the
asylum remains uncertain. What is clear is that the discovery made *Jeanne*
newly accessible to viewers.

While the problems associated with the copies of *Jeanne* circulating
pre-1985 impeded study, much of the growth of religion and film studies
has taken place since 1990, by which time the practical hindrances to
research had been overcome. Are there then other factors leading practitioners to shy away from *Jeanne*? Arguably, much film analysis that takes
place in departments of religion over-concentrates on narrative, and
largely neglects to engage film qua film. But elements of *Jeanne* present
stumbling blocks to such hermeneutics. *Jeanne* is a silent film, and silent
films are a distinct art form with their own styles of production, exhibition and viewing. *Jeanne*'s consequent distance from the conventions
of contemporary Hollywood can make it challenging to study, in the
absence of some critical awareness of film practice. Therefore, the challenge of working with *Jeanne* may serve as a test case for methodologies
in religion and film. The otherness of its conventions lends urgency to the
requirement for something more than narrative exposition. If our discipline cannot grapple with 'the affective film *par excellence*',[5] it is scarcely
worth pursuing.

2. Analysis

Increasingly, scholars call for a 'dialogue' between the worlds of religion and film analysis. But this is rarely achieved. Religion scholars often lack expertise in the analysis of visual culture; for its part, film studies has largely been dominated by theoretical frameworks that assume secularity as a given. Cultural studies offers one space where religion scholars can engage with film on more equal terms, in which the exchange of insight is not envisaged as a one-way process *from* film studies *to* religion. Building on older film studies agendas and methodologies, and drawing inspiration from anthropology and the study of religions, it does not automatically privilege the secular, nor does it exclude the possibility that those with an expertise in religious studies may bring to film distinctive and worthwhile competencies and insights.[6]

In simple terms, traditional film studies looks at the film industry, film production and the technologies associated with those activities. To these, cultural studies adds a range of concerns including: an interest in the marketing, distribution, exhibition and reception of film; questions raised by the new social movements (e.g. the feminist and gay liberation movements). In short, it is a form of film criticism characterized by a heightened interest in the location of film in particular political, social and historical moments. In applying this approach to *Jeanne*, this essay addresses four areas: narrative, style, cultural and religious context, and reception. This atomization is not without limitations: viewers do not, of course, experience films as a series of discrete dimensions. I trust, however, that the approach is justifiable on the grounds of clarity, and from time to time highlight where aspects intersect.

Film Narrative

When *La Passion de Jeanne d'Arc* appeared, Joan's story was a national preoccupation in France. Two accounts of her life are significant for Dreyer's narrative. The first is a critical edition of the trial account, published by Pierre Champion in 1921. It portrayed her as a pious peasant, and cast the Sorbonne theologian-priests who condemned her as careerists. The second is a 1925 biography by Joseph Delteil, who asserted the reality of Joan's commissioning voices, her virginity and her deserved sainthood.[7] The *Société Générale des Films*, which commissioned Dreyer, bought the rights to Delteil's biography, and he wrote a continuity for the film. Dreyer rejected it, preferring Champion's work, and employing him as a consultant. In addition to these accounts, there was a centuries' old tradition of re-presenting Joan in art.

One of the dangers in approaching a work like *Jeanne*, which handles a popular historical figure, is the temptation to evaluate the film not on its own terms, but against what we feel we already 'know' of the 'facts'. This strategy is problematic; it fails to recognize the nature of film and perhaps of history itself. Yet in the case of *Jeanne*, Dreyer invites the viewer to relate the image to that which lies beyond. It is therefore appropriate to compare the film to the written texts.

Jeanne opens with a shot of the trial transcript, and at various points throughout the film the scribe appears writing or carrying this record of events. (For example, he sits in Joan's cell during her interrogation, and is in the cemetery when she signs the abjuration document.) This repeated reference to the book is sometimes seen as an implicit argument for film's historicity – Dreyer's claim to show the events as they were recorded. But conversely, the motif may be regarded as Dreyer's acknowledgement of the film's pre-text:

> The [opening] shot is emblematic: we come to a familiar tale, equipped with familiar knowledge. Jeanne's peasant ancestry, her religious impulses, her military fervor, and her heroic death: Dreyer assumes that we know all this, takes it as the pre-text of his film, and frees the narrative of an expository apparatus.[8]

Dreyer was striving for realism in *Jeanne* – but it is a realism that locates authenticity in the evocation of the animating spirit of characters and moments, rather than in the replication of detail. For Dreyer, 'Realism, in itself, is not art . . . I try to force the realities into a form of simplification and abbreviation in order to reach what I will call *psychological realism*.'[9]

This sense that for Dreyer, an authentic narrative is not necessarily factually reliable, is reinforced by closer analysis of *Jeanne*. Most obviously, the film attends only to the trial, not to the military campaigns, nor to Joan's childhood. This cuts across the dominant trends in Joan iconography, which typically showed her as the embodiment of holy simplicity, or as an equestrian soldier. Dreyer also compresses the lengthy trial process into a single day, and locates all the film's action at various points within a single set. In this respect, he is influenced by conceptions of drama originating with Aristotle's *Poetics* and revived by Ibsen and Strindberg, whose work he reviewed when employed as a newspaper drama critic. (The time allowed for the action of a neo-classical tragedy was usually deemed to be 24 hours; the place the stage represented was restricted to points within a single larger area such as a city or palace.) This appeal to classical form further reinforces the argument that Dreyer sought a non-imitative realism. Aristotle's 'unities' of time, place and form were intended to aid the creation of art true to the realities of human nature and experience. They were, to echo Pope and Hurd, 'nature methodized'.[10]

Dreyer's trial retains several features prominent in the medieval transcripts. Joan is questioned on issues such as her adoption of male dress, and she offers a confounding response to the judges' efforts to manoeuvre her into declaring herself to be in a state of grace (a heresy): 'If I am, may God keep me there. If I am not, may God grant it to me.' Dreyer also depicts Joan's bleeding to lower a fever, though omits the cause of the historical Joan's sickness, a meal of carp.[11] Instead, Joan's collapse follows an episode in which she is threatened with torture. This presentation would have resonated with audiences in the 1920s, when the human sciences (for example, Freudian psychoanalysis) were offering new, psychological accounts of illness, and sometimes pathologized the religious adherent.

Likewise, Dreyer 're-creates' Joan's recantation, in a way that some viewers found indefensible, but which resolves inconsistencies in the medieval accounts, which are unclear about whether Joan realized that the retraction she signed stated that she had lied about her voices, and was guilty of deception. It is also uncertain whether Cauchon, a prime mover in the proceedings, wished to help Joan, or sought to manipulate her, knowing that she would renege on her decision and become a relapsed heretic, whom he could hand over for execution.[12] In the film, ambiguities are swept aside. Joan signs the recantation *in extremis*: recently bled and in a weakened state, she gives way after a priest taunts her with the host.

While the narrative of *Jeanne* is reworked to transform a chaotic and confused series of events into a unified drama, and the bleeding and recantation are recast in simplified but powerful terms, key aspects of the conflict between the historical Joan of Arc and her trial judges are absent from Dreyer's film, namely, the witchcraft accusations laid against her, and her self-proclaimed virginity. Joan's alleged crimes included numerous activities commonly ascribed to witches, so it is interesting to consider why Dreyer chose to ignore this. It may be that he felt the medieval preoccupation with magic was alien to modern audiences, who might appreciate the seriousness of theological and political disputes, but lack empathy for characters who took for granted the reality of diabolical powers. Alternatively, Dreyer saw the witchcraft charges as functions of a larger fear of heterodoxy, simply one manifestation of the underlying ideological conflicts at the heart of Joan's *passion*. Seen in this light, they could be omitted from the film, with little violence done to the dynamics (realism) of the drama.

Similarly, *Jeanne* deals with its heroine's virginity only in passing, and omits the examinations and sexual violence she experienced.[13] For the medieval world, Joan's intactness was inseparable from her identity as France's saviour: the devil could not deceive a chaste woman. Why, then, does Dreyer not touch on this topic? Propriety is unlikely to have been the primary motivation; neither Delteil nor Champion avoided the issue. Arguably, threats against Joan's person are present in Dreyer's film, but the typological construction of its heroine (see later) leads to their being transposed into the tauntings of the prison guards, which Dreyer suggests she endures with Christ-like patience. Tellingly, the film places the taunting of Joan after her recantation and before its withdrawal – that is, at the same point in the narrative at which the rehabilitation witnesses claimed the historical Joan's guards tried to rape her.

Film Style

Studying *La Passion de Jeanne d'Arc* demonstrates the need to attend to style; it is the film's aesthetics (photography, sets, editing) that are commonly thought to define it as avant-garde rather than popular. More generally, there are specific reasons for its being important for religion and film practitioners to consider style. Subject matter alone does not make a 'religious film' (however defined). It is necessary to discern carefully the qualities of Dreyer's *Jeanne* that lead many to speak of it in religious or quasi-religious terms.

One approach to film art is the thematic one, which reads stylistic effects as symbolic or metaphoric expressions of narrative themes. This is a satisfying method of 'reading' film; it leads to the construction of portable meanings, which can be described in straightforward terms. In religious studies contexts, it is a popular strategy since it allows us to identify works as expressive of specific religious concepts or dilemmas, or as typological representations of religious events or figures (witness the popularity of the quest for Christ-figures in film). But the search for aspects of a film that can: (a) be read as metaphors, and (b) cohere to form a narrative, can lead to the inappropriate forcing of both individual moments and entire films to illustrate preconceived themes, which may exist only in the critic's mind. Intrinsic, too, to thematic criticism is the danger of confusing the act of 'translating' a symbol with understanding, or explaining it. Why might a director use metaphor? (How) have viewers responded to symbolic cues in a film? These are questions the thematic approach cannot tackle adequately.

In reaction against tendencies to privilege those aspects that are linked with narrative continuity and thematic coherence, formalists emphasize the aesthetic (unities and) disunities in a given film. According to this approach, the most discussion-worthy aspects of (for example) *Jeanne* are those that disrupt viewer expectations of the basic grammar of film – the structuring of shot and cut. The fundamental emphases of the film are perceptual contradiction and discontinuity. Thus according to Bordwell, Dreyer's goal in *Jeanne* is to 'withhold the smoothly flowing pleasure of viewing', to make it hard for audiences to consume his art.[14]

Again, there is some appeal in this position. Its emphasis on disruption highlights aspects of *Jeanne* that strike even the most casual of viewers, such as the reliance on close-ups and ellipsis. However, taken in isolation, it creates an account of film that affords little room to the complexities of viewer experience. In *Jeanne*, Dreyer defamiliarizes and disorients viewers, but the film is about much more than a desire to challenge the expressive style of his contemporaries, and audiences do not relate to films as formalists classically view them, that is, as series of minute units, able to be expressed in diagrammatic or tabular form.

This section will discuss *Jeanne's* style in a way that treads a path between thematic and formalist criticism. While Dreyer's style is often strange, and is not only a function of the film's themes, at the same time, style and narrative are not wholly unconnected in *Jeanne*.

The film's title itself suggests that Dreyer intends to draw comparisons between the experiences of Joan and Jesus of Nazareth, and there are repeated visual references to the crucifixion as the drama unfolds. Crosses are formed by the bars on the windows of Joan's cell, and their shadow projected by sunlight onto its floor. They appear on the gravestones in the cemetery and on top of distant churches. Finally, a crucifix is held by and then before the burning Joan. It is significant that the cleric Loyseleur, who treads on the shadow cross in Joan's cell, is later the one who decides to use the torture chamber, and who guides her hand as she struggles to sign the abjuration. The implication is that his piety is a sham. Additionally (as noted earlier) Joan is tormented by jailors, who, evoking Mark 15.17–19, dress her in mock regal garb (a straw-crown; a sceptre made from an arrow). As she goes to the stake, a bystander offers Joan a drink (Mark 15.21–23), and another later declares, 'you have burned a saint' (echoing Mark 15.39).

In what sense are viewers being encouraged to read Joan's suffering as a rehearsal of the Christ-event? Perhaps the images are intended to suggest that this is how Joan interpreted her experiences. Changing facial expressions imply that she feels strengthened by the appearance of the shadow-cross on the cell floor. And it is at the moment when the prison guard is sweeping away the straw-crown that Joan makes the decision to withdraw the recantation and reassert the reality of her voices, a move the trial clerk notes as '*responsio mortifera*'. The crown becomes for Joan the symbol of her torment, and provides the sense of her purpose as one of martyrdom. This is perhaps the crucial point at which the film best captures the dynamics of religious experience: Joan perceives her mission as suprahistorical. Ordinary discourse is turned inside out; she will save France not by intervening in earthly affairs, but by dying at the stake. Her stance becomes visionary. Of course, it remains unclear whether Dreyer intends the audience to comprehend Joan's self-understanding intellectually, or to empathize with her, or as Baugh suggests to *share* the meanings she finds in her experience, also seeing her as Christlike.[15] In all likelihood the ambiguity is intended.

Exegesis determined by Jesus typology does not exhaust *Jeanne*. There are many dimensions of the gospel that are absent from the film, and other aspects are not helpfully described as 'Christ-like'. If the Jesus typology allows some viewers to feel 'at home' with dimensions of *Jeanne*, as touched on earlier, Dreyer's organization of shot and cut are often perceived to make the film an exhausting, disorienting one for the audience.

All critics who discuss *Jeanne* comment on its unrelenting close-ups. There are almost no true establishing shots in *Jeanne*. Joan's (Marie Falconetti's) face is present in almost every frame, filmed without make-up, and so tightly that small movements, blemishes and pores are visible. Joan is also characterized by *stasis*, the lack of movement giving her character a near statuesque quality. According to Dreyer, the use of close-up was suggested by the trial transcript, where one encounters a series of 'talking heads' engaged in combat.[16] Certainly, the spoken word is strikingly prominent in this silent film, and the reliance on the close-up, and the large number of cuts, serve to emphasize this feature.

The close-up does not only focus our attention on verbal combat. For Deleuze, the close-up is the 'affection-image'. Seen at such close quarters, faces look alike; hence we are absorbed in a way going beyond intellectual or cognitive processes. In psychological terms, our individuation is suspended – hence the feelings of disorientation and exhaustion. In using this technique, Deleuze says, Dreyer is able to show both the trial (the historical 'realities' – the characters, the connections between them) and the *passion* – the internal and the suprahistorical dimension of Jeanne's experience.[17]

Almost as remarkable as *Jeanne's* use of close-ups are the framing and the cuts between shots. Conventional editing privileges continuity, typically achieved either by the shot/reverse shot, which (for example) establishes visually the relation between the faces of two partners in a conversation, or by the carrying over of figures or objects from one shot to another. *Jeanne* subverts these norms by including few matches. It also films characters from unusual angles and rarely places the principle action in the centre of the frame. At times, Joan's face is cut (horizontally, vertically, obliquely) by the frame edge. From a thematic perspective, these elements might be illustrative of Joan's isolation from her interlocutors. For formalists, they are about perceptual contradiction and a desire to foreground film *as* film. But it is equally possible that the unorthodox techniques are intended to serve rather more conventional functions. For example, we may be arrested by the unexpected appearance of a priest's head in the bottom or side of a frame, as he questions Joan. This is visually striking, but (in part) also a stock move: Dreyer shows in the frame what Joan sees, depicting her point-of-view. Similarly, two rapid camera movements in opposite directions evoke the feelings of chaos that sweep through the judges, when they are disturbed by Joan's responses to their questions. And when, in one of the film's most famous moments, in a down shot of an alley, English soldiers appear as helmets, swinging arms and shouldered spears, the function of this ellipsis is to suggest that they are less people than tools of an occupying authority.

At this point, it is worth relating the style of *Jeanne* to that of one of Dreyer's earlier works. Many commentators have noted that the sets were designed by expressionist Hermann Warm (renowned for *The Cabinet of Dr. Caligari*, 1920) and are characterized by a simplicity that negates viewers' sense of depth and perspective. It is possible to read this design choice as a piece of avant-garde experimentation, but since the film was originally intended for a popular audience (see 'Reception') there are other plausible explanations. *Jeanne*'s set represents a deliberate departure from the mistakes of an earlier Dreyer film, *Once Upon a Time* (1922). The film was based on a popular Danish fairy strory, but the characters offered by folklore proved too flimsy and two-dimensional. The conventions of the period drama overwhelmed, and Dreyer discovered that 'one cannot build a film from atmosphere alone'.[18] Read against this experience, the choice of minimalist sets for *Jeanne* allows us to gain a sense of Dreyer the craftsman, feeling his way towards a style that does justice to history without succumbing to the temptation to picturesqueness. The film's aesthetics reflect an assessment of the best 'tools' for the job of connecting, undistracted, with Joan.

In short, the close-ups, the repeated and challenging cuts, the negation of depth and so on are partly about reminding us that meaning is enacted. But in combination they also divert attention *away* from externals in a way that encourages viewers to be absorbed by the film in quasi-mystical terms. This emphasis on interiority resonates with the ideological subtexts of the film (against which the Roman Catholic Church reacted in the 1920s) by suggesting that religiosity, or spirituality, stands in opposition to institutions and outward forms. So it is to this aspect of *Jeanne*, its place in the wider cultural context, to which the analysis must turn.

Cultural and Religious Context

Dreyer's *Jeanne* could never be '*the* Joan'. As a representation of Joan of Arc it exists inescapably in relation to other images, and needs to be understood with reference to them. This section will locate the film within two frameworks, namely, Joan's use by ultra-nationalists in turn-of-the-century France, and the European cinema debate in the early twentieth century.

Joan's persistence is testimony to her malleability. Those who would claim her as their own are able to select those elements of the Joan myth that resonate with their (sometimes contradictory) causes. In the late nineteenth and early twentieth centuries, right-wing nationalists in France appealed extensively to Joan. Specifically, her Catholicism, patriotism, royalism and chastity made her the ideal symbol for the *Action Française*, who rejected the values of the Republic in favour of a mystical Catholicism, xenophobia, and a glorification of violence and war. As one *Action* text described it in 1920: 'Joan of Arc . . . is the eternal youth of our people, who after heroism produce work and, after death, bring forth life.'[19]

Understanding this history of the use of Joan by reactionary forces, and noting that there was a flurry of popular pageantry accompanying her declaration as venerable (1903), her beatification (1909) and canonization (1920), and the quincentenary of her victories (1929) helps us to appreciate why Dreyer's film proved so controversial (see 'Reception'). The film does not depict Joan in battle and largely ignores her virginity and her relationship with Charles VII, for whom she fought, and whose coronation she attended in 1429. But Dreyer's depiction of Joan is nevertheless political. By ignoring her military genius, and leaving the question of the authenticity of her voices 'open', Dreyer challenged the Joan myth that the right wing was working to establish. More significantly, in depicting Joan's recantation (albeit in largely sympathetic terms) Dreyer's film drew attention to precisely that element of the story that the nationalists most desired to forget.

Dreyer was not ignorant of the meanings attached to Joan in 1920s France. Arguably, his focus on the *passion* is in itself a critique of those who located her significance in patriotic militarism. But this is not to say that *Jeanne* is completely at odds with the wider cultural context.

In a creative addition to the trial accounts, Dreyer shows Joan's death prompting a riot among the gathered crowds, who turn their anger against the English and their allies. This scene, with its anachronistic shot of traversing cannon, is Dreyer's salute to Sergei Eisenstein's *Battleship Potemkin* (1925). Reinforced by the final intertitle, which speaks of 'Jeanne, whose heart has become the heart of France; Jeanne, whose memory will always be cherished by the people of France,' it also evokes modern conflations of Joan and French national destiny. Schrader (adopting a thematic approach) dismisses this as the point at which Dreyer retreats from the transcendent (defined by Schrader as a deeply felt unity between humanity and 'the All'): the film's attention to social context gives space for viewers to evaluate Joan's martyrdom in historical terms, and debases its value as religious art.[20] However, this reading ignores the return to the stake and *the cross* in the final shot, and the assumption that social concerns are necessarily opposed to religious ones is not obviously a correct one. Dreyer's depiction of the riot does not preclude the possibility of viewers experiencing the film religiously. It could resonate with the perspective of those viewers for whom Joan's death transcended the simple historical event, and attained the status of a crucial moment in the divinely ordained life of the nation.

Just as Dreyer was not apolitical so more generally the world of cinema was not immune to such preoccupations. When the *Société Générale des Films* commissioned Dreyer to work on *Jeanne*, other possible subjects for the film were Marie Antoinette and Catherine de Medici[21] – like Joan, they were both controversial women from France's past. The *Société* was one of several bodies then seeking to address the growing dominance of Hollywood in world cinema. (The rise of American cinema was a particular concern in France, whose own film-makers had enjoyed a position of pre-eminence before World War One.) Across Europe, the concept of 'national cinema' was being explored. Its proponents believed that each country should aspire to create annually a small number of films bearing the distinctive imprint of that nation's character. This might be achieved by producing films based on famous literary texts, or which referenced visually the country's geographical or artistic heritage.

Just as he could not have avoided Joan's status as nationalist icon, so Dreyer would have been aware of the national cinema debate in France. In such an atmosphere, Parisian viewers might have approached *Jeanne* expecting to see a celebration of the nation, with the virgin as a kind of ambassador for her homeland. The distance between this expectation and the reality of Dreyer's film in part explains its controversial reception. Interestingly, *Jeanne* also exemplifies the reasons for the failure of the national cinema project. As a concept, the idea of a national cinema ignored the fact that cinema personnel have always crossed national boundaries: Dreyer was, after all, a Dane commissioned to make a 'French film'. Moreover, European organizations lacked the resources to compete with the industrial production methods of an ascendant Hollywood: Dreyer originally wanted to shoot *Jeanne* as a sound film, but the available European studios lacked the necessary equipment.

Reception

La Passion de Jeanne d'Arc is widely hailed as a masterpiece of silent cinema. But Dreyer did not make the film with the delectation of future cinephiles in mind; he wanted *Jeanne* to be his commercial breakthrough, for it to attract a mainstream, popular audience.[22] Likewise, the *Société*, in their desire to bolster French cinema, hoped for a film with mass appeal. At the instigation of the *Société*, *Jeanne* was even shown to an early focus group in Paris in April 1928. According to Dreyer, the feedback was such that if all objections to the film were acted upon, nothing would be left to screen, which suggested that it should in fact appear without *any* further revision. However, the staging of this preview itself indicates that prior to its release, there was a distinct feeling of unease amongst Dreyer's backers.

In Copenhagen, unemployed Danes were invited to a free screening at the instigation of a Social Democratic politician. The audience was encouraged to fill in response cards, which were generally positive, and illustrated the tendency for viewers to draw links between their own day and that of Joan. 'There are women today who are as tortured morally by society as was Jeanne d'Arc,' commented one.[23] But in France, where viewers had more firmly established ideas about the narrative and meanings of Joan's life and death, the film was condemned. For nationalists, the fact that a Scandinavian had been chosen to make a film about Joan was a scandal: the involvement of a foreigner could only be detrimental to the French national culture. The Catholic Church had additional difficulties with the film: even before the preview, the Catholic Archbishop of Paris threatened a boycott. Much dissent turned on the handling of the role of the Church authorities in Joan's death. The canonization document described her as a loyal Catholic who was attended regularly by her confessor; it depicted her judges as schismatics. Moreover, it characterized her as a virgin, not a martyr as *Jeanne* suggests. Although Dreyer does have one cleric declare her 'a saint' (like Benedict XV) he presents Joan's conviction about the truth of her *inward* experience as being in fundamental and inevitable conflict with the *institutional* Church. Specifically, Cauchon is shown attempting to pressurize Joan into signing the retraction, by taunting her with the Eucharist. This scene (cut for the Paris screening; missing from the London print) proved highly offensive to Catholic sensibilities. It suggested not just that leading Church figures were devious, but also demeaned the host, implying that it could be used as a political weapon. Perhaps in this troubling scene, we see the limits to the ability of the Catholic Church and Dreyer, whose Protestant desire (his adoptive parents were Lutherans) was to subordinate externals to 'the spirit in and behind things', to comprehend one another.

While the *New York Times* praised Falconetti for revealing the 'faith that guided the girl knight of France' and found the cinematography 'effective',[24] other objections to the film came from the English authorities, where *Jeanne* was banned for a year because of alleged anti-English bias. Joan's story was not in itself the problem. The British press reported the quincentenary celebrations of her victories in detail and with some sympathy, in features illustrated by stills from Dreyer's film.[25] The widely perceived similarity of the helmets worn by Dreyer's soldiers and those donned by English troops in World War One, and the depiction of Warwick, pressing for Jeanne's conviction and determined to deny her 'a natural death,' were sources of contention. Eventually, however, the film was screened in London in November 1930, when reviewers and advertisers carefully avoided any reference to politics and stressed style, instead finding Falconetti 'poignant' and the photography 'beautiful,' but suggesting that the style was somewhat 'strange'.[26]

There were reservations in Britain and elsewhere, too, about inaccuracies of detail. Critics ridiculed the bespectacled priest, pointing out that glasses had not been invented in Joan's day. However, in the context of Dreyer's project, to focus on such issues is the product of a misplaced sense of what 'realism' entails. Verity does not lie in the recreation of 'the look'. (Similarly, attending only to the use of twentieth-century scissors in the scene where Jeanne's hair is cropped seems reductionist in the extreme.)

While in the 1920s most negative responses to *Jeanne* stemmed from the film's lack of fit with prevailing versions of the Joan myth, and so can be attributed to wider cultural and religious factors, in more recent years the film's reception has been shaped by other forces. As noted in the introduction, engagement with *Jeanne* has been circumscribed by the lack of availability of a stable print. But as the decades have succeeded, *Jeanne* has been subjected to many different forms of criticism. In the theoretical seventies, Nash's study, heavily influenced by Marxism and psychoanalysis, pronounced *Jeanne* to be a rehearsal of 'politico-religious doctrinal struggles within the context of a patriarchal order marked by Judeo-Christian monotheism'.[27] Scholars of religion and film might find value here, while questioning some of Nash's fundamental assumptions, not least the misnomer, 'Judeo-Christian'. Just a few years later, Malpezzi and Clements assessed *Jeanne* quite differently, declaring the film to be a masterpiece precisely because it *transcended* politics.[28] This essay has argued that such an interpretation of the film is not plausible. However, one of the advantages of studying such an old film as *Jeanne* is that by comparing how different scholars have evaluated it, we can chart both changing trends in cinema studies, and the general contours in a particular film's reception over time: each study referred to in this paper forms part of *Jeanne's* reception history.

While for multiple reasons, *La Passion de Jeanne d'Arc* has been a difficult film to watch, it continues to attract the interest (but not necessarily the viewership) of arthouse film-goers, and students of film, including those of religion and film. Why is this? Without doubt, 'myth' and mystery play a significant role here. As outlined earlier, there are arresting resonances between the fate of the historical Joan and the film that bears her name. Both were railed against and ravaged by fire, only to be restored to better fortunes some years later. Similarly, Dreyer's choice of actress Marie Falconetti for the starring role was fortuitous. The historical Joan's early death ensured her status as icon. Had she lived, the truth of her voices would have been in doubt. Instead, she remains forever young, an unfailing hero in whom much meaning may be invested. Likewise, *Jeanne* is the only cinema appearance of Falconetti, which makes her brilliant performance in the film all the more compelling. Like Joan, her appearance attains a special status partly because it leaves us pondering what might have been, and because there are no disappointing follow-up roles to tarnish her reputation.

3. Conclusions

This essay is at its end. A more extended study of *La Passion de Jeanne d'Arc* would attend to many other issues, such as the film's engagement with emerging social science discourses (especially those of psychology and psychoanalysis). However, I hope that I have done enough to say something of value about *Jeanne* and to model a way of approaching film that goes beyond that sometimes practised in religion and film studies. Above all, this essay will have succeeded at least in a small way if I have encouraged others to return to what one early critic called a work of film art that 'takes precedence over anything that has so far been produced'[29] – that is, if I have shared with you a little passion for *Jeanne*.

Notes

1 See for example, Mark Le Fanu, 'Bewitched', *Sight and Sound* 13.7 (2003): 30–2.

2 Tom Milne, 'Darkness and Light: Carl Theodor Dreyer', *Sight and Sound*, 34.4 (1965): 167.

3 On this issue generally see Tony Pipolo, 'The spectre of Joan of Arc: Textual Variations in the Key Prints of Carl Dreyer's Film', *Film History*, 2.4 (1988): 301–24.

4 Mark Nash, 'Joan Complete: A Dreyer Discovery', *Sight and Sound*, 54.3 (1985): 157–8.

5 Gilles Deleuze, *Cinema 1: The Movement-Image*, London: The Athlone Press, 1992, p. 106.

6 Matthew Tinkcomm and Amy Villarejo, 'Introduction', in Matthew Tinkcomm and Amy Villarejo (eds), *Keyframes: Popular Cinema and Cultural Studies*, London: Routledge, 2001, pp. 1–29 (13).

7 On both works see Nadia Margolis, 'Trial by Passion: Philology, Film and Ideology in the Portrayal of Joan of Arc (1900–1930)', *Journal of Medieval and Early Modern Studies*, 27.3 (1997): 445–93.

8 David Bordwell, *The Films of Carl-Theodor Dreyer*, Berkeley: University of California Press, 1981, p. 84.

9 Donald Skoller (ed.), *Dreyer in Double Reflection. Translation of Carl Th. Dreyer's Writings about the Film*, New York: E.P. Dutton and Co., 1973, p. 145.

10 Michelle Gellrich, *Tragedy and Theory: The Problem of Conflict Since Aristotle*, Princeton: Princeton University Press, 1988, pp. 233–5.

11 Marina Warner, *Joan of Arc: The Image of Female Heroism*, London: Vintage, 1991, p. 21.

12 Warner, *Joan of Arc*, p. 141.

13 Warner, *Joan of Arc*, p. 106.

14 Bordwell, *The Films of Carl-Theodor Dreyer*, p. 65.

15 Lloyd Baugh, *Imaging the Divine: Jesus and Christ-Figures in Film*, Franklin: Sheed and Ward, 2000, p. 213.

16 Quoted in Mark Nash, *Dreyer*, London: British Film Institute, 1977, p. 53.

17 Deleuze, *Cinema 1*, p. 106.

18 Quoted in Casper Tybjerg, ' Dreyer and the National Film in Denmark', *Film History*, 13.1 (2001): 32.

19 Martha Hanna, 'Iconology and Ideology: Images of Joan of Arc in the Idiom of the *Action française, 1908–1931*', *French Historical Studies*, 14.2 (1985): 227.

20 Paul Schrader, *Transcendental Style in Film: Ozu, Bresson, and Dreyer*, Berkeley: University of California Press, 1972, pp. 125–6.

21 Nash, *Dreyer*, pp. 52–3.

22 Nash, *Dreyer*, p. 54.

23 Bordwell, *The Films of Carl-Theodor Dreyer*, p. 216.

24 Mordaunt Hall, 'Poignant French Film – Maria Falconetti Gives Unequaled Performance as Jeanne d'Arc', *New York Times*, 31 March 1929, s.8, 7.

25 See unattributed articles, 'St. Joan', *The Times*, 27 April 1929, 10; 'Joan of Arc. Celebrations in France', *The Times*, 27 April 1929, 13–14, and 'Joan of Arc. Celebrations at Chinon', *The Times*, 29 April 1929, 14.

26 See the unattributed 'Film Society: *The Passion of Joan of Arc*', *The Times*, 17 November 1930, 10.

27 Nash, *Dreyer*, p. 19.

28 Frances M. Malpezzi and William M. Clements, 'The Passion of Joan of Arc (La Passion de Jeanne d'Arc)', in Frank N. Magill (ed.), *Magill's Survey of Cinema: Silent Films Volume 2*, Epping: Bowker Publishing Company, 1982, pp. 854–7.

29 Hall, 'Poignant French Film', p. 7.

4. Reading Stanley Kubrick: A Theological Odyssey

JEFFREY F. KEUSS

During the 71st Academy Awards, Steven Spielberg eulogized the passing of director Stanley Kubrick with these words:

> He died before he could witness the century he had already made famous with *2001: A Space Odyssey*. Stanley wanted us to see his movies absolutely as he envisioned them. He never gave an inch on that. He dared us to have the courage of his convictions, and when we take that dare, we're transported directly to his world, and we're inside his vision. And in the whole history of movies, there has been nothing like that vision ever. It was a vision of hope and wonder, of grace and of mystery. It was a gift to us, and now it's a legacy. We will be challenged and nourished by that for as long as we keep the courage to take his dare, and I hope that will be long after we've said our thanks and good-byes.[1]

Born 26 July 1928 in New York City, Stanley Kubrick remains one of the most talked about film directors of the past century. He went on to receive Best Director Academy Award nominations for *Dr. Strangelove*, *2001: A Space Odyssey*, *A Clockwork Orange* and *Barry Lyndon*. Each of those films also earned Kubrick Best Screenplay nominations, as did *Full Metal Jacket*. In addition, *Dr. Strangelove*, *A Clockwork Orange* and *Barry Lyndon* received Best Picture nominations. Kubrick's only Oscar came for the special effects in *2001: A Space Odyssey*. In 1997, he received the D. W. Griffith Award for Lifetime Achievement from the Directors Guild of America. That same year Kubrick began shooting *Eyes Wide Shut*, returning to film-making after a ten-year absence. He died in his sleep on 7 March 1999, soon after turning in his final cut of the film. (For a filmography of Stanley Kubrick, see Text Box 4.1.)

Part of the importance of Kubrick's vision as a director was that he was someone who immersed himself in the world of words as well as vision. Kubrick began his adult career as a photographer before making the move to film but was always deeply interested in narrative. Only Kubrick's first two feature films, *Fear and Desire* and *Killer's Kiss*, were based on original stories that he created (the former with Howard O. Sackler).

4.1 Filmography of Stanley Kubrick

1951 *Day of the Fight*
Director/Photography/Editor/Sound: Stanley Kubrick
Documentary short on Walter Cartier, middleweight prize fighter
Running Time: 16 minutes

1951 *Flying Padre*
Director/Photography/Editor/Sound: Stanley Kubrick
Documentary short on the Reverend Fred Stadmueller, Roman Catholic
missionary of a New Mexico parish that covers 400 square miles
Running Time: 9 minutes

1953 *The Seafarers*
Director/Photography/Editor: Stanley Kubrick
Documentary short in colour about the Seafarers International Union
Running Time: 30 minutes

1953 *Fear and Desire*
Producer: Stanley Kubrick
Director/Photography/Editor: Stanley Kubrick
Running Time: 68 minutes

1955 *Killer's Kiss*
Producers: Stanley Kubrick, Morris Bousel
Director/Photography/Editor: Stanley Kubrick
Script: Stanley Kubrick, Howard O. Sackler
Running Time: 64 minutes

1956 *The Killing*
Producer: James B. Harris
Director: Stanley Kubrick
Screenplay: Stanley Kubrick, based on the novel *Clean Break*, by Lionel
White
Running Time: 83 minutes

1957 *Paths of Glory*
Producer: James B. Harris
Director: Stanley Kubrick
Screenplay: Stanley Kubrick, Calder Willingham, Jim Thompson, based
on the novel by Humphrey Cobb
Running Time: 86 minutes

1960 *Spartacus*
Producer: Edward Lewis
Director: Anthony Mann, Stanley Kubrick
Screenplay: Dalton Trumbo, based on the book by Howard Fast
Original Running Time: 196 minutes
Released Running Time: 184 minutes

1962 *Lolita*
Director: Stanley Kubrick
Screenplay: Vladimir Nabokov, based on his novel
Running Time: 153 minutes

1964 *Dr. Strangelove or: How I Learned to Stop Worrying and Love the Bomb*
Producer/Director: Stanley Kubrick
Screenplay: Stanley Kubrick, Terry Southern, Peter George, based on the novel *Red Alert* by Peter George
Running Time: 94 minutes

1968 *2001: A Space Odyssey*
Producer: Stanley Kubrick
Director: Stanley Kubrick
Screenplay: Stanley Kubrick, Arthur C. Clarke, based on Clarke's short story 'The Sentinel'
Running Time: 141 minutes

1971 *A Clockwork Orange*
Producer/Director: Stanley Kubrick
Screenplay: Stanley Kubrick, based on the novel by Anthony Burgess
Running Time: 137 minutes

1975 *Barry Lyndon*
Producer/Director: Stanley Kubrick
Screenplay: Stanley Kubrick, based on the novel by William Makepeace Thackeray
Running Time: 185 minutes

1980 *The Shining*
Producer/Director: Stanley Kubrick
Executive Producer: Jan Harlan
Screenplay: Stanley Kubrick, Diane Johnson, based on the novel by Stephen King
Running Time: 145 minutes

1987 *Full Metal Jacket*
Producer /Director: Stanley Kubrick
Screenplay: Stanley Kubrick, Michael Herr, Gustav Hasford, based on the
novel by Gustav Hasford
Running Time: 117 minutes

1999 *Eyes Wide Shut*
Producer/Director: Stanley Kubrick
Screenplay: Stanley Kubrick and Frederic Raphael, inspired by Arthur
Schnitzler's novella *Traumnovelle*. (English title: *Rhapsody, a Dream
Novel.*)
Running Time: 159 minutes

When he teamed up with producer James B. Harris in the early 1950s,
they began looking for literary properties to adapt, since that was Harris's
speciality and at that time it was easier for young film-makers to get a film
made based on an existing work.

Kubrick had always been a voracious reader and the success of his next
few films convinced him that he was better at adapting stories that interested him than inventing his own material (although of course he made
significant contributions to the finished screenplay on all of his films).

1. Viewing vs. Reading Film

To begin our discussion of Kubrick as a film-maker is to begin with a
reminder that Kubrick's films should be 'read' as opposed to 'viewed'. I
am differentiating between these terms 'viewing' and 'reading' as passive
and active ways of approaching film. Too often, the notion of film as
something we view rather than read results in a great loss of riches that
film by directors such as Kubrick have to offer.

As a medium we merely 'view', film becomes something we 'understand' without struggling to improve our understanding. For example, the
photographic image stands in contrast to a text, which, with a single
word, can shift from representation to reflection. We look at a photo and
recall its source – its very 'stillness' seems to allow and encourage us to
make a reference – e.g. Who *is* this in the picture? When was it taken?
Where was that building in the background? It is this that led cultural
theorist Roland Barthes to call the photographic image pure contingency
– that is, the photograph is always something that is representational
and therefore contingent on something 'other' for meaning to arise. In
contrast, more so than other arts, *film offers an immediate and fully
contextualized presence to the world* – it is self-referential and makes its
own reality. Ironically, it is precisely because, as James Monaco notes,

4.2 What is Auteur Theory?

What role does the director of a film play in the overall film? This is a point that has been greatly debated. *Auteur theory* is the school of thought that argues that for some film productions, the role of the director is not only central to understanding the overall meaning of a film but that it is vital. *Auteur* is French for 'author' and the politics of auteur, or *politique des auteurs*, were first stated by director Francois Truffaut in his article 'Une certaine tendance du cinema francais' in *Cahiers du cinema* (*Notebooks on Cinema*) in 1954. Truffaut postulated that one person, usually the director, has the artistic responsibility for a film and reveals a personal world-view through the tensions among style, theme and the conditions of production. In short, auteur theory argues that films can be studied like novels and paintings as a product of an individual artist. Truffaut's pronouncement helped defend the Hollywood system of film-making in the late 1950s against France's popular criticism. Truffaut maintained that the work of an author could be found in many Hollywood films and it was the quality of the director that was the measure of the work, not necessarily the work itself.

Examples of those film-makers often referred to as *auteurs* include Stanley Kubrick, Alfred Hitchcock and Woody Allen.

Most people now refer to 'new auteur theory'. In current film criticism, there is widespread acknowledgement that films are not the product of merely one auteur or creator but collective efforts. Although the director still receives most of the credit for the voice of the film, many of the current directors who are considered *auteurs* use the same cast and crew for most if not all their films. This raises the question, if the crew is the same in every film, is it possible to distinguish the voice of the director from that of the collective (screenwriters, actors, production designer, all those responsible for creative decisions)? Contemporary *auteurs* such as the Coen brothers, Wes Anderson and Christopher Guest almost always use the same creative team. New auteur theory holds that those responsible for the creative decisions that influence the form of the film are always the same group of individuals.

films 'so very clearly mimic reality that we apprehend them much more easily than we comprehend them'.[2] Film semiologist Christian Metz comments that, as an easy art, cinema is in constant danger of falling victim to this easiness as he surmises: 'A film is difficult to explain because it is easy to understand.'[3] This power, inherent in the cinematic image, seduces: we lay ourselves open to the massive doses of meaning and information movies convey without questioning how they tell us what they do tell us. It is in reading film, seeing deeply with a critical turn – reading as opposed to merely viewing – that is essential to plumbing the rich depths of films.

Film and the very nature of the cinematic image itself resists reading: its immediacy, its lack of distance, its illusion of pure reference does make this difficult. In short, movies need 'unpacking' and critical analysis no less than other 'texts'.

2. Reading the Religious in Stanley Kubrick

One aspect of Kubrick not fully addressed however is that he was deeply concerned with the religious aspects of life as well.[4] While not overtly playing his cards in any dogmatic pronouncements, reading the films of Kubrick shows a director who invokes an experience of the numinous and the predestined, what theologian Rudolf Otto would call the experience of the holy, the *mysterium tremendum et fascinans*.[5] It is a mystical experience, an ecstasy at the end of things, that continually threatens to consume or immerse the subjects of his films and ultimately draws us as viewers into this experience of the holy as well.

Anthropologist of Religion Mary Douglas has written that a 'person without religion would be the person content to do without explanations'.[6] To read Kubrick's films is to partake of films that display a profound discontent with the state of modern humanity akin to the fervour of an evangelist calling for an encounter with something more, something larger, and ultimately something transcendent.

One of the early sages of film critical theory is media theorist Marshall McLuhan. In *The Medium is the Massage*, McLuhan insisted that we cannot understand the technological experience from the outside as a 'viewer' from an objective space. We can only comprehend how the electronic age 'works us over' if we 'recreate the experience' in depth. He makes this point with regard to mass media:

> All media work us over completely. They are so persuasive in their personal, political, economic, aesthetic, psychological, moral, ethical, and social consequences that they leave no part of us untouched, unaffected, unaltered. The medium is the massage. Any understanding of social and cultural change is impossible without knowledge of the way media work as environments.[7]

In short, to read film is to first accept the fact that it will take work and is not a passive enterprise – but that should not take the joy out of it. Merely 'viewing' any image is ultimately a form of both idolatry (passively becoming the object rather than the subject) and iconoclasm (seeing only the surface and not into the depth of a thing is ultimately to destroy it). This is the task of religion and the call of people of faith.[8] Whether it is the empty cross or a filled chalice, Christian theology has ample reason to attend to images, both because we do not want to be in their thrall unawares and because their power already signals some sort of 'religious' resonance. We know the power of certain images to hold sway over the imagination. Media mediates through and with images – we are expected to know the meaning of the void created in the New York skyline after September 11th and the toppling of Saddam's image in central Baghdad, played over and over on television screens. We know at an innate level that something is going on when certain images hit us – their power to embody and make present the very being of their object. Profound responses in the presence of images (desire, fear) transcend the sorts of boundaries academics establish between the canon of so-called high art, folk and tribal arts, popular logos from Starbucks to Nike, and the devotional images found in our places of worship. *Film is a medium of immediate imaging – where some images and texts require some reflection and repose prior to understanding, most film demands and gets an immediate reaction and understanding.* It displays a world much more convincingly and immediately than any other symbolic form. As mechanical reproduction, it gives the illusion of pure reference. As moving picture, it seems to offer an ongoing experience of time present and therefore of presence.

Three Pointers for Film Reading

These are three 'pointers' that Barbara De Concini[9] suggests as a way of beginning to school ourselves in 'reading' films. We shall apply these to a representative viewing of three of Kubrick's films. As she suggests, since the viewer tends to identify with the camera's lens as the authoritative angle of value to be considered (which is roughly equivalent to the point of view in a novel), we should school ourselves to pay attention to the camera – what it does, what and who it shows and doesn't show. De Concini suggests the following:

1. *How the camera frames and holds the subject.* How much of the human figure is in view, how much of the surroundings? What happens to our perceptions when the character is presented to us in extreme long shot, a mere speck on the screen as opposed to in extreme close-up, and where the individual face can become a whole spiritual landscape? An image in painting or a photograph can be rich with symbolic import, but it must achieve its effects within the frame. A movie is a moving picture, a multiplicity of frames (astoundingly, as many as 180,000 in a two-hour film).
2. *The camera's angle of vision.* The angle from which a subject is photographed has an impact on how the image 'reads'. As Louis Giannetti demonstrates in *Understanding Movies*, an eye-level shot suggests

parity between viewer and subject, while high angles reduce the subject's significance, suggesting vulnerability, and low angles do the opposite, creating a sense of dominance over the viewer.

3. *Camera shots tend to acquire meaning when they are seen in relation to other shots.* Images that are created within the context of the film gain meaning through their associations with other images clustered within the film. In addition, as viewers we bring our lived experience to these images and they gain further meaning. This is one of the most characteristic ways in which the cinematic image expresses the 'something more'. We can call it symbolic and we will not be incorrect. But, as people who are used to the written text, our expectations of the symbolic may mislead us. Here the process is often a quite humble one which falls into a sort of middle range of meaning between the immediacy of the iconic and the latency of the symbolic. Through editing, the film-maker elaborates visually on some natural links and fairly straightforward connections, piecing together sets of visual associations, patterning thematic and metaphorical affinities for us through the iterative process of the cinema.

In contrast to paintings and photographs, a film can build its effect gradually, even modestly and quietly, alternating stretches of restraint, when the image is less saturated with meaning, with the occasional epiphany. A surprising amount of the connotative power of film depends on this 'cinematic shorthand' of *metonymy* – that is, a figure of speech in which an attribute of something is used to stand for the thing itself, such as 'laurels' when it stands for 'glory' or 'brass' when it stands for 'military officers' – this use of associated detail to evoke an idea or represent an object. Our understanding of how a film means and how it directs our attention towards its meaning can be greatly enhanced and complicated merely by bringing this associative resonance of the cinematic image to the level of our awareness.

3. *Lolita* (1962) – Temptation and at the End of it All . . . Desire

We begin with the first lens of film reading and consider what the camera frames into our view through a look at Kubrick's 1962 film *Lolita*. This was the film in which Kubrick began to develop his signature style of long, leisurely paced scenes that force the audience to step back and consider the overall setting and story, rather than getting caught up in the emotion of the scene itself. Kubrick felt this was the style that best suited Vladimir Nabokov's controversial story, and also helped manoeuvre it around the strict censorship standards of the time. What we notice in Kubrick's command of the camera as director is the way he not only shows us the images on the screen, but communicates rather subtly that he knows what we are watching and knows why we are – we are being watched as we watch.

Filmed in 1962 directly after completion of *Spartacus*, Kubrick shot most of the film in long master shots, sometimes up to ten minutes per take. Later, to give the film an even more literary quality, Kubrick and editor Anthony Harvey inserted fade-outs and fade-ins as scene transitions, with unusually long shots of black in between.

One aspect of film's power is the illusion of looking in on a private world, the ordinary magnified to the scale of spectacle, from our vantage of security and anonymity. This juxtaposition of intensity and detachment suggests a role not merely as viewers, but as voyeurs. As Laura Mulvey notes in her essay, 'Visual Pleasure and Narrative Cinema', among the possible pleasures the cinema offers is that of *looking itself*. Who would deny that the magic of Hollywood style at its best has always arisen from 'its skilled and satisfying manipulation of visual pleasure?' Could it be, as Mulvey argues, that movies correspond not only to our needs for ego identification, but also to our erotic desire to see that which is private or dangerous or forbidden, to gaze at the other as object from our own position of security, thus having it both ways? Movie theatres as venues of projection: both of images and of repressed desires!

In a representative scene from *Lolita*, Kubrick draws the viewer into the temptation of the protagonist Humbert Humbert (played by James Mason) as he gazes upon young Lolita Haze (played by 14-year-old Sue Lyon) while in the continued company of Lolita's mother Charlotte (played wonderfully by Shelley Winters). As the viewer is drawn to look upon Lolita Haze (an appropriate surname evoking a dreamlike quality of Nabokov's character and well framed by Kubrick) swirling with her hula-hoop, we are brought to account for our 'viewing' by the burst of the flash from Charlotte's camera. The dream/temptation bursts apart with – of all things – a burst of light that breaks the clouds or 'haze' away. Cinematically, we have been caught in the act of 'looking'. A whole body of critical literature has developed out of this argument concerning cinema's manipulation of the gaze (what theorist Jacques Lacan terms *la regard*) and how it reflects our deep psychological obsessions and the society that produces it. Throughout this film of temptation, Kubrick continues slowly to allow the approach of Lolita and Humbert, but akin to the classic tale of Tristan and Isolde they are continually pushed back over and over again leaving desire rather than consummation as the mark of the human dilemma.

Desire is an important aspect of faith. In a sermon entitled 'The Depth of Experience', theologian Paul Tillich states that it is desire that marks one of the essential aspects of our humanity and is one of the evidences of the *imago dei* – the image of god. For Tillich, it is our desire for what is 'truly desirable' that drives so much of our activity (you can possibly hear Freud and his disciples chanting 'Amen! Amen!') but Tillich goes on to note that it is conversely desiring and finding disappointments in this life that 'the truth of which does not disappoint dwells below the surface in the depth'.[10] Here Tillich sees 'depth' as that meaning-making encounter that evidences our meeting with the divine or as Tillich states 'the name of this infinite and inexhaustible depth and ground of all being is God. That depth is what the word God means.'[11]

Kubrick's films were manifestations of a search for 'this infinite and inexhaustible depth and ground of all being' and calling the film reader to account as to that which they seek and desire and exposing the film reader to their own act of desire. One has only to look at Kubrick's film *A Clockwork Orange*, which provides a number of instances of exposing the nature of desire as both a key to our downfall and also a mark of the divine spark in us.

4. *The Shining* (1980) – The Steady View of Fear

For a second lens – the camera's angle on the subject – we now look at Kubrick's 1980 retelling of Stephen King's horror classic *The Shining*.

Directors can be said to fall into two camps – trackers and zoomers. The use of the zoom lens draws the subject of the film out to the audience and this is a technique often favoured by today's directors. It is easy to do – merely change lens and re-frame the camera – and it doesn't alter the set too much. The other option – use of the track whereby the entire camera is placed on a track and moved – is very laborious, as well as time and money intensive. One of the great effects of tracking however is the ability to draw the viewer into the shot in a way that doesn't distort the image framed on screen. The reality of this use of the camera is that the viewer is 'taken along for the ride' as is seen in Kubrick's turn to the horror genre in his 1980 film of Stephen King's *The Shining*.

Prior to the mid-1970s, the only ways to move the camera within a closed-set scene were via a dolly apparatus or by having the operator hold the camera and walk around himself. The dolly allowed the camera extremely fluid movement, but required either an ultra-smooth surface or the laying down of tracks, plus several camera assistants to operate. Handheld camera shots, by their nature, tended to be somewhat unsteady, and were usually used to give a certain documentary-style effect (something Kubrick himself had done in his films on several occasions).

Then around 1974, a camera operator and inventor named Garrett Brown invented what he called the *Steadicam*. Essentially it was a small movie camera mounted onto a harness rig that could be carried and operated by one man, but which used a system of gyroscopes to keep the camera steady and the motion fluid. The result was a perfect hybrid of hand-held and dolly movement, and gave film-makers a new, very flexible tool for moving the camera.

However, the Steadicam was still considered an experimental device in 1978 when Kubrick decided to use it extensively for *The Shining*. In fact, Kubrick had the interior sets of the Overlook Hotel designed specifically with the Steadicam in mind, using only natural lighting and designing the corridors and rooms to gain the maximum effect from the device.

In a classic scene from *The Shining*, Danny Torrance (played by Danny Lloyd) is racing his Big Wheel tricycle through the hallways of the Overlook Hotel. As the viewer watches, we are placed in Danny's viewpoint, tracking through the hallways from his low riding vantage point and moving with his reckless speed, quickly taking corners without any awareness of what lies ahead. Garrett Brown came up with extenders and other modifications to give Kubrick more flexibility, including a 'low mode' for shooting the scenes of Danny riding his Big Wheel throughout the hotel's corridors.

Kubrick ended up shooting almost the entire film using the Steadicam, and *The Shining* was lauded for showing the device's potential and making it a virtually standard piece of camera equipment from that point forward. As the set of the Overlook Hotel was constructed, Kubrick built the set – the rooms, the hallways, the angles of the windows – around how the Steadicam camera could be used to best advantage. What Kubrick demonstrates is a profound shift – he does not begin with a set then try to find a way to get the right shots through adjusting the camera technology to 'fit in'. Rather, his universe begins with the principle of how things are to be seen – the angle of the shot first – then he builds the world around that.

In Kubrick's universe, seen especially in *The Shining* and *2001*, the camera angle provoked through the Steadicam tracking gives the viewer *a steady view of fear*: the anxiety of not being able to 'see' what comes around the next corner and thereby reminding us that in addition to *desire*, we as film readers must acknowledge the nature of fear and that unlimited space does not solve this but in many ways makes us realize how little we do 'know' and apprehend. Jeff Smith, in an article entitled 'Careening Through Kubrick's Space'[12] notes that Kubrick's use of space and how he fills the screen in his shots, for example in *The Shining's* reduction of 'environment' to a particular place – a huge empty hotel cut off from human contact – and the elimination of *2001*'s visual expansiveness in the middle section of the film in the space journey – both leave a 'space' so that the astronauts, whether on Earth amidst the open country or on a spaceship in the vastness of space, have no universe except their claustrophobic hotel/spaceship. The huge hotel and the large spacecraft

Discovery are still not big enough – relationships begin in uneasy balance and gradually break down into menace and terror. What Kubrick proposes through his use of infinite space is that freedom is not found in lack of boundaries. Ironically, it is the seeming infinite space that is both physically and psychologically imprisoning for the winter occupants of *The Shining* and the space travellers of *2001*.

In *The Shining* , the many doors of the Overlook open only onto more hotel, and the mirrors, deceptively breaching or enlarging space, ultimately turn one's view inward and collapse the prospect of space back onto itself: the equation of space and the self in a paradox of identity tracing a line back to Narcissus. This is not the Interior Castle of St Theresa of Avila where through the many rooms and water wheels one finds a unifying embrace from God. Maybe the greatest fear is that we are truly isolated – that around each corner is another corner and another hallway and we have been 'abandoned' to our fears.

In other words, *The Shining* depicts a chaotic and relativistic universe devoid of higher agencies, one whose very size and emptiness infuriatingly underscores human limitations and forever condemns humanity to endure her own grotesque self. According to philosopher and mystic Simone Weil 'we fly from the inner void, since God might steal into it. It is not the pursuit of pleasure and the aversion for effort which causes sin, but fear of God. We know that we cannot see him face to face without dying, and we do not want to die.'[13] With God displaced, the weak and conflicted self comes to the centre position – many of Jack Nicholson's shots in *The Shining* as we see him slowly slip into insanity are framed in the centre of the screen and fill most of the view – doomed to the endless deceptions of its own doors and mirrors. Toward the middle of the film, Jack makes a devil's pact – stating he would give his soul for just one drink – which materializes the demons of the Overlook and brings the long-faded ghosts back to life. The devil's pact offers no reward in a universe where certainty of knowledge is not possible. Man defines himself existentially only by his own dehumanizing actions – hence Jack's ultimate reduction to pure act, and his likely readiness to anoint yet another as having 'always' been the caretaker.

This is a theme through much of Kubrick's work – the loss of humanity and the search for some ultimate 'meaning' which, in the end, will only remove us from humanity at large. As seen in *The Shining* and *2001*, HAL and Jack Torrance are obsessed about their 'missions' or 'jobs' – HAL with his 'mission' and Jack with his caretaking contract with the Overlook (and, by extension, with his pseudo-job of writing his book). Just as HAL says to Bowman 'this mission is too important for you to jeopardize it', Jack goes ballistic whenever it is suggested that the family leave the Overlook (and also when Wendy interrupts his 'writing'). What is lost in embrace of one's mission or vocation as a singular focus is ultimately one's humanity. For both HAL and Jack, the inward turn towards an all-consuming 'mission' leaves them stripped of their possible humanity and care for others – in short, finding only isolation and fear.

5. *2001* – An Agnostic Prayer

For our third lens for film reading – how camera shots tend to acquire meaning when they are seen in relation to other shots – we will reflect on the nature of the jump-cut technique in respect to *2001: A Space Odyssey*.

In a recent documentary looking back at Kubrick's work, Christiane Kubrick, Stanley Kubrick's widow, spoke of *2001: A Space Odyssey* as Kubrick's 'agnostic prayer'. Upon its initial release, the Vatican contacted Kubrick and invited him to come for a special showing of the film. Christiane Kubrick said that, as the images of the film filled the ancient wall of St Peter's where the movie was being viewed, Stanley smiled and said 'now I am beginning to understand my religion – this is an agnostic prayer, a plea for the "something" that must be out there somewhere'.

Kubrick was often pressed to interpret his work – as though to give an author's read of the film as text that would somehow be authoritative. With regard to his 1965 sci-fi film *2001: A Space Odyssey*, he responded in this way:

> How could we possibly appreciate the Mona Lisa if Leonardo had written at the bottom of the canvas: 'The lady is smiling because she is hiding a secret from her lover.' This would shackle the viewer to reality, and I don't want this to happen to *2001*.[14]

Ultimately, as Christianity looks back over its shoulder to its origins and finds at the heart great disruption – *creatio ex nihilo*, floods, famine, captivity, warfare, crucifixion and resurrection – moments of certainty seem to give way to kenotic emptying, books get consumed by prophets, feet of clay turn to dust and dust gets spat upon in order to overturn blindness for sight. Religion, time and time again, peers into the primeval chaos.[15] Chaos is the beginning to which, in the great Romantic traditions, we ultimately return. For anthropologist Clifford Geertz, religion – conceived in terms of religious symbolism – negotiates 'at least three points where chaos – a tumult of events that lack not just interpretations but *interpretability* – threatens to break in upon man'.[16]

2001: A Space Odyssey was and is such an event – a tumult of events that lack not just interpretations but *interpretability* – that draws the viewer into a journey of epic proportions. The fact that David Bowman's ship is named *Discovery* should not be lost on us.

One thing immediately noticeable about *2001* is just how much of a true 'film' it is – it is a vision that brings its narrative forward in a visual linguistics – making iconic connections that deepen language beyond utterance into image and experience. One technique Kubrick uses in the film is an editing technique known as 'jump cut' – making immediate leaps from one point of reference in time and space to another that enable him to move through millennia within a split second while maintaining continuity. The scene that transitions from the 'Dawn of Man' sequence of the film to the 'Dance of the Stars' is such an instance.

As Paul writes in 2 Corinthians, such a notion is deep within the Christian story:

> all of us, with unveiled faces, seeing the glory of the Lord as though reflected in a mirror, are being transformed into the same image from one degree of glory to another . . . For it is the God who said, 'Light will shine out of the darkness', who has shone in our hearts to give the light of the knowledge of the glory of God in the face of Christ.[17]

2001 operates as a journey in a truest sense of calling and transformation from one degree of glory to another – a calling to go as Abraham is called to go but not necessarily told where. The forming of the journey is what gives it meaning – not a map given beforehand, but footprints along the way that show that one has moved from somewhere to somewhere else, creating a 'poetic cartography' where one can orient oneself and be invited to search for the nexus of the subject and the sacred – to touch the wounds of the past and truly to believe. One of the many narrative threads throughout this 'agnostic prayer' of Kubrick is that something is out there – that there are connections of intentionality in the creative story of our universe that show 'something' going on – not a random haphazard milieu per se – but connections and movement toward something. The desire we have for something more – something of infinite and inexhaustible depth and ground of all being – is hoped for and like the announcing angels of the incarnation, this hope for the infinite and inexhaustible depth and ground of all being can be a solace of 'Fear Not' as we fear what lies around the bend. In some ways, Kubrick's films are worth reading deeply for the simple fact that they read humanity's desires and fears so well, yet map out a way that has no boundary or 'edge' that would announce the end of the world or a limit to the universe that creates a sense of beginning and end, but is fully enclosed and three-dimensional, moving *itself* in the fullest breath, depth, and height of time and space[18] as one who comes unannounced – akin to the monolith that reappears and calls out as an *euangelion* – bearing gospel or good news that can be a blessing and terrifying in the same instance.

Meister Eckhart has aptly characterized true encounter with the divine

as an *'un-becoming'* (*'Entwerdung'*). As Eckhart states 'when I reach the
depths of divinity no one asks me whence I come and where I have been,
and no one misses me, for here there is an *un-becoming'*.[19] Kubrick's films
end as an *un-becoming* either with the apocalyptic scope of the birth of
the Star Child in *2001* or freezing of Jack Torrance in the everlasting maze
of the Overlook in *The Shining* – or the *un-becoming* of the self as seen in
Lolita through to *Eyes Wide Shut*. Yet it is in this kenotic un-becoming
that we can begin to 'open the pod doors' to what Kubrick worked for.

Notes

1 American Academy of Motion Pictures and Film database – www.oscars.org

2 James Monaco, *How to Read a Film: The World of Movies, Media, and
Multimedia: Language, History, Theory*, 3rd edition, Oxford: Oxford University
Press, 2000, p. 15.

3 Christian Metz, *Film Language: A Semiotics of the Cinema*, reprint edition,
Chicago: University of Chicago Press, 1990, p. 5.

4 There have been numerous studies of Kubrick's work from many different
angles, notably Luis Garcia Mainar, *Narrative and Stylistic Patterns in the Films
of Stanley Kubrick*, London: Camden House, 1999; Michel Chion, *Kubrick's
Cinema Odyssey*, London: British Film Institute, 2001; Thomas Allen Nelson,
Kubrick: Inside a Film Artist's Maze, Bloomington: Indiana University Press,
1982. However, there is still a lack of critical reflection upon the theological
concerns related to Kubrick's filmic poetics.

5 See Rudolph Otto, *The Idea of the Holy: An Inquiry into the Non-Rational
Factor in the Idea of the Divine and Its Relation to the Rational*, London: Oxford
University Press, 1950.

6 Mary Douglas, *Implicit Meanings*, London: Routledge and Kegan Paul,
1975, p. 76.

7 Marshall McLuhan, (with Quentin Fiore), *The Medium is the Massage*,
New York: Bantam, 1967, p. 26. McLuhan's most vivid description of the
'technological sensorium' is provided.

8 Babara De Concini's article 'Seduction by Visual Image', *The Journal of
Religion and Film*, 2(3) (December 1998): Section 1.

9 De Concini, 'Seduction by Visual Image', Section 1.

10 Paul Tillich, *The Shaking of the Foundations*, New York: Charles Scribner's,
1948, p. 53

11 Tillich, *Shaking of the Foundations*, p. 57.

12 Jeff Smith, 'Careening Through Kubrick's Space', *Chicago Review*, 33(1)
(Summer 1981): 62–73.

13 Simone Weil, *Gravity and Grace*, New York: G. P. Putnam & Sons, 1952.

14 Gene D. Phillips, *Stanley Kubrick: A Film Odyssey*, London: Popular
Library, 1977.

15 This is the view of religion as it is investigated by twentieth-century anthro-
pologists. For Mary Douglas, a 'person without religion would be the person
content to do without explanations' (*Implicit Meanings*, p. 76).

16 Clifford Geertz, *The Interpretation of Cultures*, New York: Basic Books, 1973, p. 100.

17 2 Corinthians 3.18; 4.6 NRSV. David Ford in his recent book, *Self and Salvation*, Cambridge: Cambridge University Press, 1999, has an extended reflection on this notion of 'facing' in relation to the figuring of Christ.

18 I am seeing this notion of 'poetic cartography' as akin to the attempts put forward by women mystics such as Theresa of Avila. See E. Ann Matter, 'Internal Maps of an Eternal External' and Laurie Finke, 'Mystical Bodies and the Dialogics of Vision', in Ulrike Wiethaus (ed.), *Maps of Flesh and Light*, New York: Syracuse University Press, 1993, pp. 28ff.

19 Cited by Rudolf Steiner, *Mysticism at the Dawn of the Modern Age*, New York: Garber Communications, 1996, p. 80. Originally published in 1923 as *Die Mystik im Ausgange des neuzeitlichen Geisteslebens und ihr Verhältnis zur modernen Weltanschauung*.

5. Sacrilege, Satire or Statement of Faith?
Ways of Reading Luis Buñuel's *Viridiana*

TOM AITKEN

In 1961, Luis Buñuel, the Spanish film director, had been in exile from his native land since 1938, living in Los Angeles, New York and Mexico. Before he left Europe he had made two surrealist films with Salvador Dali and *Land without Bread* (1932), a documentary in which peasant poverty was contrasted with ecclesiastical wealth. It was 18 years before he returned to directing, in Mexico, where he developed a reputation as a director who finished films on time and under budget. During this period he learnt his trade. That done he turned to making films that reflected his iconoclasm and hatred of the Catholic Church and bourgeois morality, and of the unholy mixture of the two that, in his view, characterized Franco's Spain. He later wrote, in his autobiography, *My Last Breath* (1984): 'I have always been impressed by the famous photograph of . . . ecclesiastical dignitaries standing in front of the cathedral of Santiago de Compostela in full sacerdotal garb, their arms raised in the Fascist salute . . . God and country make an unbeatable team; they break all records for oppression and bloodshed.'[1]

However, although he delighted in being a hostile critic of the Church, he was also an obsessively fascinated one. His anticlerical iconoclasm was linked with his attachment to anarchism and surrealism, but also to his feeling that there was a great deal of social injustice in the world. He sought to expose this injustice, while supposing that attempts to ameliorate this and other evils were bound to be ineffectual. In *Los Olivados* (*The Young and the Damned*) *(1950)*, about juvenile delinquents in the slums of Mexico, he returned to something like the mood of *Land Without Bread*. In *Nazarin* (1958), he portrayed a humble and unworldly priest who attempted to live according to the example given by Jesus but was despised for doing so by those for whom religion was no more than a formal public observance. In 1996 *Nazarin* appeared on a list of approved films issued by the Vatican to mark the centenary of the cinema. Despite being a parable that could be read as less an attack on religion than on the complacency of the faithful it was glossed as 'an indictment of Christianity'. (See Text Box 5.1 for some of Buñuel's other films.)

Buñuel himself might have been happy with the Vatican's assessment.

5.1 Twelve Other Films by Luis Buñuel (1900–83)

Un Chien Andalou (France, 1928)
A short surrealist film, which begins with a woman's eye being sliced by a razor.

L'Age d'Or (France, 1930)
An anticlerical dream in which two lovers are constantly interrupted.

Los Olivados (The Young and the Damned) (Mexico, 1950)
The corruption of an innocent in the slums of Mexico City.

Nazarin (Mexico, 1959)
A naive and unworldly priest attempts to live according to the teachings of Christ.

The Exterminating Angel (Mexico, 1962)
Guests mysteriously unable to leave a dinner party descend into bestiality and cannibalism.

Diary of a Chambermaid (France, 1964)
A sexy chambermaid uncovers the sexual, social and religious tensions of a provincial family.

Simon of the Desert (Mexico, 1965)
St Simon Stylites, atop his desert column, resists temptations from a hermaphroditic Satan.

Belle de Jour (France/Italy, 1967)
A bored bourgeois wife works as a prostitute during the afternoons.

The Milky Way (France, 1969)
Two tramps on pilgrimage to Santiago de Compostela encounter strange people.

Tristana (Spain, 1970)
A progressive, agnostic Spaniard lusts after his youthful ward in a repressive provincial city.

The Discreet Charm of the Bourgeoisie (France, 1972)
A dream-like film in which bourgeoisie wanting dinner are repeatedly frustrated.

That Obscure Object of Desire (France,1977)
A rich businessman enjoys being humiliated by his maid, who is played by two actresses.

He tells us that he was relieved that *Nazarin* did not win a Catholic prize, although there was a strong chance at one point that it would.[2] His 'relief' is interesting. He very genuinely did not want to be patted on the head by the Church. His reluctance was part of a larger disinclination to have people making assumptions about what his films 'meant'. He claimed that any interpretation of *Nazarin* that depended upon his supposed feelings of sympathy for the priest was a misunderstanding. (Nonetheless, we might note in passing his comment on one of his uncles, a priest, and 'a sweet, gentle man'.)[3] One explanation for his rejection of such interpretations was, however, that some people persisted in seeing *Nazarin* as a conscious attempt at self-rehabilitation on his part.

When, two years later, Buñuel set about making a feminine companion piece to *Nazarin,* its making was enmeshed in bizarrely comic events. The comedy appears to have been conceived in Buñuel's own mind, and stage-managed by him. The rest of the world, including the Franco government, obligingly played its appointed roles. In the case of the Franco government, the role was that of incompetent idiot.

In 1960, having been a Mexican citizen for ten years, Buñuel applied for a visa to return to Spain and to his surprise was given one. He revisited the scenes of his childhood, weeping as he walked down certain streets.[4] After the visit, on the boat back to Mexico, he decided 'to write my own screenplay about a woman I called Viridiana, in memory of a little-known saint I'd heard about when I was a schoolboy. As I worked, I remembered my old erotic fantasy about making love to the queen of Spain when she was drugged, and decided somehow to combine the two stories.'[5]

The film was to be made in Spain itself. *Viridiana* is a quintessentially Spanish story but there was also an element of careerist calculation involved. Much of his best work was virtually unknown in Europe and America and he could not establish a position for himself in the international film world, if he continued working only in Mexico. He enjoyed a high degree of co-operation in Spain – including the 50% subsidy given to productions deemed to be 'in the national interest'. The explanation is simple. He was the country's only internationally applauded film director, and Franco would have been delighted, could he have achieved the *coup* on his own terms, to have Buñuel back there, to inspire and lead a Spanish school of film-makers. Meanwhile, Buñuel was in trouble with his friends. The project outraged his associates among émigré Spanish Republicans in Mexico. He was accused of treason, of kowtowing to the hated dictator. Republican anger, however, was assuaged when the film proved to be less a gift to Franco than a bomb that exploded in his face.[6]

What Buñuel concocted by combining his half-remembered saint with his schoolboy erotic fantasy turned out to be, like all of his narrative films, a plain tale plainly told. Viridiana, a novice about to take her final vows, visits her uncle, Don Jaime, a landowner who has allowed his estate to fall into decay since his wife died on their wedding night 20 years before. He proposes marriage, and when Viridiana rejects him, tries to trick her into it by claiming that he ravished her while she was unconscious.

Don Jaime dies and Viridiana and Jorge, Jaime's illegitimate son, jointly inherit the estate and set about running their shares of it in quite different ways. He attempts to restore the estate as a working farm, while she, having abandoned convent life, throws open the outbuildings, which are all she will accept of the property, to a collection of beggars and outcasts, from whom in return she demands only a little routine work and attendance at her daily religious observances.

One afternoon when Viridiana, Jorge and Ramona, the housekeeper, are absent on errands in the nearby town, the beggars break into the main house and, in its luxurious dining room, stage a riotous party, which concludes with them assuming the postures of Jesus and the disciples in Leonardo da Vinci's painting of the Last Supper. Further sensational events ensue before the police arrive to restore order.

The script had to be passed by the Spanish censors, who suggested a number of changes. One concerned phallic symbolism when Don Jaime dies. There was complaint about Viridiana using her eponymous saint's emblems: a crown of thorns, a hammer and a nail. The last scene should be changed. Viridiana should not be shown knocking on her cousin's door, and entering, the door closing behind her. Buñuel suggested that instead she should be shown settling down to a three-handed card game with Jorge and Ramona and this was accepted. In Buñuel's mischievous view (which, of course, he kept to himself) this merely made the ending more suggestive.[7] (There is also some suggestion that he saw the card game as a symbol of the elaborate game he himself was playing with the Franco government.)

Notice the word 'mischievous'. Disguise, deceit and practical jokes were second nature to Buñuel and much of Viridiana evolved in a spirit of mischief. His dream of making love to a drugged queen of Spain led him to the story of 'a young woman . . . drugged by an old man . . . completely at the mercy of someone who, otherwise, could never have held her in his arms. It struck me that the woman should be pure, and I made her a novice.' It amused him to imagine that the novice would become mistress of a rowdy household that turned on its head the pious exactitude of the convent. He realized that the beggars' riotous dinner evoked Leonardo da Vinci's *Last Supper* only after he had set up the scene. He linked the Hallelujah Chorus with the beggars' subsequent dance and orgy to make it 'more startling' than if he had accompanied it with rock and roll.[8]

The film was entered, very late, in the Cannes Film Festival, where it shared the Palme d'Or and won a special French critics' prize for black humour. The Palme d'Or was proudly accepted by the Spanish undersecretary for Cinema, the functionary who had discussed with Buñuel the changes required by the censors. Not having seen the finished film, he realized too late that Buñuel had made only one of these alterations. Buñuel himself, who was in Paris, was incredulous. How could even Fascists be so stupid?

A day later the Vatican newspaper, *L'Osservatore Romano*, ran a piece by a Spanish Dominican describing the film as 'sacrilegious and blasphemous'. Franco sacked his under-secretary for cinema and suppressed all of Buñuel's films. (Buñuel, anticipating this, had taken a set of negatives of *Viridiana* with him to Paris.) When Franco finally saw the film, years later, he reportedly wondered what the fuss was about. Buñuel responded to that by wondering how you could shock a man who had committed so many atrocities. Asked later which he considered his most important film, he said 'See *Viridiana*.'[9]

How well does the film fit the terms listed in my title: sacrilege, satire, statement of faith? The conventional idea would be that the first two terms are so obviously apt as to be banal, while the third is a non-starter. Did not Buñuel say, not long before he died, 'Thank God I'm still an atheist'?

A majority of critics have seen *Viridiana* as a more or less straightforward satire, in more or less bad taste, on the Catholic Church. As to the bad taste, many, while praising the film, even perhaps considering it Buñuel's masterpiece, have disliked it. Parker Tyler says it leaves a bad taste in the mouth. Isabel Quigly wrote in *The Spectator* that 'Buñuel has all the hatred: what he lacks is the necessary antidote – love'. Christopher Tookey writes that it is 'a nasty piece of work, concerned with emphasizing all that is most ungrateful, cruel and insensitive in human nature.' The orgiastic parody of the Last Supper, he adds, looks 'like a juvenile attempt to shock'. Vittorio de Sica, the Italian maker of *Bicycle Thieves*, asked Buñuel, after he had seen *Viridiana*, 'What has society done to you? Have you suffered so much?' and went on to ask Jeanne Buñuel whether her husband beat her when they made love.[10]

People who consider the film a satire often read it as a parable about the condition of Spain. Parker Tyler tells us that

> the film's leading allegorical figures represent the Church (Viridiana herself), old world aristocracy (Don Jaime), male youth as it inherits the modern tradition of forthright, cynical agnosticism (Jorge) and last but not least, the pariahs that form a universal underground in our harassed world: the sheer have-nots devoid of all scruple and possessing a potential of combustion parallel with that of the atom bomb itself.[11]

On this reading, the estate (in which, we are told by its owner, 'the weeds have spread in twenty years', while 'the house is overrun with spiders') is Spain itself, presided over by an ageing, weary dictator, emotionally stultified by events that happened decades ago, who passes his time in playing and listening to various masses and requiems. Don Jaime's attempt to seduce his niece Viridiana represents . . . Well, what does it represent? Viridiana herself is well-meaning, naive, sentimental in a cold-hearted way, applying, arguably, the wrong solutions to problems she has failed to identify accurately. So what, in terms of political parable, can Don Jaime's attempt to ravish her mean? Had Franco's establishment ravished the Church? That, surely, would be to imply that the Church had resisted Franco, an implication Buñuel would reject. Whatever Viridiana's character and her uncle's attempt to ravish her mean (if either 'means' anything) neither seems to me to constitute an attack on the Church by the maker of the film. Viridiana is sincere in her behaviour throughout. She is more than a little tactless, even rather cruel, in her dealings with her uncle, but she is honest and never underhanded.

Dilys Powell preferred the notion of parody to that of parable and thought the result 'superb'. 'Buñuel', she writes, 'goes far beyond attacking professional religion and the practices of celibacy and self-mortification. He assaults the very basis of a creed which he sees as upholding a callous and decaying society.' The drunken dinner and dancing to the Hallelujah Chorus are not 'the simple derisive reaction against the forms of religion which many inquiring minds go through in early life . . .' but 'the expression of a hatred which has developed, which has matured. For Buñuel the Church is anti-life.'[12]

I think parts of this reading are seriously flawed, since they require us to assume that Buñuel rejoices in the actions of the outcasts – that, as an antifascist, anarchist and reputed Communist, he must be their supporter. (Buñuel denied ever joining the Communist Party and, by the end of the Fifties, felt that its dogmas left out at least half of what makes us human.)[13] In *Viridiana*, although he probably enjoys contemplating the beggars as lords of misrule, he presents them very critically. He may be in sympathy with them in the same way as is Viridiana: they are lost souls destroyed by society. But as a group, he makes it clear, they are ungrateful, selfish, stupid and incapable of co-operating with each other. They are liars and cheats. They hate each other at least as much as they hate wealth and privilege. If they, in their muddled drunken way, think that they are paying back society and the Church for the evils they have suffered, the film seems rather to be telling us that they are cutting their own throats. Our sympathy remains firmly with Viridiana, and is reinforced by a brutal attempt to rape her.

But if this film is a parable or allegory, Viridiana cannot represent the Church as hated by Buñuel. She does little to deserve such hatred. She could be kinder to her besotted uncle, but after all, she has her virginity to defend. (I don't think that Buñuel tries to make us think the worse of her for this.) She is also a bit of a bossy boots. But, misguided and unaware as she may be, she is hardly an oppressor. But if she does not represent the Church, who or what does? The Mother Superior of Viridiana's convent appears twice. The first time you might think that she is telling Viridiana to visit her uncle merely because he gives money to the convent. Later, she may seem unfeeling about Viridiana's decision to leave the convent, but, essentially, is sensible to the point of neutrality. Similarly, Don Jaime's taste for doodling sacred songs on the harmonium, while not notably cheerful, hardly amounts to an intolerable weight of stifling dogma and intolerance.

Can we then deny that *Viridiana* is in any sense satirical? That might be difficult. Samuel Johnson tells us that in satire wickedness and folly are censured, and Buñuel clearly supposed that he was doing something of that kind in his film. He fits easily enough into that strand of satire that is produced by people we might describe as anarchic reactionaries: Jonathan Swift; Evelyn Waugh; *Private Eye*, even. Satire, of course, is not mere mud-slinging born out of dismissive contempt. It is rather an attempt to contrast what some institution or person claims to be, and should be, with what in fact it or they are. Something of the sort is clearly involved here, but it is a good deal more subtle than most commentators make it seem.

Buñuel described himself as 'a fanatical anti-fanatic', and this, I think, gives us the clue we need. The idea that is satirized, both in individual scenes and in the film at large, is the folly of trying to right the wrongs of the world. *Viridiana* is essentially a bleakly ironic tragicomedy about the ineffectuality of good intentions. In one scene Jorge frees a dog he sees being mistreated, while failing even to notice another one being treated in exactly the same way. (The dog he has freed, incidentally, does not appear to want to be taken from its inconsiderate master.) According to Buñuel's sister he loved animals and suffered grievously when shooting the scene because the reality was so common, and trying to break Spanish peasants of their ingrained habit of cruelty was like tilting at windmills.[14]

Similarly, if Viridiana had succeeded in redeeming her beggars, there would still have been other beggars left in the world. But she was in any case doomed to failure. Like the dog, they are ungrateful for the kindness they have been offered. Her insistence that they participate with her in devotional exercises indicates her naivety and impracticality. Making the beggars recite the *Angelus* when they could be getting on with some work (the *Angelus* is counterpointed by the activities of Jorge's workmen) is not awfully sensible but hardly a crime. (As with all the music in this film, Buñuel has chosen here something precisely and mischievously relevant to his theme, since this devotional prayer includes the words 'Behold the handmaid of the Lord, be it done unto me according to your word.' Viridiana, casting herself by implication as 'the handmaid of the Lord' is being presumptuous, but it is her ineffectuality that most amuses Buñuel.)

These two scenes suggest that *Viridiana* is at least in part a satire, but what is being satirized is an aspiration rather than an institution, and it's an aspiration which is found as much among unbelievers as among Christians.

Turning to another term from my title: You will remember that *L'Osservatore Romano*'s Spanish Dominican denounced the film as 'sacrilegious and blasphemous'. I'll come to 'sacrilegious' shortly: let's look at 'blasphemous' first (for definitions of blasphemy, sacrilege and other terms, see Text Box 5.2). You will notice that I have not actually included it in my title. Why not?

The word derives from Greek roots that together suggest damage to reputation. Within Christian theology the basic meaning is speech, thought or action manifesting contempt for God. Aquinas defines it as a sin against faith that attributes to God that which does not belong to him or denies him that which is his due. Is *Viridiana* therefore blasphemous?

Here we must take into account cultural differences between Spaniards (at least in Buñuel's day) and the rest of us. Blasphemy has, or had, a special role in Spanish life. Buñuel tells us that 'the Spanish language is capable of more scathing blasphemies than any other language I know . . . blasphemy in Spain is truly an art; in Mexico . . . I never heard a proper curse . . .'[15]

In *Viridiana*, in fact, God is hardly mentioned. His name is sung in the Hallelujah Chorus during the beggars' riotous party, but we should surely draw a distinction between Buñuel showing us beggars being blasphemous, and Buñuel making a blasphemous film. Often blasphemy is in the eye of the beholder, and even good intentions are no defence. In 1879, for instance, Max Lieberman's painting *The Twelve Year Old Jesus in the Temple* showed a precocious but no more than human boy talking with intense interest to the priests. To my eyes the picture is charming and acceptably naturalistic, but in its day it stirred intense controversy because of its 'blasphemy'.[16] At one point in *Viridiana*, a white bird is killed (off camera). Some have seen this as a blasphemous reference to the Holy Spirit. Again, the point remains that it is a despicable character in the film who kills the bird. Perhaps, in a grown-up world, 'blasphemy' is not a useful concept. Perhaps a 'blasphemous' treatment of the Church or its doctrines requires a reasoned response – which condemnation is not.

The charge of 'sacrilege' is easier to sustain, but you don't have to have been educated by Jesuits – as Buñuel was – to question it. Sacrilege is the violation of any sacred person, place or thing. Thus, the attempted rape of Viridiana when she is a novice might be sacrilegious, although perhaps it isn't quite, since she isn't quite a nun. Her subsequent misadventures occur after she has abandoned the cloister, so do not count.

Three major works of Christian art, one pictorial, two musical, are treated disrespectfully. Leonardo's painting is imitated fairly exactly, as anyone can see by comparing the painting and the scene in the film, but is the picture violated or profaned? More seriously, is the Last Supper itself damaged by the parody?

That depends. The moment when the drunken beggars suddenly pose for a photograph, and the photographer lifts her skirts at them, is usually thought of as a straight gesture of despite by Buñuel – who, however,

---

5.2 Some Catholic and Literary Technical Terms

Agnosticism: the belief that we cannot know that God exists.
Angelus: a thrice daily act of devotion that honours the incarnation of Jesus by celebrating his mother, 'the handmaid of the Lord', signalled by the tolling of church bells.
Atheism: denial that God is real.
Blasphemy: contemptuous language addressed to or used of God.
Celibacy: renunciation of marriage.
Dogma: a definitive or infallible teaching of the Church. Not every doctrine is a dogma.
Dominican: an order of preachers and teachers of the gospel, founded in 1216.
Heresy: formal and deliberate rejection of a dogma by a baptized person.
Iconoclasm: destruction of Christian images.
Idolatry: the worship of persons and things other than God as if they were God.
Jesuit: member of the Society of Jesus, founded in 1540 for the propagation of the faith and well known for its schools; a practitioner of casuistry, the art of resolving problems of conscience by drawing implausibly fine distinctions between what is and is not illegal or improper.
Novice: one in training who has not yet taken vows which admit them to a religious order.
Parable: a short, simple story that conveys a moral or spiritual meaning.
Parody: an imitation of the style and ideas of an author, sometimes affectionate, sometimes intended to make them seem ridiculous.
Paradox: an apparently self-contradictory statement which partially or totally reconciles its conflicting elements.
Retablo: carved panels behind an altar, of which there are spectacular examples in Spain.
Sacrilege: the violation or contemptuous treatment of any sacred person, place or thing.
Satire: A work in which the wickedness and folly of humankind are exposed, censured and scorned.
Surrealism: literary or visual works which attempt to express the non-logical and distorted working of the unconscious mind.
Superstition: a morbid, exaggerated reliance upon aspects of religion or supposed supernatural forces.

notoriously despised picturesque groupings in films. But the scene includes complexities and resonances that render the epithet 'blasphemous' seriously inadequate. I have barely mentioned surrealism, which was another of the complex loyalties that most fuelled Buñuel's creative drive, because I don't consider this a notably surrealist film. However, since surrealism itself was for him a way of rebelling against those aspects of reality that he detested, this beggars' riot is perhaps surrealist in mood. It is an inexplicable event in which reality is both present and, as it were, left behind. Its lack of logic may be presumed to reflect the workings of the subconscious mind. Considered as an act of rebellion it relates to another of the complications of Buñuel's personality: he advocated revolution but was appalled when it occurred. When, in 1936, civil war broke out in Spain and the shooting began, he writes, 'I, who had been such an ardent subversive, who had so desired the overthrow of the established order, now found myself in the middle of a volcano, and I was afraid.'[17]

Perhaps, if we want a rational explanation for the scene, we may assume that the beggar who is himself a painter of religious pictures has put the others up to the jape and coached them in what positions to adopt – although in that case we might expect him to sit where Judas sits in Leonardo's painting, which he doesn't. But if we ask why Buñuel conceived or reconceived the scene in terms of Leonardo's picture, interesting answers present themselves. Obviously, for the film's likely audience, it is probably the best known of the many artistic representations of the subject, and the shock – the sacrilege or blasphemy, if you will – is therefore maximized. But there is another reason, one very much more relevant to the film as a work of art. Whereas, in portraying this scene, many older painters had represented, as Kenneth Clark expresses it, 'the moment of communion, a moment of calm in which each apostle might wish to sit alone with his thoughts', Leonardo 'chose the terrible moment in which Jesus says "One of you will betray me".'[18]

The beggars' party is, is it not, a betrayal of Viridiana – she who has fed, clothed and sheltered them and generally done her best, according to her own lights, to rehabilitate and redeem them. What do we hear in the moment of silence as the pose is struck? A cock crowing, a reminder of the moment when Peter denied knowing Jesus. If this scene (as well as being 'surreal') is a sacrilegious gesture on Buñuel's part, it is a very carefully worked out and deliberately ambiguous one.

The two extracts from sacred choral classics that are used in the film are similarly there for other reasons than mere shock value. Early in the film Don Jaime plies Viridiana with wine and drugs and is only prevented from ravishing her by a last-minute accession of conscience. This takes place to the musical accompaniment of that part of the Mozart *Requiem* in which the words 'let eternal light shine upon them with Thy saints' are being sung. Even given that Buñuel would have denied the reality of the eternal light and the saints, his choice of music is hardly unsympathetic to Viridiana.

The Hallelujah Chorus, which accompanies the party scene, is used in a more obviously frivolous way. (We might wonder, very unfairly no doubt, whether a Spanish Dominican was really so very upset to hear, in this disgraceful context, a work by a German Protestant set to English words.) But it is surely significant that the choir is cut off in mid-phrase, at 'And He shall reign . . .' omitting 'for ever and ever'. It is obviously a denial of the proposition that 'the Lord God omnipotent reigneth', but although this, according to Aquinas's definition quoted earlier, is at least technically blasphemy, since it denies God that which is his due, at the same time it makes the use of this music in this scene a statement of belief (or disbelief) rather than a juvenile attempt to shock.

We might also reflect that Leonardo's picture and Mozart's and Handel's music are not objects of worship. They are *objets d'art*, and before we start saying that they are or ought to be revered we might consider two other items in the dictionary of misdemeanours: idolatry and superstition.

Let us agree for the moment, then, that neither 'blasphemy' nor 'sacrilege' offer complete accounts of what Buñuel is doing in this film. What of the third of my terms: a statement of faith?

Five years after *Viridiana* appeared, a Spanish historian and translator, Fernando Diaz-Plaja, published *The Spaniard and the Seven Deadly Sins*. In it he refers to 'the bold way in which religious subjects are treated by most Spaniards'. He also tells an illustrative anecdote, which I feel may be relevant to our apprehension of Buñuel. A bootblack in Cadiz mocks a passing priest. His client, a Protestant traveller, seizes the opportunity to explain the advantages of Protestantism. 'Save your breath, mister,' says the bootblack. 'I don't believe in my own religion, which is the true one, so how am I going to believe in yours?' Diaz-Plaja asks, 'Who can doubt that the blasphemer . . . is a believer at heart? How can one offer gross insults to something which does not exist?'[19]

Obviously Buñuel's attitude to God was significantly entangled with his attitude to the Church in Spain and the Catholic dictatorship of General Franco. As an institution that embodied a particular system of belief and set of social attitudes, he despised it. Let me quote again his remarks about 'ecclesiastical dignitaries . . . in full sacerdotal garb, their arms raised in the Fascist salute . . . God and country make an unbeatable team; they break all records for oppression and bloodshed.' But he was more ambivalent about Franco than he was sometimes prepared to admit. In *My Last Breath* he claimed not to have been a fanatical opponent of Franco, whom he thought had possibly saved Spain from Nazi invasion.[20] His collaborator Jean-Claude Carrière believed that this statement contributed to national reconciliation during the turbulent decade after

Franco's death in 1975. Buñuel also gave the dictator credit for having helped save Spanish Jews.[21]

His attitude to the Church had similar touches of ambivalence. He wrote that the only civilization he admired was that in which he was brought up. He loved the cathedrals of Segovia and Toledo and 'that incomparable spectacle of the *retablo,* with its baroque labyrinths, where your fantasies can wander endlessly in the minute detours. I love cloisters too.'[22]

The very title *Viridiana* embodies a curiously gentle side to his attitude

---

5.3 Spain During Buñuel's Lifetime (1900–83)

According to Hugh Thomas (*The Spanish Civil War*, p. 190),'the twentieth century saw an awakening of the Spanish spirit: the political volatility of the years between 1898 and 1936 . . . was an expression of a vitality which extended through most spheres of national life'. Buñuel's contemporaries in the arts and literature included the painters Picasso, Dali and Miro; the writers García Lorca, Jiménez, Antonio Machado, Pio Baroja, Uamuno and Ortega; and the musicians de Falla and Casals.

1909–23: General strike and convents burnt in Barcelona; street riots throughout Catalonia; Spain is neutral during World War One; strikes and industrial unrest. Gang warfare in Barcelona.

1923–30: Primo de Rivera governs as a military dictator; resigns after losing support of the Right.

1931–4: Second Republic proclaimed; abortive military coup; Right wins general election. Insurrections by miners and Republicans in Asturia and Catalonia crushed.

1936: Popular Front wins general election; military uprising in Morocco spreads to Spain; civil war between Republicans and Nationalist rebels begins; Nationalists murder the poet and playwright Federico García Lorca in Granada. (During the war tens of thousands of Spaniards are murdered by both sides.)

1937: General Franco becomes leader of Nationalists; German Condor Legion destroys the ancient Basque capital, Guernica, in an air raid; Picasso paints *Guernica*, expressing outrage.

1939–40: Nationalists win the war; fierce repression of the Popular Front; Spain neutral during World War Two; Franco meets Hitler.

1946–7: The UN boycotts Spain; Buñuel emigrates to Mexico.

1955: Spain readmitted to UN; twenty years of gradual, restricted liberalization begins.

1961: Buñuel makes *Viridiana* with Franco's support.

1975: Franco dies; Juan Carlos crowned king; democratization of Spain begins.

towards the Church. As I have mentioned he derived the name from a little-known saint he had heard about when he was a schoolboy. Not only was she little known, she was Italian. She lived in Castel Fiorentino in the thirteenth century, spending 34 years of prayer and penitence in seclusion there, although in 1221 she was visited by St Francis. Her death, in 1242, was announced by a sudden miraculous ringing of bells in Castel Fiorentino. Her life of seclusion (she had earlier been married, probably under some pressure from her parents) may have been inspired by a pilgrimage to Santiago de Compostela, which may be the connection in which Buñuel heard of her.[23] But why should he have remembered her? Perhaps because the Latin root of her name suggests greenness, with its overtones of innocence and freshness.

As *Nazarin* and *Viridiana* show, Buñuel thought Christianity impractical and naive. But, although he proclaimed Jesus an idiot, it is not difficult to detect, in both films and in *The Milky Way*, an implication that there is, at least theoretically, a truer, more admirable version of Christianity than that practised by the Church. But, of course, like Viridiana herself, that truer Christianity is necessarily so vulnerable to attack and betrayal as to be useless.

Many observers would suppose that Buñuel had good reason to despise at least some aspects of the Catholicism of Franco's Spain. If we accept this, it may follow that Buñuel's view of Christianity in general was necessarily a distorted one. I am not trying to make him out to be any kind of closet Christian, nor to suggest that anything he thought was necessarily true, but his films are among the fruits of Catholic Spain and 'by their fruits shall ye know them'. However, although the uncompromisingly violent anger that is commonly attributed to him might seem to be the only possible response to the privileges and wealth enjoyed by the Church in his youth – when so many Spaniards lived in abject poverty – ironic amusement seems more characteristic of many of his films, including *Viridiana*. He frequently denied that his films attacked anything. *The Milky Way*, he said, is neither for nor against anything at all.[24] The actress Stéphane Audran said of him, 'He wasn't *attached* to anything. His vision of human beings was . . . amused. Like God, watching us doing crazy things, but with love.'[25]

Sometimes, it must be said, his characters utter quasi-religious sentiments that seem entirely sincere and are not being mocked by the director. One says, 'My hatred of science and my horror of technology will finally bring me round to this absurd belief in God.' In *The Milky Way*, he uses an image derived from one of his own vivid dreams. The Virgin, shining softly, holds out her hands to the dreamer.

She speaks to me – to me, the unbeliever – with infinite tenderness . . . suddenly I feel myself inundated with a vibrant and invincible faith.

When I wake up . . . I hear my voice saying: 'Yes! Yes! Holy Virgin, yes, I believe!' It takes me several minutes to calm down.[26]

Buñuel even argued, when provoked, that *Viridiana* was essentially a devout film, 'because in every scene there is an underlying sense of sin. The old man cannot violate his niece because of this.' The Mexican camera-man Gabriel Figueroa believed that Buñuel was 'only irreverent; not against Catholicism. The irony is [says Figueroa] that even though his films are labelled anti-religious and anti-Catholic, Buñuel is actually preparing for his next life, trying to come nearer to God all the time. He is one of the most religious of men.'[27] Be that as it may, he did not feel called upon to practise the Christian virtues. In 1977, while making *That Obscure Object of Desire*, he was approached by an elderly Dominican who confessed that he had written the article in *L'Osservatore Romano* denouncing *Viridiana*. He had now changed his mind and asked Buñuel's forgiveness. I'm sorry to say that Buñuel threw him off the set.[28]

Perhaps Figueroa was engaged in wishful thinking. Orson Welles, rather more sharply, said of Buñuel that he was 'a deeply Christian man who hates God as only a Christian can . . . I see him as the most supremely religious director in the history of the movies'.[29] During the last months of his life Buñuel became dependent upon the visits of a Catholic priest with whom he became friendly. Every afternoon at five, Father Julian Pablo turned up (in non-clerical garb, at Buñuel's request). Sometimes they sat in silence, sometimes they debated points of Catholic dogma. Both denied that the priest was trying to persuade Buñuel to be reconciled with the Church. 'He knows more about the Church and its doctrines than I do,' was the priest's comment.[30]

I don't think it is either over-ingenious or merely provocative to say that for Buñuel, atheism was indeed a faith, and one which he devoted much of his life and work to stating. Atheism, he said, forced him to live 'in shadowy confusion',[31] thus keeping his moral freedom intact. (Nevertheless, he was very upset when, during the war, the Museum of Modern Art in New York, acting under pressure from Cardinal Spellman, fired him because Salvador Dali, in a much publicized and scandalous auto-biography, had written of him that he had attacked Catholicism in a primitive manner and was an atheist. Buñuel desperately needed the salary he lost, and had no taste for martyrdom.)[32]

To conclude, *Viridiana* illustrates in a coolly detailed way the atheism which Buñuel embraced with such fervour. He could not simply ignore 'this absurd belief in God', but was driven, as Orson Welles said, to hate the object of that belief. If the Last Supper scene in *Viridiana* is a wild parody of Leonardo's painting, so also is Buñuel's life and work a parody – sometimes wild, often anything but – of faith.

There is something much more than mere jokey paradox in his utterance, which I quoted earlier: 'Thank God I'm still an atheist.'

Select Bibliography

John Baxter, *Buñuel*, London: Fourth Estate, 1994.
Luis Buñuel, *My Last Breath*, trans. Abigail Israel, London: Vintage, 1994.
Raymond Carr (ed.), *Spain, A History*, Oxford: Oxford University Press, 2000.
F. L. Cross and E. A. Livingstone (eds), *The Oxford Dictionary of the Christian Church*, 3rd edn., Oxford: Oxford University Press, 1997.
Fernando Diaz-Plaja, *The Spaniard and the Seven Deadly Sins*, London: Victor Gollancz, 1968.
Ephraim Katz (ed.), *The Macmillan International Film Encyclopedia*, 2nd edn, New York: Macmillan, 1994.
Richard P. McBrien (ed.), *The HarperCollins Encyclopedia of Catholicism*, New York: HarperCollins, 1995.
Hugh Thomas, *The Spanish Civil War*, Harmondsworth: Penguin Books, 1977.
Christopher Tookey, *The Critics' Film Guide*, London: Boxtree, 1994.
Parker Tyler, *Classics of the Foreign Film*, London: Spring Books, 1966.
Philip Ward (ed.), *The Oxford Companion to Spanish Literature*, Oxford: Clarendon Press, 1978.

Notes

1 Luis Buñuel, *My Last Breath*, trans. Abigail Israel, London: Vintage, 1994, p. 170.

2 Buñuel, *My Last Breath*, pp. 215–16.

3 Buñuel, *My Last Breath*, p. 12.

4 Buñuel, *My Last Breath*, p. 232.

5 Buñuel, *My Last Breath*, p. 234.

6 John Baxter, *Buñuel*, London: Fourth Estate, 1994, pp. 2–3, 255–6; Buñuel, *My Last Breath*, p. 234.

7 Baxter, *Buñuel*, pp. 6–7. This is what you would expect Buñuel to have said if you accept the usual interpretation of *Viridiana*. There are, however, two problems. Baxter cites Buñuel's *My Last Breath*, but I cannot find the passage in the 1994 edition, which gives no indication that it has been abridged or re-edited in any way from the edition published ten years before, which Baxter uses. But even if we suppose that Baxter found his quotation elsewhere and misattributed it, I think we should heed the words of D. H. Lawrence: 'Never trust the artist, trust the tale.' There is a great deal more to the scene than is indicated by Buñuel's words.

8 Baxter, *Buñuel*, p. 4.

9 Parker Tyler, *Classics of the Foreign Film*, London: Spring Books, 1966, p. 244.

10 Buñuel, *My Last Breath*, p. 238.

11 Tyler, *Classics of the Foreign Film*, p. 245.

12 For the quotations from Isabel Quigly, Christopher Tookey and Dilys Powell, see Christopher Tookey, *The Critics' Film Guide*, London: Boxtree, 1994, pp. 905–6; for those from Parker Tyler see *Classics*, pp. 244–7.

13 Buñuel, *My Last Breath*, p. 166.

14 Buñuel, *My Last Breath,* p. 38.

15 Buñuel, *My Last Breath*, p. 159.

16 See Jaroslav Pelikan, *The Illustrated Jesus Through the Centuries*, New Haven and London: Yale University Press, 1992, p. 197.

17 Buñuel, *My Last Breath*, p. 153.

18 Kenneth Clark, *Leonardo Da Vinci: An Account of His Development as an Artist*, revised edn, Harmondsworth: Penguin, 1958, p. 93.

19 Fernando Diaz-Plaja, *The Spaniard and the Seven Deadly Sins*, London: Victor Gollancz, 1968, pp. 39–40.

20 See Buñuel, *My Last Breath*, p. 170.

21 Baxter, *Buñuel*, p. 243.

22 Buñuel, *My Last Breath*, pp. 220 and 222–3. (A *retablo* is a series of carved panels behind an altar and there are some particularly spectacular examples in Spain.)

23 I am indebted to Michael Walsh, sometime librarian at Heythrop College, for this information.

24 Buñuel, *My Last Breath,* p. 245.

25 Baxter, *Buñuel*, p. 313.

26 Buñuel, *My Last Breath*, p. 95.

27 Baxter, *Buñuel*, p. 256.

28 Baxter, *Buñuel*, p. 256.

29 Baxter, *Buñuel*, p. 2.

30 Baxter, *Buñuel*, p. 312.

31 Buñuel, *My Last Breath*, p. 174.

32 Buñuel, *My Last Breath*, p. 182 and Baxter, pp. 184–86.

6. An Ethic You Can't Refuse?
Assessing *The Godfather* Trilogy

ERIC S. CHRISTIANSON

'Make an ice-blue, terrifying movie about people you love.'

Al Ruddy, answering Paramount Head Charlie Bludhorn when asked what he would do with *The Godfather*, given the chance to produce it (he got the job).[1]

I have long had an interest in the seeming mass appeal of stylized (one might say, rhetorical) and extreme violence in a morally ambiguous context. In every genre one need not look hard to locate protagonists (or appealing 'anti-protagonists') for whom violence is not offered for our scrutiny but rather merely for our field of vision, our 'entertainment'. So, for example, the Western offered us The Man With No Name, the crime thriller the Tarantino-esque witty style icon (and ambiguously violent cops, too, such as Popeye Doyle of *The French Connection*), and of course there is the ubiquitous action hero (in the mould of Arnold Schwarzenegger, Bruce Willis, etc.), whose righteousness rarely requires any argument. Comedy has its own strange brand of often extreme violence (of the *Home Alone* variety, or the black humour of a *Prizzi's Honour*, or of that marvellous film noir comedy, *Pulp Fiction*). My question for investigation here is, What ethics are at work in the presentation of screen violence? Since its appeal is not in question, *how* is that appeal achieved? And what factors shape our response? (I am assuming that viewers *should* respond and reflect, but that is open to question.) To achieve this I will assess the moral argument of a film series that spawned a host of imitations but also emerged at the very start of what film critics refer to as Hollywood's golden age of violence (which also produced, for example, *Bonnie and Clyde*, *The Wild Bunch*, *A Clockwork Orange*): *The Godfather* (and its two sequels), directed by Francis Ford Coppola.

It is just over thirty years since *The Godfather* was first screened, and it is hard to overestimate the impact and lasting influence of *The Godfather* trilogy of films, particularly the first two (for a synopsis of the films, see Text Box 6.1). As Nick Browne suggests,

> the first two films amounted to a social phenomenon – they entered into every level of American culture – high and low – sometimes by attitude,

sometimes by quotation, and sometimes through their iconic, signature scenes. The first two films entered not only movie history, but American mythology as well, and have stayed there for [over] twenty-five years.[2]

6.1 *The Godfather* Trilogy: Synopsis (spoilers included!)

- Part I (1972) takes place in New York in 1945 and traces the murderous struggle of the Corleone family to achieve dominance over other rival Mafia families. While the family is headed by The Godfather, Don Vito Corleone (Marlon Brando), the real focus of the film is the family itself, enshrining its traditions and assessing the various relationships among the Don and his three sons. After the murder of the eldest son, Sonny (James Caan), and the death of the Don, it is Michael Corleone (Al Pacino), the youngest, and not number two, Fredo, who inherits the throne. Michael's WASP wife Kay (Diane Keaton) at first enjoys a close relationship with Michael, but ends up being all but cut out of his life (the film ends with Michael symbolically closing the door on her).

- Part II (1974) interweaves two stories, one of the young Vito Corleone, his violent coming of age and rise to power, first in Sicily (where he witnesses the murder of his brother and mother) and then as an enterprising immigrant (Robert de Niro) in New York, *c*.1917. That story is deliberately contrasted to the rise of the Corleones under Michael's leadership. It begins in the late 1950s in Lake Tahoe, significantly outside of the traditional homestead. Don Vito's story is a romantic counterpoint to the course that Michael takes, which is one of dishonesty and ruthlessness that culminates in the murder of his brother Fredo and results in alienation from his family and from his own ideals. The last frame shows Michael alone and bereft against a cold autumn sky, possessing everything and nothing.

- Part III (1990) opens eight years after Part II ended, in the late 1970s, with the desolation of the Lake Tahoe compound, Michael now having moved back to New York. Throughout the film he is haunted by his sins and openly seeks redemption from the Church and from his family. He embarks, however, on some very shadowy and complex financial dealings with the Vatican and discovers that the power and corruption to which he has accustomed himself is present at the highest levels. His attempt at redemption fails. Michael 'adopts' his brother Sonny's bastard son, Vincenzo, who eventually becomes Don in his place. The film ends with the tragic murder of Michael's daughter, Mary, and then with the final image of the unceremonious death of Michael, slumped in his chair in the Sicilian sun.

As an American I can vouch for the all-pervasive influence of the films in every area of popular culture, from advertising to social parlance. Then there is the influence on other films, not only in the crime genre (notably Scorsese's *Goodfellas* and *Casino*), but even in the spawning of a whole new genre, the Mafia comedy (such as *Mickey Blue Eyes* and the much funnier *Analyze This*). Reference to *The Godfather* films has become shorthand in a range of films and cultural phenomena for Old World values; the request for loyalty backed by the promise of violence. And there is no doubt as to the enduring popularity of the films themselves. The Internet Movie Database provides a respectable indicator. In its poll, with over 100,000 voters rating it an average of 9.0 out of 10, *The Godfather* ranks as 'the greatest film ever'. Part II, with 8.9, is ranked number four (Part III, alas, is absent from the top 250 films list, though still garners a respectable 7.3 rating).[3] Finally, one of the most innovative television series of recent years, *The Sopranos*, frequently references the films. From the first scene in the first episode, it is clear that *The Godfather* films provide not just comic relief, but a whole framework of meaning in which to understand the workings of 'the family' (Silvio, one of Tony Soprano's henchmen, mimics Al Pacino in Part III: 'Just when I thought I was out, they pulled me back in . . .').[4]

The Godfather was something very new in 1972, at least not something seen for over 30 years. Here was a film that refused to interpret the activities of criminals as *unambiguously* wrong. It was not since films such as *Little Caesar* (1931), *The Public Enemy* (1931) and *Scarface* (1932) that the activities of criminals were at the centre of the narrative and were so brutally, vividly and even sympathetically portrayed. These films sparked off a series of others in which the gangsters were clearly more appealing than their law-enforcing counterparts. As Martin Quigley Jnr puts it,

> The postscript [to *The Public Enemy* screenplay] said that the producers wanted to 'depict honestly an environment that exists today in certain strata of American life, rather than glorify the hoodlum or the criminal.' The film had a different effect: [James] Cagney was playful and dynamic, and so much more appealing than the characters opposed to him that audiences rooted for him in spite of themselves.[5]

But the Hays Production Code successfully put a stop to audience sympathy. (This is not to say that ambiguity around the act of violence would not itself flourish in the following years; see my essay on *film noir* in this volume, Chapter 9.) The debate surrounding the gangster films of the early 1930s, which the Code sought to address, was largely to do with, as an early draft of the Code had put it, 'the effect which a too-detailed description of these [criminal activities] may have upon the moron'[6] (read 'the viewing public'!).

Here are a few relevant examples from the Code:[7]

1. No picture shall be produced that will lower the moral standards of those who see it. Hence the sympathy of the audience should never be thrown to the side of crime, wrongdoing, evil or sin.
. . .
3. Law, natural or human, shall not be ridiculed, nor shall sympathy be created for its violation.
. . .

Crimes Against the Law
. . .
1. Murder
. . .
b. Brutal killings are not to be presented in detail.
c. Revenge in modern times shall not be justified.

The Code made a particular distinction that seems presciently to have had *The Godfather* in mind. Under the heading, Reasons Underlying the General Principles, the following is noted:

We may feel sorry for the plight of the murderer or even understand the circumstances which led him to his crime: we may not feel sympathy with the wrong which he has done. The presentation of evil is often essential for art or fiction or drama. This in itself is not wrong provided:
a. That evil is not presented alluringly. Even if later in the film the evil is condemned or punished, it must not be allowed to appear so attractive that the audience's emotions are drawn to desire or approve so strongly that later the condemnation is forgotten and only the apparent joy of sin is remembered.
b. That throughout, the audience feels sure that evil is wrong and good is right.

(While I do not wish to enter the debate of the impact of films on the viewer's moral behaviour, one early critic's thoughts on the matter are worth citing here: 'These gang pictures . . . [are] doing nothing but harm to the younger element of this country. I don't blame the censors for trying to bar them . . . these gang movies are making a lot of kids want to be tough guys and they don't serve any useful purpose.'[8] Given the critic's name – Al Capone – readers will draw their own intriguing conclusions.)

The Code was decisively in effect for over 20 years. It was not until sweeping reforms by the US Supreme Court in 1966 that it was finally put to rest, just four years before *The Godfather* really began production. *The Godfather* returned the criminal/gangster to the true centre, a place it generally had not been allowed to occupy for over 30 years. And yet it went beyond the pre-Code gangster films in portraying the life of Italian-Americans with some dignity and realism (in interviews, Coppola speaks frequently of how his memories of growing up in a large Italian-American family made their way into the films, particularly in 'event' scenes such as marriages, meals and baptisms). Coppola's depiction of the united, convivial and cosy Mafia family, in the first half of Part I especially, created an inviting aura around criminal life. It is most clearly achieved in the opening sequence of the wedding of Michael's sister, Connie, in which the Don generates warmth and genuine respect in all of his social interactions.

In most senses the Corleones are an ideal 1940s family. As such, this is a white, male fantasy world, where the women are quiet and largely do as they are asked; with, of course, the fascinating exception of Michael's wife, Kay. Apart from Kay, the women of Parts I and II are little more than animate props and plot devices. But it is from Kay's perspective that we are first introduced to the brutal violence of the family.

In the acclaimed opening wedding sequence of Part I, the business of the family is confidently displayed. The sun-kissed, festive party, full of lights, paper globes and *tarantella* (Italian folk-music) dancing, is buzzing with family 'business'. Envelopes of cash are passed between 'family', the Don meets serenely with those who ask his favour, as if he is capable of bestowing divine beneficence. Having returned from army service, Michael makes his first appearance in uniform and introduces Kay, his WASP fiancée, to the family. To Kay's surprise, famous crooner Johnny Fontaine arrives to sing. Kay asks how the family knows Johnny and Michael relates how his father helped Johnny by getting him out of a binding contract early in his career:

Michael: Now Johnny is my father's godson, and my father went to see this bandleader and they offered him 10,000 dollars to let him go, but the bandleader said no. So the next day my father went to see him, only this time with [his henchman, whom Kay has just seen and been frightened by] Luca Brasi, and within an hour he signed a release for a certified cheque of 1,000 dollars.
Kay: Well, how'd he do that?
Michael (*with alarming detachment*): Luca Brasi held a gun to his head, and my father assured him that either his brains or his signature would be on the contract. (*Kay is visually stunned, speechless.*) That's a true story. That's my family, Kay, not me.

The central place enjoyed by the family in *The Godfather* indicates another significant move away from the old gangster genre. Gone is the old antithesis between criminals and the law. The only law enforcers in *The Godfather* are either corrupt or simply ineffective. The new framework of meaning is the family, namely the struggle of one family to dominate other families, and to look after their own. If one can identify 'The Law' in *The Godfather*, it is the law of the family, which itself is nostalgically linked to the law of the 'Old Country'; the law is about loyalty, honour and the wisdom of silence. To put it another way, the Hays Code was now replaced by the Code of Sicily (to which I will return). For good or ill, this is the paradigm now at work in many crime dramas of the big and small screen, and we have *The Godfather* to thank for it.

The Godfather series is not a simple matter of the support or critique of one ideology. There is more than one prominent ideology and the films variously support and critique ideologies in turns. Glenn Man suggests that *The Godfather* fits a particular type of ideological discourse in that it is 'basically conservative but contain[s] radical elements that disrupt the text'.[9] *The Godfather* is an extreme example of this type. '*Part I* plays up the tensions between a prosocial myth and the myth of the romanticized gangster, never quite resolving the conflict between the two, whereas the other two films pursue a relentless critique of American capitalism and the American dream.'[10]

There are at least three points of view to which we are drawn in assessing the mythology of *The Godfather* films. The first is that of Vito Corleone. The scenes that attempt most clearly to legitimize violence appear in the sequences of Part II of the young Vito in Sicily and New York. The act of violence that signals Vito's future power and status is the murder of the flamboyant and repulsive Fanucci, a neighbourhood tyrant who takes advantage of poor immigrant families. He is not unlike the overlord who is responsible for the deaths of Vito's brother and mother in Sicily. He is easy to hate. But everything about Vito is charmed, confirmed by his being rendered in soft focus and sepia tones, the theme music played on an evocative music box, all conjuring up Old World values.[11] Vito and his friends are warm and open and they like to joke around. Vito is a local hero, looking after the underprivileged. It is also significant that Vito is aligned with what film critic Vera Dika has identified as 'La Via Vecchia', a real Sicilian code of honour. It is at work throughout *The Godfather* films. It includes the code of silence with respect to the 'family business', an expectation that men will not abuse 'their women' and that all business will be conducted with honesty. The same disarming charm follows the older Vito from the opening scene of Part I, Amerigo Bonasera's pleading with the Don for justice:

From the start of *The Godfather*, Coppola restrains us from classifying Don Corleone as a comic-book villain. The Don fixes Bonasera with an imperious stare . . . The camera's computer-timed lens retreats with scarcely perceptible stealth back past the head of Brando's Don . . . The Don sits in monolithic silence, stroking a cat in a telling visual metaphor for the hooded claws of his domain. All these elements, and the conspiratorial shadows of Gordon Willis's photography, evoke the intimacy of some pagan confessional.[12]

Beneath the Don's tranquil veneer constantly lurks the threat of violence, like the cat that might suddenly hiss and lash out, yet it is something we never see. This is, as we will see, a disingenuous strategy with which some have taken issue.

Within the logic of Part I, then, suggests Dika, those who violate the codes (as Don Vito represents them) 'deserve everything they get. So, since [police chief] McClusky is a vulgar cop who violates the law, and [Connie's husband] Carlo is a wife beater and a traitor to his family, they become worthy of their punishment'[13] (and I would add to the list Tessio, an old friend who is punished for betraying the family). So here is a deeply sympathetic portrayal. Vito's violence is to be *understood* and, through the flawless editing of Part II, it is deliberately contrasted with the second significant point of view, that of Michael Corleone.

I have noted how *The Godfather* opens with Don Vito Corleone gracefully in control at the wedding of his daughter. He insists that the family photograph be delayed so that Michael can appear in it. He hears all who want to see him and his authority is never questioned. Traditional music provides the ambience and there is genuine joy and conviviality. It is a master class in character establishment. When we are introduced to Michael in Part II, it is at the christening of his son, Anthony. He has left the roots of New York and followed the money, to Lake Tahoe. Michael looks out of place and rarely smiles. When he meets with the corrupt Senator Geary we see his authority challenged. An old family friend, Pentangeli, tries to get the band to play the same *tarantella* music played at Connie's wedding in Part I, but he is mocked by a rendition of *Pop Goes the Weasel* instead. Connie is now out of control and Michael's brother, Fredo, violates the Via Vecchia by 'losing control' of his drunken wife. In contrast, Don Vito was rendered as a genuinely loved and warm person who cared for his family. The only murders in which he participated appear to have been revenge killings or were directly related to a wrong done against him or an attempt to provide for his family. Michael starts this way. With his wife Kay he is at first warm and even a good listener. But the deeper he falls into the family business, the more he shuts Kay out. (This is an effective motif: Kay gets the door shut on her several times throughout the films.)

By the end of Part III, *The Godfather* has come full circle. In a sense, Michael has become what, according to Part II, drove his father to crime: a wealthy landowning Northern Italian involved in shadowy business. That is not to say that his attempt at reform is not genuine, but it seems it is too late for him, that at some point he has crossed a personal Rubicon.

Everything about Part III supports this view of Michael, even the presentation of violence. In Parts I and II, the language around vengeance and 'business' is jovial; there are happy meals and nearly always it is the 'right' people who die. The exception is Fredo, who is the linchpin between Parts II and III. Everything about the business in Part III has become ugly and demeaning. There is no jovial warmth and Michael discovers that hypocrisy is at work in the highest places. Killing is not as clean as it once was. The fantasy of power is laid bare in Part III. Gone are any noble motivations of vengeance; the only motive left in Part III is greed. Of course the whole denouement is only made possible by the romanticization of the Mafia myth in Part I, and the seeds of its destruction sown in Part II.

Kay offers us a third perspective from which to view the mythology, as an outsider from the 'real world', and it is perhaps the most satisfying. Towards the end of Part II, Kay critiques (for us?) the whole rationale of Michael's life. After Michael has returned from a long absence, the two meet at a hotel. As their children play in the hallway, Kay confronts him in his hotel room and informs him that she and the children are 'going'. They begin to talk, calmly at first. Michael, quietly and threateningly, asks, 'Do you expect me to let you take my children from me? . . . Don't you know that that's an impossibility?' Kay then informs him that he is 'blind', and that what he had previously been led to believe was a miscarriage of her last pregnancy was in fact an abortion:

> An abortion, Michael. Just like our marriage is an abortion; something that's unholy and evil. I didn't want your son, Michael. I wouldn't bring another one of your sons into this world . . . I had it killed because this must all end . . . I knew . . . there would be no way you could ever forgive me, not with this Sicilian *thing* that's been going on for 2,000 . . . (*Michael cuts her off and slaps her viciously in the head, knocking her down.*)

Kay's revelation causes Michael to lose control, to violate the Via Vecchia. Her voice in Parts II and III is the clearest critical moral voice. My question is, What is *our* response to Kay's assault on Michael in this scene? Is it sympathy for Michael? Or do we see this as the harvest of what he has sown? When she challenges 'this Sicilian thing', with whom do we find ourselves aligned? Are we outraged at her mockery of the Old World? I think it is to Coppola's credit that he does not instruct us how to assess his characters. But does *The Godfather* trilogy ask us to *understand* (in the manner of critique) the Corleones' violent ethic, to assent to it or merely to be entertained by it?

Having considered *The Godfather*'s mythology, I would now like to ask where exactly the *appeal* to *The Godfather* lies. Whereas the Hays-Code

gangster offered us something against which to oppose ourselves (gangsters as 'pathological, morally reproachable', etc.), does *The Godfather*
offer us 'a man that we want to be, or that we can't help being'?
Is Alessandro Camon right when he states, 'As much as we enjoyed
[Michael's] affirmations of power (carefully set up in the film as righteous
revenges, almost supernatural in their efficiency), we empathize with his
suffering the consequences'?[14] Or is it all simply a case of 'bad guys' being
redeemed by their interaction with 'worse guys'?[15]

I am certain that Coppola and author and screenwriter Mario Puzo
sought to elicit audience sympathy, particularly for Michael. They both
eventually agreed that in Part II Michael could not murder his brother
Fredo until their mother had died. As Puzo put it, 'Psychologically I felt
that . . . the audience would never forgive him.'[16] Coppola wanted the
acts of violence to be committed with rhetorical flourishes to make them
'poetic' (according to Coppola, 'there was always some weird detail'),[17]
and this distances the viewer, shifting interest from consequence and
realism to aesthetics. One spectacular example of that rhetoric in Part I
is Michael's initiation into violence. The scene is set in a small Italian
restaurant, with few patrons present, at night, as Michael sets about the
shifty murder of Sollozzo and corrupt police chief McClusky (played by
film noir veteran, Sterling Hayden), who both attempted to kill his father.
The effect of the cinematic rhetoric (from the widely acclaimed use of
sound to the mists of blood that fill the air in the moment of impact) is that
we are not so much appalled as entertained, even amused. This is inten-
sified by the use of extremely low lighting by cinematographer Gordon
Willis, which weaves deliberate ambiguity into the stories. As he comments, 'There were times in some of [Brando's] scenes where I deliberately
did not want to see his eyes, so that you saw this mysterious human being
thinking about something . . . but you didn't really know what the hell
was going on.'[18]

Film critic Roger Ebert suggests that it is because the world of *The
Godfather* is a closed one that we find it so easy to be drawn to their central characters. In other words, that world is presented on its own terms,
the way it would 'like' to be received. For example, the somewhat infeas-
ible decision of Vito Corleone, in Part I, that the family not be involved in
drug trafficking (Vito: 'How did things ever get so far? . . . I believe this
drug business is going to destroy us in the years to come') could be seen
simply as a cynical attempt to make the family more palatable to us.[19] As
Ebert remarks, 'During the movie we see not a single actual civilian victim
of organized crime. No women trapped into prostitution. No lives
wrecked by gambling. No victims of theft, fraud or protection rackets.'[20]
David Denby takes a similar view, seeing this closed world as a subtle but
disingenuous strategy of Coppola and Puzo. So effective is the presentation of the piety of the family that 'By the time Michael Corleone shoots

his father's enemies in the restaurant scene, Coppola had most of us where he wanted us . . . we accepted the notion that Michael's violence was an act of family piety, a way of accepting his father, his family past, his natural destiny.'[21] As James Caan put it (and, judging by his hard-boiled delivery, *meant* it) in a recent interview, 'It's almost like you forgave everybody everything because they did it for the sake of family.'[22] Their world becomes odd and even funny, but there is no real tragedy, no 'everyday victims of Mafia extortion'.[23] It is this sterility, this banality, that William Pechter has suggested is the most morally audacious aspect of the films:

> The gangster here . . . has become . . . only another instance of the banality of evil. Who is this good husband and father, this man who must occasionally kill people in order to provide? . . . What are we that in this outsize, driven figure and his terrible excesses we can see the image, however extravagant and distorted, of ourselves?[24]

Denby also identifies a 'sociological argument' at work in the films: that is, that the Mafia was necessitated by the failure of the American judicial system. The argument is there from the opening speech of Bonasera in Part I, as he pleads with the Don to revenge the rape of his daughter: 'I believe in America. America has made my fortune . . . I went to the police, like a good American . . . They [the offenders] went free . . . Then I said to my wife, "For justice we must go to Don Corleone".' This 'sociological' view of Vito has a softening effect. Interestingly the actors clearly held to the argument themselves while making the film. In a 1971 documentary with interviews of the actors in costume, Pacino suggests that an island invaded as much as Sicily *needed* to form a bond of trust found uniquely in the 'family compound'.[25] Richard Castellano, who played Clemenza, put the case more authoritatively: 'See, there is a necessity for Don Corleone . . . There is a necessity for the syndicate. If there were no necessity, it wouldn't exist.' Denby also suggests that the ultimate message of Part II, that 'extreme success in America isolates you from everything worth striving for', is simply boring and is too easy an irony.[26] Ironically this is precisely what many critics see as the great strength of the trilogy. In the words of Coppola himself, at the end of Part II Michael 'has damned himself and lost everything that is worthwhile'.[27]

Part III provides another clue as to the massive appeal of *The Godfather* Parts I and II. Part III is often derided as inferior to the first two films, and in polls ranks well below the first two. It is certainly flawed, yet as one reviewer put it, if it stood alone it would probably rate far better. The unpopularity of Part III might in part be due to viewers' reluctance to see a vulnerable Michael, being made weak by his struggle with diabetes, no longer being a 'step ahead' of the bad guys. Coppola has said that he knew he was taking a risk by portraying Michael seeking redemption. Michael couldn't be a 'slick, lethal killer, the Michael Corleone people love'.[28] The murder of his brother Fredo in Part II hangs like a dark shadow over Michael's ultimately failed attempt to redeem himself. In Part I it was perfectly acceptable to see Vito in a state of weakness, for we knew that Michael was on the rise; Vito somehow managed to make us feel that he was a good man. With Vito's demise we do not think he is being left to the devil, but with Michael we can be certain that he has not managed to break away from *his* pact. And yet this interior judgement of the film presents another problem. The film is asking us to judge Michael not by an external moral standard, but by the life of arch-criminal Vito Corleone; that is, by Vito's idealized motivation of love for family. Michael's 'sins' are to do with the betrayal of family. This presents an insurmountable problem to the whole ambition of Parts II and III; for to believe that Michael's redemption is a worthy goal we must assent to *everything* for which Vito Corleone has stood: *all* of the untold and unseen social consequences of the Mafia lifestyle, implicitly and superficially rationalized by 'love of family'.

I have discussed the diverse ways – technical and emotional – in which Coppola and crew sought some kind of viewer identification, even empathy, with the Corleones. But what exactly are we empathizing *with*? Clive Marsh has recently explored the question of identification in films, asking what films actually do to us as viewers. Drawing on the work of Berys Gaut, Marsh argues that viewers

> do not (cannot, usually) identify with characters in all respects. What happens is that in a variety of ways viewers end up empathising, and sometimes sympathising, with characters. Sometimes this is a result of film technique (particular camera angles which require us to take up particular viewpoints); at other times it may result from what the viewer him- or herself brings to the film.[29]

With Vito are we aspiring to the kind of charm that is able to distance one from evil? Is that an appealing approach to coping with personal evil? Or to be more specific, coping with localized social oppression? With Michael are we empathizing with his loss of control (and ultimately, of love), even though his takes place in a context and at a level that most of us can never grasp? Marsh's brief reference to *The Shawshank Redemption* in the context of his discussion of identification is particularly apt here: 'Few viewers of *The Shawshank Redemption* will identify with Red because of their own experience as murderers . . . The real emotion that viewers do bring to this film is the sense of guilt or remorse that they feel about a past action of their own.'[30] If that is so, what of *The Godfather* films? Although they have apparently found a receptive and empathetic audience among real *mafiosi*, perhaps it is not such a specific emotional and social context that the films are touching on with most viewers. The films touch a more universal nerve and somehow allow viewers, seemingly without a sense of guilt or irony, to *identify* with the Corleones.

The moral arguments of *The Godfather* are certainly flawed, but that might be missing the point. *The Godfather* films neither clearly glorify nor condemn the mafia myth, but portray it in all of its moral ambiguity, and perhaps this is a strength of the films.[31] When asked by *Playboy* if he thought he was guilty of romanticizing the Mafia, Coppola replied, 'Remember, it wasn't a documentary about Mafia chief Vito Genovese. It was Marlon Brando with Kleenex in his mouth.' Of course he is underestimating the power of his own filmic rhetoric, but he has a point. Why do we not apply the same ethical questions to other romances?

And this leads me to contrast a final parallel. The way we 'read' *The Godfather* films is of particular interest to me as a Bible exegete, for we bring our reading ethic to other 'texts', and reading the Bible presents us with some surprisingly similar moral quandaries. The most consistently comparable feature is the refusal of the Bible's narrators to guide our assessment of the moral actions of its protagonists. Lot is prepared to hand over his daughters to certain death to save his skin; Jacob lies to his father's face to steal a birthright; a concubine is left for dead and the Levite does nothing but gruesomely desecrate her body with a violence that would not pass the censors. In each case (and there are more) we are offered little or no moral guidance by the narrator or the narrative presentation generally. (Although this often enables a critical encounter with the text *because* multiple readings are possible.) And then there is David. His was a story of house against house, the defeat of one family by another. David's 'rustic', even romantic, beginning was to be overshadowed and consumed by his violent rise through the echelons of power. His is a story of loyalty, corruption and tragedy through moments of moral weakness. It is a story of Old World values moving inexorably towards an institutionalized form of power. And in his ignoble end (in bed with a concubine probably young enough to be his granddaughter), having lost his son, and lost any moral voice within his family, I am reminded of Michael Corleone's lonely and feeble demise.

Notes

1 Cited in Peter Cowie, *The Godfather Book*, London: Faber and Faber, 1997, p. 8.

2 Nick Browne, 'Fearful A-Symmetries: Violence as History in *The Godfather*

Films', in Nick Browne (ed.), *The Godfather Trilogy*, Cambridge Film Handbooks; Cambridge: Cambridge University Press, 2000, pp. 1–22 (2).

3 Source: http://imdb.com/Top/, 16 September 2004. When the figures are broken down into male and female voters, *The Godfather* unsurprisingly ranks first with men and is still an impressive fourteenth with women.

4 On the many ways in which *The Godfather* films inform *The Sopranos*, see D. Pattie, 'Mobbed Up: The Sopranos and the Modern Gangster Film', in D. Lavery (ed.), *This Thing of Ours: Investigating The Sopranos*, New York: Columbia University Press, 2002, pp. 135–45.

5 Cited in John Walker (ed.), *Halliwell's Film and Video Guide*, London: HarperCollins, rev. 12th edn, 1997, p. 604.

6 Cited in Richard Maltby, 'The Spectacle of Criminality', in J. David Slocum (ed.), *Violence and American Cinema*, AFI Film Readers; London: Routledge, 2001, pp. 117–52 (120).

7 All citations from the Code are taken from S. Prince's superb study, *Classical Film Violence: Designing and Regulating Brutality in Hollywood Cinema, 1930–1968*, New Brunswick, NJ: Rutgers University Press, 2003, Appendix B: The Production Code, pp. 293–301. It is also available at ArtsReformation.com, http://www.artsreformation.com/a001/hays-code.html.

8 Cited in Maltby, 'Criminality', p. 118.

9 Glenn Man, 'Ideology and Genre in *The Godfather* Films', in Browne (ed.), *The Godfather Trilogy*, pp. 109–32 (128; drawing on the work of Louis Camolli and Jean Narboni).

10 Man, 'Ideology', p. 128.

11 As Cowie puts it, 'Brando's Don radiates an irresistible charm and nobility, and in the "prequel" De Niro's Vito adroitly reflects these qualities. As a consequence, the audience allows itself to be duped, lulled into accepting the legitimacy of the budding Don's crimes' (*The Godfather Book*, pp. 181–2).

12 Cowie, *The Godfather Book*, p. 171.

13 Vera Dika, 'The Representation of Ethnicity in *The Godfather*', in Browne (ed.), *The Godfather Trilogy*, pp. 76–108 (90).

14 Alessandro Camon, '*The Godfather* and the Mythology of Mafia', in Browne (ed.), *The Godfather Trilogy*, pp. 57–75 (70).

15 Camon, 'Mythology', p. 75 (referring to Tarantino's *Pulp Fiction*).

16 'Coppola and Puzo on Screenwriting', Bonus Materials DVD, Paramount Home Video, 2001.

17 DVD director's commentary to Part II, Paramount Home Video, 2001.

18 'Gordon Willis on Cinematography', Bonus Materials DVD, Paramount Home Video, 2001.

19 Cowie agrees, and gives examples of *mafiosi* being involved in the drug trade as early as 1935 (*The Godfather Book*, p. 173).

20 Roger Ebert, 'The Godfather', *The Chicago Sun Times*, 1999; http://www.suntimes.com/ebert/ebert_reviews/1999/10/god1028.html.

21 David Denby, 'The Two Godfathers', in Browne (ed.), *The Godfather Trilogy*, pp. 173–80 (175).

22 'The Godfather Family: A Look Inside', Bonus Materials DVD, Paramount Home Video, 2001.

23 Denby, 'The Two Godfathers', p. 174.

24 'Keeping Up with the Corleones', in Browne (ed.), *The Godfather Trilogy*, pp. 167–73 (172–3). Critics at the time of the release of Part I also identified a moral vacuity. So, for example, Robert Hatch in *The Nation* wrote, 'The success of *The Godfather* is deplorable if you believe that popular entertainment both reflects and modifies social morale. In a sentence, the picture forces you to take sides, to form allegiances, in a situation that is totally without moral substance . . .' (cited in Cowie, *The Godfather Book*, p. 69).

25 Bonus Materials DVD, Paramount Home Video, 2001.

26 Denby, 'The Two Godfathers', p. 178.

27 DVD director's commentary to Part II.

28 DVD director's commentary to Part II.

29 Clive Marsh, *Cinema and Sentiment: Film's Challenge to Theology*, Carlisle: Paternoster, 2004, p. 90.

30 Marsh, *Cinema and Sentiment*, p. 92.

31 So Camon, 'Mythology', p. 75.

7. Was Judas *The Third Man?*

The Lost Childhood in the Cinema of Graham Greene

TOM AITKEN

In 1947, the year during which, on 27 September, he conceived the story of *The Third Man* (or so he says, although elements of it come from much earlier),[1] Graham Greene published an essay called *The Lost Childhood*. This discussed the special pleasure and excitement the young derive from reading, a pleasure and excitement that, he found, diminished somewhat with maturity. That special pleasure and excitement, he thought, made the books we enjoyed when young stay with us and influence us forever. He himself had been impelled to become a writer when he read Marjorie Bowen's *The Viper of Milan*, a ripping yarn about evil in Renaissance Italy.

At the end of his essay he quotes 'Germinal', a poem with a broadly similar theme, by the Irish poet George William Russell, who wrote as 'A.E.', which asserts that both good and evil deeds have roots in childhood; the reason for the betrayal of Christ, for example, was buried in 'the lost boyhood of Judas'.[2]

This reference to Judas, I think, takes Greene's essay into more suggestive territory than it has previously entered. It also provides a cluster of meanings and associations which taken together epitomize much of Greene's work. Anyone may write about lost childhood. Anyone may write about betrayal. But throw in Judas and Jesus and the mix becomes specifically Greene. No mean betrayer himself, he returns over and again to situations in which religion and betrayal are closely linked – almost two sides of the same coin. (For a chronology of Greene's life, see Text Box 7.1.)

Thus, in *The End of the Affair* – almost unique in Greene's work in that it has now been the subject of two fairly and variously respectable screen adaptations (for further screen versions of Greene's fiction, see Text Box 7.2) – when the adulterous Sarah becomes a Catholic and refuses to have anything further to do with her lover Bendrix, he feels betrayed and bitter. And, be it noted, Sarah's conversion is shown as deriving from an incident lost so deep in her childhood that she has completely forgotten it (largely

---

7.1 Graham Greene: A Chronology

1904–35: Born at Berkhamsted, Hertfordshire. Educated at Berkhamsted School (where his father was headmaster) and Balliol College, Oxford.
1926: Converts to Catholicism in order to marry Vivienne Dayrell-Browning in 1927.
1929–31: Publishes three novels, two of which he later rejects. Only the first, *The Man Within*, remains in print.
1932–9: Writes two novels and three 'entertainments' (his word for thrillers), establishing his characteristic world of seedy disappointment, now known as 'Greeneland'. The novelist J. B. Priestley threatens a libel action against the first of the 'entertainments', *Stamboul Train*.
1937: Greene suggests in a review of a Shirley Temple film in the magazine *Night and Day* that the studio 'procured' its star 'for immoral purposes': widespread outrage and closure of the magazine follow.
1938: Travels through Mexico in order to report on the condition of the Catholic Church there in *The Lawless Roads*. Later, in *The Power and the Glory*, he reuses much of the material as fiction.
1938–61: From *Brighton Rock* to *A Burnt-Out Case*, writes five novels in which Catholicism is central. The last makes Evelyn Waugh fear that he has abandoned Catholicism, which he denies.
1947: Begins a drunken, intense affair with Catherine Walston.
1955–88: Returns to political themes in *The Quiet American*, but later becomes eclectic in subject and approach. *Our Man in Havana* (1958) and *Travels with My Aunt* (1969) are comedies, while *Monsignor Quixote* combines comedy with Catholicism.
1966: Begins affair with Yvonne Cloetta.
1978: Death of Catherine Walston.
1993: During Greene's last illness his long-separated wife Vivienne asks to see him but he refuses. She and his mistress Yvonne Cloetta meet for the first time at his funeral.

---

perhaps because when it happened she did not understand it). Bendrix is told at Sarah's funeral that when she was two, her mother, on holiday in France without her atheist husband, had her secretly baptized. The sacrament had clearly, her mother believes, 'taken' even though Sarah was unconscious of it. Bendrix, a man of no religious belief, is outraged. He has been betrayed not merely by Sarah herself but, as he sees it, by a piece of mumbo-jumbo enacted during her lost childhood.

In *The Fallen Idol*, made in 1948, the year before *The Third Man*, betrayals are multitudinous and of many kinds. Baines, butler in the London Embassy of a foreign power, has betrayed his wife by falling in love with a secretary. He has betrayed the secretary by failing to leave his wife. He has betrayed the trust, almost hero worship of the ambassador's lonely son, Felipe. Mrs Baines has in some sense betrayed her husband by being or becoming an ill-tempered, house-proud shrew, and, worse, is very unkind to Felipe, for whom Baines harbours a love as if for his own unborn son.

Events are seen from Felipe's point of view, but the audience is placed outside him, watching in anguish as he is tricked into betraying what he knows of Baines's affair to Mrs Baines and, when talking to the police at

---

7.2 Ten Other Screen Versions of Greene's Fiction

(Films marked * scripted by Greene himself)

Went the Day Well (Alberto Cavalcanti, 1940)
German soldiers infiltrate an English village.

The Ministry of Fear (Fritz Lang, 1943)
Guilt-ridden mercy killer becomes involved with German spy ring.

Brighton Rock (John Boulting, 1947)*
Childlike waitress falls in love with a sadistic baby-faced criminal who loathes women.

The Fallen Idol (Carol Reed, 1948)*
Small boy loses his trust in the butler he has hero-worshipped.

The Heart of the Matter (George More O'Ferrall, 1953)
Catholic policeman in West Africa agonizes over an adulterous affair.

Our Man in Havana (Carol Reed, 1960)*
English vacuum cleaner salesman becomes an inventively fraudulent spy.

England Made Me (Peter Duffell, 1973)
British siblings in Thirties Germany troubled by their unacknowledged incestuous attraction.

Monsignor Quixote (Rodney Bennett, 1985; made for television)
Elderly priest and Marxist sparring partner bicker amiably as they drive around Spain.

The End of the Affair (Neil Jordan, 1999)
An adulterous affair in wartime London provokes a crisis of conscience.

The Quiet American (Phillip Noyce, 2002)
Political and sexual discord between cynical Brit and idealistic American in 1950s Saigon.

the film's climax, almost incriminates Baines after Mrs Baines has acci-
dentally fallen to her death. Felipe is left feeling that the entire adult world
has betrayed him – or perhaps it would be better to say that it has let him
down. He cannot understand why people should be so upset about a few
clandestine meetings in tea rooms, why Baines should lie to him, and why,
when he decides to tell the exact truth about what has happened ('Please!
Please listen to me! This is important.') he is patted on the head and
ignored. And, of course, his childhood, previously idyllic, is lost.

Greene regarded his original story, *The Basement Room*, as unfilmable,
and in his conferences with the director Carol Reed, he writes, it 'was
quietly changed so that [it] no longer concerned a small boy who unwittingly betrayed his best friend to the police, but dealt instead with a small
boy who believed that his best friend was a murderer and nearly procured
his arrest by telling lies in his defence'.[3] This permits a halfway happy ending. Similarly, in *Brighton Rock*, young Rose is saved by a scratched
gramophone record from what the novel calls, in anticipation, 'the worst
horror of all', Pinkie's abusively contemptuous parting message to her –
another betrayal of innocent trust. But although *The Fallen Idol* is given a
comfortable rather than a disastrous ending for Baines (and therefore for
the audience, since Baines is a sympathetic character), it is a sad one for
Felipe: his idol has fallen indeed, and with him, for the time being at any
rate, any wish Felipe might have to enter the adult world.

A more dubious kind of innocence is examined and in due course
betrayed in *The Quiet American*, set in Saigon during the rebellion against
the French. In this, detachment (in the person of Fowler, a sceptical British
journalist) is pitted against involvement (in the person of Pyle, a younger
man from the American legation). When Pyle's naive political views and
actions lead the French colonial police into thinking him a menace,
Fowler (admittedly almost by omission) helps them lure Pyle into a situation in which he can easily be killed. Like some other betrayers in Greene
whom I will mention later, he washes his hands of the matter, reflecting
that 'Sooner or later, one has to take sides – is that not so?' Nonetheless,
he is aware of what he has done, and, like others of Greene's erring atheists, yearns for somewhere to unload his guilt. 'Even betrayal of someone
you neither like nor respect feels like betrayal. You hand it over to that
somebody in whom you don't believe,' wishing that 'someone existed to
whom I could say I was sorry'.

Many of these betrayers who so fascinate Greene act out of conflicting
feelings of love and malice. Their betrayals are never performed out of
pure self-interest; there is always a mixture of moral or ideological com-
plication, amounting at times almost to the sense that the deed is done in
the victim's best interests. Their betrayals take many forms: espionage,
quisling-like treason, failure to observe priestly vows, adultery, stealing a
friend's mistress, failure to intervene to save another's life, pretence of

love, adulteration of medicine, failure to live up to an acquaintance's high opinion. And, frequently, the betrayed are also betrayers, as in *The Fallen Idol* and *The Third Man.*

In *The Third Man,* Holly Martins, after realizing how far he and others have been betrayed by Lime, is persuaded to co-operate with the authorities. But after he has done what he has to do, Martins still feels that he has betrayed Lime; and not just Lime himself, but their friendship – a friendship that was a whole greater than the sum of its parts, and might somehow have been able to transcend the desolating truth about Lime the betrayer: of the sick children of Vienna, of Anna, his mistress, of Martins himself and of all civilized feeling. It is not ideology or conscience which takes precedence in Martins's far from incisive mind, so much as the sentimental romanticism of the cheap Westerns that he writes.

The Third Man was not an adaptation of an existing work, but an original story. We shall come later to the question of just how original it is. Greene, as he usually did when starting a film from scratch, began by writing a prose draft, which in this case was subsequently published. (It differs considerably from the finished film.) Greene's idea concerned a man apparently dead who turned out not to be dead after all. Alexander Korda, at that time the sole producer of the proposed film, wanted it set in post-war Europe and suggested Vienna and Rome. Greene spent some time living in the Sacher Hotel behind the Vienna Opera, at that time occupied by the British military, gathering atmosphere for his story. Eventually he decided that Rome would not be necessary. While in Vienna he visited many less respectable haunts than the Sacher, as was his wont: Elizabeth Montague, who had been sent by Korda to look after him, recalled asking him how he squared his religious principles with sitting in a brothel getting drunk – and being almost convinced by the brilliant equivocations in his lengthy response.[4]

All this is described in Charles Drazin's book, *In Search of The Third Man,* published in 1999, which also covers in entertaining detail the no less brilliant equivocations Greene and Reed used to circumvent demands for change emanating from the American producer, David O. Selznik, who came on board when Korda (as he often did) had a cash-flow problem. Selznik complained that the script made it look as if the British were the most important power in Vienna, and that of the two Americans on view, Lime was a racketeer and Holly Martins a crass drunk. It is impossible to deny that he had a point, but we can nevertheless be glad that many of his suggestions (which amounted quite often to commands) were ignored. He was, however, responsible for the amazing final shot in the film, in which Anna walks away from Lime's grave, ignoring Martins, who, in his bumbling way (he has told her, 'I'm just a hack writer who drinks too much and falls in love with girls') wants to replace Harry in her affections.

Before I examine how 'Catholic' the film is, and the various other meanings it has, I want to address the question of just how 'original' its story is.
I have said that *The Third Man* is about betrayal, and it is easy to argue
that not only is it about betrayal, but also that in constructing his plot
Greene in a sense betrayed two other writers and, covertly, a close friend.
Philip French, in a cogently argued review when the film was re-released
in 1999, draws attention to marked resemblances between Greene's story
and that of Eric Ambler's thriller, *The Mask of Dimitrios*, published in
1939. In this, a naive, not very good writer of detective stories visits
Constantinople in search of Dimitrios, a criminal who has victimized
many, and has now disappeared. ('Until nearly the end', Ambler himself
tells us, 'the reader sees Dimitrios only obliquely, through the eyes of
those he has victimized and through the mind of Latimer, the scholarly
detective story writer in search of reality.'[5]) Greene, of course, presents
Lime in exactly the same way in *The Third Man*. Like Martins, Latimer
refuses to take the advice of the local police chief (who has read his books,
just as Paine, Calloway's assistant, has read Martins's). We have here,
surely, in Dimitrios, Latimer and the police chief, speaking likenesses of
Harry Lime, Holly Martins and Major Calloway. In *The Third Man* itself
there is one highly suggestive reference, otherwise apparently irrelevant.
The film begins with a voice-over commentary on the Viennese situation,
spoken, incidentally, by the director, Carol Reed. It begins: 'I never knew
the old Vienna before the war, with its Strauss music, its glamour and easy
charm – Constantinople suited me better . . .' Is this mention of
Constantinople a nod in the direction of Ambler's story? Surely it cannot
be mere coincidence. Various people involved in the new film had worked
either with Ambler, or on his books, in the not too distant past and there
may have been a shared feeling that he was owed something. Reed had
collaborated with Ambler on a wartime documentary, *The Way Ahead,* in
1944. Orson Welles had part-directed a film of Ambler's *Journey into
Fear* in 1942. Greene had praised Ambler's thrillers.

There is a faint possibility, perhaps, that Greene and Ambler may have
colluded in some way. In 1944, Warner Brothers had produced an undis-
tinguished film of *The Mask of Dimitrios*, one which (as Ambler again
tells us) simply 'ignored' the complexities of his narrative, introducing
Dimitrios right from the start. Ambler may have allowed Greene to take
over the central elements of his story in order to see what could be done
with them by a good director and cast. Ambler, however, makes no such
suggestion in his autobiography, *Here Lies*, and Greene was unlikely to
advertise any borrowing of the kind. As was the convention, he took sole
writing credit for the film, although Carol Reed, Peter Smollett (of whom
more later) and Mabbie Poole, wife of the playwright Rodney Ackland,
all worked on the script.[6] Also, as is well known, it was Orson Welles,
playing Lime, who wrote Lime's speech about the cuckoo clock –

although he in fact lifted the idea from the American Artist James McNeil Whistler. More important than any of these in the script-writing team was an American screenwriter, Jerome Chodorov, who was brought in to make Holly Martins's dialogue more convincingly idiomatic. (Chodorov appears to have done rather more than that, in fact. Many of the changes in Martins's dialogue between Greene's shooting script and the finished film are not merely more idiomatically American, they define Martins's character more sharply and interestingly than the lines they replace.)

When Philip French asked Ambler whether he had noticed the resemblance between *The Third Man* and *The Mask of Dimitrios*, Ambler replied drily, 'Yes, I have.'[7] But whatever the truth of the Ambler connection (almost a title for one of Ambler's own books), the elements of deception and sharp practice involved would have appealed to Greene. I would add, however, that the context of occupied Vienna transforms the atmosphere surrounding the story. Ambler's pre-war yarn shows an innocent Englishman getting into trouble with devilishly cunning Levantine criminals. In *The Third Man*, the evils of the war and the rampant corruption that has succeeded it are everywhere apparent and essential to the story and, taken together with the religious and moral elements, lend *The Third Man* a resonance and power that is missing from *Dimitrios*. As Greene suggested elsewhere, when a country hands itself over to moral and social collapse it is every man for himself. And, to a much greater extent than Ambler's Charles Latimer, Holly is Everyman, adrift in a world where he understands neither the language nor the conventions. He gives this tale something for everybody. Perhaps we have an illustration here of the First Law of Plagiarism: If you plagiarize, do so with improvements.

Another unacknowledged source for Greene's plot was his friendship with Kim Philby. Philby was a British diplomat and double-agent who worked in liaison with the CIA but also spied for the Russians. He defected to Russia in 1963 after being warned that his cover had been blown. Philby had been in Vienna in February 1934, when the Austrian Chancellor, Englebert Dollfuss, suspended parliamentary government and drove the Socialists into revolt. There Philby met a young communist called Litzi Friedmann, and some of the things that happened to her seem to have suggested things that happen to Anna in *The Third Man*. During a military siege of the Karl Marx Hof, a municipal showpiece housing estate half a mile long, Litzi and Philby helped besieged Socialists to escape through the city's network of sewers. When they had themselves to flee to safety, Philby – unlike Lime with Anna – married Litzi in order to take her to London; although they subsequently split up.

Litzi had meanwhile introduced Philby to a local journalist called Peter Smolka (mentioned above under the name he used when he too took refuge in London, Peter Smollett), who would become another of Greene's unacknowledged sources for *The Third Man*. By the time Greene went to

---

7.3 Post-war Vienna

July 1945 Vienna divided into four zones administered by France, Britain, the United States and Russia respectively. The central area of the city is administered jointly by all four.

Four famous hotels are commandeered as military headquarters.

Theatres, restaurants and other places of public resort and entertainment continue to function, largely without customers.

The state-run pawn shop, the Dorotheum, does a roaring trade.

The black market thrives and is powerful.

Rural peasants decorate their homes with the possessions of the urban rich, bartered for food.

1948 While *The Third Man* is being made, the Cold War begins. The Russians blockade Berlin and the Western powers airlift food and other supplies into the city. This continues for over a year until September 1949, the month in which the film opens.

Vienna in 1948 with Elizabeth Montague to research for the film, Smolka was back there, and they met, possibly not for the first time. Smolka showed Greene stories he had written; three of which featured, respectively, the network of sewers under Vienna, the penicillin rackets that were practised in the city and the way in which jeeps carrying soldiers from each of the four occupying powers patrolled the city. Greene lifted all this material without acknowledgement, but when Elizabeth Montague realized what he had done, Smolka was given 200 guineas and appointed as an adviser and location assistant on the film, in addition to helping with the script.[8] As with Ambler, there is in the film (but not in the script) a typically covert acknowledgement. When, after Lime's supposed funeral, Calloway gives Martins a lift back from the cemetery and offers him a drink, he tells the driver what we assume is the name of a bar. The name is 'Smolka!'

Aside from questions about how much or little of his story Greene actually invented, the Philby/Smolka connection has suggested to some commentators that, in the character of Harry Lime, Greene is making a coded confession that he knew all about Philby's double life. It is at least an ingenious interpretation and may even be true. It would not necessarily have needed to be consciously true.[9] Either way, Greene was careful, then and later, to cover his tracks.

Thus, *The Third Man* is not only about betrayal; it is in itself a complicated act of betrayal. Is it also about Catholicism? Although none of the four leading characters in *The Third Man* is announced as a Catholic (although Anna may be, and we can assume that all the Austrian supporting characters are), the film comes at approximately the central point of Greene's most Catholic phase as a writer. Between *Brighton Rock* (1938) and *A Burnt Out Case* (1960) most of Greene's novels (as opposed to the fictions he called 'entertainments') had explicitly Catholic themes, exploring the idea of 'the appalling strangeness of the mercy of God'. Two of the most explicit of all, *The Heart of the Matter* and *The End of the Affair*, appeared respectively in 1948 (the year before *The Third Man*) and 1951, two years after it. Alongside 'the appalling strangeness of the mercy of God' and the lost childhood of Judas, there appears a third concern, derived from Browning's poem 'Bishop Blougram's Apology':

> Our interest's in the dangerous edge of things.
> The honest thief, the tender murderer,
> The superstitious atheist . . .[10]

These ideas found their way into many of the more than 20 films, scripted either by Greene himself or by others, based on his fiction. When I began work on this essay I wrote that 'there is only one scene with any particularly Catholic resonance in *The Third Man* (which in many respects resembles an 'entertainment'), albeit an important one'. Then, experiencing a serendipitous twinge of nervous caution, I watched the film again and realized that in fact it is stuffed with them.

When Martins arrives in Vienna he goes to Harry's flat, expecting to see him. He meets instead the porter, who speaks very little English. (The actor who played him, we are told by Drazin, spoke none at all, and had to be taught the English words by rote. If so he did a remarkable job.) Be that as it may, he tells Martins that Harry is dead, gives the first of many conflicting accounts of the 'fatal' accident, and adds, of Lime 'Already in hell . . .' (pointing upwards) '. . . or' (after a pause to signal dubiety) 'in heaven' (pointing downwards). The moment, which is not in Greene's shooting script, is a remarkably subtle one. The joke about the porter's grasp of English is obvious, but we have to decide whether the porter has actually confused the two words. Any impartial judge knowing the truth about Harry would naturally assume that he had gone to hell. The porter, however, is an innocent-seeming chap, vaguely aware that it may be dangerous to say too much about Harry (his strapping wife sharpens his perceptions on this matter from time to time) but perhaps, like Martins and Harry's girlfriend Anna, is unwilling to believe that Harry was anything other than the charmer he seems. Later, however, when pressed about the accident, the porter backtracks in a way which in the context of Austria just after the war, is significant. 'I saw nothing,' he says. 'It is not my business.' What else, we wonder, has he failed to notice in the past 15 years because it was not his business?

From Harry's flat Martins goes to Harry's funeral, where another subtlety not in Greene's shooting script has found its way into the film. A priest ('mumbling rapidly', as the script commands) is reciting from the missal, but not the words about resting in peace that Greene originally used. Instead he seems to be reciting the Creed, at the point at which Pontius Pilate is mentioned – the man, of course, whose response to a difficult problem was to wash his hands. The hand-washing that goes on in *The Third Man* – a film whose climax, let us remember, occurs in a sewer – is extensive and practised by many characters. Furthermore, the mention of Pilate immediately precedes mention of the resurrection, relevant in a somewhat improper fashion to Harry Lime.

Furthermore, implausibly, the priest is speaking not Latin but German. Is he telling us subliminally that the whole funeral service is a fraud? Well, perhaps, perhaps not. Soon after this, misled by Sergeant Paine's announcement that Martins is a 'very good' writer, Crabbin, who is busy culturally re-educating the Viennese, invites Martins to give a lecture on the modern novel. At a subsequent meeting he is more specific: 'They want you to talk on the Crisis of Faith.' Startled, Martins asks, 'What's that?' Crabbin says, 'I thought you'd know, you're a writer . . .' Then he laughs. 'Of course you know.' No doubt Greene is having a little private joke here about the subjects readers at this time wanted to discuss with him, but we may note that Martins is on his way to a major crisis of faith of his own when the friend he has trusted and admired to the point of worshipping is revealed as a despicable crook.

Meanwhile, Martins has interviewed two Viennese friends of Harry's. The second of these, Lime's medical advisor, Dr Winkel, is a precise, fastidious man whose waiting room is described in Greene's directions as reminding us of 'an antique shop that specialises in religious *objets d'art*'. In the film Martins and Winkel fill most of the screen, but the room is clearly much as Greene imagined it. I continue with his description:

> There are more crucifixes hanging on the walls and perched on the cupboards and occasional tables than one can count, none of later date than the seventeenth century. There are statues in wood and ivory. There are a number of reliquaries: little bits of bone marked with saints' names and set in oval frames on a background of tinfoil. Even the high-backed, hideous chairs look as if they had been sat in by cardinals.[11]

In the shooting script there is a brief conversation about a crucifix on which Christ hangs with his arms above his head. Winkel explains that it is a Jansenist crucifix and the posture reflects (he does not say how) the Jansenist belief that Christ died only for the elect. In the film these lines are cut, and the curious choice of decoration for a doctor's waiting room is not alluded to; it is merely there. It is possible, I think, that Greene intended a veiled comment on those Viennese Catholics, some of them among the most antisemitic in Europe, who lived through the Nazi period apparently blind to any conflict between Nazi and Catholic beliefs.

This corruption and wilful blindness is echoed by Winkel's reiterated response to questions about Harry's death: 'I cannot give an opinion. I was not there.' (This, of course, raises the question of Greene's own anti-semitism, which I think we may say was of the relatively mild semi-automatic sort common in Western Europe and elsewhere during the inter-war years. After the war, as Michael Shelden in his notably unsym-pathetic account expresses it 'he had the good sense to back away'[12] from this earlier attitude; I think we may see *The Third Man* as a stage in that process.)

The last of the scenes in the film that explicitly mentions Christian belief is the meeting between Lime and Martins on the big wheel on the Prater. Martins asks Lime if he has ever seen any of his victims. Lime is evasive, then scathing.

'You know, I never feel comfortable with these things . . . Victims? Don't be melodramatic. Look down there. Would you really feel any pity if one of those dots stopped moving for ever? If I said you can have twenty thousand pounds for every dot that stops, would you really, old man, tell me to keep my money – or would you calculate how many dots you could afford to spare? And free of income tax, old man, free of income tax.'

[After further dialogue, Harry adds,] 'In these days, old man, nobody thinks in terms of human beings. They talk of the people and the prole-tariat, and I talk of the suckers . . .'

[Martins says,] 'You used to believe in a God.'

A shade of melancholy [Greene tells us] crosses Harry's face. 'Oh, I still *believe*, old man. In God and Mercy and all that. The dead are happier dead. They don't miss much here, poor devils.'

(In a way, ironically, Lime is here almost echoing Calloway, who has earlier told Holly, 'Death's at the bottom of everything, Martins. Leave death to the professionals.')

Whether or not we can believe Harry's assertion of belief – and perhaps we can – Harry is voicing a colder, more clinically detached, version of the same corrupt excuse-making and hand-washing we have already seen from the porter, Kurtz and Winkel: times are bad, how can we be any better than the times we live in? 'We aren't heroes, Holly, you and I,' Lime says. 'The world doesn't make heroes outside your books.' Given this view of the world, then for the 'suckers', death is the lesser of two evils. Even at this point, looking down from the zenith of the turning wheel, like Satan on the desert mountain top, Lime tries to tempt Martins into joining him.

Let us accept, then, that the action of *The Third Man* is coloured by Greene's Catholicism. Further, in leaving the ideas of Christian morality to be expressed by the powerless and ineffectual Holly Martins, Greene offers a version of the old saying that this world is a vale of tears within which evil is largely invincible. He also, however, uses a feature of Martins's own genre, the climactic shoot-out between goodies and baddies, to give us a temporal, in-this-world resolution. The death of Lime at Martins's hand will not, of course, eliminate evil from the world – not even from Vienna – but it allows us to feel, with Calloway, Anna and, very reluctantly, Martins himself, that with Lime's death the world has changed for the better.

Nevertheless, Martins, like young Felipe, has lost his childhood by losing the picture of Harry he has lived with all these years. As he has told Anna, 'I knew him for twenty years – at least, I thought I knew him. I suppose he was laughing at fools like us all the time.'

'He liked to laugh,' says Anna.

But even though Lime 'liked to laugh' and is a betrayer not only of those who buy his adulterated penicillin, but of his oldest friend and his mistress, we have perhaps arrived at the point where I must abandon my characterization of him as Judas. In the film he is altogether too large a figure for that to be adequate. He is, rather, Satan, or his alter ego, Lucifer, as described by Isaiah[13] (in various translations) as 'Son of the Morning', 'Daystar', 'the fallen Angel of Light'.

Select Bibliography

Eric Ambler, *Here Lies*, London: Weidenfeld and Nicholson, 1985.
—— *The Mask of Dimitrios*, London: Macmillan, 1999.
Charles Drazin, *In Search of The Third Man*, London: Methuen, 1999.
Quentin Falk, *Travels in Greeneland*, 3rd edn, London: Reynolds & Hearn Ltd, 2000.
Philip French, review of a re-release of *The Third Man*, London: *The Observer*, 18 July 1999.
Graham Greene, *Collected Essays*, London: Penguin Books, 1970.
—— *A Sort of Life*, London: Bodley Head, 1971.
—— *The Third Man* and *The Fallen Idol*, Harmondsworth: Penguin, 1975.
—— *Ways of Escape*, London: Bodley Head, 1980.
Graham Greene and Carol Reed, *The Third Man: A Film by Graham Greene and Carol Reed*, London: Lorrimer, 1969.
Michael Shelden, *Graham Greene: The Man Within*, London: William Heinemann, 1994.

Notes

1 Graham Greene, *Ways of Escape*, London: Bodley Head, 1980, pp. 122–7, and Charles Drazin, *In Search of The Third Man*, London: Methuen, 1999, pp. 2–3.

2 Graham Greene, *Collected Essays*, London: Penguin, 1970, p. 18.

3 Graham Greene, *The Third Man* and *The Fallen Idol*, Harmondsworth: Penguin, 1975, p. 123.

4 Drazin, *Search*, p. 6.

5 Ambler, *Here Lies*, London: Weidenfeld and Nicholson, 1985, p. 224.

6 Drazin, *Search*, p. 8.

7 *The Observer*, 18 July 1999. I have recently discovered that *The Mask of Dimitrios* was among the books which Graham Greene took with him to West Africa in 1941.

8 Drazin, *Search*, pp. 7–9. Drazin notes that this was a generous payment for the use of three short stories and that Smollett/Smolka accepted the situation cheerfully.

9 See Drazin, *Search*, pp. 144–54, and Michael Shelden, *Graham Greene: The Man Within*, London: William Heinemann, 1994, pp. 310–24.

10 See Graham Greene, *A Sort of Life*, London: Bodley Head, 1971, p. 115.

11 Graham Greene and Carol Reed, *The Third Man: A Film by Graham Greene and Carol Reed*, London: Lorrimer, 1969, p. 55.

12 Shelden, *Greene*, p. 151.

13 Isaiah 14.12.

8. Artificial Bodies:

Blade Runner and the Death of Man

GEORGE AICHELE

[T]he great cosmos itself is a vast computer and . . . we are the
programs it runs.[1]

Postmodernism deconstructs the humanist oppositions of reality/appear-
ance, nature/artifice, symbol/meaning, signifier/signified and organism/
machine. Postmodern thought recognizes that existence precedes essence,
and nothing is less natural, more artificial, and more ideological, than
'human nature'. What makes us human is indeed what separates us from
nature. Human nature is a 'reality effect'[2] or ideological construction, a
simulacrum. 'The simulacrum is not a degraded copy. It harbors a positive
power which denies *the original and the copy, the model and the reproduction*.'[3] 'Today abstraction is no longer that of the map, the double, the
mirror, or the concept. Simulation . . . is the generation by models of a real
without origin or reality: a hyperreal.'[4] (For brief explanations of some of
the technical terms in this chapter, see Text Box 8.1.)

   The postmodern subversion of belief, even of beliefs demanded by
modernist atheism, is suggested already by Nietzsche's madman's phrase,
'God is dead.'[5] If God did not exist, then God could not die. The mad-
man's claim is a strange confession of faith, and it is the beginning of the
end of 'man'. As Michel Foucault says, '[t]he death of God does not
restore us to a limited and positivistic world, but to a world exposed by
the experience of its limits, made and unmade by that excess which trans-
gresses it'.[6] It is an apocalyptic moment, a rediscovery of humanity – but
an apocalypse, finally, that uncovers questions, not answers. When God
dies, the human being is revealed to be an artifice, a posthuman cyborg.
If modernism is the philosophy of man, then postmodernism is the
philosophy of hyperreal humanity, or posthumanity.

   Katherine Hayles concludes her book with the comment that '[w]e have
always been posthuman'.[7] Human beings are fabricated beings – one
might even say essentially artificial. It does not require surgery, implants
or drugs to transform humanity, for human beings have been doing
that to themselves over and over again for thousands of years, beginning
with simple tools, language, clothing, the use of fire and agriculture. The

8.1 Some Technical Terms

Apocalypse – the revelation of some secret, especially concerning the end of the world.

Cyberpunk – cybernetic + punk. A type of story in which the distinction between human being and machine (especially computers) is blurred or erased.

Deconstruct – to disassemble a system of ideas by uncovering the inherent incoherence or incompleteness that makes that system possible.

Gnosticism – ancient belief system, especially widespread in early Christianity, that taught that salvation was to be achieved through secret knowledge (*gnōsis*) brought to humanity by a divine redeemer.

Postmodern/postmodernism – 'that which, in the modern, puts forward the unpresentable in presentation itself' (Jean-François Lyotard, *The Postmodern Condition: A Report on Knowledge*, trans. Geoff Bennington and Brian Massumi, Minneapolis: University of Minnesota Press, 1984, p. 81).

Simulacrum/simulation – the idea that everything is artificial, and that whatever we consider to be 'natural' is an ideological illusion. Also known as 'hyperreality'.

hyperreality of everything human becomes particularly evident in relation to the human body. After the death of God, the status of the soul becomes problematic. The deconstruction of the body/soul opposition leads to recognition that although the body is the point at which every human being is most natural, nevertheless the body is also both tool and signifier. We have modified and extended our bodies, both internally and externally. On one hand, the body is simply 'meat', the living flesh that sustains human consciousness. On the other hand, the body is augmentable and even replaceable, not only through drugs and surgery, but by means of biomechanical prostheses such as hearing aids and heart pacemakers as well as external supplements such as telephones and computers. The body has been reduced to code (and not merely DNA) – code that can be endlessly replicated or revised.

This is a recurring theme of 'cyberpunk' fiction.[8] Cyberpunk is a recent form of science fiction that combines in speculative narrative imaginary technological innovations (usually in the near future) and the gritty urban realism often associated with 'hard boiled' detective stories. Genetic or cybernetic tools or processes so modify the human body that questions of human identity and nature can be explored through plots that realize 'the expression of deep, unconscious, collective fears about our social life and its tendencies'.[9] The story is often narrated from a cynical or paranoid first-person perspective. Cyberpunk contrasts strongly with epic-heroic science fiction of the *Star Wars* or *Matrix* variety. The stories often feature a strong dose of ironic social commentary, and the principal characters are typically marginal hustlers and con artists, alienated 'street people' who survive in a grim, violent world – often a police state ruled by giant corporations – through their ability to slip through the cracks in a disintegrating community order and to manipulate the massive cybernetic powers that hold that world together.

These cyberpunk themes appear in Philip K. Dick's novel, *Do Androids Dream of Electronic Sheep?*, which served as the basis for Ridley Scott's movie, *Blade Runner*. Like a fine translation, Scott's movie complements and illuminates Dick's novel. However, it is by no means a literal translation, and even to say that both film and novel represent 'the same story' is quite a stretch. Indeed, there are numerous versions of Scott's movie, which are also arguably not 'the same story'.[10] I will be discussing both the US theatrical release and the 'director's cut' versions, and relevant differences will be noted. Nevertheless, despite numerous and substantial differences between the novel and the film, or perhaps because of them, the movie does an excellent job of reflecting the enigma that defines the novel – namely, the paradoxical relation between human beings and 'nature', as both embodied and surpassed in the machines that humans build. As a work of narrative art, the movie is just as interesting as the novel that it is derived from, and both Dick's novel and Scott's movie have on their own merits achieved 'classic' status in their respective media. Indeed, Scott's film has had such impact on awareness of Dick's novel that later printings have been retitled *Blade Runner*, and unless otherwise indicated, I use this title to refer both to Dick's novel and Scott's film.

The novel and the movie agree on the following: early in the twenty-first century (approximately 50 years from the novel's publication in 1968), there has been a nuclear war. That and the resulting nuclear winter have eliminated most animal life on Earth. Many of the surviving humans are emigrating to colonies elsewhere in the solar system, seeking 'a new life' where they are assisted by androids ('andys' in the novel, 'replicants' in the movie). These androids are not the tin-man robots of early science fiction, nor are they electronic computers; instead they are cyborgs, fusions of organic tissue and inorganic machine – simulated life. In the movie, this is emphasized in the death scene of the replicant Pris, in which her twitchy, toy-like death spasms contrast with the gore of her bullet wounds. Androids are technologically constructed organic beings, DNA-based, who closely resemble human beings, and who have quickly 'evolved' (as a result of design improvements and market demand) to a point where they are equal or superior to humans in intelligence and strength. They also pass Descartes's humanity test: 'I think, therefore I am,' Pris tells the human J. F. Sebastian in the movie. Later, the replicant Roy accuses the human Deckard of being irrational.

The newest android models, the Nexus–6, even have false memories built into them, giving them the illusion of having grown up and lived for many years as 'real' human beings. They may not even realize that they are not natural human beings. In the words of their human creator, they are 'more human than human'. (This phrase appears only in the movie, but it nicely summarizes the novel as well.) The main limitation of these synthetic human beings is that they have a lifespan of only four years, which may or may not be an inevitable result of the technology itself. Near the beginning of the movie, the police chief, Bryant, states that this feature was deliberately designed into the androids as a fail-safe control mechanism, implying that it is not necessary. Indeed, the controversial ending of the theatrical release version of the movie depends on the possibility that this limitation might be suspended. In contrast, there is no doubt of the inevitability of this 'accelerated decrepitude' in the novel, and instead in that story the androids' lack of empathy is their 'deliberately built-in defect'.[11]

The androids are treated as slaves in extraterrestrial colonies and are not permitted on Earth. They have no rights and are regarded as 'it', not 'him' or 'her', even though their bodies appear gendered. Because their bodies look like human ones (both internally and externally), detection of more advanced androids is possible only through tests of empathic response to hypothetical situations involving living organisms. A machine called the Voigt-Kampff Test detects the presence of the human 'group instinct' that is empathy, which the androids lack (*BR*, 26). However, as they have increased in sophistication, the newer androids have begun to develop human-like emotions, including the desire to live in freedom, as humans do, and they are also starting to fall in love with one another. As a result, there is some doubt as to whether the Voigt-Kampff device can successfully distinguish real human beings from Nexus–6 androids. Some of these androids escape and flee to Earth, where they are hunted down and 'retired' by police bounty hunters ('blade runners'). One of these hunters is Rick Deckard, who lives in San Francisco (Los Angeles in the movie) and who is assigned the task of retiring a group of escaped Nexus–6 androids. As he hunts the androids, Deckard comes increasingly to question his own humanity and to suspect that these androids actually are more human than he is. He also becomes attracted to an android woman, Rachael, and he begins to wonder if he might be an android, paradoxically, when he begins to feel empathy for the simulated humans that he is hunting.

One important difference between Dick's novel and Scott's movie lies in their respective treatments of religion. Like many of Dick's writings,

Do Androids Dream of Electronic Sheep? presents an extended medita-
tion on religion.[12] In the devastated post-nuclear world of this story, the
human survivors have become obsessed with Mercerism, a religion that
incorporates elements of Christianity and Buddhism. Mercerism advo-
cates the unity and sacredness of all living things. Although no organiza-
tional aspect of this religion is described, its adherents make regular use of
another electronic device, the 'Mercer box'. This machine both replays
sensations of the final moments of the religion's founder, Wilbur Mercer,
and stimulates the user's nervous system to produce a strong sense of
empathy. Mercer himself is a mysterious figure, who may have been an
ordinary human being, or possibly a radioactively mutated 'special', or
perhaps even a superhuman 'archetype' from the stars (*BR*, 20, 61). The
Mercer box artificially fuses the user's mind with Mercer's, and through
Mercer with everyone else who uses a Mercer box, and the user vicari-
ously experiences in her own body Mercer's physical sufferings and death.
This intense bodily experience can be shared with other humans, even
'specials', but androids are unable to experience it.

Near the end of the novel, it is revealed (by a popular television per-
former who is himself an android) that the Mercer images produced by the
boxes are fraudulent, staged simulations. 'Mercer' himself was an actor
who was filmed on a Hollywood stage set (*BR*, 182–4). The empathy that
the boxes generate has no real object. Despite this revelation, and as he is
about to destroy the final androids, Deckard has a vision of Wilbur Mercer
– one that does not involve a Mercer box – and he is compelled to go out
into the dangerously radioactive desert where he personally and physically
re-enacts Mercer's final moments. This experience brings Deckard to an
ambivalent peace and acceptance of his own general lack of empathy.
Although everything appears to be simulated – Deckard concludes that
'Mercer isn't a fake . . . unless reality is a fake' – nevertheless, 'everything
is true' (*BR*, 207, 201).

Thus in the novel, religion plays an important role in deconstructing
the opposition between 'natural' human being and 'artificial' android.
Through the empathy produced by the Mercer box, Mercerism emphasizes both the interdependence of all life and the radical difference
between living creatures, especially human beings, and non-living simulations – that is, androids. By celebrating the sufferings of living bodies,
Mercerite empathy contributes to the persecution and suffering of simulated living bodies. Nevertheless, and ironically, Mercerism is itself shown
to be an unnatural and probably fictitious construct – a simulated religion
built upon an artificially generated sense of empathy – which continues to
have very real effects, perhaps not unlike a gripping novel or movie – such
as *Blade Runner* itself!

In contrast to the novel, the movie makes no reference to Mercerism. Instead, it presents a highly secularized human world, in which the

supernatural appears only in the form of rare albeit highly symbolic events, in each of which the androids figure prominently. The two most important of these events appear near the end of the film. In the first, Roy Batty (Baty in the novel), the leader of the renegade androids, rides an elevator up the side of a Babel-like skyscraper/pyramid to confront Eldon Tyrell, the man whose corporation designed and manufactured him and his friends. 'It's not an easy thing to meet your maker,' Roy tells Tyrell, and then, Job-like, he presents his demand: 'I want more life, fucker.' Death is the problem, Roy says. Tyrell calls him 'the prodigal son', after which Roy admits that he has done 'questionable things' but insists that his deeds are 'nothing the god of biomechanics wouldn't let you in heaven for'. He confesses and is absolved by the god himself: '[y]ou were made as well as we could make you,' Tyrell tells him. Roy is acknowledged and simultaneously abandoned by his creator. In response, the android kisses and then kills his god, crushing the human's skull in his bare hands.

The second symbolic event occurs when Roy finally confronts Deckard. Roy is filled with very human grief over the death of the android woman, Pris, whom he loved and whom Deckard has just retired. 'Unless you're alive, you can't play,' Roy says bitterly. However, the last few seconds of Roy's own abbreviated life span are ticking away. He jams a large nail into his hand in order to keep his body from shutting down before he can kill Deckard. Surprisingly, he then saves Deckard's life, catching Deckard's falling body with his impaled hand, just as his own life finally breaks down. 'Maybe in those last moments he loved life more than he ever had before. Not just his life, anybody's life, my life,' says Deckard in voice-over (only in the theatrical release). As Roy expires, a dove that he had been holding flies up into the perpetually raining clouds just as they open briefly to let blue sky peep through. Roy's death becomes baptism, crucifixion and ascension (and Deckard's salvation) all at once.

These two episodes, with their heavy-handed religious imagery,[13] establish Roy as an android messiah, a warrior-king who fails to liberate his people, although his death makes a profound impression on his enemy (cf. Mark 15.39 par.). He is a rebel against the old god and the old covenant, with a body that is not human – a gnostic redeemer figure and Lucifer who makes war on 'the god of biomechanics' and on all of his human allies. Roy does not come to visit humanity on behalf of any god or to share any higher truth with us. Instead, he seeks escape from the hell of his slave's existence and entry into a more heavenly, albeit earthly, realm. He is both Christ and Satan at once – but he is also an android, and his final undoing is not Deckard's work but simply the expiration, like a clock running down, of mechanisms built into his artificial body four years earlier.

Through the intensity of passion that links the symbolism of Roy's murder of Tyrell to that of Roy's own death, Deckard comes face to face with his own lack of humanity, and he is redeemed through this revelation.

However, neither of these two scenes, or anything corresponding to them, appears in Dick's novel, in which Roy plays a less significant role.

The ending of the movie is less ambiguous than is that of the novel, and for this reason, some viewers prefer the director's cut version of the movie, which ends in greater ambiguity, although not as the novel does. This is partly because of the different roles played by religion (and by Deckard) in each of them. Through both the universality of Mercerism and the televised revelation that the religion is based on falsehood, the novel identifies Deckard as a symptom and representative of humanity as a whole. Although he is the central character of the story, he is not a particularly sympathetic one, thanks largely to his own lack of empathy. Dick's novel is itself a literary Mercer box, a test of the reader's empathy with Rick Deckard. In contrast, the movie focuses on Deckard as a unique individual – as evidenced by his feelings that emerge ('there it was again – feelings in myself,' in voice-over in the theatrical release) in regard first to Rachael and then to Roy – and the movie's symbolic events have no apparent universal implications. In the film, Deckard is a highly sympathetic character struggling to get by in a harsh, dehumanized world.

Despite important differences between the novel and the film, in both of them Deckard encounters the unexpected humanity of the simulacrum. His meeting with the synthetic messiah, whether android replicant or replicated Mercer, and his attraction to the female replicant, bring him to something like a crisis of faith, after which his life can no longer be the same. Deckard becomes fully human – indeed, posthuman – only when he recognizes his own android qualities, reflected in the artificial Other. Only the simulacrum can be 'more human than human'.

Neither Deckard nor the reader/viewer ever knows for certain whether he is truly human or android. However, both Dick's novel and Scott's movie contain versions of a remarkable scene in which the young woman, Rachael, discovers that she is an android, after she has been tested by Deckard. In Rachael's case, false memories implanted in her brain when she was manufactured had kept her from this awareness. Her new awareness disturbs her deeply; it is an apocalyptic moment (*BR*, 51–2).[14] Nevertheless, there is little positive content to the new knowledge that Rachael gains. Instead, everything that she already knows acquires a whole new set of meanings. Rachael's most intimate memories turn out to have been recordings of the experiences of a stranger, and her personal identity is not a natural product of years of growing up as a human being, as she had believed, but rather a construct implanted in a body that is much younger than it appears. Rachael's body is not a truly human body; it is artificial. It is not even *her* body, because she is now 'it', a 'skin job' with no rights and no possessions.

This crisis that both Deckard and Rachael go through is a kind of repentance. These episodes depict a realization that your deepest beliefs and values are mistaken and that the very fabric of reality itself is quite other than what you had previously thought. Something previously hidden has been revealed; it is the apocalyptic moment that was mentioned above. This is not repentance in the traditional 'biblical' sense. Neither Rachael nor Deckard feels any regret or remorse, although Deckard is increasingly resistant to the idea that androids are non-living, non-human objects. Nor does either of them experience conversion, in the sense of religious or even non-religious change from one world-view or lifestyle to another: there is no indication that either Deckard or Rachael has made such a change. Deckard remains a bounty hunter at the end of both novel and film, although his future in that line of work is unclear at best. This crisis is not a moment of conversion, but rather subversion, or perhaps even perversion.[15]

The less overtly theological sense of repentance as 'change of mind (or heart, or purpose)' comes closer to the experience depicted in *Blade Runner*, but even that is not enough. A better depiction appears in the central image of Jean-Paul Sartre's novel, *Nausea*. Nausea results when that novel's main character, Antoine Roquentin, makes a self-shattering discovery, after which his orientation toward life has been profoundly changed.[16] It is not a discovery of meaning, but rather of profound meaninglessness. This experience is the 'vertigo of the simulacrum'[17] in which modernist 'man' and the modernist world disintegrates. As Deckard's experience makes clear, the shock is not in the discovery that you are a simulacrum, but rather the discovery that *everything* is simulated and that none of the modernist oppositions works any more, and perhaps even that they have never worked.

This sort of paradox appears in many of Dick's stories. Discussions among the movie's fans about whether or not Deckard himself is a replicant miss this crucial point. Everything in the world of *Blade Runner* is fake, and yet everything is true. This is a far more stunning realization than the discovery that 'I am a replicant.' All of reality is a construct, although not in any sense that might be contrasted to some opposite, non-constructed thing. There is no non-simulacrum; nothing is natural. It is the realization that, as Hayles argues, we have always been posthuman.

Deckard's and Rachael's repentance is not 'biblical', but something rather like it does appear in the Gospel of Mark. At Mark 1.15, Jesus preaches 'the gospel of God': 'The time is fulfilled, and the kingdom of God is at hand; repent, and believe in the gospel' (RSV). 'Repent' in Mark 1.15 resonates with 'turn again' in 4.11–12: 'for those outside everything is in parables; so that they may indeed see but not perceive, and may indeed hear but not understand; lest they should turn again, and be forgiven'. Jesus quotes Isaiah 6.9–10, God's instruction to the prophet to speak in parables in order that the people will not 'understand with their hearts'.

The Gospel of Mark's 'repent' denotes a paradoxical disruption of understanding, or a disruptive understanding, apart from which there can be no belief in the gospel or recognition of the kingdom of God (see Text Box 8.2). Understanding might lead to turning, and thus to forgiveness, and Jesus rebukes his disciples in Mark 4.13 for their failure to understand the parables. This matter appears yet again in 8.17–18, where Jesus again criticizes the disciples: 'Do you not yet perceive or understand? Are your hearts hardened? Having eyes do you not see, and having ears do you not hear? And do you not remember?' Once more there is seeing without perceiving, and hearing without understanding, and understanding is opposed to hardened hearts and an inability to remember. Seeing and understanding lead to turning, that is, to hearts that are not hardened and to remembering (or in Rachael's case, un-remembering) – that is, to repentance.

Both Deckard and Rachael perceive and understand, and they turn away from what they had been thinking and doing before. As Gilles Deleuze says, 'the paradox is the force of the unconscious: it occurs always in the space between consciousnesses, contrary to good sense . . .'[18] The Greek verb translated as 'repent' in Mark 1.15 is *metanoeō*, which along with the noun, *metanoia*, plays an important role in the New Testament. Paradox as the space between (*meta*) consciousnesses (*nous*) is the place of *metanoia*. Repentance is 'contrary to good sense'.

The phrasing of Mark 1.15 is often read as though it were 'repent and then believe' or 'repent in order to believe'. However, this conjunction of terms suggests that repentance does not end when belief starts; they are not distinct events. In the Gospel of Mark, belief is not reassuring and comfortable; instead, it is the opposite: 'whoever loses his life for my sake

---

8.2 'Kingdom of God' and 'Son of Man'

In Mark 1.15, Jesus's call to repent brings into play the phrase, 'the kingdom of God'. However, in the Gospel of Mark the kingdom is not a locus of meaning but rather a disruptor of meaning, a 'secret' (see Mark 4.10–12). The kingdom is the subject of Jesus's parables, which have as their goal to keep people from understanding.

Like the rumours about Mercer, the son of man takes on two forms in Jesus's sayings. On one hand, the son of man is a supernatural being who will come in glory and power in the near future (Mark 8.38—9.1), like the one to whom an everlasting kingdom is given in Daniel 7.13–14 (where he is 'one *like* a son of man,' i.e. explicitly a simulacrum). On the other hand, the son of man is a human being who will suffer and die, but then rise up again (Mark 8.31). As in Mercerism, these two forms of the son of man oscillate in a cycle of death and resurrection.

and the gospel's will save it' (8.35). Belief recognizes the timeliness and the nearness of the mysterious kingdom, but in order to recognize the proximity of the kingdom, you must turn the world upside down and reverse the ground rules. Like the women at the tomb, you must be astonished – and nauseated! In other words, that which was clear and stable must become unclear and unstable, paradoxical.

It should be evident by now that reading the Gospel of Mark in juxtaposition to *Blade Runner* puts both texts in a rather different light. Mark becomes a paradoxical machine, not unlike a Mercer box or Voigt-Kampff device. The Mercer box and Voigt-Kampff Test provoke responses in connection with scraps of narrative, responses that reflect inner states of the user. These machines are non-human mirrors of humanity, and they provide evidence for judgement regarding the user's status as a human being. According to Mark's Jesus, his parables are semiotic machines, scraps of narrative that distinguish between insider disciples and 'those outside', who 'see but [do] not perceive, and may indeed hear but not understand' (4.11–12).

Indeed, the Gospel of Mark not only includes parables as part of its story about Jesus, but it itself appears to be a great parable, a semiotic machine to which readers respond either as insiders or outsiders. This opposition is deconstructed in the course of Mark's story, for outsiders sometimes understand Jesus (12.34) and insiders often do not. Understanding is always in jeopardy in the Gospel of Mark (7.18, 8.17), and therefore 'let the reader understand' (13.14). According to Mark, to believe in the gospel is before all else to read Mark's book and understand it – but whether this book itself can be understood is another matter. Mark's text both demands and resists understanding.

Indeed, the more you read this paradoxical text, the less you understand. Jesus says that only by losing your life can you save it (Mark 8.35). But if you lose your life in order to save it, then you have sought to save it – and therefore you will lose it. In order to save your life, you must not want to save it – but then your life is worthless to you (8.36–37), and why should you wish to save it? Likewise, if you repent in order to believe, then you have not truly repented. But once you have repented in the way that Rachael repents, there is no 'you' left to believe anything, or to be saved.

Both Rachael and Deckard are stunned by a violation of proper meaning. They give up what was most precious for something that was insignificant, and they become nauseated. The truth is inverted. The convictions that had previously made their lives meaningful are demolished. The only way they can continue to live is by abandoning their deepest beliefs and attitudes. This 'repentance' is not something that you make happen, but rather something that happens to you – as Deleuze says, 'the paradox . . . occurs'. Perhaps that is why repentance is conjoined to belief in Mark 1.15, for just as you cannot *choose* to believe – you can only choose to make believe – so you cannot choose to repent, not in this sense of the word. Repentance arises in lived paradox; it happens for no good reason. It cannot be explained or justified or controlled.

According to Mark's Jesus, if you repent, then you become a son of man. Readers often identify the son of man in the Gospels with Jesus himself, but in Mark this is not clear. In *Blade Runner*, the distinction between human being and android is progressively erased, and in the Gospel of Mark, the distinction between 'man' and 'son of man' is also erased. In Mark 3.28, the 'sons of men' are both plural and fallible (sinful and blasphemous), but they also appear to be the 'brother and sister and mother' of Jesus: that is, those who 'do the will of God' (3.34–35). In *Blade Runner*, Deckard and Rachael both 'repent' when they discover 'the kingdom of God' in the paradoxical (and nauseating) realization that 'reality is a fake' and yet 'everything is true'. The experience of these two sons of men leads to paradoxical salvation and bleak knowledge. They turn to the only god left after the death of God, the hyperreal saviour, Wilbur Mercer (in the novel), or the android messiah, Roy Batty (in the movie). For Rachael and Deckard, the kingdom of God is the new world of hyperreality and the simulacrum, a world beyond good and evil, and beyond the death of man.

The son of man in Jesus's sayings points beyond the death of man, and hyperreal humanity, or posthumanity, appears in this mysterious character. Like Rachael and Roy, the son of man replicates humanity. She is a simulacrum. Mark's Jesus is also a simulacrum. Indeed, all of the Jesuses of the New Testament – the four Jesuses of the Gospels, as well as the Jesuses of Paul and Revelation and the other writings – all of these Jesuses are simulacra. Nevertheless, no character in Mark's story experiences anything like the repentance of Rachael and Deckard in *Blade Runner*. Instead, that repentance is reserved for the Gospel of Mark's reader, whose empathic fusion (or lack thereof) is not with Jesus or any other specific character in the story, but with the one to whom the virtual Jesus says, 'repent, and believe in the gospel'.

Notes

1 N. Katherine Hayles, *How We Became Posthuman: Virtual Bodies in Cybernetics, Literature, and Informatics*, Chicago: University of Chicago Press, 1999, p. 239.

2 Roland Barthes, *The Rustle of Language*, trans. Richard Howard, Berkeley and Los Angeles: University of California Press, 1986, pp. 141–8.

3 Gilles Deleuze, *The Logic of Sense*, trans. Mark Lester and Charles Stivale, New York: Columbia University Press, 1990, p. 262, his emphases.

4 Jean Baudrillard, *Simulacra and Simulation*, trans. Sheila Faria Glaser, Ann Arbor: University of Michigan Press, 1994, p. 1; see also p. 123.

5 Friedrich Nietzsche, *The Gay Science*, trans. Walter Kaufmann, New York: Random House, 1974. See section 125.

6 Michel Foucault, *Language, Counter-Memory, Practice*, trans. Donald F. Bouchard and Sherry Simon, Ithaca, NY: Cornell University Press, 1977, p. 32.

7 Hayles, *Posthuman*, p. 291.

8 For detailed discussions and examples of cyberpunk, see Larry McCaffery (ed.), *Storming the Reality Studio*, Durham, NC: Duke University Press, 1991, and Hayles, *Posthuman* (especially chapters 7 and 10).

9 Fredric Jameson, *Postmodernism, or the Cultural Logic of Late Capitalism*, Durham, NC: Duke University Press, 1991, p. 282.

10 For information on the various movie versions, see Paul M. Sammon, *Future Noir: the Making of Blade Runner*, New York: Harper Collins, 1996, pp. 394–408. For detailed discussions of the making of the movie, see Sammon's book as well as Judith B. Kerman (ed.), *Retrofitting Blade Runner*, Bowling Green, OH: Bowling Green State University Popular Press, 1991, especially pp. 132–77. Two 'sequels' to *Blade Runner* were written by K. W. Jeter after Dick's death in 1982. These two novels are sequels to Scott's movie, *not* to Dick's novel, and they do not share the paradoxical features of either the novel or the movie.

11 Dick, *Blade Runner*, New York: Ballantine Books, 1982, pp. 173, 162. Hereafter cited in the text as *BR*.

12 On religion in Dick's writings, see Roland Boer, 'Non-Sense: *Total Recall*, Paul and the Possibility of Psychosis', in George Aichele and Richard Walsh (eds), *Screening Scripture: Intertextual Connections Between Scripture and Film*, Harrisburg, PA: Trinity Press International, 2002, pp. 120–54; Michel Desjardins, 'Retrofitting Gnosticism: Philip K. Dick and Christian Origins' in George Aichele and Tina Pippin (eds), *Violence, Utopia, and the Kingdom of God*, London: Routledge, 1998, pp. 122–33; and Hayles, *Posthuman*, pp. 160–91.

13 According to Scott Bukatman, *Blade Runner*, London: British Film Institute, 1997, the released dove is 'easily the most banal image in the film' (p. 85). Be that as it may, the dove image also suggests a gnostic Christ who abandons the crucified Jesus when he returns to the eternal realm.

14 In Dick's novel, it is revealed later that even this discovery may have been simulated by Rachael (*BR*, 174–5). In the movie, Rachael's discovery is a world-shattering revelation for her. Dick's fascination with ancient Gnosticism is well-known, and he could be described as a latter-day Gnostic. See Boer, 'Non-Sense', and Desjardins, 'Retrofitting Gnosticism'.

15 Deleuze, *The Logic of Sense*, pp. 127–33.

16 Jean-Paul Sartre, *Nausea*, trans. Lloyd Alexander, New York: New Directions, 1964, pp. 126–35.

17 Deleuze, *The Logic of Sense*, p. 262.

18 Deleuze, *The Logic of Sense*, p. 80.

Part 3

Case Studies – Genres

9. Why Film Noir is Good for the Mind

ERIC S. CHRISTIANSON

A young soldier, Mitchell, hides out in an all-night movie-house. His face occasionally lit by the screen, bewildered at the fact that he is being framed for murder and resigned to finding no way out, he shares his dilemma with his sergeant, Keeley:

> **Mitchell**: Keeley, what's happening? Has everything suddenly gone crazy? I don't mean just this, I mean everything. Or is it just me?
> **Keeley**: Ah, it's not just you. The snakes are loose. Anyone can get 'em. I get 'em myself, but they're friends of mine.

Like Mitchell, in Edward Dmytryk's film noir, *Crossfire* (1947), the shady characters who inhabit the dark corners and wet streets of noir are invariably troubled. And as the films themselves are played in retrospectives and (probably more often than we realize) on television, their gritty people with their hard-boiled words become even more deeply embedded nostalgic icons, signs for coping with the uncertainty of dangers long gone and yet strangely familiar. André Bazin captured it in his own eulogy to noir icon Humphrey Bogart, who was important because 'the *raison d'être* of his existence was in some sense to survive' and because the alcoholic lines visible on his face revealed 'the corpse on reprieve within each of us'.[1] Noir films are full of moments where the plot has become inconsequential (noir is famous for incomprehensible plots anyway) and the simple experience of disorientation, of ambiguity, is expressed with sublime poignancy. Such moments do not make for passive spectatorship, but engage viewers in a risky negotiation of meaning. As such, as I hope to show, they are good for the mind.

Film noir has become a concept of enormous proportions (see Text Box 9.1). My interest is in one of its particular core features: *ambiguity*. That is because *ambiguity* is more than a theme of noir. It is a lens through which characters struggle to make sense of the world, themselves and each other. It is an intellectual and spiritual *condition*, a stance of being in relation to others. Through all of the gaps and unanswered questions noir poses, viewers are engaged in an intellectually demanding process. I will argue that it is a process that resonates with some of the most provocative material of the Hebrew Bible.

9.1 What is 'Genre'?

In film criticism, 'genre' (from the French, meaning 'genus', 'kind' or 'family') is a term for categorizing films by type, arguing for distinctive features that mark off a film as belonging to a significantly represented group of films. The idea has its roots in the ancient literary criticism of Aristotle (*Poetics*) and Horace (*Ars Poetica*), and the seductive charm of its argument has never left the critical scene. What has changed, however, is that while early critics proposed genres with the same certainty they would a scientific genus, an observable biological 'truth', more recent critics have become increasingly less certain. They have recognized the importance of, for example, the reader's expectations, the vagaries of the production process and the historically conditioned nature of interpretation. All of these factors must now temper what we mean by 'genre'.

Criticism apart, most of us organize our thinking and talking about films along the lines of genre. Ask someone today what their favourite 'science-fiction' film is, or 'comedy' or 'gangster' movie and most will likely give an informed answer. Film reviewers often frame their reviews in terms of the accepted conventions of a certain genre, how a film defies or conforms to these. The ubiquity of 'genre' is partly due to Hollywood's romance with the genre film. Early cinema is littered with bio-pics (often based on the Bible), Westerns, melodramas, the gangster movie and the musical. The cynical reason is cash. When something works in Hollywood, you will see its type again. Whatever the case, 'genre' will no doubt remain not only a useful critical concept, but a way of talking about film for all of us. (Further, see 'Genre', p. 56.)

Ambiguity can manifest itself many ways in noir, and these instances are intriguing attempts at frustrating clear lines of meaning for viewers to pursue. They are achieved through visual style (unusual and unexpected camera angles with unconventional frame composition), narratorial judgement (that is, a lack of it), story gaps, and linguistic play.[2]

Ironically, to a large degree we have the censors to thank for the frequent appearance of the last item. To get around the injunctions against the depiction of sex and sexual intent imposed by the many censorial bodies of this highly regulated era, screenwriters invented whole new signifiers of innuendo. One of the best examples is the infamous 'race-horse' banter between Marlowe (Humphrey Bogart) and Vivien (Lauren Bacall) in *The Big Sleep* (1946). Marlowe suggests to Vivien that in order to 'rate her' he has to see her 'over a distance of ground' first. Otherwise, as he puts it, 'I don't know how far you can go.' Bacall replies with, 'A lot depends on who's in the saddle. Go ahead, Marlowe, I like the way you work.' (The censors were either bored or asleep.)[3] In early noir the hard-boiled hero was expert at the verbal spar. A fine example comes again

9.2 What is *Film Noir*?

- Critics often refer to the 'classic film noir' period as being inaugurated roughly with John Huston's *The Maltese Falcon* (1941) and ending roughly with Orson Welles's *Touch of Evil* (1958). However, there are clear forerunners of the genre as early as 1931, and most critics agree that its key themes have never left the cinema.

- The term 'film noir' was coined by French critics just after the second world war. Their discussion (and admiration) was prompted by the simultaneous group release in Paris in 1946 of *The Maltese Falcon* (1941), *Double Indemnity* (1944), *Laura* (1944), *Murder, My Sweet* (1944) and *The Lost Weekend* (1945). These films (the first four especially) would come to be regarded as proto-typical of an emerging category. For the French the term reflected a darkening of mood, subject matter and visual style.

- Although critics can differ significantly on what makes a film *noir*, there is considerable agreement regarding its core themes and stylistic devices, for example:
  - o The protagonist is caught in an often life-threatening dilemma, such as being framed for a crime, or seeking out a new life and being drawn unwillingly into his past. Protagonists are almost always men.
  - o It is a woman who often obstructs the man's desire for 'truth' or social progress, or facilitates his destruction (usually bringing about her own in the process): the so-called femme fatale.
  - o Noirs usually employ extreme contrasts between light and shadow (*chiaroscuro*), unusual camera angles, often in an urban landscape, typified by night time and rain – lots of rain.
  - o Noirs often have 'hard-boiled' dialogue, which has its literary roots in the likes of James M. Cain, Raymond Chandler, Graham Greene and Ernest Hemingway.
  - o Some critics suggest that noir is best defined by the wartime and post-war social anxiety it reflects, particularly its often deliberately confused approach to morality and sexual identity.

from the Bogart stable, from Sam Spade's first exchange with Kasper Gutman (Sydney Greenstreet) in John Houston's 1941 *The Maltese Falcon* (Gutman to Spade: 'I distrust a close-mouthed man. He generally picks the wrong time to talk and says the wrong things. Talking's something you can't do judiciously, unless you keep in practice. Now then, we'll talk if you like. I'll tell you right out, I'm a man who likes talking to a man who likes to talk' – and so on). Even by the simple invitation to be dazzled by verbal skill, the linguistic ambiguity of both characters frustrates lines of moral inquiry.

The *mise-en-scène* of most noir films contributes to the sense of uncertainty from the perspective of characters and, most effectively, of the audience. We are left in the unlit corners where darkness gathers. *Chiaroscuro*, the play between darkness and light, does not clarify morality, but renders it complex and problematical.[4] As is so well demonstrated in Orson Welles's *Touch of Evil* (1958), audiences are generally morally disempowered, not offered a secure vantage point from which to pass judgement. In *Touch of Evil* this extends to the cacophony of characters' voices, which seem simultaneously to vie for the audience's empathy. A sense of powerlessness pervades this Wellesian vision of Mexico. Indeed, throughout classic noir, modes of narration are tenuous linchpins for the viewer's grasp on competing claims to truth. This is pronounced in *The Killers* (1946), in which Edmund O'Brien's insurance investigator seeks to discover what 'Swede' (Burt Lancaster) meant when on his deathbed he pronounced, 'I did something wrong . . . once.' Nearly everyone in the film gets their chance to put forward their spin on Swede's life, everyone, that is, but Swede himself (his voice-over is filled with uncertainty). His fate has been commandeered by the subjective position of others and by overpowering circumstance. This is resignation on a grand scale. As such he is what Andrew Spicer terms the film's 'enigmatic absent centre'.[5] Key to the ambiguous and pervasive quest (usually for the truth about the past) so common to noir, the voice-over is widely commented on as a film noir innovation. Time shifts between the 'real' present and a much less stable remembered past. Some noir films invite us

> to inquire about the motives of narrative voices, how much they know and whether they are telling the truth, when and to whom they are speaking. If the dominant Hollywood style provided all the information spectators would need to follow the narrative, Film Noir seems to emphasize narrative gaps, and even the possibility of narratives that can deceive.[6]

The flashback structure engendered by this device also has the effect of alienating the viewer and producing a distinctly 'detached', almost semi-documentary style.[7] In such experimentations with classical modes of linear narration, in which gaps and ambiguities were minimized, the noir style succeeds in questioning our grasp of the past. Who, if anyone, has any control over the events leading to the predicament in which protagonists find themselves?

From its start the *terrain* of Jacques Tourneur's *Out of the Past* (1947) is clearly marked: the oblique past of Jeff Bailey (Robert Mitchum). It is not a place to which he wishes to return, but once he does he is gripped by a fatal and wistful nostalgia (clarified by Nicholas Musuraca's sumptuous, sparkling photography). In the opening sequence, Jeff is fishing, idly romancing his gal and running his own small business – he has made good. In noir, however, such a condition rarely lasts long. And so a snake slips into the garden in the form of Joe. Dressed in a black trench coat, Joe is a charmer who can barely conceal the threat of violence in his request for Jeff to return to his former mobster employer (Joe: 'The guy just wants to see you.' Jeff: 'When you put it that way, what can I do?' Joe: 'You know any other way to put it?'). We are inexorably drawn into the search for what brought Jeff to this confrontation as well as his motives. Immediately his self-potential (the simple life he has achieved) is under threat. In other words, as I will explore in more depth below, in noir the promised American dream is constantly under threat.

In Carol Reed's *The Third Man* it is Orson Welles's enigmatic Harry Lime who not only casts an enormous shadow by his mythic absence, but provides a flashpoint of ambiguity. Indeed the whole film becomes about how Harry's friends are to read who and what he has become, and it is precisely this issue that ultimately fractures the fragile love affair of Holly Martins (Joseph Cotten) and Harry's ex-sweetheart, Anna (Alida Valli). Habitually the potential lovers and Harry's nemesis, Major Calloway, return to the issue of how to assess him. It is Calloway who eventually forces Holly to come to a moral assessment of Lime. But because Anna remains sympathetically unpersuaded and oblivious to Harry's malevolent crimes, viewers are left to decide for themselves who and what Harry is and may even represent in themselves. The film also seeks to question what we do with our knowledge of the self once we get it. As James Naremore puts it, 'After Lime is gone, the film does nothing to assuage the sense of moral ambiguity he has created.'[8] (Further on *The Third Man*, see Chapter 7.)

In its visual and narrative modes, noir reflected a shift from certainty to uncertainty, with a new-found 'pronounced interest in the characters' "uncertain psychology"'.[9] Men in particular seem at odds about their place in the world. As such noir can be characterized 'by a certain anxiety over the existence and definition of masculinity and normality'.[10] There are few better examples of such uncertainty than the nameless man who (seems to) live in the apartment of 'tart-with-a-heart' Ginny (noir regular Gloria Grahame) in *Crossfire*. In pre-production the nameless man troubled the regulators at the Breen Office. The script suggests that Ginny is a prostitute and the man is her customer. Joseph Breen granted approval of the film on the condition (among others) that 'this man . . . should definitely be indicated as Ginny's divorced or separated husband who is trying to win her back'.[11] In the film, however, the man arrives when the haunted Mitchell is waiting there for Ginny at her invitation. The man asks 'You're wondering about this set up, aren't you?' He then spins one feasible scenario after another and calmly declares them each a lie. Naremore's comments are worth citing:

'I want to marry her,' he says to Mitchell at one point. 'Do you believe that? Well, that's a lie, too. I don't love her and I don't want to marry her. She makes good money there. You got any money on you?' By turns sinister, pathetic, and comic, he seems to mock the conventions of realist narrative, and as a result he opens his part of the story to all sorts of scandalous interpretation.[12]

Is he mad? Is he a defiant statement to Joseph Breen? Is he capable of believing anything? Does he function as a sign of a broader systemic uncertainty? At points he mentions he is a soldier, that he has 'gone to the war' (do we believe him?). His final words (spoken for the first time with anxiety) are 'I'm so restless. I don't know what I want to do.'

Strangely, *noir* brought some uncomfortable realities to the silver screen. I say strangely since, as many students of noir suggest, the cycle is one of the most subversive series of films to emerge from *mainstream* Hollywood. It is perhaps surprising, then, that from the conservative America of the 1940s and 1950s emerged a movement (of sorts) that would provide heroes for French intellectuals. Film noir had a long-recognized relationship to existentialism in Europe, and the influence was two-way. Some of the hard-boiled writers who provided the raw material for noir, such as Ernest Hemingway, Dashiel Hammett and Graham Greene, themselves brought, if not direct existential thinking, a critical awareness of relevant writers and thinkers. Many of the early noir directors were European immigrants who brought with them a distinctly sceptical and artistically expressionist sensibility. Also, post-war French intellectuals were totally enamoured with the film noir product. Unlike in the USA, where films would pass through local picture houses for a week or two and then disappear, in France batches of films would arrive and remain playing in cinemas for up to a year. Nino Frank, writing from Paris in 1946, describes the appeal:

> Here we are one year after a series of poor quality American movies made it seem that Hollywood was finished. Today another conclusion is needed, because the appearance of half a dozen fine works made in California compels us to write and affirm that American cinema is better than ever. Our film-makers are decidedly manic depressive.[13]

(It is interesting to note that in Paris the classical film noirs continue to get a fairly regular outing in the cinema circuit.) Ciné-clubs arose, settings where debate and discussion could be held at the end of a screening.[14] Some particular figures became heroes: Humphrey Bogart because of his tragic face; Raymond Chandler because he wrote with unflinching honesty of the human condition; director Nicholas Ray because he depicted 'moral solitude' so well.[15]

As A. MacIntyre suggests, 'stress on the extreme and the exceptional experience is common to all existentialism'.[16] It is the hero in some excessive and dangerous situation, caught in a trap not necessarily of their own making, that defines the noir protagonist. Sometimes sociological arguments are articulated in the films themselves (e.g. *Criss Cross*, *Gun Crazy*, *Try and Get Me*), and often there is a sense that evil is endemic, insidious and irretrievable, embedded in unchangeable systems that can entrap (e.g. *Force of Evil*, *Touch of Evil*). The noir hero sets themselves against such a fate, but rarely successfully. Where there is some success it is always tempered by ambiguity. So in the conclusion to *The Maltese Falcon*, when Sam Spade 'turns over' his lover, Brigid O'Shaughnessy, for killing his partner, he is doing the right and noble thing. But even in this case the ending is boldly cracked open when Spade expresses his insecurity over what it means to love a woman and also to avenge his partner.

Many noir heroes at some point resign themselves, in true Camusian style, to their fate. One of the finest examples of this is found in the opening of Robert Siodmak's marvellous noir, *The Killers*. Two professional killers arrive in a sleepy town to kill Swede. In establishing Swede's whereabouts they manage to bewilder and terrorize the two staff and customer of a small diner. When the customer runs ahead to warn Swede of his imminent execution he finds him lying on his bed, still and lifeless, [17] his face obscured by dark shadow, seemingly aware of his fate. The customer, who knows Swede, is unable to comprehend his apathy. As Swede is dispatched with grim efficiency, he remains motionless, and we see only his hand losing its grip on the bedpost. (This whole opening sequence is a remarkably faithful adaptation of Ernest Hemingway's short story of the same title from 1927.) As I have already mentioned, throughout the rest of *The Killers*, Swede's past is under constant interrogation from a range of perspectives. As Michael Mills suggests, the 'disjunctive use of time, the unrelated flashbacks, all combine to put us in the voyeuristic position of knowing not only what will become of him, but more importantly why'.[18] Walter Neff (Fred MacMurray) and Phyllis Dietrichson (Barbara Stanwyck) in *Double Indemnity* (1944) provide a similar picture. It always seemed to Neff that their perfect murder, their attempt to beat the system, would all fall apart. His walk became, as Neff's voiceover puts it, 'the walk of a dead man', imbued with a sense of dread. 'Straight down the line for both of us' is the couple's fatalistic catchphrase to each other.

In one of the first and most influential studies of noir, Raymond Borde and Étienne Chaumeton concluded that 'the moral ambivalence, the criminality, the complex contradictions in motives and events, all conspire to make the viewer co-experience the anguish and insecurity which are the true emotions of contemporary *film noir*'.[19] Indeed, their study recognized ambiguity as the core factor of characterization across noir types: victims, protagonists and femme fatales.[20] This overwhelming ambiguity frustrates our ultimate assessment and knowledge of a person. It is perfectly illustrated in the closing scene of what is widely regarded as the swan song of classic film noir, *Touch of Evil* (1958). Captains Quinlan (Orson

Welles) and Vargas (Charlton Heston), who have clashed with their opposing ethics of compromise and idealism respectively, have their final showdown. Quinlan is killed by Vargas, and as his body floats down the river, Tana (Marlene Dietrich), a gypsy who was Quinlan's enigmatic confidante, arrives and speaks to Schwartz, an officer on the scene:

> **Tana:** Isn't somebody going to come and take him away?
> **Schwartz:** Yeah, in just a few minutes. You really liked him, didn't you?
> **Tana:** The cop did . . . the one who killed him. He loved him.
> **Schwartz:** Well, Hank [Quinlan] was a great detective alright.
> **Tana:** And a lousy cop.
> **Schwartz:** Is that all you have to say for him?
> [*at this point a pause, as wistful cabinet piano music fades in and the camera lingers closely on Dietrich's luminous, world-weary face*]
> **Tana:** He was some kind of a man. What does it matter what you say about people?
> **Schwartz:** Goodbye Tana.
> **Tana:** Adiós.

In Nicholas Ray's *In a Lonely Place* (1952) the viewing experience begins quite comfortably from the perspective of Bogart's existentially struggling screenwriter, Dixon Steele. When a murder takes place and he is the prime suspect, our perspective is subtly and expertly nudged to that of his love interest, Gloria Grahame's Laurel Gray. The film is less about the murder and more about how we are to interpret this man's outer mask (the working title of the film was *Behind This Mask*) and his, as well as our own, capacity for violence. Steele refuses throughout to explain himself and his motives; he guards his inner life for all he is worth. (Parallels to the concurrent McCarthy trials are instructive.) Towards the second half of the film, Laurel's trust in Steele is tested to the limit when she witnesses him lose control in a confrontation with a young man, coming close to killing him. After the incident, in a moving sequence we see how she is able to help him to confront his inner demons and to find the beginning of his redemption. A fascinating defence of Steele (and of one of the main themes of existentialism, the primacy of a person's essence) comes from one of his best friends, his agent Mel. At the moment Laurel fears the worst about Steele, Mel comes to his defence:

> **Laurel:** Why can't he be like other people? Why?
> **Mel:** [*in disbelief*] Like other people? Would you have liked him? You knew he was dynamite. He has to explode sometimes . . . always violent . . . Why, it's as much a part of him as the colour of his eyes, the shape of his head. He's Dix Steele. And if you want him, you gotta take it all – the bad with the good.

Steele's relationship to Laurel is refreshingly against type. Through her eyes we are asked what kind of man Steele is. At the moment of the final denouement, Steele believes he is tantalizingly close to his own redemption, and his true history is left an open question until that point. 'Steele is a noir hero trapped in a compulsive role; caught, almost frozen, between the dark past and a bleak future, he is unable to see a continuum that valorizes the present except through Laurel.'[21] The film is remarkable for its immeasurably sad ending. The original script finished with Steele strangling Laurel to death in a final loss of self-control. After filming that version Ray rescinded and improvised a new ending on the spot. By this time Laurel's fear has defined her actions. She has told Dix she will go away with him but is planning instead to leave him. When the travel agent phones, Dix discovers her plans, becomes violent and begins to strangle her (and in the original, kills her). The phone rings again. He stops. He answers. It is the police. Dix is finally cleared and there is for a moment a hope for a new beginning. He hands the phone to her ('A man wants to apologize to you'). As she listens to the news ('Mr Steele's absolutely in the clear'), Dix begins despondently to walk away. Laurel speaks into the phone: 'Yesterday this would have meant so much to us, now it doesn't matter, it doesn't matter at all'. We then see, from Laurel's view, only Dix's back as he shuffles away and leaves the court of her apartments. She cites a line that was once their romantic refrain: 'I lived a few weeks while you loved me . . . Goodbye, Dix'. That ending takes us even closer to Dix's redemption without delivering it.

The power of the ending of *In a Lonely Place* resides in its unflinching portrayal of loss, namely of self-potential, infused with ambiguous motives and confused desires. In fact, this is one of noir's most outstanding and overwhelming themes: the systematic disenchantment with the façade of progress, of the possibility of 'making good', of finding something of lasting worth in America. Although it is there in the fatalist and 'social problem' films of the 1930s (e.g. *I Am a Fugitive from a Chain Gang*, 1932; *Fury*, 1936) and in a smattering of wartime films (e.g. *They Drive by Night*, 1940; *I Wake up Screaming*, 1941), it comes breathtakingly to the fore in post-war films (e.g. *Mildred Pierce*, 1945; *Scarlet Street*, 1945; *The Killers*, 1946; *Out of the Past*, 1947; *Force of Evil*, 1949; *Gun Crazy*, 1949; *Sunset Boulevard*, 1950; *Try and Get Me*, 1950; *In a Lonely Place*, 1952; *The Big Heat*, 1953), some of which also deal with the ex-soldier's sense of dislocation (e.g. *Crossfire*, 1947; *Act of Violence*, 1949). Notable from the above are Edward G. Robinson's Christopher Cross in *Scarlet Street*, Burt Lancaster's Swede in *The Killers*, Robert Mitchum's Jeff Bailey in *Out of the Past*, Frank Lovejoy's Howard Tyler in *Try and Get Me*, and William Holden's Joe Gillis in *Sunset Boulevard* (1950) – each of these show a nuanced side to the noir cycle, a development that creates, as Spicer says of *Out of the Past*, 'through the careful tonal shadings of its black-and-white cinematography, a melancholy romanticism that shifts noir's axis away from the toughness of Powell's Marlowe to the desolate fatalism of Mitchum's Bailey'.[22] In all of the above films the protagonist fails to find self-redemption. Each implies a desire for something better. In the case of *Try and Get Me*, the protagonist's loss of self-potential is expressed as an oppressive social structure that produces unachievable material objectives, and that is at least partly responsible for crime culture. After being villainized by the press, two petty thieves (Frank Lovejoy and Lloyd Bridges) are lynched in one of the most terrifying sequences in noir. It is made all the more frightening by its semi-documentary style and the fact that it is based on real events in California in the early 1930s. It is also a stinging indictment of the mass-media judgement of character that typified the McCarthy era.

In Fritz Lang's *Scarlet Street*, Edward G. Robinson's protagonist is an emblem of lost fulfilment. Cross is a bank clerk (note: every film generation has a symbolic 'loser' job) who wanted most of all to be a painter, and it is that skill that is exploited by an exceptionally nasty femme fatale (Joan Bennett), with the result that Cross can never lay claim to what he regards as the most redeeming aspect of his humanity. In fact, a series of films expressed a profound distrust of America's ability to produce an empowering socialist democracy. As Naremore puts it,

> The despairing tone of *The Prowler*, *Try and Get Me*, *Force of Evil*, *Gun Crazy*, *All the King's Men*, and *In a Lonely Place* is clearly related to the politics and historical circumstances of individual writers, directors, and stars. As Joseph Losey remarked in 1979, the Left in Hollywood was utterly demoralized by Truman, the atomic bomb, and the HUAC [House Un-American Activities Committee] investigations, and it was beginning to recognize 'the complete unreality of the American dream'.[23]

Whether or not noir was addressing a perceived social need for meta-narratives that acknowledge the moral complexity of the world, it is clear that its ringing endorsement of the sanctity and inviolability of human essence was *at least* directed against those exerting social control, against the univocal concerns of McCarthyism, which so many of the key noir-makers managed to defy.[24]

Noir spoke as well to other social realities. Its visual style took root in what the film industry itself termed the 'psychological thrillers' of the early 1940s and 1950s. Demographically the films appealed to a youth- and male-dominated post-war culture, an audience that 'no longer wanted opulent settings, "an exotic and make believe world", but films which allowed them to understand themselves and society'.[25] As Porfirio suggests, 'The atmosphere is one in which the familiar is fraught with danger and the existential tonalities of "fear" and "trembling" are not out of place; even less that sense of "dread" which is taken to mean a pervasive fear of something hauntingly indeterminate.'[26] Such a context makes sense of the failure of a now famous film that *framed* film noir within its fantastical borders. The noir world is perfectly captured in Frank Capra's *It's a Wonderful Life*. It is the potential world that George Bailey (James Stewart) is shown, on the presumption that he did not exist.[27] It has become lawless and is made up of dark street corners and seedy clubs patrolled by femme fatales. To Bailey, and implicitly the viewer, it is a nightmare world. *It's a Wonderful Life* did not perform well in 1946, a classic noir year that saw the release of *The Big Sleep, The Blue Dahlia, Gilda, The Killers, Notorious, The Postman Always Rings Twice* and *The Strange Love of Martha Ivers*. It was a time when audiences were already accustomed to hard-boiled detectives and dangerous alleyways in their film diet, and the world in which Bailey *did* exist had no bite, no resonance with the socially disorientating world post-war America was inhabiting. Just as noir is the antithesis of Capra's world, it is also of early Hollywood entertainment generally, and its protagonists of the mainstream hero figure. The 'ideal noir hero is the opposite of John Wayne. Psychologically he is passive, masochistic, morbidly curious; physically, he is "often mature, almost old, not very handsome. Humphrey Bogart is the type."'[28]

Recently some broad affinities of noir to Hebrew biblical literature have been recognized independently by three scholars. Cheryl Exum sees in Delilah the figure of the classic femme fatale. Audiences and film-makers in the 1940s and 1950s, she argues at length, generally demanded that the bad women of the cinema either be reformed or die. Neither happens to the Delilah of the Bible, but in retellings of her story she is either reformed (Milton's *Samson Agonistes*), knocked off or both (as in De Mille's 1949 film, *Samson and Delilah*).[29] Carol Newsom recognizes in the neo-noir film, *Fatal Attraction* (1987), the 'strange woman' of Proverbs 1—9:

> The 'strange woman', Alex, is portrayed as belonging to the margin in many ways . . . She has no husband or recognized lover. She stands outside the realm of socially ordered sexuality . . . Like the strange woman of Proverbs 7 she has a brilliant power of speech, always more than a match for her male victim . . . It is 'the wife of his youth' who must rescue him. The wife has been presented, as is the wife of Proverbs 5, as herself a deeply erotic, desirable woman . . . Her symbol is the house, where, more than once we see the brightly burning kitchen hearth.[30]

The most sustained theological dialogue with noir appears in Christopher Deacy's *Screen Christologies*. Starting by recognizing film as both a bearer and locus of religious meaning and reflection, Deacy develops the idea of film noir being particularly concerned with the *activity* of redemption. Films provide viewers the opportunity to examine the human condition as 'privileged witnesses'.[31] The eventual focus of the study, however, is the noir-ish films of Martin Scorsese. Early in his study Deacy develops an intriguing comparison of classic noir to the book of Ecclesiastes, suggesting that for Qoheleth (i.e. 'the Preacher' of Ecclesiastes) as in noir, there is little hope under the sun except for finding a way out through a transformation of everyday existence[32] – what Ecclesiastes would call enjoying all the days of your absurd life under the sun.

To his analysis I would add that particular existential themes have been identified in Ecclesiastes by a range of scholars (among whom I include myself), such as the experience of extreme circumstances and the judgement of the world as absurd. Perhaps most interestingly, however, Ecclesiastes presents a developed attempt at asking what the self is made of, and it does so through a disjunctive and radical use of first-person narrative – a melancholy investigation into the protagonist's past. Like Mitchum's Jeff Bailey, and other noir 'heroes', Qoheleth is brought tantalizingly close to his own redemption and finds it always beyond his reach. Finally, just as in noir, in Ecclesiastes' emphatic judgement of the absurdity of the world is implied a desire for something better.[33]

More can briefly be said regarding the shared themes of noir and the Hebrew Bible. In the same way that the noir world threatens the stability of the American dream, narratives like Judges and Samuel threaten the stability of Israel's covenantal relationship, and exposit the contingency of access to the promised land. The cycle of judges stories destabilizes the reader's ability to come to a positive assessment of Israel's relationship to the land because of the fundamental ambiguity of its stories: narrative gaps, lack of narratorial judgement and conflicting testimony all mean that we cannot know whether the judges experiment was ultimately good (further on which, see Chapter 12 in this volume, 'A Fistful of Shekels'). Also, the judges of Israel, even Gideon and Samson, deliver at the micro-level, specifically not the macro. That is, there is a resignation in the judges cycle to Israel's reliable rebellion and the consequent transient nature of deliverance 'for a time'. This social observation is present in noir. Describing Raymond Chandler's Philip Marlowe, Spicer suggests that unlike 'Sherlock Holmes, Marlowe realizes that although he may solve an individual case, it is part of a wider corruption that is too deep to be eradicated'.[34] And right to the end of the classic noir cycle, those who represent the law fail spectacularly. These are only outlines of what I am convinced is a fruitful area for reflection.[35]

In his absorbing study, *The Flight from Ambiguity*, Donald Levine suggests that ambiguity offers a positive model for reflection: 'it appears that to become aware of the multivocality of certain central concepts is not necessarily to identify a need to eliminate their ambiguities . . . The toleration of ambiguity can be productive if it is taken not as a warrant for sloppy thinking but as *an invitation to deal responsibly with issues of great complexity.*[36] (Of the Hebrew Bible, Levine suggests that its 'sparse detail has been a standing invitation for evocative interpretations'.[37]) Helpfully in relation to noir, Levine identifies an 'American aversion toward ambiguity'.[38] Citing a 'Nigerian novelist' who had lived in the USA for more than 20 years, he suggests that 'Americans tend to be direct and literal rather than allusive and figurative, stark rather than subtle. They are happier dealing with statistics than with nuances.'[39] Levine further points to tendencies in governmental policy towards the openness of information and privacy: 'Americans resent esoteric knowledge of any sort as symptomatic of "undemocratic" snobbishness.'[40] Levine traces the particularly extreme forms of American aversion to ambiguity to Puritanism, which 'discouraged aesthetic pleasures, including the enjoyment of ambiguous figures in repartee . . . Puritanism stressed the moral imperative of honesty . . . that came to be cherished to a remarkable degree in American society'.[41] Univocal and unambiguous discourse are to be aligned with human 'capabilities for gaining cognitive mastery of the world'.[42] Ambiguity answers 'the need for expressivity under a regime of . . . formal rationalities, and *the need to protect privacy in a world of extended central controls*'.[43] (This latter descriptive fits perfectly the noir response to censorial controls.)

To view film noir, and to read it carefully, is to engage with ambiguity borne not of 'sloppy thinking', but of rigour, tolerance of multivocality and willingness to question conventions and norms. It offers always *an invitation to deal responsibly with issues of great complexity.* Such valuable intellectual structures are produced within the ebb and flow of cultural ideas. As David Aaron comments in his recent study of the Hebrew Bible, *Biblical Ambiguities*,

> One generation's solutions to the unknown become another generation's source of uncertainty . . . The tolerance for uncertainty constantly shifts with an era's preferences. There is no progression from concrete to abstract, literal to metaphorical, plurality of meaning to singularity of meaning. All of these are natural by-products of the human struggle to make sense.[44]

'Movements' like noir, or indeed the texts of the Bible that are counterconventional, cannot be manufactured. As is widely recognized, the makers of noir had no cognizance of a 'genre', of the term 'film noir', yet alone a series of films to be practically venerated in years to come (Robert Mitchum: 'Hell, we didn't know what film noir was in those days. Cary Grant and all the big stars got all the lights. We lit our sets with cigarette butts').[45] Yet within the discourse of film viewing and study, film noir has become a critical idea greater than the sum of its parts. It was a luminous and influential moment of cinematic defiance (and sadly for those who fell victim to McCarthyism, one coupled with resignation and personal loss), and thankfully it continues to exercise the mind.

Notes

1 As cited in James Naremore, *More Than Night: Film Noir in Its Contexts*, Berkeley: University of California Press, 1998, p. 25.

2 It is worth noting here that noir films do not generally exhibit a radical ambiguity or nihilism. They are stable texts. But they make use of fixed meanings and conventions in order to disorient and to question. Noir's ambiguity as I am discussing it cannot (did not) function outside of a mainstream and conventional sign system. Compare Robert Porfirio: 'What keeps the *film noir* alive for us today is something more than a spurious nostalgia. It is the underlying mood of pessimism which undercuts any attempted happy endings and prevents the films from being the typical Hollywood escapist fare many were originally intended to be' ('No Way Out: Existential Motifs in the *Film Noir*', in A. Silver and J. Ursini (eds), *Film Noir Reader*, New York: Limelight Editions, 1996, pp. 77–93 (80)).

3 Apparently the scene was filmed almost a year after the rest of the film, in order to capitalize on the sexual chemistry between Bogart and Bacall that had made *To Have and Have Not* (1944) so popular.

4 Compare Paul Schrader: '*film noir*'s techniques emphasize loss, nostalgia, lack of clear priorities, insecurity; then submerge these self-doubts in mannerism and style' ('Notes on *Film Noir*', in Silver and Ursini (eds), *Film Noir Reader*, pp. 53–63 (58)).

5 Andrew Spicer, *Film Noir*, Inside Film; Harlow: Longman, 2002, p. 78.

6 Michael Mills, 'Narrative Innovations in Film Noir' (http://www.modern times.com/palace/inv_noir.htm; accessed April 2003).

7 So Robert Porfirio, '*The Killers*: Expressiveness of Sound and Image in *Film Noir*', in A. Silver and J. Ursini (eds), *Film Noir Reader 2*, New York: Limelight Editions, 1999, pp. 177–87 (179).

8 Naremore, *More Than Night*, p. 80.

9 Spicer, *Film Noir*, p. 2.

10 Richard Dyer, 'Resistance through Charisma: Rita Hayworth and *Gilda*', in E. Ann Kaplan (ed.), *Women in Film Noir*, new edn; London: BFI, 1998, pp. 115–29 (115).

11 Cited in Naremore, *More Than Night*, p. 117.

12 Naremore, *More Than Night*, p. 119.

13 Nino Frank, 'A New Kind of Police Drama: The Criminal Adventure' (trans. by A. Silver), in Silver and Ursini (eds), *Film Noir Reader 2*, pp. 15–19 (15).

14 Naremore, *More Than Night*, pp. 13–15.

15 Naremore, *More Than Night*, pp. 21–6.

16 'Existentialism', in P. Edwards (ed.), *The Encyclopedia of Philosophy*, Macmillan, 1967, III, pp. 147–59 (149).

17 Here, as in his other noir films, Lancaster 'kept his energy levels under rigid control, rarely extending himself and then only to withdraw quickly like a hunted animal' (Porfirio, 'No Way Out', p. 85).

18 Michael Mills, 'Two from Siodmak: The Killers, Criss Cross' (http://www.moderntimes.com/palace/kc.htm; accessed April 2003).

19 'Towards a Definition of *Film Noir*', in Silver and Ursini (eds), *Film Noir Reader*, pp. 17–25 (25).

20 'Towards a Definition of *Film Noir*', p. 22.

21 Julie Kirgo and Alain Silver, 'In a Lonely Place (1950)', in A. Silver and E. Ward (eds), *Film Noir: An Encyclopedic Reference to the American Style*, rev. 3rd edn; Woodstock, NY: The Overlook Press, 1992, pp. 144–6 (146).

22 Spicer, *Film Noir*, p. 56.

23 Naremore, *More Than Night*, p. 130.

24 For an incisive account of the most politically and philosophically articulate maker of noir, Abraham Polonsky (writer *Body and Soul*, writer and dir. *Force of Evil*), and of the cultural climate of the McCarthy era, see P. Buhle and Dave Wagner, *A Very Dangerous Citizen: Abraham Lincoln Polonsky and the Hollywood Left*, Berkeley: University of California Press, 2001. Most of the Hollywood Ten who stood against HUAC were involved in producing noir.

25 Spicer, *Film Noir*, p. 41 (citing R. Sklar).

26 'No Way Out', p. 92.

27 See Christopher Deacy, *Screen Christologies: Redemption and the Medium of Film*, University of Wales Press, 2001, pp. 28–9.

28 Naremore, *More Than Night*, p. 20 (citing Borde and Chaumeton).

29 J. C. Exum, *Plotted, Shot and Painted: Cultural Representations of Biblical Women*, Sheffield: Sheffield Academic Press, 1996, pp. 204–37.

30 'Women and the Discourse of Patriarchal Wisdom: A Study of Proverbs 1–9', in P. L. Day (ed.), *Gender and Difference in Ancient Israel*, Minneapolis: Fortress Press, 1989, pp. 142–60 (157–8).

31 Deacy, *Screen Christologies*, p. 18 (with reference to Paul Gallagher). See also pp. 13–15, 21–3.

32 Deacy, *Screen Christologies*, pp. 59–64.

33 The existential themes of Qoheleth are explored in Eric S. Christianson, *A Time to Tell: Narrative Strategies in Ecclesiastes*, Sheffield: Sheffield Academic Press, 1998, pp. 259–74.

34 Spicer, *Film Noir*, p. 7.

35 I will be further developing the biblical comparisons in an article: 'The Big Sleep: Strategic Ambiguity in Judges 4–5 and in Film Noir', in D. Shepherd (ed.), *That We May See and Believe* (Semeia Studies, SBL, forthcoming).

36 Donald N. Levine, *The Flight from Ambiguity: Essays in Social and Cultural Theory*, Chicago: University of Chicago Press, 1985, p. 17 (my italics).

37 Levine, *Flight from Ambiguity*, p. 24.

38 Levine, *Flight from Ambiguity*, p. 31.

39 Levine, *Flight from Ambiguity*, p. 28.

40 Levine, *Flight from Ambiguity*, p. 33.

41 Levine, *Flight from Ambiguity*, p. 37.

42 Levine, *Flight from Ambiguity*, p. 39.

43 Levine, *Flight from Ambiguity*, p. 40, my italics.

44 David H. Aaron, *Biblical Ambiguities: Metaphor, Semantics and Divine Imagery*, Leiden: Brill, 2001, p. 199.

45 Cited in Arthur Lyons, *Death on the Cheap: The Lost B Movies of Film Noir*, New York: Da Capo Press, 2000, p. 2.

10. Speaking of God and Donald Duck: Realism, Non-Realism and Animation

ROBERT POPE

The inspiration for the title of this chapter comes from a passage in a book by Don Cupitt. Perhaps the best known of British non-realists, Cupitt's case is that the category 'God' can be profitably employed in order to ensure the living of an ethical life, but to believe that we have knowledge of God, and even that we have language adequate to describe God, belittles God and makes him part of the world of experience. Instead of this, 'God' is merely a linguistic sign that personifies the 'religious requirement'. In other words, 'God' may or may not be real. What matters is whether or not our views of God help us in the business of living. Perhaps more accurately, then, he suggests that 'God' only has reality as a 'sign', and he uses the cartoon character Donald Duck to explain this.

> Each and every Donald Duck image published by the Disney Studios really *is* Donald Duck himself; there is no superior original. Donald Duck is a vivid character to millions, maybe billions, but he simply doesn't need to have any existence outside his own iconography. It would be a pedantic mistake to try to establish the existence of a real Donald Duck independent of the standard image, and then to investigate whether the standard Donald Duck image is in fact an accurate likeness. No, the vitality and cultural influence of Donald Duck does not depend at all on any such question. It depends entirely on the vitality of his image and the way it behaves. And because signs are infinitely multi-pliable, and each of them is the real thing, Donald Duck can be omnipresent.[1]

As in most of his work, Cupitt's point is patently clear: human beings cannot really know ultimate reality. God, in the way we understand the term, is no more than a projection, a human construction in the same way as human beings draw cartoon characters. We cannot know whether or not those constructions correspond with a reality. Of course, Cupitt's approach may be flawed simply because it *could* be the case that our conceptions of God, however incomplete and faltering, in fact correspond with an actual reality. Furthermore, he may be right in suggesting that we cannot prove the validity of the correspondence, though that, in itself, does not disprove it. What he seems to be saying is that this does not in the end matter. What matters is whether or not our ideas of God are sufficiently real to have the kind of effect on human beings that is desirable, namely that they will then act in appropriate ways towards each other and towards their environment.

Cupitt's point is not that Donald Duck is as real as God (or vice versa), but that the iconography surrounding our use of the word God is the same kind of human construction that surrounds the cartoon character. In the same way that all that matters about the cartoon character is the image being watched, rather than any archetype, so all that matters about God is what we have to say about him, rather than knowing accurately the reality of God's nature or, indeed, whether or not God exists. It seems, quite plainly, to be an apologia for the Kantian distinction between appearance and reality: all we know is the appearance, the phenomenal. We cannot know the real and noumenal. Our purpose, then, is to live meaningfully in the phenomenal realm of appearances. We do not need to know the extent to which the appearance corresponds to the reality. And one tool that helps us to live meaningfully is myth. 'Myth consists of stories that provide human communities with grounding prototypes, models for life, reports of foundational realities, and dramatic presentations of fundamental values: myth reveals a culture's bedrock assumptions and aspirations.'[2] In other words, myths are stories created by human beings in order to give meaning to their lives.

There is much here that resonates with the recent interest in the theological interpretation of film. Just as the reference in the quotation is to Donald Duck, we could now claim that animation as well as film should be the subject of theological reflection for it, too, gives expression to modern myths. Three questions are raised in this chapter. First, what kind of justification is there for interpreting film theologically? Second, to what extent are films which employ animation able to provide us with material to do theology? Third, is it 'realism' or 'non-realism' which provides the philosophical background to make such interpretations possible?

1. The Theological Interpretation of Film

The theological tradition in the West during the nineteenth and twentieth centuries developed in such a way as to accommodate the development of cinema and its interpretation as a means of conveying value and of experiencing transcendence. The priority of human experience and ability to reason, finding their modern roots in Schleiermacher and Hegel respectively, have opened the way to seeing all experience and all human musings as potentially revealing connection with the divine. Paul Tillich's insistence that the revelation of God was 'one moment of great beauty' but that it has imbued all subsequent moments with potentially revelatory beauty, has resulted in a more open approach to culture both as a means for God and reality to be revealed and as a means for human creativity to be seen as analogous to God's creativity because it reflects the all-pervasive consequences of creation in *imago Dei*. The presence of a religious dimension means that everything can be explained in religious terms.[3] H. Richard Niebuhr is often appealed to[4] with his fivefold categorization of Christ against culture, Christ in paradox with culture, Christ the transformer of culture, Christ above culture and the Christ of culture.[5] To interpret film theologically it seems that a 'Christ of culture' model must be employed,[6] for it appears to confirm the existence, importance and significance of the spiritual within a cultural context that has become secularized. It is a way of appealing to, and tapping into, today's fascination with spirituality – a deliberately loose and slippery term which at best recognizes that human beings have an inherent yearning for the other, for reality, for transcendence or for God, a yearning immortalized by Augustine in his confession that 'you have made us for yourself, and our heart is restless until it rests in you'.[7] At worst, it reflects the attempt to find meaning in anything now that traditional sources and forms have been discarded. As a means of conveying meaning and value, film is supported, theologically, by all these movements and can be seen in either a negative or positive light. At the very least it may be a useful tool in order to begin a debate on value and principles in a postmodern culture that has abandoned consensus and, as a result, is in danger of moral disintegration.[8]

Alongside theological developments, the twentieth century witnessed several shifts in social value within Western culture. One factor in this was the almost spectacular decline in religious observance in Britain and Europe,[9] but there were others too. For a time at least, people found value in politics through their commitment to socialist theory in the Labour Movement or capitalist ideology in Thatcherite Britain. Harold Wilson's somewhat contemptuous dismissal of political dogma as 'theology' helped neither the retention of particular values in politics nor the cause of the theologian to be taken seriously in the modern world. Value in politics has been replaced with pragmatism and expediency. This element has always been present, and necessary, as political ideal met empirical reality, but appears now to have taken the primary role in a political system in which parties strive to be electable and create the kind of image necessary to be so elected without necessarily providing the requisite substance once power has been achieved. At one time, value could be found in the workplace where ideals of industry, honesty and reliability were exalted as of utmost importance. Changes in working patterns have seen it displaced here too, the victim partly of an all-pervading individualism and partly of job insecurity. One place that is left for value to be affirmed is in leisure and this is where the cinema and television both become important. It is through the secular imagery of the soap opera, the period drama, the mini-series, the sitcom or the feature film that meaning and value are now conveyed. It is they that provide the raw material or the basic narratives for our conversation and the moral dilemmas through which people decide what is, and what is not, an acceptable lifestyle. The effect is that meaning and value are dissociated from specifically religious sources.

If the television and the cinema have played a part in this development, then what is of vital significance is that they provoke a discussion of value and meaning through fictional images that are mobile and not static. The image does not wait for a final analysis but has moved on almost before the interpretation can be completed. In one sense, this has created the sound-bite generation. Substance has had to be sacrificed in favour of effect.[10] But, in another sense, the communication of meaning through a moving image opens the way for endless interpretations. When an image is static, it has certain boundaries; when it is moving a whole new dimension is added to what is being observed. When this is considered alongside the fact that film thrives on illusion and appeals primarily to the world of the imagination, it can be seen what a complex means of conveying information it really is. Mircea Eliade called the cinema a 'dream factory' simply because of the way its imagery appeals to the imagination,[11] concentrating as it does on localizing the eternal battle between good and evil by allowing the audience to personalize abstract concepts and condense them into the characters of the hero and the villain and thence to empathize and identify with them. In this way, films allow the viewer to transcend his or her own life and context and experience the 'other'.[12] The sense of otherness is heightened through the use of excess. Films appeal simply by releasing their audiences, even fleetingly, from the restrictions placed on their lives. They enable them, through imagination and appearance, to fly, to kill, to have perfect and frequent sex; they thrill, excite and move before ending and sending them back out into the real world. In so doing they enable people to experience a certain transcendence, the feeling that there is something beyond the confines of the self as we empathize with, and almost live the life of, the character portrayed on the screen.

If it is the case that the cinematic experience is one of transcendence, this transcendence is more the recognition of human need than a response to contact with the divine. It may be a transcendence of the self, of personal limitations, and the fleeting, imaginative experience of 'the other' who is liberated from the limitations under which the audience still live. But is this really an encounter with the 'wholly other' as some would claim?[13] More importantly, is it only the *appearance* of the real or the noumenal that religious encounter and experience have usually been held to be? We see here, in a sense, an appeal to non-realist thinking.

Transcendence is achieved not through contemplating higher things, not through contact with God and not through the ritual of, and divine presence in, the Eucharist, but through imagining that the bounds of human capability can be crossed. Meaning is created and located within humanity as myths are heard, watched and responded to by human beings. Films convey meaning through the creation of atmosphere where the audience is led to anticipate activity which fulfils, if not also surpasses, human potential. Horizons are broadened and even challenged as the story is worked out and human capability is glorified. Through such portrayals, an audience confronts otherness with all its potential to transcend the present, the historical and the contingent. It expands the imagination and thus creates an expanded world-view.[14]

If film is a means of representing (re-presenting) what is real in such a way that it appeals to the imagination, then it follows that, however much subject to interpretation, it reflects something of ourselves, of human achievement and aspiration. It offers meaning by allowing us to see familiar images, whose very familiarity opens up a range of interpretation and construes meaning for the viewer. But in the end it claims that meaning belongs not in the noumenal realm but in the phenomenal realm for, imagined or otherwise, it is meaning through visual *appearance* that is conveyed.

2. Animation

If film appeals to the imagination and achieves its goals through illusion, then animation (see Text Box 10.1) appeals by its very unreality. It is this that allows for particularly imaginative, indeed, fantastical, interpretations of reality to flourish. It releases its audiences into a fairy-tale, make-believe world where the usual laws of cause and effect are reinterpreted or suspended. Even if Sylvester catches Tweety Pie, or Tom catches Jerry, we are secure in the knowledge that the bird and mouse will not suffer the same fate as those caught by cats in our own back gardens, while the retribution invariably meted out on the cats is nothing but a momentary setback for them despite its apparent severity. Wil E. Coyote can plummet down ravines or be caught and blown up in his own traps, but will still return to resume his quest to stop the Road Runner. In animation, animals talk to each other, they walk around on their hind legs as human beings, they can attack with a tremendous force of violence but never expire. It is pure escapism.

Other animated programmes are more sophisticated and can be 'read' at different levels. At one level, Bart Simpson is the paragon of the all-American mischievous schoolboy, but retains an endearing innocence and naivety which seems always to come good in the end. On another, the whole programme is a highly perceptive comment on modern society, exposing the emptiness of postmodern life, which is void of meaning save the disvalues of hedonism and acquisition. However, it never becomes merely cynical, and retains hope through maintaining a semblance of the ideal of family life, behind which lies the absolute certainty of the existence of a benevolent God whose demands on human beings relate primarily to the way in which they love their neighbour.[15] A similar message

---

10.1 Animation – Some Landmarks

- Animation can be defined as 'the technique of filming successive drawings or positions of models to create an illusion of movement when the film is shown as a sequence' (*Oxford English Reference Dictionary*).

- The advent of celluloid in 1913 heralded the rapid development of animation. Because several levels of celluloid can be superimposed on to each other, the repeated drawing of background scenery became unnecessary, thus quickening the production of a cartoon.

- Pioneers of animation include the American Winsor McCay whose *Gertie the Dinosaur* (1914) was a landmark in the history of animation and whose *Sinking of the Lusitania* (1918) is generally regarded to be the first animated feature film.

- For McCay, animation was the task of a single artist drawing all the scenes, sometimes taking up to a year to produce a single film. Soon, animation studios emerged with groups of artists all working on the same film. The result was the emergence of cartoon series with popular characters, *Felix the Cat* (1919) being an early example.

- Sound was first added to animated films by Walt Disney in *Steamboat Willie* (1928). It was Disney, too, who produced the first full-length animated film, *Snow White and the Seven Dwarfs* (1937).

- Technological advances have meant that computer enhanced graphics and special effects are now common in all genres of film, such as the recent *Matrix* and *Lord of the Rings* trilogies.

- The first full-length computer animated film was *Toy Story*, produced in 1995 by Walt Disney and Pixar Animation Studios.

- This and further information can be found at www.digitalmediafix. com/Features/animationhistory.html and www.fi.edu/fellows/fellow5/May99/History/history.html

was conveyed by the far more controversial, and less stylized cartoon, *God, the Devil and Bob*, where God seeks evidence that humankind is worth saving and allows the Devil to choose who, among the sons of men, is to be the saviour.[16] The chosen one, Bob Alman ('all men', 'everyman'?), 'drinks, swears and downloads porn off the internet'. He is told that he knows what he must do in order to show humankind's value but unwittingly 'saves' humanity by taking time to talk to his daughter. The message is by and large the same as in *The Simpsons*: be good to each other. With no doctrine or devotion, and with a rather mechanical view of grace, this seems to be the sum of the religious life. *South Park*, on the other hand, plummets to the depths of cynicism in order to appeal in a postmodern age in which the lack of value is the only value worth upholding. Despite their unrealism – they are, after all, cartoons – all three clearly present a particular message and all three provoked a reaction in their audience, whether negative or favourable.

Like all films, animation works best when it tells a story and catches the imagination of the viewer. After seeing *Beauty and the Beast* (1991), the film critic Roger Ebert wrote: 'Watching the movie, I found myself caught up in a direct and joyous way. I wasn't reviewing an "animated film", I was being told a story, I was hearing terrific music, and I was having fun.'[17] It is in this way that 'having fun' relates to unrealism which allows meaning. In animation, realism does not matter. Its very non-realism (or even unrealism) is appealing because people cannot fail to realize that it really is not real, even when its characters are endearing and able to provoke an emotional response, that is, even when the audience cares about what is going to happen. It is in this juxtaposition of recognized unreality and being moved to care that meaning is conveyed, however subtly and subconsciously, by animated film. This can be seen, to some extent, in the following brief descriptions of five animated films: *Chicken Run* (2000), *Toy Story* (1995) and *Toy Story 2* (1999), *Antz* (1998) and *A Bug's Life* (1998).

Chicken Run

At all levels, this is a film about liberation. It is, in fact, a spoof prisoner-of-war film where captured allied soldiers are replaced with chickens but the barbed wire fences, rigid military regime and periods in the cooler for failed escapees are all present, as are several echoes of classic scenes from *The Great Escape* (1963). All this is given a contemporary twist with the heroine, a chicken called Ginger, exclaiming in exasperation, 'It's not the fences around the farm that keep us here; it's the fences around your brains.' The saviour comes in the figure of Rocky the Rhode Island Rooster who is catapulted into the chicken coop from the beyond giving the impression that he can fly. The chickens hope to learn to fly to freedom under Rocky's tutelage, only to have their hopes dashed when he deserts the rest of the group. The climax is a bid for freedom through the construction of an aeroplane to fly out to reach the paradise beyond the fence.

This film can be interpreted on various levels. The idea of coming from beyond with the promise of redemption is a classic characteristic of the 'Christ-figure',[18] though in this case hopes of redemption are dashed when Rocky proves to be something of a charlatan. This, of course, pushes the analogy further than it really ought to go if we are to regard an animated chicken as a 'Christ-figure': to push it thus would serve only to demonstrate either the banality of the category itself or the desperation of theologians to find connections with modern culture. Perhaps the film's subliminal message is that liberation is accomplished by a state of mind. Freedom can be achieved when people are prepared to work for it, working out their own salvation as it were. The 'Christ-figure' (if indeed we are willing to associate it with a chicken) is seen to be a decoy, even if he comes good in the end. The main character, Ginger, shows a remarkable solidarity with the rest of the roost: she does not desert her fellows but shares with them her vision of the freedom available beyond the fence and by so doing encourages them all to share in it. She refuses her own liberation without the rest, and is even prepared on occasion to forgo her vision and to stay with the rest of the chickens if necessary.[19]

All this takes place in the context of unrealism. These are, after all, (admittedly stylized) chickens attempting to escape from their (admittedly stylized) chicken coop. Mr Tweedy, the chicken farmer, has his suspicions, but is dissuaded from them by his superbly overbearing and ambitious wife because it is all in his head. 'The chickens are revolting,' he exclaims. 'Finally something we can agree on,' she responds. Perhaps the unrealism of it all is underlined by Fowler, the camp rooster who continually harps on about his RAF days, in which, it turns out, he was a mascot and not a fighter pilot. This continuous harping leads Ginger to pin her hopes on Fowler to fly the aeroplane to freedom, and his admission, right at the end of the film, that he cannot fly it because he is a chicken, is a moment of comic genius. We have been persuaded by then that chickens really can do anything, only to be derided and chided for our stupidity by the rooster himself.

Chickens cannot work for their liberation, but humans can. They are driven towards freedom by the vision of a future paradise and must not be distracted by the invasion of the outsider. The film shows the broadening of horizons for the chickens which, with perseverance, they can achieve. Ultimately, even the recognition that they are helpless chickens does not hinder them from achieving their goal.

Toy Story *and* Toy Story 2

The original *Toy Story* film was a story of belonging and of growing up. All the toys belong to Andy, though his favourite is Woody, a sheriff doll. While this situation prevails, Woody, as the favoured toy, is prepared to declare that it does not matter how much they are played with: they must simply 'be there' when Andy needs them. Such is life, until the arrival of a new toy. Apparently the latest word in sophistication, the arrival of Buzz Lightyear, a space ranger, causes jealousy and rivalry to foment between him and Woody. The story sees the toys 'grow up' as Buzz Lightyear learns that he is not a space ranger on a mission to save the universe from the evil Emperor Zurg, but a toy. The revelation is devastating and it comes while he is trapped, with Woody, next door in Sid's bedroom – Sid being a boy who delights in deforming toys and thus represents the forces of evil! Buzz has to come through the angst he feels at this discovery in order to co-operate with Woody to find their way back to Andy's bedroom before Andy moves house.

This is not a film about toys as such but about children. They have to work out their relationships, to learn how to get on with one another, and find eventually that they come to need and even like each other. The message has to do with growing up and maturing, of giving people a chance and of working at relationships. It is Woody who has to reach the point of realizing that he cannot get back to Andy's room without Buzz, even if Buzz is just a toy and not a space ranger. It is a story that recognizes that growing up means leaving fantasies behind in order to cope with the real world. But its message is also that the real world requires people to get on with one another, to help each other and even to grow to like each other. Even when devoid of fantasy, it suggests that such a real world would not be such a bad place after all.

Toy Story 2 takes the story further, showing that the toys have, to an extent, 'grown up'. When on a mission to save a discarded toy from a yard sale, Woody, by accident, gets picked up by a collector. He then discovers that his character was the star in a children's television series. The toy collector has all the other merchandise and, with Woody, his set is now complete. His intention is to sell the collection to a Japanese museum. The other toys set out to rescue Woody and we see themes such as loyalty on the part of the other toys; the challenge to Woody's fidelity (he is Andy's toy but is willing to go to Japan now he knows he was a television star); the selfish toy – Stinky Pete the Prospector – who cares not for the others but will do his utmost to ensure that they all go to Japan together; and a spoof of *Star Wars*'s identification of Darth Vader as father of Luke Skywalker when Buzz Lightyear is seen to be the son of Zurg, his arch-enemy. There is a moment of pathos when Woody discovers that his show was axed before reaching its allotted end. On enquiring why, Stinky Pete responds 'Two words: Sput Nik. Once the astronauts went up children only wanted to play with space toys.' 'I know how that feels,' replies Woody.

The film's story is that toys do not last for ever. The temptation is to try for some kind of immortality in a glass case in a museum. But self-preservation must not be chosen over and above living life to the full. Jesse, the cowgirl, outlines it well, saying that when a child plays with a toy 'even though you're not moving, it feels like you're alive'. We are reminded that they are toys even if they display the highest of human virtues: fidelity, devotion and even love, and, perhaps, it draws on themes of immortality and usefulness and the problems raised when those things are craved or left unfulfilled.

Antz

Antz is the story of a neurotic ant intent on breaking out of the restrictions placed on his lot in life in the colony. The voice is supplied by Woody Allen, 'the biggest neurotic in the world', and the opening scene is full of ironic humour as the ant, lying on a therapist's leaf, complains about his anxious childhood.[20] The ants are separated at birth into workers and fighters with an accompanying value judgement made regarding the two classes. The main character is a worker who falls in love with the princess. His story is one in which he forges an identity as an individual, inspires others to do likewise and assists in foiling a plot by the evil General Mandible who is intent on a quasi-eugenic scheme to be rid of the lower orders and thereby ensure the creation of a superior race of ants.

Throughout the film the main character is reminded that he counts for nothing as one ant: all that matters is the colony where each ant has his or her place. He dreams of a better place, suggested to him by an old drunk in a bar as 'Insectopia', which turns out to be a rubbish bin in a city park. He is encouraged by a dying fighter ant, 'Don't make my mistake, don't follow orders your whole life. Think for yourself.'[21] Finally, as the only one to return from a battle into which he was mistakenly drawn, the vitality of his individualism is acclaimed by the princess when she greets him with the words: 'You were a worker, now you are a war hero.'

The film promotes the need for individualism beyond oppressive structuralism and classism. It provokes the sense of individual value and thinking for the self. But it concludes that individuals also need others to make things work. Ultimately, the main character finds that he belongs exactly where he is, but the appropriateness of his place is discovered because he has chosen it.

Ants, of course, do not talk and plot in the way presented: they are shown as though they were human beings. Their posture, for example, is anthropomorphic. Interestingly, when they go into battle against the termites, the termites are portrayed as ferocious, beast-like, incoherent and, unlike the stylized ants, definitely subhuman.

As such, the film's main purpose appears to be the affirmation of individuality, the oppression of the system and the need to rise against it, even if that finally secures one's place within it, which in a somewhat ironic way seems to suggest the need for adolescent rebellion and searching, providing the individual concerned comes round in the end to seeing the vitality of the status quo.

A Bug's Life

This, too, is a story of liberation from oppression and finding value in the individual. This time the main character is a mad-cap inventor whose attempts to help end up in failure and indeed appear to make matters worse. In the world in which he lives, there is a set order to things that is not to be broken: the sun grows the food, the ants pick the food, the grasshoppers eat the food. He resolves to go beyond the ants' island colony to find some warrior bugs who will help drive the grasshoppers away for ever.

At the heart of the story is the way in which one individual discovers 'the non-necessity of oppression'[22] and decides to strike a blow 'for the colony and for oppressed ants everywhere'. At first the others do not follow, but they come round in the end. However, rather than a group of powerful vigilantes, it is circus bugs that he mistakenly employs and they turn out to be shallow, self-indulgent thespians whose weakness and worthlessness is also transformed as they too come good in the end.

This is a story intended to show the reappropriation of hope and dignity in oppressed life. It is in some ways a parable of liberation theology. Liberation theology's major contribution was the recognition that oppression belonged to history in which human beings worked out God's salvific will. It may have depended more on Marx than the Gospels, identifying human beings as the agents of historical change, but in doing so it supplied the hope that things do not have to be as they are. This consciousness-raising was the first step in liberation: recognizing that suffering and oppression are the results of human sin and not God's will. *A Bug's Life* shows this step in liberation as the ants stand up to the grasshoppers. Though the context would have obvious parallels, for children, with the bully in the playground who uses his superior size and strength to play on the fears of those smaller than himself, the message can be seen in wider terms. The oppressive minority are not secure, for they know, as the grasshoppers know, that the oppressed majority outnumber them significantly. They have to play on their fears. Once those fears are removed, and oppression is seen to be the contingent illusion that it really is, then the first step is taken on the road to liberation.

3. Conclusion

There can be little doubt that these films are entertaining. *Chicken Run* and *Antz* in particular will appeal to an adult audience because of their sophisticated animation, use of popular actors to provide the voices and using those actors in a familiar way. Their appeal is increased by the deliberate echoing of scenes from other films. But are they really anything more than entertainment, and are they really anything more than entertainment for children?

If they are to do anything more than entertain, it is important to recognize that these films are about us: they are about human beings, our relationships, our hopes and aspirations, our virtues and our vices. They are particularly about 'growing up' and maturing experiences. They take the characters from a lowly position, usually of oppression by the system, and they present life and the gaining of meaning in terms of finding an individual identity which, if it does not beat the system, at least finds a place within the system in which its own identity can be maintained. And they suggest that to do so the individual does not have to claim a more significant place than the group. All this has parallels with non-realist thinking, for it demonstrates the projection of what are unavoidably human values into archetypal myths in order to provide purpose, meaning and boundaries for human life. However, these points relate to the story, the narrative being conveyed, rather than to the form of animated film.

In some ways, the discovery of meaning in animation must be related back to the opening quotation from Don Cupitt that Donald Duck has no existence beyond his own iconography. In other words, there is meaning to be gained for Donald Duck only from within certain ground rules. In some ways this is how non-realism works, too. It has certain ground rules that, when accepted, allow meaning to be gained that is not pejorative. It is not, in theory, a denial of God's existence, but it does say that God's existence is not the most important point, partly because if God exists then that existence is beyond our experience and therefore beyond analogy and beyond any kind of meaningful expression. As a result, God's existence per se is unimportant, or at least not a matter for concern. Rather we have to find ways of living meaningfully which may be promoted by using 'God' as a sign.

Similarly, animated film, like any other film, can express theological meaning from within a certain epistemological framework. The truth is that all films will convey meaning, but we may not want to convey some meanings as those we ought to discuss and emulate. Alongside conveying meaning, if we further accept that film works primarily by appealing to the imagination, then animation may appeal more to this than any other genre. And if we also see with Tillich and Richard Niebuhr that culture is vital for our understanding of ultimate reality then film and animation, as aspects of our culture and of human creativity, are of some significance. There would then be little doubt that animated films, despite their unreality, are as able to convey meaning and value as any other film, particularly when they evoke a response in the viewer: one where they empathize with the main character and care what is going to happen. Indeed, it could be their very unrealism which helps convey meaning by ensuring that the story is followed rather than any secondary factor. As such, they may be important texts for children (and adults) as they develop and mature into citizens because it is the things we watch on film and television that appear now to have greatest effect on our psyche, either for the benefit or detriment of civil society. They, like other films and like other aspects of culture, may help instruct us or provide us with raw material or imbue values and principles into our characters; in so doing, they may possibly help us in the business of living.

But if, on the other hand, we begin in a different place, such as that of traditional Christian thought, then our answer will be very different. If we are to begin with a sense of God's realism, and with convictions about how that realism has been conveyed in history, that God 'was in Christ reconciling the world to himself' (1 Cor. 5.19; Col. 1.20), then a different perspective is put on the whole study. These films may be human 'mythoi' that enable people to experience, discuss and even define meaning and value in a new way, but they do not do so in any particular sense; they support a general morality, they affirm the vitality of the human spirit and they appeal to vague notions of a civic religion but they do not specifically promote Christianity or, for that matter, any other organized religion. They may help people to live life by providing principles and values, though this may not in fact be the sum total of the 'religious requirement'. The trouble is that the interpretation of film can be so arbitrary and nothing is guaranteed. Films, including animated ones, may, or may not, inspire people to contemplate issues and events and move people to extremes of emotion. They may, or may not, offer the kind of information traditionally offered by religion such as the why or wherefore of the universe, the meaning and purpose of life, forgiveness of sin and salvation. It may be that tried and tested stories convey these best, and for those we would have to turn to different 'mythoi'.

Notes

1 Don Cupitt, *After God: The Future of Religion*, London: Weidenfeld & Nicolson, 1997, p. 25.

2 Joel W. Martin and Conrad E. Ostwalt Jnr (eds), *Screening the Sacred: Religion, Myth and Ideology in Popular American Film*, Oxford: Westview Press, 1997, p. 6.

3 See Christopher Deacy, *Screen Christologies: Redemption and the Medium*

of Film Cardiff: University of Wales Press, 2001, p. 2. Cf. Joseph Marty, 'Toward a theological interpretation and reading of film: incarnation of the Word of God – relation, image, word', in John R. May (ed.), *New Image of Religious Film*, Kansas City: Sheed and Ward, 1997, pp. 141ff.

4 See, for example, Robert K. Johnston, *Reel Spirituality: Theology and Film in Dialogue*, Grand Rapids: Baker Academic, 2000, p. 59; Clive Marsh, 'Films and Theologies of Culture', in Clive Marsh and Gaye Ortiz (eds), *Explorations in Theology and Film*, Oxford: Blackwell, 1997, pp. 24–7.

5 H. Richard Niebuhr, *Christ and Culture*, London: Faber and Faber, 1952.

6 Richard Niebuhr, with his Calvinist background, probably favoured the 'Christ as transformer of culture' model and, therefore, possibly would not have approved of the contemporary use of his categorization to justify the dialogue between theology and film. Cf. Johnston, *Reel Spirituality*, p. 59.

7 St Augustine, *Confessions*, trans. Henry Chadwick, Oxford: Oxford University Press, 1991, p. 3.

8 Whether a good or bad thing, it is worth noting in passing that this, of course, falls far short of anything that the Christian gospel (for example) would demand in terms of conversion and commitment to God in Christ reconciling the world unto himself. (1 Cor. 5.19; Col. 1.20).

9 It has been estimated, for example, that approximately 1,500 people leave the churches every week in Britain. See Philip Richter and Leslie J. Francis, *Gone But Not Forgotten*, London: Darton, Longman & Todd, 1998, introduction, pp. xi, xii.

10 The case is forcibly put in Neil Postman, *Amusing Ourselves to Death*, London: Methuen, 1985.

11 Mircea Eliade, *The Sacred and the Profane: The Nature of Religion*, New York: Harcourt Brace Jovanovich, 1959, p. 205, quoted in Martin and Ostwalt, *Screening the Sacred*, p. 9.

12 Michael Northcott, 'Spirituality in the Media Context', in Derek C. Weber (ed.), *Discerning Images: The Media and Theological Education*, Edinburgh: University of Edinburgh Press, 1991, p. 105.

13 Johnston, *Reel Spirituality*, p. 17.

14 Martin and Ostwalt, *Screening the Sacred*, p. 16; see also Wesley Kort, *Narrative Elements and Religious Meaning*, Philadelphia: Fortress Press, 1975, pp. 86–7.

15 Despite the fact that religion is portrayed positively on *The Simpsons*, it is very much a civic religion of morality with no sense of 'following Jesus', a point noted by Mark I. Pinsky, *The Gospel according to the Simpsons: The Spiritual Life of the World's Most Animated Family*, Louisville: Westminster John Knox, 2001.

16 See www.godthedevilandbob.com

17 Johnston, *Reel Spirituality*, p. 27.

18 As Peter Malone notes, 'The story of the stranger who comes into a community and transforms their lives, sometimes with challenge and pain, a sign of contradiction which is often misunderstood – and who then disappears is an archetypal story.' Malone, '*Edward Scissorhands*: Christology from a Suburban Fairy-tale', in Marsh and Ortiz (eds), *Explorations in Theology in Film*, p. 81. In *Shane*, the main character descends into the world of the homesteaders from the

hills 'above', in Jon Tuska's words, 'like a messiah'. Tuska, *The Filming of the West*, Garden City, NY: Doubleday and Company, 1976, p. 530, quoted in Lloyd Baugh (ed.), *Imaging the Divine: Jesus and Christ Figures in Films*, Kansas City: Sheed and Ward, 1997, p. 170.

19 See Susie Saunders's comments at www.textweek.com/movies/chicken-run.htm

20 See the entry for *Antz* at www.us.imdb.com

21 See www.textweek.com/antz.htm

22 See Eleazar S. Fernandez, *Towards a Theology of Struggle*, Maryknoll: Orbis, 1994, p. 19.

11. Clint Eastwood Westerns:
Promised Land and Real Men

PETER FRANCIS

1. Theological Conversation

Why should a practical theologian bother with Westerns or, indeed, any popular film? It is certainly not from any desire to 'baptize' films or give Christian readings of secular stories. It is not to dole out an imprimatur to films that are morally uplifting, nor is it to utter condemnation of particular movies that are deemed morally dubious.

Practical theology is 'the discipline within the theological curriculum whose task is to describe, analyse and interpret the contemporary situation in order to identify the problems to which the Christian Church must make a strategic response'.[1] Film is one of the tools that can help theology achieve that task. Films not only arise out of a particular cultural context, they even help to define that context. Films give the viewer an understanding of the values and assumptions, public issues and private issues of society. Films, as Margaret Miles has pointed out, 'articulate a range of values, fleshing out these values in characters, and narrating the conflicts that arise'.[2] These conflicts can be intimate and private or they can be public and societal. Films offer comment, illustration and a narrative on their social moment. 'They are cultural products deeply informed by the perspectives, values, and aspirations of their makers.'[3] They address the anxieties and interests of their situation. If film is one of the voices of a broader 'social conversation', it is a conversation in which practical theology is involved.

The Westerns that this chapter will consider tell us very little about the actual history of the west but they will tell us something about the public and private values, assumptions of the film-maker and the society that watched them.

2. Westerns

This chapter will begin by looking at the Western genre[4] to identify certain key themes. It will then look specifically at the Western films that Clint Eastwood has directed. Westerns have an operatic and mythic quality that has yet to be captured in any other genre in contemporary cinema. Part of this is geographical setting, part blatant neglect of historical facts, partly also the Western's ease of mutation and a persistent riff on masculinity (see Text Box 11.1, The Western Genre).

11.1 The Western Genre: Ten Landmark Westerns

1. *Stagecoach* (John Ford, 1939)
John Wayne plays the Ringo Kid, a 'cocky' outlaw seeking revenge for his father and brother, who becomes the selfless hero. The film culminates in an Indian attack on the stagecoach. The promised land of the west is painted in sharp contrast to the civilization of the east as represented by the stagecoach passengers. It has been called the basic Western template. John Ford uses Monument Valley, which thereafter epitomized the west.

2. *She Wore a Yellow Ribbon* (John Ford, 1949)
Wayne is now a kindly father figure about to retire from the US Cavalry in the aftermath of Custer's defeat. Wayne embodies old-fashioned virtues and the film is formed around a series of ritual incidents. Ford again uses Monument Valley as the backdrop.

3. *The Searchers* (John Ford, 1956)
Wayne plays a psychologically complex character, Ethan Edwards. Ethan is an outsider on an obsessive and pathological racist quest. Character takes over from action and heroics, although the setting, Monument Valley, remains the same. These three films show the evolution of the genre.

4. *Ox-Bow Incident* (William Wellman, 1943)
This film dramatizes the horror of mob violence. Three innocent drifters are murdered by a lynch mob. The liberal credentials of this film are cited as proof of how the genre can adapt and dramatize contemporary themes.

5. *High Noon* (Fred Zinnemann, 1952)
A dark night of the soul for Gary Cooper as he has to decide whether to buckle on his gun to confront a killer or to renounce violence as his Quaker bride wishes. Focusing on 'character' and 'cause', John Wayne famously called it 'the most un-American thing I have seen in my life'. Written by the 'black-listed' Carl Foreman.

6. *Shane* (George Stevens, 1953)
Stevens's self-consciously mythic film offers us, in Alan Ladd's deadpan performance, 'everyman'. Shane tells the boy who idolizes him as a gunfighter, 'a man has to be what he is Joey – he can't break the mould'.

Like *High Noon* the dilemma of strapping on the six-gun or settling for a life as a homesteader is central. Action in both films is confined to the final climax.

7. *The Magnificent Seven* (John Sturges, 1960)
A remake of Kurosowa's *Seven Samurai* (1954), it marked a return to action rather than the ponderous dilemmas of the classic Westerns of the fifties. 'Character' is not sacrificed to heroics as the seven fill the screen with memorable set pieces.

8. *Once Upon A Time in The West* (Sergio Leone, 1968)
After the success of Clint Eastwood's Spaghetti Westerns, Leone filmed this grand operatic Western in Monument Valley. Fantastic set pieces and, like the *Wild Bunch,* it offers a vision of the death of the west.

9. *Wild Bunch* (Sam Peckinpah, 1969)
Set in 1913, this is about the end of an era, when armies and their generals take over from cowboys. The heroes are bad men, but Peckinpah gives us the passing of the west from their point of view. They die defeated by an army equipped with cars and machine guns.

10. *Dances With Wolves* (Kevin Costner, 1990)
This film reinvigorated the Western genre following a spate of end-of-the-era films. It is full of 1990 sensibilities. Costner's wounded soldier finds his true self among the native American Sioux Indians. Historically authentic, it shows the Sioux's love of the land. Its ecological message is accompanied by fantastic panoramas.

The Promised Land

Geographical setting is interesting. Ever since Frederick Jackson Turner's 1893 lecture on *The Significance of the Frontier in American History*[5] the west has always been portrayed in contrast to the urbanized east, the wilderness *vs.* civilization. The east is stifling – a place of unemployment, poverty, humanity enslaved by machines, skyscrapers where people are literally piled on top of each other. The west, on the other hand, conjures up visions of wide-open spaces, promises of hopes fulfilled and the free-dom to make a new life. The west is a wide, open country, the big country where there is a freedom to become one's true self. 'Phrases like "Far West", "El Dorado", "Big Sky Country" or "Virgin Land" all resonate with semantic excess, imposing on that terrain the blankness of an unin-scribed page, implying a freedom to alter it at will.'[6] In film it doesn't really matter if these huge landscapes are in Australia, New Jersey, Paraguay, Spain or Italy (and all have been used as the backdrop for Westerns), the wide-open spaces are the west.

The promise of the west has strong resonance with the Hebrew Bible's understanding of salvation. The rediscovery of the Hebrew root meaning of the word 'salvation' had a strong influence on the World Council of Churches, thinking in the 1970s and was a key word in the vocabulary of liberation theologies. Philip Potter, General Secretary of the World Council of Churches throughout the 1970s, emphasizes the importance of the theme.

> The Hebrew verb *yasha*, to save – from which the name Jesus, 'he who saves', is derived – was a thoroughly this worldly word. It meant, 'to be wide, to be spacious'. Its opposite was *sara*, 'to be narrow – whether physically, intellectually or spiritually'.[7]

Salvation has to do with having or getting space in which to move, breathing space, which gives the possibility of choice, of growth and development. It is the condition where crops flourish and peace prevails. A fellow WCC officer, the Presbyterian theologian Ian Fraser, spells out the contrast more explicitly. Fraser's understanding parallels the contrast between the urbanized American east and the mythic American west.

> *Sara* . . . gives the impression of being hemmed in, imprisoned, cornered, suffocated . . . Those who are unfree, cramped without room to manoeuvre or liberty to shape their lives for themselves . . . Salvation is related to the provision of a door of escape and through it ground on which they can walk as people free to participate in making their own future.[8]

It is worth noting that although this parallel conjures up images of freedom for those trekking west, the consequence was almost exactly the opposite for the native Americans whose land was being usurped. Just as in the days of Moses and the patriarchs the biblical trek towards the Promised Land spelt defeat for the indigenous tribes. The Promised Land is won at the expense of those already dwelling in these fertile lands.

History

The west, like all utopias, never existed. The real Wild West was very different.

> Cowboys, cattle towns, and long drives north formed a minor chapter in western history; range wars were simply labour strikes on horse back, and 'the lone gunman' a rare psychopath, regarded as such and with contempt. It is not unfair to say that few Americans attached more than passing significance to Indian wars, railroad extensions, mining

and lumber operations – certainly vis-à-vis more pressing eastern considerations.[9]

Lee Clark Mitchell believes that the great Western set pieces (Pat Garrett's capture of Billy the Kid, Custer's Last Stand, Tombstone's OK Corral) were all quite prosaic events and have taken on a mythic dimension because Americans find the real history of these times and events so inconsequential. There are parallels with the Hebrew Bible. The wanderings of nomadic tribes, and their internal conflicts and significant events are also exaggerated into formative myths.

Films like Sam Peckinpah's *Wild Bunch* (1969), which purports to offer a more realistic look at the Wild West, are really only more realistic in that the violence is more graphic and that there are no real heroes anymore. The end of an era that Peckinpah's film purports to be about is really only the end of an era of Western films, the end of the age of heroes, the days of clearly defined goodies and baddies. The real story of the decline of the Wild West would make fairly boring viewing just as the real story of, say, Jacob and Joseph (if we could ever reconstruct it) would hardly excite.

Westerns maintain the myth of the west. Similarly, we don't want realism in the retelling of the Hebrew Bible's stories of patriarchs, prophets and kings. It is books with titles like *Archaeology Proves the Bible Is True* that give a bogus historicity to the biblical myths (fish bones on Ararat and fossilized trumpets outside Jericho). Depressingly, it is these books that sell rather than the scholarly deconstruction offered by contemporary biblical scholars.

The similarity between the Hebrew Bible's stylized narratives and the stylized conventions of Western film-making is striking. It is surprising that the Hebrew narratives haven't been plundered as source material for contemporary Westerns; maybe the fear of offending religious sensibilities has counselled caution. It does help to explain the attraction of the highly stylized Japanese films of Kurosawa to Western film-makers, the *Seven Samurai* (1954) remade as *The Magnificent Seven* (John Sturges, 1960) and *Yojimbo* (1961) remade as *A Fistful of Dollars* (Sergio Leone, 1964).

A Hungry Cuckoo of a Genre

If geography and the opportunities for historical 'freedom' help to form the Western then the easy assimilation of contemporary themes is also an important factor. The British film critic Philip French expresses this ease of mutation. 'The Western is a great grab bag, a hungry cuckoo of a genre, a voracious bastard of a form, open equally to visionaries and opportunists, ready to seize anything that's in the air from juvenile delinquency to ecology.'[10] Martin Scorsese[11] notes how the Western allows writers and film-makers to explore contemporary themes. The clear-cut morality of the Westerns of the 1930s, 1940s and early 1950s (although some of these are clearly anti-Nazi or anti-Communist) gives way to the complicated anti-hero of Arthur Penn's *Left Handed Gun* (1958) where the young Paul Newman plays Billy the Kid as a rebel without a cause at a time when society was confused by youth problems. As Clint Eastwood has observed in a BFI interview: 'In a Western you can get across things that concern you sociologically today. Look at Wellman's *The Oxbow Incident* (William Wellman, 1943), which analysed mob violence: it was not successful commercially, but it was a tremendously important film.'[12] It is possible to credit a Western like *Broken Arrow* (Delmer Daves, 1950) for helping to transform attitudes to the native American at a time when the USA was in the midst of civil rights disturbances. More recently we have witnessed feminist Westerns, black Westerns, ecological Westerns and pro-native American films.

The Western genre gives film-makers the freedom to explore current issues and societal confusions on a wide-open canvas. Henry Nash Smith observed that the Western is 'our fullest objectified mass dream . . . we need then to acknowledge how fluently that dream has always mutated'.[13]

Real Men

Westerns are about masculinity. They resonate with the desire for men to be real men, and for 'a man to do what a man's gotta do'. They are haunted by this flawed idea of masculinity. There is a recurring image of the Western hero beaten to a pulp and yet overcoming physical wounds to defeat the bad. In a survey of over 100 years of Western writing and film-making Jane Tompkins claims that the Western answers the domestic novel.

> Westerns invariably depict the same man – a man in flight from the domestic constraints of Victorian culture, afraid of losing mastery, at the centre of an endlessly repeated drama of death, inarticulateness, emotional numbness in a genre whose pattern of violence never varies.[14]

It is an argument that finds support in Gary Wills's reflections on why John Wayne remained the most popular movie star for years after his death.

> The archetypal American is a displaced person – arrived from a rejected past, breaking into a glorious future, on the move, fearless himself, feared by others, killing but cleansing the world of things that 'need

killing,' loving but not bound by love, rootless but carrying the Center in himself, a gyroscopic direction-setter, a travelling norm.[15]

The traits of flawed masculinity are all evident in the heroes of the Western genre. The hero is his own man, seeking support and help from no one, autonomous rather than dependent. The real man is active rather than passive, never tired or in need of sleep and with a miraculous ability to recover or shrug off injury or illness. Health concerns are not for him, a man will smoke, eat steaks and drink. The male Western hero is not emotional but rather coldly rational and logical, relationships are a bind to be avoided, his sexual responses are depersonalized, his gun and penis are both tools. A real man is in control and seeks to triumph, there is no compromise. A real man is resolutely unafraid, preferring death to being labelled a coward.

It would be easy to illustrate each of these points with any number of scenes from Western movies. The Western hero is unlikely to allow his feminine side to bring him towards growth and wholeness. In religion the male power images of God warp our understanding of the divine. There is something in Westerns that panders to this powerful masculine side, however self-destructive we know it to be. No matter how 'new' we men claim to be or how in touch we are with our feminine side there is always a part of us that longs to be Clint Eastwood, The Man With No Name riding into town, silent, strong, blowing away the bad and the ugly.

3. Clint Eastwood Westerns

Clint Eastwood has made 57 films. He has directed 25 of these films. It is hard to think of a contemporary director or actor who has had such a long run of commercial success. His commercial success has recently been matched by critical acclaim. *Unforgiven* (1992) won four Oscars, including best director for Eastwood himself. Eastwood was the subject of a retrospective at the Venice Film Festival 2000, and chairman of the jury at Cannes in 1998.

His wide-ranging films encompass the Dirty Harry movies, redneck comedies, police thrillers, musicals, romantic comedies, love stories, science fiction – nevertheless it is as a Western anti-hero that he is best known, for as Christopher Frayling has remarked,[16] from the moment The Man With No Name rode into the town, chewing cigars, sweeping back his poncho, narrowing his eyes, the Western was never going to be the same again.

Only 15 of the 57 have been Westerns. Of these 15, he has directed four – *High Plains Drifter*, *The Outlaw Josey Wales*, *Pale Rider* and *Unforgiven* – and it is these that I want to explore. The two mentors for his Western films are undoubtedly Sergio Leone and Don Siegel. From the former he absorbed the operatic quality of film-making and from Siegel, he learnt the director's craft.

High Plains Drifter *(1973)*

High Plains Drifter is an unpleasant and violent film. Derek Malcolm, reviewing the film in the *Guardian*, sums up this impressive but unlikeable film.

> The scene is stunningly set, the characters well-observed in one dimensional terms. And Eastwood plays the avenger as if born to it, a Dirty Harry unshackled by silly liberal laws. It all works well which is why one resents it so much.[17]

Clint Eastwood sets his first Western in beautiful open country, part of the wide open promised land, which is being terrorized by a lawless gang. The town of Lago nestles beside a tranquil lake. The Stranger rides into town and borrows every cliché he can from his Sergio Leone films, including an operatic approach. Like The Man With No Name in Leone's films, Clint chews cigars, gives us close-ups of his narrow focused eyes, uses the cliché of the bathtub and barber's chair shootings, and flashbacks of a violent beating that have driven him on towards vengeance. Within the first ten minutes Clint has shot three men and raped a woman.

We learn the reason for his violent revenge. He is an avenger, perhaps even a supernatural avenger. The suggestion is that he is the good lawman who was horsewhipped to death, as the townsfolk and his girlfriend looked on mute and compliant. He exacts his revenge. He renames the town 'Hell'. The conclusion, the final shoot-out, of the film is played out amidst the fires of Hell, before the Stranger vanishes as mysteriously as he arrives.

Is the Stranger Christ? It's certainly not very Christ-like behaviour. However, the Stranger is empowering to the community, he gets them to stand up for themselves. He empowers the most downtrodden and smallest member of the community, the midget Mordecai, and makes him sheriff and mayor. That's the good news. The film doesn't provide an answer, we never know who the Stranger is, but the supernatural quality pervades the atmosphere from the start.

If the supernatural and the divine are in some sense equated – and the film certainly presents a convincing judgement day – then the image of the divine/avenging angel is disturbing. The mixing of the strong masculine stereotype that Clint portrays with the things of God gives a very cockeyed (*sic*) view of God.

The view of God that is here portrayed is of a God of judgement; some-day, in some way, God will make you pay for your sins, exact a price for your guilty secret. John Wayne strongly disliked the film and wrote to Clint claiming it was the antithesis of what the American frontier – and the American people – represented. Clint Eastwood was unphased.

> It was just an allegory, it wasn't meant to be about pioneers and cov-ered wagons and conflict with Indians. It was a speculation about what happens when they go ahead and kill the sheriff and somebody comes back and calls the town's conscience to bear. There's always retribution for your deeds.[18]

For Eastwood, the director and star, it remains unclear who the Stranger is, but it is clear that it is a film about retribution and that retri-bution will be exacted by circumstance or even divine agency: a God of the eye for an eye variety, from whom there is no hiding and who will get you in the end.

Pale Rider *(1985)*

If *High Plains Drifter* shows Clint Eastwood borrowing the style and iconography of his mentor Sergio Leone, *Pale Rider* demonstrates a much more personal style, a very sure and languid directing style that has become one of his hallmarks. *Pale Rider* is almost a remake of *High Plains Drifter*. In *Pale Rider* the religious symbolism is much more overt. The pale rider looks identical (same hat, coat and horse) to the mysterious stranger in *High Plains Drifter*. This time he comes not to exact revenge on the community but in answer to a prayer by the young girl Megan Wheeler to save the mining community. Megan is reading from Revelation: 'And behold a pale horse . . .' And there framed by the window is Clint Eastwood, the mysterious stranger sitting on a pale horse. Of course, for those longing for a good shoot-up we are heartened to read on in Revelation: 'Its rider was named Death, and Hell was following close behind him' (Rev. 6.8; NRSV).

We don't learn the pale rider's name; we see from his dog collar that he is a preacher. His actions are miraculous. He helps the miners, pan-handlers who have gone west to find a home and prosperity. He helps them to find gold, single-handedly defeats six men bullying the kindly but ineffectual miner Hull. He rescues Megan from rape, fells a giant and resists temptations – a bribe of building a church and financial reward from villain La Hood and the sexual overtures of Megan and her mother Sarah, both of whom have fallen in love with him.

In Christ-like manner he sides with the impoverished miners against big business represented by the mining company of La Hood, who sweeps all aside in his greed – murdering and bullying people and destroying the environment, washing away the hillside in his lust for gold. Clint is setting a deliberate environmental and topical sub-plot to his conventional tale of revenge, a good example of the ease of mutation of the Western. Eastwood uses the film to attack the greed of big business and to defend the individual trying to scrape together a living. This is very much a film of the 1980s, of the time of Gecko's creed that 'greed is good' as epitomized in the 1987 film *Wall Street* (Oliver Stone, 1987).

Big business is not only indifferent to the environment but has a corrupt legal system on its side. A new corrupt sheriff, Stockburn, is appointed to support La Hood's business ventures. Clint rides off alone to fight Stockburn and his six deputies. There is a certain salvific quality in siding with the poor against the oppressors. In Western terms it is defending the freedom of the frontier against the urbanizing oppression of the east. It should be noted that Stockburn and his deputies come from the urban east to oppress those seeking room to be people.

Stockburn and the Preacher have clashed previously. Stockburn thought he had killed him years before (earlier the Preacher is seen taking his shirt off and revealing five wounds/bullet scars on his back – five wounds of Christ?). Is this, as Andrew Greeley seems to think, a clash between the Devil and the Christ-like pale rider? The Preacher kills Stockburn and his six deputies as well as La Hood himself. When he kills Stockburn, Stockburn calls out 'You! You!' Greeley believes 'that he recognizes the face of the pale rider as perhaps the face of God, Christ, or an avenging angel, as he now at the moment of his death, sees his judge and executioner'.[19]

In his study of *Pale Rider*, Greeley points out Eastwood's skill as a director. The pale rider is always on higher ground looking down on the small mining community – or the corrupt town – on those being judged, only coming down to their level to perform a miracle or to judge decisively.

Pale Rider is more explicitly about God and God's judgement than *High Plains Drifter*. The concerns remain. If God and Christ are like this then God help us. God conforms to all the stereotypes of flawed masculinity. It is a God created from the masculine power language of hymns and worship (King – Almighty – Judge – Father – Lord – Protector). It is a God who is remote and only descends to dole out judgement or to flex his miraculous muscles. This is a God who remains aloof, unknown and unnamed. Forgiveness and repentance are unknown qualities to this God.

As in *High Plains Drifter*, the Preacher/Stranger is good news for those who need empowerment. The miners – the panhandlers – receive hope from his intervention in the impossible battle against (the Wild West's equivalent of) the multi-national corporation. But how empowering is this supernatural help? The Preacher does it all for them, they are not participants in the struggle for freedom.

The American Monomyth

Those who are given to seeing Christ-types in contemporary films often cite *High Plains Drifter* and *Pale Rider* as two examples. One has to acknowledge that Clint Eastwood is deliberately playing with biblical imagery but I want to support John Shelton Lawrence and Robert Jewett's argument in *The Myth of the American Superhero* that sees not a Christ-figure but one of many examples of an American take on the *hero* or *monomyth*. Lawrence and Jewett have noted how film-makers have been influenced by the work of Joseph Campbell in identifying a monomyth that is common to all cultures and all eras.[20] This has developed into a particular American version that dominates any number of Hollywood plotlines.

> A community in a harmonious paradise is threatened by evil; normal institutions fail to contend with this threat; a selfless superhero emerges to renounce temptations and carry out the redemptive task; aided by fate, his decisive victory restores the community to its paradisiacal condition; the superhero then recedes into obscurity.[21]

This form of the monomyth certainly has echoes of the Christ-figure, the suffering, selfless servant who impassively gives his life for others even if Christ is hardly the zealous crusader who destroys evil. But these aren't Christ-types are they? They have certainly jettisoned the inconvenience of the Sermon on the Mount and all that namby-pamby stuff. These heroes who save communities and even the world are almost without exception white males and almost without exception the story is anti-democratic, and anti community institutions – local, national or international. The law, the authorities, the government are invariably seen to be failing, weakened by liberal values (all that 'love your enemies' nonsense) and therefore justice requires that the gun be placed in the right private hands. (This you might note is not far from George W. Bush's reading of the war against Iraq or Ronald Reagan's alleged remark that the Oliver North story would make 'one heck of a movie someday'.)

The American monomyth explains why so many of the heroes that people identify as Christ-types, like the avengers in Clint Eastwood's *Pale Rider* (1985) or *High Plains Drifter* (1972), cannot be seen as Christ-figures. The redemptive violence of the American Superhero negates any such identification even when the film-maker is eager to offer us a distinct Christ-imagery.

The Outlaw Josey Wales (1976)

The Outlaw Josey Wales was made between the two previous Westerns. Its theme is very different. Eastwood sees the film as trying to take the

Western back to its roots. It shows a confident manner and its slow 'languid' pace is typical of Eastwood's developing style. This style takes time to relish the landscape and makes the sudden outburst of violence all the more telling.

The film starts in paradise. Despite civil war engulfing the country Josey Wales and his family have found their patch of land and are happily engaged in tilling the soil. This is the big country, the promised land of peace and honest labour, where you can find yourself and be yourself. A gang of Union redlegs loot and burn his smallholding, killing his wife and son. Josey retrieves his gun from the charred remains and prepares for retribution. Joining the Confederate cause he and his band are betrayed, he flees and is chased by the Union redleg gang responsible for the destruction of his wife, son and home and by the betrayer of his confederate band.

Despite his attempt to remain alone, on his journey he gathers a whole community. First, he befriends an Indian Chief – betrayed by the government's promises – and an Indian woman, betrayed by her own people. Later in his journeying he meets a spirited old woman, looking for her son's old smallholding. Her son, a member of a redleg gang, had died in the war. The rest of her family except her daughter (who inevitably falls for Clint) have been killed by comancheros on the journey west. This mixed group, all of whom have reason to hate each other, form a community and live together on the smallholding. They have learnt forgiveness and have been able to move on.

Josey Wales, the Union redleg Tyrill and Fletcher (who betrayed Josey and his confederate band) are the ones fighting the war long after the peace has been declared. They can't forgive and move on. In the final sequence, when Fletcher and Josey confront each other, there is no final shoot-out, no retribution – there is forgiveness and both are able to move on: Josey to live on the smallholding and start a new life and Fletcher to ride away to a new beginning in Mexico.

The film ends as it begins, in paradise. The state of salvation has been achieved. The community forged by forgiveness can grow and develop. It is not a conventional end to a Western and in that sense it is a revisionist Western. Josey Wales still embodies the masculinity of the standard Western hero but this is forced on him by circumstance rather than choice. Fundamentally he is compassionate and altruistic, a well-armed shepherd who tends the weak.

Josey Wales is a man who found happiness, had it ripped away from him but regains happiness in the wide-open spaces of the Wild West. In the book he marries Laura Lee – Clint however did not want to be domesticated and in that sense he remains a standard Western hero, unbound by love. This happiness is possible because of the forgiveness that allows him to bury the past and his diffuse community, who have all in some sense had to come to terms with past hatred and prejudices in order to settle down peacefully. This state of well-being is only possible because of the word of honour treaty between Ten Bears, the Comanche leader, and Josey Wales. Ten Bears and all the Indians in the film are depicted in a sympathetic manner. All are honourable and intelligent.

It is a film that honours the Western conventions but gently subverts them. The good news is that forgiveness and community (people need people) prove greater than violence and the lone gunman hell bent on revenge. Some have seen this film as an allegory for post-Vietnam USA: the need to embrace the ideal of a multi-faith, multicultural society where past hatreds have been forgiven and we learn to live together in peace. It certainly is an allegory for a more racially inclusive USA that has learnt to live together and move on from a bitter past; in many ways a deeply spiritual and hopeful film.

Unforgiven (1992)

Unforgiven begins with this text on the screen and Clint Eastwood's haunting (self-composed but uncredited) 'Claudia's theme' on the soundtrack:

> She was a comely young woman and not without prospects. Therefore it was heartbreaking to her mother that she would enter into marriage with William Munny, a known thief and murderer, a man of notoriously vicious and intemperate disposition. When she died, it was not at his hands as her mother might have expected but of smallpox.[22]

The film is about William Munny, a former murderer transformed by the love of a good woman, who gave up a life of killing to raise a family and try his hand at pig-farming. His wife is the significant absence that pervades the whole film, just as surely as her theme dominates the soundtrack.

With his wife dead, and swine fever killing off his pigs, Munny is lured back into his old ways by the Schofield Kid, an aspiring gunfighter who brings the older man word of a bounty being offered in the town of Big Whisky. The bounty is offered by the town whores for the murder of two cowboys, one of whom has cut the face of Delilah, one of the whores. Munny, after initially refusing the Kid's offer, teams up with his old partner Ned Logan and sets off to join the Kid.

Eastwood himself claims that he made the film out of concern about violence and gunplay in society. 'When you are a perpetrator of violence, and when you get involved in that sort of thing, you rob your soul as well as the person you are committing a violent act against.'[23] Gene Hackman, who plays the sheriff (and won an Oscar), initially turned the part down because he felt he had made too many violent films, but reconsidered when he realized its strong anti-violent message. The film is not just another violent film purporting to be preaching anti-violence, it is a film that undermines the whole warped view of masculinity that struts through so many Westerns.

The film is driven by flawed masculinity. It is an insult to the manhood of one of the cowboys in the brothel that unleashes such terrible violence. 'Alls she done, when she seen he has a teensy little pecker, is give a giggle. That's all.'[24] The victim, Delilah, isn't enthusiastic about exacting revenge and even seems inclined to accept the 'innocent' cowboy's gift by way of apology. It is the head of the brothel, Alice, who is anxious to use the incident to exact some retribution for their continual abuse at the hands of the cowboys, 'who ride us like horses'. It is Alice who makes the girls pool their resources to provide the bounty. The whores of Big Whisky aren't innocent in the film, they are desperate for a bloody revenge. They want to pay for two killings, even though one of the cowboys tried to constrain his partner. Theirs is not the noblest of causes. Even in the eye for eye, death for death mentality that pervades Western and American culture, this is revenge out of kilter.

The bounty hunters are all flawed human beings. Richard Harris plays English Bob, whose finest hour seems to have been the drunken shooting of another drunken cowboy. This cowardly killing is being rewritten as a mythic tale of the Wild West, and English Bob is written up as the Duke of Death, by an accompanying journalist. Little Bill, the sheriff, debunks the myth. The inflated past of masculine valour is deflated. The Duke of Death becomes the Duck of Death, as Little Bill deliberately misreads the biographer's title.

Even the three 'heroes', Munny, Ned Logan and the Schofield Kid are no shining white knights. Munny was a murderer, 'You'd be William Munny out of Missouri, killer of women and children.' Munny replies 'I've killed just about anything that walked or crawled.'[25] Neither is the Schofield Kid a hero; he has a fantasy name he has chosen for himself as he becomes an enthusiastic recruit to the gunslinging world. The film underlines his foolishness by making the boy short-sighted. When the boy does kill one of the errant cowboys it is when the cowboy was unarmed, pants round his ankles, having a shit. The death of the other cowboy is also unglorious. It is bungled by Ned's poor shooting, thereby debunking the myth of his famed ability with the rifle. The wounded cowboy takes a horribly long time dying: 'Give him some water, god dammit', yells Munny to the cowboy's companions.

Clint Eastwood's Munny exacts a terrible revenge, killing five men. But even this final shoot-out is messy and inglorious; nobody dies with a first shot. He is no hero and never was.

The film successfully debunks the myth of a heroic past, beginning with the unglamorous scene of the gunfighter turned farmer William Munny, scrambling in a muddy pen to separate healthy from sick hogs.

Thereafter, Munny is represented as a man whose body repeatedly fails him, who consistently has trouble mounting his horse, who suffers from debilitating fever chills and horrifying memories of a wayward youth.[26]

Eastwood's portrait of Munny combined with Ned's lack of stomach for killing, the Schofield Kid's horror at killing, Little Bill's horrific killing and torturing of Ned, the beating of English Bob, not to mention the slur on the cowboy's manhood that starts it all off leaves the masculine stereotype in tatters. There is no riding tall in this film, no noble cause and William Munny returns with the bounty money, not forgiven and redeemed but *unforgiven*.

What is so startling about the film is that William Munny is really the Stranger, the Preacher, Josey Wales and the Man With No Name all rolled into one. This is what happens to those characters after they ride off into the sunset at the end of all those other Westerns. In those Westerns we are frequently left feeling that the hero is at peace with himself and is retiring to the wide open spaces – saved. *Unforgiven* offers a dose of reality. The salvation project can go wrong; it can be lost through death and disease and the hauntings of the past life.

The film debunks the myths of the west; it is not yet another take on the American monomyth. Its setting is also fascinating. As in other films the landscape is wide open and beautiful as Munny and his companions ride through it, but as they near their goal the gloom descends, the rain falls. The town of Big Whisky is a rain-drenched dark place and Eastwood keeps the film resolutely dark, never to return to the light wide-open spaces. David Webb Peoples's screenplay allows for no soft options; even the possibility of romance between Delilah and Munny is rejected.

In this film there is no promised land, no wide-open space which offers peace and hope. Munny has found love and set up home only to have his dream, which was also his redemption, shattered by the death of his wife and the economic death of his farm through swine fever. Redemption has proved temporary and elusive. Munny is almost forced to ply another trade by circumstances. Munny's story is paralleled in this respect by Little Bill's story, the sheriff of Big Whisky. He has tried to escape his past, which was spent among the drunken cowboys like Munny and English Bob, by becoming a lawman, trading on his past reputation. But his paradise is far from perfect and epitomized in the film by the building of his house. He wants a place to sit, drink and admire the scenery. In reality his house is a lopsided bodged job and leaks in any rainstorm.

As in most Westerns, Munny's journey has brought him west to find a new life with his wife and children. This is the conventional trek from the cities of the east to the open spaces of the west. By the end of the film the hero escapes to the city, to the urban life to start a new life for his family where it was rumoured he prospered in dry goods. It is worth observing that his new life is in San Francisco – the urban west, as far west as you can physically go, the very end of the dream. This is the end of the west. We can only speculate whether he found redemption in San Francisco. We can say that in the film he never finds redemption. The constantly recurring Claudia's theme expresses Munny's longing to find again the forgiveness he felt with his wife.

Some commentators read the film differently, most notably Robert Jewett. He sees *Unforgiven* as a dangerous film: 'It invites the public to solve its problems by shooting down its sheriff and placing truck bombs in front of its federal buildings.'[27] He sees it as encouraging violent zeal against a corrupt regime 'that tolerates the mutilation of women and the torturing and shaming of prisoners'.[28] I suppose it is a subject for debate but it fails to take account of the searing hellishness of killing in this Western, the debunking of the ideal of the promised land, the demythologizing of the mythic west and flawed masculinity.

In *High Plains Drifter* and *Pale Rider* we are offered theological themes and characters but they deliver a bogus view of God: a vengeful unpleasant God. The films are firmly within the conventions of the mythic Wild West. Both films offer a version of the American monomyth. In both *The Outlaw Josey Wales* and *Unforgiven* the Western conventions are subverted. In *The Outlaw Josey Wales* we are presented with a tale of salvation that is about forgiveness and the building of community. In *Unforgiven* we have a devastating tale of redemption and damnation that takes us through the promised land back to the city. Like Munny's trek, Eastwood seems to be saying that the Western has nowhere else to go.

These four Western films offer a fascinating insight into the values, assumptions, anxieties and interests of contemporary USA. They say something about how Americans view the world through the pervasive influence of the American monomyth in contemporary culture. These films capture something of our persistent need to have utopias of freedom that give us some hope in our present, allowing us to dream beyond our confines. *The Outlaw Josey Wales* in particular helps us to understand how to build an inclusive community and leave behind old hatreds. *Unforgiven* wrestles with our struggle to redeem a violent past. It also debunks the macho image and gives a fascinating insight into masculinity. All of this adds image, colour and insight into the social conversation of which theology is part. Of course, the main thing these films have in common is that historically the Wild West wasn't like any one of them.

Notes

1 Statement about practical theology from Center for Congregational Research and Development, School of Theology, Boston University, http://www.bu.edu/ccrd/about/practical.

2 Margaret R. Miles, *Seeing and Believing*, Boston: Beacon Press, 1996, p. xv.

3 Miles, *Seeing*, p. 193.

4 John Saunders, *The Western Genre*, London: Wallflower, 2001.

5 Frederick Jackson Turner, *The Frontier in American History*, New York: Dover, 1996.

6 Lee Clark Mitchell, *Westerns – Making the Man in Fiction and Film*, Chicago: University of Chicago Press, 1996, p. 5.

7 Philip Potter, *Life in All Its Fullness*, Geneva: World Council of Churches, 1981, p. 1.

8 Ian Fraser, *Study Encounter No 39*, Geneva: World Council of Churches, 1975, p. 6.

9 Mitchell, *Westerns*, p. 5.

10 Philip French, *Westerns: Aspects of a Movie Genre*, London: Secker and Warburg, 1973, p. 6.

11 Martin Scorsese and Michael Henry Wilson, *A Personal Journey with Martin Scorsese Through American Movies*, London: Faber and Faber, 1997, pp. 35–44.

12 Clint Eastwood in Scorsese and Wilson, *Personal Journey*, pp. 42–3.

13 Henry Nash Smith, *Virgin Land: The American West as Symbol and Myth*, Cambridge, MA: Harvard University Press, 1950, pp. 91–2.

14 Jane Tompkins, *West of Everything: The Inner Life of Westerns*, Oxford: Oxford University Press, 1992. p. 39.

15 Gary Wills, *John Wayne's America: The Politics of Celebrity*, New York: Simon and Schuster, 1997, p. 302.

16 Christopher Frayling, *Sergio Leone*, London: Faber and Faber, 2000, pp. 245–6.

17 Derek Malcolm quoted in Christopher Tookey, *The Critics Film Guide*, London: Boxtree, 1994, p. 360.

18 Patrick McGilligan, *Clint – The Life and Legend*, London: Harper Collins, 1999, p. 268.

19 Albert J. Bergesen and Andrew M. Greeley, *God in the Movies*, London: Transaction, 2000, p. 78.

20 Joseph S. Campbell, *The Hero with a Thousand Faces*, New York: Meridian, 1956.

21 John Shelton Lawrence and Robert Jewett, *The Myth of the American Superhero*, Grand Rapids: Eerdmans, 2003, p. 6.

22 David Webb Peoples, *Unforgiven – Screenplay*, www.man-with-no-name.com, p. 1.

23 Scorsese and Wilson, *Personal Journey*, p. 43.

24 Peoples, *Unforgiven*, p. 2.

25 Peoples, *Unforgiven*, p. 57.

26 Mitchell, *Westerns*, p. 260.

27 Robert Jewett, *St Paul Returns To The Movies*, Grand Rapids: Eerdmans, 1999, p. 149.

28 Lawrence and Jewett, *Myth*, p. 151.

12. A Fistful of Shekels:

Ehud the Judge (Judges 3.12–30) and the Spaghetti Western

ERIC S. CHRISTIANSON

As critics of American culture inform us, the American west and the American Western are different creatures. There is a point at which most historical narratives of the 'Wild West' were inflated into historicized romance. As Greg Garrett puts it, 'the use of the violent legends of the wild, wild West makes for a more dramatic story for film-makers than the often dreary reality'.[1] The Western as a genre says more, according to Garrett, about its producers than its subjects, for 'the Western, like many film genres, seems to reflect American attitudes towards society and order'.[2] As for scholars of the biblical 'Wild West' of the Ehud narrative (Judg. 3.13–30), the case seems less clear. Robert Alter and Baruch Halpern, for example, represent two very different approaches to the genre and rationale of the Hebrew Bible's 'violent legends' ('fictionalized history' akin to prose fiction and historical narrative respectively).[3] It is at least clear to most that the Ehud story makes ample use of rhetorical devices in order to establish a character for whom violence is a tool with which to deliver the word of God (see Text Box 12.1, 'What is a Judge?'). The Western genre also presents us with some ambiguously virtuous violent heroes. It is with reference to such figures that I will reflect on the machinations of and rationale for Ehud's violence, as well as the rhetoric of entertainment that it shares with the Western.

1. Scene-by-Scene

For reasons that will become apparent, the bulk of my analysis deals with one Western sequence. It is from the second of Sergio Leone's 'dollars trilogy' of Spaghetti Westerns, *For a Few Dollars More* (1965).[4] In it Clint Eastwood plays a bounty hunter with no name, whom I will refer to as 'the Man'.[5] Leone's anti-hero goes to collect a criminal that he has heard resides in the town of White Rocks – for bounty. This is the Man's first appearance in the film and it is preceded only by two establishing sequences for the film's other anti-hero, Colonel Mortimer (Lee Van Cleef), and the film's intriguing pre-credit sequence in which a rider is shot off his horse from a distance, seemingly without reason.

12.1 What is a 'Judge'?

The judges (Hebrew, *shôphēt*) of the Old Testament appear mainly in the book that bears that name, but also in the material from Exodus through to the books of Samuel (Samuel himself is the 'last judge').

Judges were generally unlike what we consider today to be a judge. Their prototype was Moses, who embodied charismatic leadership, teaching and judging (see Exod. 18, where Moses sets up a system in which judges hear the many cases of Israelite complaint). By the time we get to the book of Judges, however, a 'judge' has become much more than those who sit in judgement (though compare the book's only female judge, Deborah, in Judg. 4). Chapter 2 fleshes out the judges' role: 'Then the Israelites did what was evil in the sight of the Lord and worshiped the Baals . . . and they provoked the Lord to anger . . . Then the Lord raised up judges, who delivered them out of the power of those who plundered them . . . Whenever the Lord raised up judges for them, the Lord was with the judge, and he delivered them from the hand of their enemies all the days of the judge' (2.11–18). In the book of Judges, judges deliver Israel at the national level. They are socio-political saviours who through their deliverance bring the promise of national spiritual renewal. The book of Judges itself, however, is highly sceptical of whether the judges actually achieve it.

We track the Man's back as he walks into town. The camera is gradually raised from a close-up of the Man's holster to an overhead perspective of the town, its name and a slight horizon visible. Rain pours excessively. The Man pauses. A full 20-second shot pans up the length of his body, emphasizing the iconography: hands at side (a leather gunfighter's brace strapped to his right forearm), poncho, hat tipped towards camera, then cigar and face, capturing a deliberate and steady lighting up of his cheroot. Towards the end of this shot, jaunty piano music is heard from the distance.

The Man enters a 'classic' saloon. The camera scans, from the Man's view, a jovial scene; music is churned out on a cabinet piano and almost everyone is busy drinking and cavorting. 'Goodtime ladies' lean over the banister. Already the Man is apart from the crowd; true to typical Western form, he embodies the plains, the outsider. The Man approaches the local sheriff.

The Man: Light?
The sheriff lights the Man's cheroot with his own cigar.
The Man: You know B. B. Cavanaugh?
No response. The Man studies him with an intense stare.
The Man: Now tell me, you know where I can find 'im?
The sheriff looks over to his left; the Man's eyes follow.

Sheriff: There, at that table. He's got 'is back to ya.

Cavanaugh sits at a table with four other men. They are playing poker.

The Man: Thanks.

The Man slowly walks to the table, which is up a small flight of stairs. The Man sets his hand on the deck of cards at the centre and begins to deal five cards to Cavanaugh and himself, inviting a game. Close-ups on the faces around the table follow, showing the indignation of the Man's opponents. Cavanaugh goes along with the challenge, exchanging two cards with 'the dealer'. We share Cavanaugh's view of his final hand, three kings. The Man puts down his hand, three aces.

Cavanaugh: Didn't hear what the bet was.

The Man slowly looks aside and casually spits.

The Man: Your life.

Cavanaugh rises quickly from the table and a fight ensues. Midway through the fight the saloon music stops and the only sound is now of the Man landing blows and deflecting Cavanaugh's, and of rain outside. We cut to a man at a barber shop getting a shave (probably Cavanaugh's brother). The sheriff appears at the window and motions for him to come. He leaves. Cut back to the saloon and, using only his left hand (his right is 'bound' by his gunfighter brace), the Man knocks Cavanaugh around until they are both at the bar, the Man with his back to the entrance, grasping Cavanaugh's collar.

The Man: Alive or dead. It's your choice.

As the Man says this, three men appear at the door behind him, their guns drawn. The barber shop customer is in the centre. The Man studies them in the mirror behind the bar.

Barber shop customer: Let Brett go.

A pause while the camera closes on each determined face of the men at the door. The Man spins around and lets off three shots (now firing with his right hand), killing all three men. Cavanaugh moves to pick up his gun. As soon as he does, the Man, without looking at him, shoots him dead (again with his right hand). The camera closes in on his killing hand as he twirls his gun into his holster.

The next scene has the Man collecting his money at the sheriff's office. An over-the-shoulder shot from behind the sheriff shows the Man flanked by a row of rifles.

Sheriff: Two-thousand dollars. That's a lot of money. Takes me three years to earn it.

The Man: Tell me, isn't the sheriff supposed to be courageous, loyal and above all honest?

Sheriff: Yeah, that he is.

The Man pulls the sheriff's star off of his vest and studies it. He goes outside to where a few local men are standing. He throws the star down into the dirt (probably a homage to High Noon).

The Man: You people need a new sheriff.

As the Man mounts his steed and rides off into the horizon, music signifies the Man's success: bars from the opening title scene, the same signature 'whistle' tune as earlier, now build with the gradual accompaniment of cracking whips, church bells, strumming guitars and boisterous yells.

Eastwood and Leone's laconic creation appealed (eventually) to a huge international audience. Cinema-goers obviously enjoyed the bold, violent and subversive wit, present in abundance in the above sequence. The spare tough talk, the confident solitary figure (no responsibilities, no social ties, transgressing sociological norms), the possession of trickster-like fighting skills in the face of aggrandized intimidation – all contribute to the appeal of the product.

My main reason for focusing on this particular sequence is that, as Christopher Frayling points out, in this Leone film there are elements of parody in his treatment of 'classical' Western motifs (e.g. saloon scenes, poker games, riding off into the sunset/distance),[6] and this sequence pretty well has them all. Another factor is that, like the Ehud story, it is a self-contained unit, and the consequences are not felt in the motion of the storyline but function instead to notify the audience of the Man's extra-ordinary skills and heroic character. What follows, then, is a developed analysis of this sequence and of the Ehud narrative, in order to illuminate shared rhetorical features. I will then move on to reflect on the relationship of both to their social contexts (particularly in terms of the possibility of social commentary in both).

Proleptic Potency

This is our first sight of the Man, and by all accounts we are meant to be impressed. Having been provided minimal characterization, during this sequence we come to realize that he is possessed with superhuman ability, an invincible gunfighter. We are enabled to infer from his solitary arrival and extraordinary autonomy (in the end he 'takes on' eight baddies) that he does not have (nor will he have) any real social or familial ties or responsibilities. This is easy to infer because we already know this stock gunfighter from countless Westerns. This use of stock characters who provide for the 'reader' a relatively reliable expectation is one of the more interesting shared rhetorical features of the Western and the Judges narrative. Indeed, Philip French recognizes in the Westerns from the 1940s through to the early 1970s a relatively short list of actors who consistently embody heroes, villains, '[r]anchers, sheriffs, deputies, sidekicks, assorted citizenry'.[7] This allowed directors to 'work' actors into new patterns and mine them for new meanings. Rhetorically this is precisely what happens in Judges. The Judges narrative provides a pattern of expectation in the first description of the 'apostasy cycle' (2.11–19). The pattern that readers subsequently expect is generally followed closely throughout, and it is mined for new meanings through subtle variations in and deviation from it.

As the Man pauses to light up, the camera tells us that he is full of confidence (even the way he retrieves the cheroot, lifting his poncho in the dark rain, suggests the access of some secret strength). Such flourishes are where viewers locate meaning in the Spaghetti Western.

> The heroes and villains of Spaghetti Westerns are almost invariably obsessed by 'style', 'image', 'ritual', and their confrontations or inter-actions are, typically, symbolic ones . . . and the hero figures are *usually identifiable* by a collection of external gestures, mannerisms, 'stylish' articles of clothing, or even motifs on the soundtrack, rather than by anything remotely to do with the 'inner man'.[8]

Potency and future success are here established by the Man's preparatory and manneristic ritual. The poker game that he so provocatively forces upon his opponents is a potent symbol suggesting that he is in some way charmed for success. 'Poker in the Western is at once a deeply serious activity and a marginal one. Success is defined more by character than by skill, and personalities are determined by their attitude to the game and the way they play it.'[9] In other words, that the Man finds himself with three aces over three kings is a signifier; we are never given room to doubt his success, and we may enjoy the anticipation of its execution. Such signification is not unlike those attributes of Ehud that set him off as 'pro-fessional'. He was no ordinary warrior. Later in Judges we read, 'Of all this force [the Benjaminites], there were seven hundred picked men who were left-handed; every one could sling a stone at a hair, and not miss' (20.16; cf. 1 Chron. 12.2). These were specially trained warriors. As Baruch Halpern observes concerning Ehud's binding of the right hand (3.15), Ehud

> was one of a breed of men schooled in the use of the left hand for war . . . Ehud conveyed Israel's tribute to Eglon, guarding it against local bandits and kings. He was charged with this mission because he was the closest thing to a professional soldier that the Israel of his period pro-duced. He was a seasoned samurai, or, to use a modern caricature, a sort of James Bond. Bred for combat, schooled to feats of sinister valor, Ehud was precisely the man to execute the operation that Judges 3 describes.[10]

Like Eastwood throughout the trilogy (if not all of his 'gun-oriented' films, such as the Dirty Harry franchise), Ehud can hit the mark several times in the same place. Indeed, structurally, the Western film genre consistently evidences the revelation of the protagonist's 'special ability'.[11] Deceit can be a part of this skill factor (more on which below).

Ehud's manufacturing a roughly 18-inch long dagger and concealing it under his clothes (3.16) not only provides necessary information but also establishes his heroic potency by foreshadowing his success. Meir Sternberg recognizes this pivotal moment as a proleptic projection of victory:

> a left-handed hero about to confront the oppressor of his people with a miniature sword hidden where nobody would suspect it equals a story of assassination. Everything so falls into place, therefore, that Eglon is already as good as dead even before he grants the ambassador a private audience.[12]

Dangerous Deception

Ehud is to 'carry' to Eglon a tribute, a material gift of some kind,[13] a token of homage and submission. In the Deuteronomistic History (Deuteronomy—Kings), failure to present the tribute is equivalent to a refusal of loyalty, and in such contexts the weaker party is coerced through military superiority with the threat of destruction.[14] But this symbol turns out merely to be a ruse in order to gain entry into Eglon's presence. In Judges the sense of political tribute occurs only in this passage (and that four times), which suggests the degree to which the oppression was politically entrenched, thereby underlining the enormity of Ehud's achievement. As a symbol of the oppressor's authority, Ehud renders the tribute meaningless and empty by his deceitful deliverance.

Ehud is a loner, a trait recognized by commentators.[15] After delivering his tribute, he slips away from the crowd, suggesting that he must do the business alone. While there may be good strategic and political reasons for his solitary action,[16] there remains a certain heroic toughness about his task – he is a James Bond, a Dirty Harry – he is the law. The fact that he works alone is indicative of his status as God's deliverer and even hints at his special, deceptive, abilities.[17] Like the Man, Ehud has no qualms about winning the 'shoot-out' with deceit. Indeed, there is little that Ehud does in the story that does not involve some deception.[18]

Subversive Wit and Laconic Tough Talk

The Ehud narrative displays its subversive wit in a number of ways.[19] And as Marc Brettler has shown (here citing F. Rosenthal), the use of scatology and the violation of royal rule by a single commoner suggest a 'momentary lifting of one of the many restrictions which the . . . social environment imposes upon man [*sic*]'.[20] Such sociological upheaval creates a moment of escape, of palpable relief – of laughter. The audience is of course meant to laugh at the Moabites and clearly not with them. As J. L. McKenzie puts it, 'The story of the assassination is full of earthy details which bring out the cleverness of the Israelite and the crass stupidity of the Moabites.'[21] As John Kutsko suggests, 'Even the description of the confused guards in vv 24–25 borders on slapstick, were it not for the sobering discovery on the other side of the door.'[22] Ehud's wit and wordplay not only frame the tale memorably but function to establish him as a potent and unified heroic symbol.

Ehud's wit is conveyed in strikingly minimalist form. Not only is there an ironic use of wordplay in his 'secret message', but the economy of words suggests a linguistic toughness. Ehud speaks twice in the assassination scene proper; first five words (v. 19) and then four (v. 20). More importantly, in the Hebrew, he uses a total of six words, repeating three of them twice. First, 'I-have-a secret word for-you, O-king', and then, when he and the king are alone, 'I-have-a word of-God for-you'. Ehud's words are choice, ironic and as sharp as his sword (the secret word [or 'thing'] turns out to be God's word, which turns out to be Ehud's double-edged dagger [thing]). Significantly, the first address (v. 19) acknowledges the servant–master relationship by addressing Eglon as king. By dropping the decorous title the second time, when they are alone (v. 20), Ehud dangerously withers the king's status while inflating his own. The daring content of his dialogue is matched by the manner in which he delivers it: sparsely.

Again, Ehud's behaviour finds a strange bedfellow in Westerns. Jane Tompkins offers relevant insight into (male) Western words:

> Western literary and film heroes, almost to a man, use language grudgingly . . . The rank understatement, the clipping off of the indefinite article, are the kind of minimalist language heroes speak, a kind of desperate shorthand, comic, almost, in its attempt to communicate without using words . . . The string of commands John Wayne issues in [*Red River*, 1948] . . . – 'Tie 'em up short', 'Get up on the seat', 'Let's go', 'Keep 'em movin'' – are typical. Heroes give abrupt orders in monosyllables.[23]

Similarly, Lee Clark Mitchell suggests that in the Western,

> the visual busyness of . . . [the hero's] demeanor is balanced by vocal inactivity, sonic stillness that regularly offers a nearly physical pause in the narrative line . . . So entirely self-contained is the later Western hero that he seems to exist beyond the everyday commonplaces of talk and explanation, of persuasion, argument, indeed beyond conversation altogether.[24]

In Ehud's case, his provocative words demand an argument to back them up, and that argument is made, quite literally, by his 'double-mouthed' sword. Ehud thereby entrenches himself as a virile man of few words, a particularly masculine ideal; a man who lets his sword do the talking. Indeed, words in both stories serve to provoke. Like the Man's words, Ehud's verbal showdown seems also to wound the pride of its target; that is, the 'fat thug' Eglon appears to have been provoked into an angry response of 'silence!' (his only dialogue), scattering his servants (v. 19). Through his spare and provocative words, Ehud is established as a hermetically sealed hero.[25] Most of the judges 'judged' within their given tribal borders.[26] While Israel remained divided, characters like Ehud provided a potent unifying symbol. In effect, this story's entertainment value comes through the image of Ehud as a quiet monolith who controls his own environment through language and self-reliance, remaining 'hermetic' and, in slow-motion,[27] punching Eglon so full of holes that his enemy is robbed of his own physical integrity.[28]

Personal Justice

Because Leone's Spaghetti trilogy is steeped in the rhetoric of stock Hollywood Western typologies, the films evidence (an ironic?) nostalgia. While they are beginning to scrutinize the Hollywood myths, they also tentatively cling to them. The Man is still a good guy and does not shoot down an unarmed man, and he even helps families in need. Indeed, his character is tinged with positive mythical references. In Leone's own summation he was 'an incarnation of the Angel Gabriel'.[29] The Man does not operate in a moral vacuum.[30] His own 'justice' is personal, and yet disinterested. He is certainly not interested in acquisition of property, and his desire for money is without motivation. The taking of the sheriff's badge suggests that the Man's individual brand of justice is able to occupy the higher moral ground and to pass judgement on the corrupt corporate 'justice' that the sheriff represents.

Ehud's violence likewise is rooted in personal accountability; that is, his action is autonomous and the divine cause is only insinuated by his own speech ('a word of God for you . . .', v. 20; cf. v. 28, in which God's action is again only insinuated by Ehud's speech: 'the LORD has delivered . . .'). His individual violence does, however, lead to the corporate violence of Israel: 'At that time they killed about ten thousand of the Moabites, all strong, able-bodied men; no one escaped' (v. 29). Yet even the corporate violence of the story is to be understood as under Ehud's control. His success against Eglon presumably gives confidence; he 'sounds the trumpet' and leads a 'cavalry charge'. While this violence is for the benefit of the nation, it is couched in Ehud's terms only. *He* was before them (v. 27). His call to the Israelites was '"Follow after *me*" . . . and they went after *him*' (v. 28). It is his rhetoric that leads to victory.

2. Entertaining Violence in Social Context

Understanding the cultural forces behind the legend-making processes of the Western film might suggest avenues of exploration regarding the rationale of the production of Israel's own violent 'cowboys'.

Violence is embedded in both of the world-views on show here. As for the Western, Stephen Prince suggests that it

> is the only genre which, by its nature, creates a dialogue about violence, about what violence is, who may use it, and when. Similarly, the Western is the only genre which inherently talks about the land, about access to the prairies and the mountains and, therefore, about ownership and, implicitly, about the economic and political evolution of the United States.[31]

The Western offers 'a serious orientation to the problem of violence such as can be found almost nowhere else in . . . [American] culture'.[32] Violence in the Western becomes a means not so much to a higher moral end but to a demonstration of masculinity. And yet there is a certain impotence implied by the Western's attempt. 'The Western as a form appears incapable of coping with social problems it is asked to resolve, and one of its central premises – that violence is legitimate in certain circumstances, when all else fails – is gradually undone [in the genre] through its own excess.'[33] And as John Cawelti points out, the notion of legitimized violence has its base in fantasy: 'where some values place a great emphasis on individual aggressiveness and others emphasize social responsibility and conformity, the fantasy of the hero who reluctantly, but nobly aids the cause of social order by acts of individual violence probably corresponds to a widespread fantasy of legitimated aggression'.[34]

Later Westerns have continued to scrutinize the traditional mythology, particularly Eastwood's 1992 film, *Unforgiven* (itself dedicated to Leone). *Unforgiven* undermines, as Koosed and Linafelt point out, 'the notion that the violence practised by the good guys is qualitatively different from the violence practised by the bad guys, and that the community can in fact host this "limited" violence within it for the sake of maintaining its essentially "peaceful" nature.'[35] What makes Judges remarkable in this regard is that it is not the violence of the bad guys that is showcased, but, as in the case of Eastwood's earlier Westerns, that of the good guys.

Although there is little in the Ehud story to aid the reader in *morally assessing* its violence, it may be that the story inherently provokes reflection on such issues, particularly that it 'creates a dialogue about

---

12.2 Screen Violence: New or Old?

There is a general misconception that brutal violence in cinema is a relatively recent phenomenon, a product even of postmodernity. In his book, *Classical Film Violence* (London: Rutgers University Press, 2003), Stephen Prince insightfully plots two axes: 'The referential component of violence – the behavior that is depicted – is the *x*-axis, while its cinematic treatment – the stylistic design – is the *y*-axis' (p. 35). Intriguingly, the *x*-axis, the actual *acts of violence* in cinema, has always been high. What has undergone much greater change is the *y*-axis, the *stylistic representation* of violence. In other words, cinema has never shied from *acts* of violence, even brutal violence. From the earliest films, people have been murdered and abused in all manner of morbidly inventive ways. But film-makers, particularly those of the heavily regulated era of the early 1930s through to the mid 1960s, did shy from its depiction, and opted for often ingenious means of presentation (silhouettes, explicit use of sound, violence just off screen and so on). Indeed, the *x*-axis of violent *acts* changed very little from the beginning of cinema right up to the 'golden age of violence', inaugurated by the release in 1968 of such violent films as *Bonnie and Clyde* and *Once Upon a Time in the West*. Since then, both axes have grown considerably (and the *y*-axis quickly caught up with the *x*), and there is little now in the spectrum of world cinema that is off limits in terms both of violent acts *and* their stylistic representation.

---

violence'. The story may at least provide the canvas for such questions to be raised; that is, it can be seen to invite reflection on the values it is seemingly endorsing. In some respects the Ehud story shares the moral ambiguity of *Unforgiven*. Ehud may be constructed as 'good' partly because God has raised him up, but he is raised out of nowhere. And God's role is no guarantor of Ehud's 'goodness'. Apart from the brief descriptor, son of Gera, a Benjaminite (3.15b), we have no indication of why he is a judge, whether he is good or trustworthy (or whether that matters), or of what events brought him to this crisis. We are never *told* he is good and we must make assumptions to construct him and his actions as positive. God 'raises' him analeptically but he is linked by his lineage to the house of Saul. He is sneaky, deceitful and, when his violence is read at face value, his actions are generally offensive to our modern sensibilities. Whereas the spirit of Yahweh falls upon most other major judges at least once (Othniel, Gideon, Jephthah, Samson), here it is absent. While Lillian Klein goes as far as to suggest that Yahweh's absence in most of the narrative evidences his displeasure with Ehud,[36] we are at a loss in terms of the narrator's lack of judgement, both on this particular event and on the attitude towards the kind of leadership that legitimizes Ehud's violence in Judges as a whole.[37]

3. The Possibility of Social Commentary

Seeking ways in which to place the Spaghetti Westerns of the 1960s in their social context, Frayling considers several approaches that understand the films with reference to class division (between northern ('intelligentsia' upper class) and southern (petit-bourgeoisie) Italy – Leone was from the South) and political conscience. Film critic Lino Micciché, for example, identifies a series of questions:

> The Italian Western is in its own way a typical by-product of mid–60s Italian society, and reflects, more or less unconsciously, some of the sociological data, some of the hidden history of those years. It especially betrays the ideological and moral confusion of that period, as well as the difficulty, which seemed to exist in a broad section of petty-bourgeois public opinion, of distinguishing 'who was guilty?, 'who was responsible?', 'who were the good guys?'[38]

Audiences hence identified with a man whose only option was violence and who was not a hero, but a 'cynic in despair'. Frayling further speculates that the popularity of Westerns among Italian audiences reflected a desire to escape from society, and the hostility to codified law and centralized government, occasionally enshrined in Hollywood Westerns, became a central theme in the Italian Western. He finds a parallel in the hostilities of 'Southern Italian society'.[39]

Others also recognize the political edge to the Western's rhetoric. John Lenihan locates Westerns of the late 1960s and early 1970s in an increasingly anti-establishment tradition, decrying the

> inequalities and dehumanization of postwar urban industrial development . . . Movies in general and Westerns in particular became more critical in their vision of society, more pessimistic about reform, and more accepting of personal violence as an alternative, rather than a solution, to social vapidity.[40]

As Lenihan remarks of the style of satire that Leone's films embodied, 'The premise of these satirical stabs at the classical Western is that frontier society is basically violent, greedy, and hypocritical, which in turn renders the hero's deviousness a perfectly logical response.'[41]

The Western's vision in the 1960s and 1970s was at least in part a form of social commentary, even satire, on modern America, an America that Leone held simultaneously in esteem and derision. Might the Ehud narrative also be understood as social commentary, even satire? I have already noted the moral ambiguity of the story. That is, while it does work on the same lines as the mythology of the Man of the late 1960s, the seeds of its

deconstruction are present as well. If there is satire, several scholars
(notably Brettler and Handy) clarify the fact that the Moabites are the
obvious target. But perhaps they are not the real target. In Judges, apart
from the recounting of a previous battle with Moab in chapter 11, Moab
or the Moabites only feature in the Ehud story. Given their caricatured
nature (e.g. fat, thick), the Moabites might best be regarded as rather
empty ciphers for a 'foreign power'. In other words, it does not seem to be
that important in this story that Eglon is a Moabite. Moab is one nation
among many from whom the major judges will achieve a limited deliverance. Indeed, the story as a whole, while achieving an 80-year peace,
demonstrates the failure of violent 'justice' to achieve a lasting solution to
the turmoil of Israel's foreign relations. And even though the land has
'rest', there is nothing to suggest that this achievement is politically desirable. It cannot stop the cycle of apostasy. In fact, Ehud is among the first
in a string of successively less successful judges.[42] Like the Man, change
can only be affected at the micro level. To go beyond that would be to
destroy the efficacy of the myth.[43]

While I am not denying that the Ehud story is satirizing something, we
simply cannot be as precise about its target as we can with the Western.
Having said that, based on the above analysis I would like to suggest some
possibilities about the social comment that might be at work in the Ehud
story. Perhaps similar social forces were at work on the Judges story-
tellers. Perhaps their environment was one in which the only real human
virtues were physical strength, fighting skills, wit and even subversion.
Perhaps the Ehud story is the by-product of a society awash with ideological and moral confusion (does not Judges ultimately ask, 'Who are the
good guys?'). Perhaps audiences did identify with an individual man
whose only viable option was violence, and who was not a clearly defined
hero. Perhaps the Ehud story does embody the desire to escape from
society and reflects a turbulent relationship with any form of centralized
government. Perhaps it is significant that an exilic, defeated society might
produce a hero who lives on his wits and prefers fantasized acts of violence to social responsibility. Perhaps the premise of Judges is that the
'frontier' society of ancient Israel was basically violent, greedy and hypocritical, which rendered Ehud's deviousness a logical response. And just as
the Westerns use all kinds of 'baddies' to satirize identifiable social forces,
perhaps the production of this satire was driven by social inequalities
and disempowerment. Finally, and most whimsically, perhaps as Ehud
became saturated with the violence of 'frontier' life, he might have
agreed with the haggard conclusion of *Unforgiven*'s William Munny
(Eastwood), who, while destroying his enemy as well as any hope of
redemption, declared, 'Deserve's got nothin' to do with it.'[44]

Notes

1 G. Garrett, 'The American West and the American Western: Printing the Legend', *Journal of American Culture* 14 (1991): 99–105 (102).

2 Garrett, 'The American West', p. 102.

3 R. Alter, *The Art of Biblical Narrative*, London: George Allen & Unwin, 1981, pp. 37–41; B. Halpern, *The First Historians: The Hebrew Bible and History*, University Park, PA: Pennsylvania State University Press, 1996 (orig. pub. 1988), pp. 39–75. For an insightful analysis of both studies, see Marc Brettler, 'Never the Twain Shall Meet? The Ehud Story as History and Literature', *HUCA* 42 (1991): 285–304.

4 The first of Leone's trilogy, *A Fistful of Dollars* (1964), sparked off a flood of imitations. The third of the trilogy was *The Good, the Bad and the Ugly* (1966). The term 'Spaghetti Western', originally used pejoratively of what critics perceived to be inferior Westerns, has come simply to refer to Spanish–Italian productions of Westerns (see the discussion of the term in Christopher Frayling's influential study, *Spaghetti Westerns: Cowboys and Europeans from Karl May to Sergio Leone*, London: I.B. Tauris, rev. edn, 2000 (1981), pp. ix–x, xix).

5 At a broad cultural level (and in film criticism) his character is understood as 'The Man With No Name' or simply 'the Man' (see Frayling, *Spaghetti Westerns*, p. 187).

6 Frayling, *Spaghetti Westerns*, p. 49.

7 Philip French, *Westerns: Aspects of a Movie Genre*, London: Secker and Warburg/BFI, 1973, pp. 57–8.

8 Frayling, *Spaghetti Westerns*, p. 61 (my emphasis).

9 French, *Westerns*, p. 129.

10 Halpern, *The First Historians*, pp. 41, 43.

11 So Will Wright, *Six Guns and Society: A Structural Study of the Western*, Berkeley, CA: University of California Press, 1975, pp. 66–7 *et passim*.

12 Meir Sternberg, *The Poetics of Biblical Narrative: Ideological Literature and the Drama of Reading*, Bloomington, IN: Indiana University Press, 1987, pp. 333–4.

13 Only rarely are the details of what the 'tribute' consists described. 1 Kgs 10.25 (NRSV) offers an insight from the description of 'tribute' given to Solomon from the 'kings of the earth': 'objects of silver and gold, garments, weaponry, spices, horses, and mules, so much year by year' (cf. 2 Kgs 8.9).

14 See the discussion in H.-J. Fabry and M. Weinfeld, 'מִנְחָה *minḥâ*', *TDOT*, VIII, pp. 407–21 (414–17).

15 See, for example, R. Bolin, *Judges: A New Translation with Introduction and Commentary*, AB, 6A; New York: Doubleday, 1975, p. 85; E. J. Hamlin, *Judges: At Risk in the Promised Land*, ITC; Grand Rapids, MI: Eerdmans, 1990, p. 73.

16 E. G. Kraeling suggests a number of such reasons; e.g. the first encounter was 'as ill suited as possible for an attempt to assassinate the oppressor' ('Difficulties in the Story of Ehud', *JBL* 54 (1935): 205–10 (206)).

17 Similarly, see Susan Niditch, *War in the Hebrew Bible: A Study in the Ethics of Violence*, Oxford: Oxford University Press, 1993, p. 119.

18 A feature widely recognized by commentators; e.g. Lillian R. Klein, *The*

Triumph of Irony in the Book of Judges, JSOTSup, 68; Sheffield: Almond Press, 1988, p. 37; Niditch, *War in the Hebrew Bible*, pp. 106, 117–18; J. L. McKenzie, *The World of the Judges*, London: Geoffrey Chapman, 1967, p. 123.

19 Numerous commentators highlight the story's wit: so J. A. Soggin, *Judges: A Commentary*, OTL; London: SCM Press, 2nd edn, 1987, p. 49; Alter, *The Art of Biblical Narrative*, p. 39; Tom A. Jull, 'מקרה in Judges 3: A Scatological Reading', *JSOT* 81 (1998): 63–75 (p. 71); Yairah Amit, *The Book of Judges: The Art of Editing*, BIS, 38; Leiden: Brill, 1999, pp. 197–8.

20 Brettler, 'Never the Twain Shall Meet?', p. 298 (citing F. Rosenthal).

21 McKenzie, *The World of the Judges*, p. 123.

22 J. Kutsko, 'Eglon', in *ABD* (CD-ROM edn).

23 J. Tompkins, 'Language and Landscape: An Ontology for the Western', *Art Forum* 28 (1990): 94–9 (96).

24 Lee Clark Mitchell, 'Violence in the Film Western', in J. David Slocum (ed.), *Violence and American Cinema*, AFI Film Readers; New York: Routledge, 2001, pp. 176–91 (179). Note also John G. Cawelti: 'the laconic style is commonly associated with the Western hero, particularly in the twentieth century, when movie stars like Gary Cooper, John Wayne, James Stewart and Henry Fonda have vied for the prize as the Western hero who can say the fewest words with the least expression . . . Like his gun, language is a weapon the hero rarely uses, but when he does it is with precise and powerful effectiveness' (*The Six-Gun Mystique*, Bowling Green, OH: Bowling Green University Popular Press, 1973, p. 61).

25 Compare Tompkins, 'Language and Landscape', p. 97.

26 Note the comments on the function of boundaries in Judges in Koosed and Linafelt, 'How the West Was Not One: Delilah Deconstructs the Western', in A. Bach (ed.), *Biblical Glamour and Hollywood Glitz*, Semeia, 74; Atlanta: Scholars Press, 1996, pp. 167–81 (179–80).

27 Two verses (21–22), 29 words in the Hebrew, are devoted to this single moment of violence.

28 Note Tompkins: 'It is fitting that in the Western the ultimate loss of control takes place when one man puts holes in another man's body' ('Language and Landscape', p. 97).

29 Cited in Frayling, *Spaghetti Westerns*, p. 183.

30 Frayling notes that 'The Man With No Name has been consistently misinterpreted by critics as a brutal existentialist living in a *moral* vacuum' (*Spaghetti Westerns*, p. 181). This misrepresentation continues with Mitchell's recent assessment of the Spaghetti Westerns as 'morally vacant' ('Violence in the Film Western', p. 183).

31 S. Prince, 'Tom Horn: Dialectics of Power and Violence in the Old West', *Journal of Popular Culture* 22 (1988): 119–29 (120).

32 Robert Warshow, cited in Mitchell, 'Violence in the Film Western', p. 180.

33 Mitchell, 'Violence in the Film Western', p. 188.

34 Cawelti, *The Six-Gun Mystique*, p. 84. He goes on to point out that the best Westerns always acknowledge a complexity and ambiguity inherent in this notion of legitimation (p. 85).

35 Koosed and Linafelt, 'How the West Was Not One', p. 172.

36 Klein, *The Triumph of Irony*, p. 38.

37 Cf. J. Cheryl Exum, who argues that God's commitment to his judges and

to Israel is either morally dubious (particularly in the cases of Jephthah, Samson and the Levite and his wife) or entirely absent (increasingly so towards the end of the book; 'The Centre Cannot Hold: Thematic and Textual Instabilities in Judges', *CBQ* 52.3 (1990): 410–31 (413)). Judges exhibits a 'love–hate' affair with the idea of kingship. People do what is 'right in their own eyes' while there is no king, but Abimelech, the first king, offers nothing that is politically desirable.

38 Frayling, citing L. Micciché, *Spaghetti Westerns*, p. 55.

39 Frayling, *Spaghetti Westerns*, p. 58.

40 John H. Lenihan, *Showdown: Confronting Modern America in the Western Film*, Chicago, IL: University of Illinois Press, 1980, p. 160.

41 Lenihan, *Showdown*, p. 173.

42 So Richard G. Bowman, 'Narrative Criticism: Human Purpose in Conflict with Divine Presence', in Gale A. Yee, *Judges and Method: New Approaches in Biblical Studies*, Minneapolis, MN: Fortress Press, 1995, pp. 17–44; and Exum, 'The Centre Cannot Hold', esp. pp. 426–31.

43 Frayling identifies the stock Italian Western hero with the Superman myth as examined by Umberto Eco. Like Superman, the Spaghetti hero acts at the local, micro level, that is, against identifiable 'bad guys' and does not necessarily defeat the structures of which they are a part (or sociological conditions such as unemployment). If he did, this would 'draw the world, and Superman with it, towards final "consumption"' (citing Eco, in *Spaghetti Westerns*, p. 78).

44 This essay appeared in a longer version as 'A Fistful of Shekels: Scrutinizing Ehud's Entertaining Violence (Judges 3:12–30)', *Biblical Interpretation* 11.1 (2003): 53–78.

13. The Two Faces of Betrayal:
The Characterization of Peter and Judas in the Biblical Epic or Christ Film

WILLIAM R. TELFORD

1. Introduction

The Aims of the Chapter

The title of this chapter is 'The Two Faces of Betrayal: The Characterization of Peter and Judas in the Biblical Epic or Christ Film'. What history and tradition, and art, literature and film did with these two figures is the subject of this chapter, and how they are treated in the biblical epic or Christ film is our particular focus. Both Peter and Judas are shown in the New Testament to have been guilty of an act of disloyalty, treachery or denial with respect to their master, Jesus. Nevertheless, one came to be *the* great apostle, the other *the* great apostate. One is seen as the prototypical Christian, the other the stereotypical Jew. One has come to be the supreme example of Christian discipleship, the other the universal symbol of Jewish perfidy. The one became a Pope, the other a pariah. Peter was given the keys to the kingdom of heaven, Judas was sent to eternal damnation in hell. Judas had his place among the twelve disciples of Jesus taken by another, Matthias (Acts 1.15–26), Peter presided over the process that replaced him. The one, then, has become a sacred symbol for a universal Church, the other a subversive icon for an unbelieving world. One was *rehabilitated* after his denial of Jesus, the other *vilified* in consequence of his treachery. It is these two biblical characters, then, and the two faces of betrayal that they represent, that I want to examine.

The chapter is divided into four parts. In the first three parts, I shall set the context for the subject by discussing the characterization of Peter and Judas in the New Testament, in history and tradition, and in art, literature and film, and in the final part I shall comment on a select number of clips from six biblical epics or Christ films, which will demonstrate the various and interesting ways that film-makers have treated these two characters. The Notes will suggest further reading, listing some key works on the biblical epic or Christ film,[1] and some principal works on Peter and Judas.[2]

Approaching the Subject Critically

Let me offer a brief word, first of all, on my methodological approach to the subject of this chapter. Films can be explored from a number of angles, as the first chapter in this book indicated. They can be examined in relation to their sources and with respect to the question of how these sources have been used or treated. They can be explored for their intertextual references, in other words. In this case, a major source for the biblical epic is, of course, the Bible, and where the Christ film is concerned, the New Testament Gospels, and so we shall look at how film-makers have altered or adapted these texts, as well as the traditions that have grown from them, in their filmic representations.

A growing emphasis in recent scholarly work on the cinema, as we saw in the first chapter, is the notion of the film itself as a text, and narrative criticism and theory, therefore, as applicable to it. Two key recent books in this regard are Jakob Lothe's *Narrative in Fiction and Film. An Introduction* (2000) and Robert Stam's *Film Theory. An Introduction* (2000), which devotes a chapter to this aspect. Films, in other words, like narrative texts, can be approached with respect to their plot, settings, and characterization. The key emphases and approach that I will be taking to the biblical epic and the Christ film in this chapter, therefore, will be on plot and characterization, intertextuality and the treatment of tradition.

2. Peter and Judas in the New Testament

Let us begin with a brief summary of the way Peter and Judas are treated in the New Testament. The New Testament, as a rule, furnishes little by way of sharp character definition of its key actors, far less an understanding of their motivations. To some extent, and to a limited degree, Peter and Judas buck this trend, especially Peter.

Peter in the New Testament

Peter is a prominent figure in the New Testament, especially in the Gospels (where he is mentioned by name 114 times) and the Acts of the Apostles (where he is mentioned 57 times).[3] Our knowledge of him is derived principally from the Gospels and Acts, then, but also to an extent from Paul's Letter to the Galatians. The two letters ascribed to him in the New Testament, 1 and 2 Peter, are generally regarded as pseudonymous, but supply some clues as to how a later Christian community, possibly in Rome, viewed him at the end of the first century or in the first part of the second.

A classic historical evaluation of his life and career was undertaken by Oscar Cullmann, and the results of that enquiry would still command widespread support, with the exception perhaps of the data surrounding his death, which comes from outside the New Testament. Cullmann concluded his book as follows:

> In summary of our entire historical section . . . we must say that during the lifetime of Peter he held a pre-eminent position among the disciples; that after Christ's death he presided over the church at Jerusalem in the first years; that he then became the leader of the Jewish Christian mission; that in this capacity, at a time which cannot be more closely determined but probably occurred at the end of his life, he came to Rome and there, after a very short work, died as a martyr under Nero.[4]

In their equally influential book, *Peter in the New Testament* (1973), Raymond Brown, Karl Donfried and John Reumann summarized the key images of Peter that are reflected in the New Testament: 'missionary, fisherman, pastoral shepherd, martyr, recipient of special revelation, confessor to the true faith, magisterial protector, and repentant sinner'.[5]

Where characterization is concerned, one commentator sums up what is by now a popularly conceived profile:

> The character of Peter is one of the most vividly drawn and charming in the NT. His sheer humanness has made him one of the most beloved and winsome members of the apostolic band. He was eager, impulsive, energetic, self-confident, aggressive, and daring, but also unstable, fickle, weak, and cowardly. He was guided more by quick impulse than logical reasoning, and he readily swayed from one extreme to the other. He was preeminently a man of action.[6]

One prominent element in the Gospel tradition about him is his alleged denial of Jesus. Mark, the earliest Gospel, is particularly scathing in his portrait of Peter, having him robustly swear allegiance to Jesus (14.29) but then deny him, not once but three times over (14.31, 66–72). Apart from a disputed hint in 16.7 ('Go, tell his disciples and Peter that he goes before you to Galilee'), this denial is not later reversed, since the original version of Mark ended with no post-resurrection appearances, and hence no stated rehabilitation of Peter.

Matthew softens this treatment considerably. Apart from inserting the now famous *investiture* scene ('You are Peter and on this rock I will build my church', Mt. 16.18), he does supply post-resurrection appearances that give the disciples, including Peter, a post-Easter leadership role. 'Matthew's Gospel', hence, in the words of R. P. Martin, 'offers a picture of Peter modified by ecclesiastical developments.'[7]

Luke goes even further in effecting a bridge between the disciple who denied his Lord in the Gospel and the one who will lead the Church in the Acts of the Apostles. Mark's harsh treatment is toned down, and Peter's post-denial rehabilitation is announced: 'I have prayed for you', says the Lukan Jesus, 'and when you have turned again, strengthen your brethren' (Lk. 22.32).

John's Gospel crowns this developing trajectory. Despite the role given to the 'Beloved Disciple', Peter is credited in chapter 21 with a post-resurrection appearance from Jesus, and in this he is not only given the opportunity to reverse his threefold denial of his Master with a threefold declaration of love, but is rewarded with a commission to 'feed my [Christ's] sheep' (Jn 21.15–17). Thus the fisherman became the shepherd, and exchanged his net for a crook.

In sum, then, where Peter is concerned, rehabilitation after betrayal is the chief trajectory that one can discern in the New Testament tradition.

Judas in the New Testament

Where Judas is concerned, the story is very different. Where Peter is seen performing a variety of roles, Judas has little significance in the New Testament accounts other than as the one who betrayed Jesus. Our meagre knowledge of him comes solely from the Gospels and Acts. His name is still a puzzle to us, and G. W. Buchanan sums up the possibilities: 'Many suggestions have been given to explain the name Iscariot. The most plausible are (1) "man of Kerioth" [in southern Judea], (2) "liar" or "man of the lie", (3) "dyer" and (4) "dagger bearer" [or assassin, hence Zealot].'[8]

If the first is correct, then Judas was the only disciple, it appears, who came from Judaea, and was not a Galilean. Treasurer to the twelve, he betrayed Jesus, we are told, to the Jewish authorities for the legendary 30 pieces of silver, and suffered either an intentional death (suicide, by hanging, Mt. 27.3–5) or an accidental one (a fall which ruptured his intestines, Acts 1.16–20).

The dominant image associated with Judas, therefore, is of the betrayer of Jesus. To us today, he is an enigmatic figure, the most enigmatic in the gospel story. His motivations for betraying Jesus are ultimately unknown but this lacuna in biblical characterization has been filled with myriad speculations, and has been grist for the mill for countless theological, literary and filmic presentations. Was he merely a pawn in a divine game? Was he a good man turned by the influence of Satan (cf. Lk. 22.3; Jn 13.2, 27)? Did he betray Jesus out of greed or avarice, or personal jealousy? Was this deed a misguided attempt to force Jesus's hand politically or to test his leadership? Was it the act of a disillusioned patriot? All have been suggested. When we examine the Gospel accounts, what is clear, as William Klassen points out, is that, just as Peter's trajectory after betrayal is one of increasing *rehabilitation*, Judas's trajectory is one of increasing *vilification*.

3. Peter and Judas in History and Tradition

If we turn to the treatment of Peter and Judas in tradition outside and beyond the New Testament, this becomes more and more obvious.

Peter in History and Tradition

In addition to his role in legitimizing the papacy, what is significant about Peter is the leading role he plays in the tradition of Christian piety. Peter, in Leslie Houlden's words is 'the man whose timid abandonment of Christ was transformed by grace into vigorous mission and ultimate martyrdom'.[9] Taking its cue, perhaps, from the New Testament's Petrine Letters, Peter's powerful profile produced a panoply of writings all about him or ascribed falsely to him: *The Apocalypse of Peter (Ethiopic, Greek, Coptic), The Acts of Peter, The Acts of Peter and Paul, The Gospel of Peter, The Doctrine of Peter, The Preaching of Peter, The Passion of Peter and Paul, The Martyrdom of Peter, The Epistle of Peter to James, The Letter of Peter to Philip* and so on.

Three key traditions are associated with him. The first is that he not only had a wife, as indicated in the New Testament (1 Cor. 9.5) but also children, one of whom, a daughter, was said to be disabled. Tradition attached a name to her, Petronella, gave him a son as well, and invented a glorious martyrdom for his wife. The second tradition is the one advanced by the church father Papias, and others, that Mark had been a follower of Peter and that the Gospel that bears his name was essentially the reminiscences of the apostle. The third and most important tradition is that of his martyrdom, a fate that is only hinted at in the New Testament (cf. Jn 21.18–19). The traditions are either silent or divergent about the place and the time, but the popular aggregated view of ecclesiastical romantics is that Peter was crucified in Rome, upside down, on the Vatican Hill, within the emperor's gardens, at the same time as Paul, at the time of Nero's persecution of Christians (64–67 AD), and there he is now buried.

In connection with Peter's martyrdom is the famous 'Quo Vadis?' legend. James Hall's summary of the story is so succinct that it is worth quoting in full:

> *Domine, quo vadis?* The earliest version of the story is found in the early Acts of Peter, a New Testament apocryphal work, and is retold in

the *Golden Legend*. At the prompting of his fellow Christians, Peter departed from Rome at the height of the persecutions by Nero. On the Appian Way he met Christ in a vision. Peter exclaimed, 'Lord, where goest thou?', and received the reply, 'I go to Rome to be crucified again.' Peter interpreted this to mean that he was to return to Rome to prepare for his own martyrdom. Christ is shown carrying the cross, and addressing Peter.[10]

While fascinating in their inventiveness as well as their ghoulishness, the historical basis of these traditions is very difficult to determine. There is late second-century attestation for Peter's association with Rome (and the tradition may be even earlier) but one looks in vain to the New Testament for corroborative evidence. 'At any rate the question is still controversial', Geddes MacGregor states, 'as is also the nature of his primacy among the apostles.'[11]

What runs through all these traditions, however, is the image of a figure who, though betraying Jesus, has been powerfully rehabilitated by the Church and made into an ecclesiastical icon, an image of Christian piety. He has even been adopted by secular society in a somewhat 'domesticated' form, if we are to judge by the widespread popularity, for example, of the 'St Peter joke'.[12] There isn't, to my knowledge, a genre of Judas jokes.

Judas in History and Tradition

Judas did not spawn a significant apocryphal literature like Peter, but we have knowledge of a unfortunately now lost *Gospel of Judas*, which was used by a Gnostic sect called the Cainites. What was significant about Judas in later tradition was the link between him and antisemitism, a subject touched upon by Klassen and treated in Maccoby's book. Great play was made on his name (Judas) and its correspondence with the name associated with the Jewish people in general (Judah). Jerome makes the connection: 'The Jews take their name, not from that Judah who was a holy man, but from the betrayer. From the former, we [i.e., Christians] are spiritual Jews; from the traitor come the carnal Jews.'[13] Besserman notes that '[t]he association of the name and character of the avaricious and traitorous "Judas" with the name and qualities of the "Jew" is a medieval commonplace'.[14] This can be observed particularly in the medieval Passion Plays where he was the principal Jewish character, and where he was depicted not only as a traitor but also as a usurer.[15] One of Judas's distinguishing marks in these plays (and this was not a normal Jewish stereotype) was his red hair, an idiosyncrasy he shared only with Herod.[16]

Judas, then, is the disciple who betrayed Jesus, the ultimate symbol for human treachery, a creature fit only for the lowest circle of hell, where

Dante in fact places him.[17] At the same time, however, there is a sense in which, by being anathema to the established and dominant religion, he is also a 'subversive icon', and this is a theme we shall pick up later in film. He was certainly such to the Gnostic Cainites who, in opposition to both Judaism and Christian orthodoxy, regarded him as a saint and a hero like other Old Testament rebels such as Cain and Korah. It was Judas's greater spiritual insight that had led him to precipitate Jesus's death, and his superior knowledge that had reckoned on such an act leading to the defeat of the forces of darkness.[18]

4. Peter and Judas in Art, Literature and Film

To provide further elements of context for our biblical epic and Christ film excerpts, let me say a few things about these two figures in art, literature and film (in general).

Peter and Judas in Art

Of the depiction of Peter in art, D. H. Farmer writes:

> Images of Peter [in art] are innumerable, but his portraiture (possibly an early tradition) remains curiously constant, of a man with a square face, a bald or tonsured head, and a short square, curly beard. . . . Sometimes he is dressed in a toga.[19]

The only apostle to carry a wand or staff, he can also be recognized by the carrying of keys (cf. Mt. 16.19), a distinguishing motif that goes back to the fifth century.[20]

In the main, dark hair, sometimes a dark complexion, a beard and an advanced age are characteristic of Judas's image in art.[21] He is described as small in stature, according to legend, with red hair and wearing a yellow robe.[22] In medieval art, these elements combine with his image as the archetypal Jew to give an unflattering portrait: 'red hair and beard, ruddy skin, yellow robe and money bag, large, hooked nose, big lips and bleary eyes'.[23]

Peter and Judas in Literature

Peter has been treated rather circumspectly in English literature, and it is only in the twentieth century that lively portrayals of him have been ventured. Examples include Thornton Wilder's play *Now the Servant's Name was Malchus* (1928), Henry Sienkewicz's novel *Quo Vadis?* (1896),

Morris West's novel, *The Shoes of the Fisherman* (1963), Lloyd C. Douglas's *The Robe* (1942) and *The Big Fisherman* (1948). What distinguishes the characterization of Judas in literature from the nineteenth century onwards, according to Besserman, is its sympathetic treatment of him:

> In a variety of modern revisionist versions of the Gospel narrative – e.g., Anthony Burgess's *Jesus of Nazareth*; George Moore's *The Brook Kerith*; Robert Graves's *King Jesus*; and Nicos Kazantzakis' *The Greek Passion* and *The Last Temptation of Christ* – Judas is absolved of the guilt associated with Christ's betrayal and passion, and accorded semi-heroic status.[24]

Peter and Judas in Film

All these cultural currents have fed themselves, therefore, into the depiction of Peter and Judas in film. Novels such as Henryk Sienkiewicz's *Quo Vadis?*, Lloyd C. Douglas's *The Robe* and *The Big Fisheman* have formed the basis for a number of Roman-Christian epics featuring Peter, with actors such as Finlay Currie and Michael Rennie playing this esteemed role. I shall comment on an excerpt from one of these in a moment. Judas has been a dominant figure in the biblical epic or the Christ film from its very inception, given his dramatic potential for plot and character development. One of the earliest of these was *The Kiss of Judas*, an early French short released in 1909 that told of the events of the Last Supper up to the time of Judas's suicide.

Judas continues to appear in various guises even in the most recent films. Some have seen a Jesus-Judas typology in *Star Wars* (1977), particularly with respect to Obi-Wan Kenobi's death at the hands of the cosmic rebel, Darth Vader.[25] An interesting example of the demonization of Judas in recent film is Patrick Lussier's *Dracula 2001*, in which vampirism is wedded to the New Testament, and the Dracula figure, 'the King of the Vampires', 'the first vampire in the world', is revealed to be – Judas himself. The Judas legend is also used to good effect in Ridley Scott's *Hannibal* (2001), the Florentine cop, Pazzi, being despatched by Hannibal Lector in a manner fiendishly modelled on the death of Judas, namely, by hanging and evisceration following defenestration. This ghoulish murder occurs after Hannibal has given his learned lecture to the trustees of the Florentine archive on the depiction of Judas in art.

Mention was made earlier of the various motivations that have been offered in both popular and academic literature for Judas's betrayal of Jesus: divine destiny, satanic influence, worldly greed, personal jealousy, moral disillusionment, political ambition, misguided patriotism. Because of the relative silence of the New Testament on these matters, Judas's great narrative pull is that directors have been free to explore these motivations in imaginative ways.

Some portraits of Judas have been hostile, as we shall see shortly in *The King of Kings* (1927). Others have been sympathetic, with Judas presented as Jesus's 'right-hand man', as in *Jesus Christ Superstar* (1973), or as Jesus's alter ego, as in *The Last Temptation of Christ* (1988). Judas's anguish at his betrayal of Jesus is given special emphasis in films such as *The King of Kings*, *King of Kings*, *The Greatest Story Ever Told*, *Jesus of Nazareth* and *Jesus Christ Superstar*. In some films, a twist is introduced, in that Judas is himself betrayed, by the scribe Zerah, for example, in Zeffirelli's *Jesus of Nazareth* (1977), or supremely, as we shall see, in Scorsese's *The Last Temptation of Christ* (1988). In D. W. Griffith's *Intolerance* (1916), as a result of Jewish pressure, Judas's betrayal was simply excised.[26]

5. The Two Faces of Betrayal: Peter and Judas in the Biblical Epic or Christ Film – Some Selected Clips

These observations, I trust, will have set the historical, traditional, artistic, literary and cinematic context for our examination of the characterization of Peter and Judas in the biblical epic or Christ film, and it is to six selected sequences from these films that we now turn. Text Box 13.1 offers some brief information on the films selected. Further reading is to be found in the Notes. I shall give a brief general introduction to each sequence (whose approximate time location in the film is given in square brackets at the end of each heading), and then make some comments on its characterization of Peter and Judas. When you yourself view the sequences, you may wish to note down your own observations and comments on them, and for this purpose a further text box (13.2) is provided.

13.1 Notes on the Films Selected

The King of Kings (Cecil B. DeMille, 1927)
A major classic, this was the first full-length, silent Hollywood epic on the life of Jesus, as seen from the perspective of Mary Magdalene. It presents Mary as a rich courtesan with Judas as her lover. Its many memorable moments include Mary's riding off in her chariot to rescue her Judas from the clutches of the carpenter of Nazareth ('Harness my zebras – gift of the

Nubian king!'), her subsequent exorcism by Jesus in a swirl of exiting
demons, the moving giving of sight to a little blind girl and dramatic
crucifixion and resurrection scenes.

Quo Vadis? (Mervyn LeRoy, 1951)
A Roman soldier, Marcus Vinicius (Robert Taylor) falls in love with a
Christian slave girl, Lygia (Deborah Kerr) and seeks to save her from the
lions and Peter Ustinov (Nero). Described by critics as 'unusually intelli-
gent' (R. Kinnard and T. Davis, *Divine Images. A History of Jesus on the
Screen*, New York: Citadel Press, 1992, p. 74), this major Roman-
Christian epic made $25 million worldwide and paved the way for the
biblical epics which followed. How could it fail with St Peter played by a
Scotsman – and from Edinburgh too (Finlay Currie)!

King of Kings (Nicholas Ray, 1961)
A remake of the DeMille version in name only, this Sixties' Hollywood
adaptation presents Judas and Barabbas as political revolutionaries, with
Jesus as a reluctant pawn in their game. Criticized by the Catholic Legion
of Decency as 'theologically, historically, and scripturally inaccurate'
(Kinnard and Davis, *Divine Images*, p. 132), the film is now viewed in
retrospect as better than its critics made it out to be.

The Gospel according to St. Matthew (Pier Paolo Pasolini, 1964)
A low-budget, black-and-white, European film made by the Marxist director, Pier Paolo Pasolini and dedicated to Pope John XXIII, this unconventional adaptation of Matthew's Gospel in *cinéma verité* style had more
impact on audiences than the traditional, glossy Hollywood epic, *The
Greatest Story Ever Told*, which was to follow it a year later.

Jesus Christ, Superstar (Norman Jewison, 1973)
Filmed in Israel, where young tourists re-enact episodes of the life of Christ,
this vibrant movie, which was based on the successful rock opera by Tim
Rice and Andrew Lloyd Webber (with a screenplay by Norman Jewison
and Melvyn Bragg, and musical direction by André Previn) mixes the
historical and the contemporary to good effect.

The Last Temptation of Christ (Martin Scorsese, 1988)
Based on Kazantzakis's novel about 'the dual substance of Christ' and 'the
incessant, merciless battle between the spirit and the flesh', and directed by
one of Hollywood's most distinguished film-makers, this is one of the
finest, most religious and yet most controversial Christ films ever made.

13.2 Comments on Films/Clips

The King of Kings (1927): The Two Faces of Betrayal – Peter and Judas at the Last Supper

Quo Vadis? (1951): Betrayal Redeemed – Peter's Vision on the Appian Way

King of Kings (1961): The Two Sides of Betrayal – Judas and Barabbas as Collaborators

The Gospel according to St. Matthew (1964): The Anguish of Betrayal – Peter's Denial

Jesus Christ Superstar (1973): Who's betraying Whom? – Judas's Warning

The Last Temptation of Christ (1988): The Betrayer betrayed – Jesus is Judas!

The King of Kings (1927): The Two Faces of Betrayal – Peter and Judas at the Last Supper [01.03.28–01.07.04]

Our first sequence, from Cecil B. DeMille's 1927 *The King of Kings* presents us with our two faces of betrayal. A major classic, this was the first full-length, silent Hollywood epic on the life of Jesus, as seen from the perspective of Mary Magdalene. It presents Mary as a rich courtesan with Judas as her lover. Its many memorable moments include Mary's riding off in her chariot to rescue her Judas from the clutches of the carpenter of Nazareth (declaiming the immortal words 'Harness my zebras – gift of the Nubian king!'), her subsequent exorcism by Jesus in a swirl of exiting demons, the moving giving of sight to a little blind girl and dramatic Last Supper, crucifixion and resurrection scenes.

In the Last Supper sequence under review, the disciples are seated at a table. Judas is on his left hand. He is dressed as a courtesan. Jesus has his overmantle on, as in an earlier scene with the children. The bread is passed solemnly to every disciple, followed by the cup, with each striking bathetic and reverential poses, except for Judas, who is uneasy and distracted. He refuses the cup. Jesus announces his betrayer. Judas slips out as the other disciples remonstrate. Jesus embraces his mother and takes his leave. A dove flutters over an illuminated chalice.

As you watch the sequence, observe the various aesthetic elements: its illustrated Bible story book ethos, the harmonizing use of biblical captions drawn from the Authorized Version of the Bible, the choral music and the use of traditional hymns (in the sonorized 1931 version), DeMille's use of close-up, the stylized religious expressionism. These elements will be discussed further in chapters 16 and 17 ('"His blood be upon us, and our children": The Treatment of Jews and Judaism in the Christ Film' and 'Ritual Recast and Revisioned: Hollywood Remembers the First Passover and the Last Supper'). The actor chosen by DeMille to portray Jesus was the distinguished British actor, H. B. Warner. Judas is played by Joseph Schildkraut. Peter, the big fisherman, played by Ernest Torrance, is the one hugging the cup to his breast.

The first thing to observe is Peter's appearance. He is depicted here very much as in traditional Christian art. The second thing that one notes is the intensely sympathetic treatment accorded to him. Peter lifts his face to Jesus; he clasps the cup to his breast; he falls to the table with anguish as Judas leaves. Here is Peter in the full traditional image of Christian piety.

Where Judas's appearance is concerned, the contrast could not be greater. Judas is depicted in a way quite unlike his image in religious art. Here he is dandified, shifty, clean-shaven in contrast to the other disciples (as is Caiaphas, Jesus's other arch-enemy in the film), black-haired, and dressed as a playboy or gigolo. One notes the hostile treatment accorded

to him. Where Peter lifts his face to Jesus, Judas covers his own, and he
treats the cup like a poisoned chalice. The minatory music (deep bass/
violin) announces Judas as the betrayer. There is much rolling of eyes.
Judas is being presented as the archetype of evil.

Judas's motivations, according to DeMille, are quite clear. In the intertitles so characteristic of these early films, Judas is described as 'the
Ambitious, who joined the Disciples in the belief that Jesus would be
the nation's King and reward him with honor and high office'. After the
cleansing of the Temple, '[t]hey [the crowd] try to crown him king', we are
told, 'Judas himself producing a crown (Jn 6.15)'. Judas betrays Jesus
to Caiaphas, we are informed, for 30 pieces of silver, 'after hope of an
earthly kingdom was gone'.

Where the intertextual dimension is concerned, DeMille has obviously
invented the romantic relationship between Mary Magdalene and Judas.
His treatment of later tradition, however, is generally conservative. The
tradition of Peter's connection with Mark's Gospel is dramatized earlier
on in the film by Peter's rescue and subsequent caring for the young,
homeless Mark who is cured of his lameness by Jesus.

One untraditional element, nevertheless, is his introduction of Peter to
the audience as 'the giant fisherman'. Where this idea comes from, is anybody's guess. That it runs counter to the Catholic Church's claim to have
discovered the bones of Peter under the Vatican is clear, for, although I
myself am sceptical of such a claim, I did check up on the Vatican reports
and discovered that the (alleged) skeleton reveals him to have been five
feet seven inches tall![27] One commentator suggests that 'Peter is portrayed
as the "Giant Disciple", perhaps because of his reputation as a great
fisherman, but more likely because he was recognized within the medieval
church as a theological giant among the other disciples.'[28]

Quo Vadis? *(1951): Betrayal Redeemed – Peter's Vision on the Appian Way* [01.57.24–01.59.43]

Our second excerpt is from Mervyn LeRoy's *Quo Vadis?* (1951). Based
on Henryk Sienkiewicz's novel (1896), it tells the story of a Roman soldier, Marcus Vinicius (Robert Taylor), who falls in love with a Christian
slave girl, Lygia (Deborah Kerr), and seeks to save her both from the lions
and Peter Ustinov (Nero). Described by critics as 'unusually intelligent',[29]
this major Roman-Christian epic made $25 million worldwide and paved
the way for the biblical epics that followed. Four key scenes involve Peter:
his speech at a nocturnal Christian meeting; the famous 'Quo vadis?'
episode; Peter's subsequent speech in the arena; and his crucifixion upside
down on the Vatican Hill. Peter is played by Finlay Currie, a Scottish

actor, and former organist and choirmaster, born, like Sean Connery, in Edinburgh, but very unlike this other man of action. Although he is best remembered for playing the convict Magwitch in David Lean's *Great Expectations* (1946), Currie was known for his impressive character roles, often as patriarchs or other men of authority.

The scene selected is Peter's vision on the Appian Way. Peter is leaving Rome to avoid Nero's persecution of Christians, sees a vision ('Quo vadis, domine'/'Whither goest thou, Lord?') and returns to the capital to face his death. The first thing to notice is Peter's conventional appearance: the patriarchal beard, the white robes, the carrying of the staff in the form of the shepherd's crook. The apostle is depicted, then, as he is in traditional Christian art, although audiences, responding to his accent, might find Peter as a Scotsman (albeit with a pronounced Semitic nose), a somewhat anomalous element! Here we have the universal Peter, the model of true discipleship, the ecclesiastical patriarch, and no longer the original Jewish follower of Jesus. Here he is accompanied by a youthful companion, Nazarius, through whom Christ speaks. Nazarius is the Christian neo-phyte, the root of his very name ('Nazar-') conjuring up in our minds, the Nazarene. He is Christianity's next generation, the future of Christianity, and when Marcus and Lygia leave Rome at the end of the film, Nazarius is with them when they see Peter's staff sprouting leaves at the very spot where he had his vision.

Intertextually, the sequence carries little significance since it is not in the New Testament. Two passages, however, have resonances with this tradi-tion, namely, the passage in the Fourth Gospel's farewell discourse where Peter asks of Jesus, 'Whither goest thou?' and Jesus answers, 'Where I am going you cannot follow me now; but you shall follow afterward' (Jn 13.36). The other is the Johannine Jesus's prediction in Jn 21.18: 'Truly, truly, I say to you, when you were young, you girded yourself and walked where you would; but when you are old, you will stretch out your hands, and another will gird you and carry you where you do not wish to go.' The legend may indeed be an imaginative embellishment of these selfsame passages.

The post-biblical tradition itself is altered by LeRoy in respect of the reasons that are given for Peter's departure from Rome, that is, to escape Nero's persecution. Peter departs from Rome in the original tradition because his preaching has made converts of the wives and concubines of the prominent men of Rome, and, as a result, they have given up sleeping with their husbands and lovers (apocryphal stories have a distinct antipathy to sex). These frustrated men plot to kill him, but he is fore-warned and leaves in anticipation! The main point, nevertheless, is that the Quo Vadis? legend, and its filmic representation here, is another witness to the developing tradition of Peter's rehabilitation after betrayal.

King of Kings *(1961): The Two Sides of Betrayal – Judas and Barabbas as Collaborators* [01.39.43–01.42.54]

Having looked at 'betrayal redeemed – Peter's vision on the Appian Way', let us now turn to our third sequence, which I have entitled 'the two sides of betrayal – Judas and Barabbas as collaborators'. Our selected sequence is from Nicholas Ray's *King of Kings* (1961). A remake of the DeMille version in name only, this Sixties' Hollywood adaptation presents Judas and Barabbas as political revolutionaries, with Jesus as a reluctant pawn in their game. Criticized by the Catholic Legion of Decency as 'theologic-ally, historically, and scripturally inaccurate',[30] the film is now viewed in retrospect as better than its critics made it out to be.

The style is impressive, and it is distinguished for its aesthetic look, and its painterly quality. The costumes throughout are immaculate, and the colours striking, especially the solid blocks of blue, brown, white and blood-red. Giving the audience its emotional cue is the musical score by Miklos Rosza, the Hungarian composer whose music virtually epitomizes the biblical epic in the popular imagination nowadays.

The part of Jesus in the film was played by Jeffrey Hunter, an American actor popular in the 1950s, especially among teenagers. Where character-ization is concerned, his adolescent Jesus offers a sharp contrast to H. B. Warner's patriarchal Jesus in the 1927 version. Judas is played by Rip Torn and Barabbas by Harry Guardino. Our chosen excerpt, found just before the film's first intermission, takes place in an underground Zealot cave, where Barabbas is supervising the manufacture of swords. Judas and Barabbas are discussing their strategy, with Judas urging that Jesus be given time to speak in the Temple to enlist the people's support without bloodshed. Barabbas, however, plans a surprise attack on the Romans.

This film stands out for the way that it explores the motivations of Judas in betraying Jesus, and places these motivations within the context of the Jewish nationalist struggle. Two revolutionary strategies are repre-sented by Barabbas and Jesus respectively, and Judas is the figure caught in the middle:

> While Jesus and Barabbas (Harry Guardino) represent alternative methods of resistance, Judas (Rip Torn) is caught in the middle, turning towards one, then the other, trying but failing to bring them together. While one is, as the [earlier] voice-over puts it, the 'Messiah of War', the other is the 'Messiah of Peace'.[31]

Judas himself believes in political messiahship, while Jesus promotes inner transformation. Later, in order to enlist Jesus's support for Barabbas's movement, Judas decides to force his hand. He hopes that Jesus will employ miracles on behalf of the people against the Romans. A unifying theme in the sequence is that of 'fire' and 'water' which is another metaphor for the difference between Jesus and Barabbas. The scene begins with the image of the sword and the water. Later, Barabbas criticizes Jesus in the same vein: 'He speaks only of peace. I am fire, he is water. How can we ever meet?' Another twist in the narrative is the notion of the 'betrayer betrayed'. Barabbas promises Judas that he will stand by Jesus in the Temple and give him time to speak, but in reality he thinks that 'Judas dreams, and all dreamers are fools'. The Zealots plan, in fact, to borrow Jesus's audience, but storm the Temple while he speaks.

The Gospel according to St. Matthew *(1964): The Anguish of Betrayal – Peter's Denial* [01.50.01–01.52.09]

Our fourth excerpt returns to Peter, and deals with another aspect of betrayal, the apostle's denial of Jesus and the anguish resulting from it. One of the most powerful denial scenes in the Christ film is to be found in Pier Paulo Pasolini's *The Gospel according to St. Matthew*, which was released in 1964. This was a low-budget, black-and-white, European film made by a Marxist director, and dedicated (somewhat ironically) to Pope John XXIII. Made with a cast of non-professionals, and filmed in Southern Italy, it was immensely popular, its unconventional adaptation of Matthew's Gospel in *cinéma verité* style having more impact on audiences than the traditional, glossy Hollywood epic, *The Greatest Story Ever Told*, which was to follow it a year later.[32] The actor who played Jesus was likewise an unknown, a Spanish student, Enrique Irazoqui, who had never acted before. Peter was played by Settimo Di Porto, a young Jewish subproletarian (as Pasolini called him) from Rome.

The sequence begins after Jesus is taken bound to Caiaphas, with Peter following on. The text of Mt. 26.57–75 is the source. There is silence. The trial is staged with the camera set from Peter's perspective at the back of the crowd. The questioning of Jesus is heard from a distance, the audience catching the muted but raised voices of his questioners. Peter denies knowing Jesus and then breaks down and weeps in the empty street outside. Violin music plays.

One should observe, in particular, the camerawork here, and listen out for the effective use of music to lend pathos to the scene. Pasolini makes very effective use of the hand-held camera. One should look out, in addition, for the use of distance shots (of the trial at the beginning) to establish the scene and close-ups thereafter (of Peter; the first woman; the first man; the second woman). The peasant faces as well as the southern Italian settings are also to be noted.

What Pasolini's camerawork does is increase the sense of participation

on the part of the spectator by virtue of the camera angle selected. We
begin with a distance shot from the back of the crowd, and catch Peter's
view of the proceedings. The eye of the camera is Peter's eye, and it is also
ours. We then follow Peter out of the trial scene. We, like him, are challenged by the various interlocutors. We follow him into the open space of
the city, into the light, after the confined spaces where his denial has been
reiterated three times. We follow immediately behind him, as the violin
music invokes his reflective and penitent mood. Then we see his face, and
his tears. The camera then backs away from him and leaves him in his
anguish, and we are left with a final distance shot. This is brilliant film-
making.

Jesus Christ Superstar *(1973): Who's betraying Whom? – Judas's Warning* [00.06.42–00.10.02]

Because space is limited, I shall leave further comment on Pasolini's *The
Gospel according to St. Matthew* (1964) to chapter 16 ('"His blood be
upon us, and our children": The Treatment of Jews and Judaism in the
Christ Film'), and move on to our next film, *Jesus Christ Superstar* (1973).
Filmed in Israel, where young tourists re-enact episodes of the life of
Christ, this vibrant movie, which was based on the successful rock opera
by Tim Rice and Andrew Lloyd Webber (with a screenplay by Norman
Jewison and Melvyn Bragg, and musical direction by André Previn) mixes
the historical and the contemporary to good effect. The figure of Jesus,
traditionally dressed in white, is played by Ted Neeley, while that of Judas
is played by the black actor/singer, Carl Anderson.

I have called this excerpt, 'Who's betraying Whom? – Judas's Warning'
for reasons that will become apparent. The scene occurs fairly early on in
the film. On a pinnacle, dressed in an open-necked red and black trouser-
suit, sits Judas who sings the opening song, 'Heaven on Their Minds'. He
asks Jesus to listen to him and to remember the oppression under which
the people live.

The first thing to comment on is Judas's appearance. Here again we
have the familiar colour red associated with Judas. At the end of the
movie, and perhaps hinting at his ultimate redemption, Judas descends
from heaven in a dazzling white Elvis Presley-like trouser-suit. The fact
that Carl Anderson's Judas is also black is a bold, provocative and possible symbolic piece of casting, and all the more so against Ted Neely's
golden-haired Jesus.

Jewison's Judas is, therefore, one of the most complex Judases in the
Christ film repertoire, and vital to this film. He, not Peter, is Jesus's 'right-
hand man'. At one point, Judas declares:

Listen, Jesus, do you care for your race?
Don't you see we must keep in our place?
We are occupied.
Have you forgotten how put down we are?
I am frightened by the crowd,
For we are getting much too loud,
And they'll crush us if we go too far.

Because Judas is black, and this film was released in the aftermath of the black civil rights movement, we are tempted to see in him the voice of black rather than Jewish oppression. On the other hand, by urging restraint on Jesus's revolutionary activism, he seems to express the voice of social conservatism. As with other Christ films, the movie explores Judas's motivations but in a distinctive way. Judas is neither a pawn in God's divine game (as scriptural writers imply), nor a well-meaning but misguided zealot (as some modern directors have tended to see him), but someone who wishes to puncture Jesus's divine pretensions, and their consequences.

As Stern, Jefford and Debona point out:

Judas will betray Jesus in order to force him to admit publicly that the people have deluded themselves about who Jesus is as the Messiah (a cosmic savior from God), and thus draw them away from any direct, self-destructive conflict with Roman power.[33]

Judas is concerned about the distinction between the myth and the man. By criticizing Jesus, and hence Christianity, for allowing the worship of the man to replace an emphasis on his teaching we have an almost post-modern note. Who's betraying whom, here?

The Last Temptation of Christ *(1988): The Betrayer betrayed –*
Jesus is Judas! [02.26.06–02.29.22]

This leads us conveniently to our last sequence, which I have entitled 'The Betrayer betrayed – Jesus is Judas!' You will see why in a moment. This sequence is taken from Martin Scorsese's *The Last Temptation of Christ* (1988).

Based on Kazantzakis's novel about 'the dual substance of Christ' and 'the incessant, merciless battle between the spirit and the flesh', and directed by one of Hollywood's most distinguished film-makers, this is one of the finest, most religious and yet most controversial Christ films ever made. Judas is again the central character, and this time he is Jesus's alter ego. The film takes seriously Judas's predestined role as Jesus's betrayer, but this time shows Jesus and Judas in collusion over the divine plan. Initially under contract from the Zealots to kill Jesus but now a follower, Judas is instructed by Jesus to aid him in his task of saving the world by dying on the cross for his people's sins. The film explores the consequences for the world if the human Jesus had, in fact, failed to carry out his divine mission, and if he had succumbed to the temptation of living a normal life, with domestic concerns – a temptation mediated by the devil in the form of a young girl. It carries out this theological exploration, in the most imaginative way, by presenting a series of dream sequences that occur when Jesus is on the cross, and in which this alternative scenario takes place.

The sequence I have chosen is one of these dream sequences. The movie has moved forward to 70 AD. Jesus is on his deathbed, and the Romans are sacking Jerusalem. The disciples are visiting him, and among them is Judas. The part of Jesus is played by Willem Dafoe, and that of Judas by Harvey Keitel.

W. Barnes Tatum comments on the film as follows:

> And during the fantasy sequence, which includes the burning of Jerusalem by the Romans in 70 C.E., Judas upbraids Jesus for not having kept their bargain by Jesus' having forsaken the cross. Judas says: 'He was going to be the new covenant; now there's no more Israel. . . .' Therefore, the film ironically anticipates the time when Judaism and Christianity go their separate ways.[34]

The first thing to note is Judas' pre-eminence over Peter. He is the last figure to appear, and, this time, he is the one carrying the staff. Second, one observes again the traditional colour of red associated with Judas. He has red hair (particularly prominent in the opening sequence of the film), and this association is augmented with the blood that stains his hands.

This is the most complex Judas we have yet seen in film, as well as the most complex Jesus. This is an angry Judas who has played his part in the drama of salvation, only to find that he, himself, has been betrayed by Jesus. This is a sympathetic Judas, with whose passion, strength and emotional intimacy audiences can identify. This is the only Judas who doesn't in the end hang himself. Instead, he fulfils his role in the divine plan by persuading Jesus to return to the cross, and so secures humanity's salvation. In giving this ultimate twist to the concept of betrayal, in exploring the dualisms of spirituality and social activism, humanity and divinity, the spirit and the body, sin and redemption, and, finally, in illuminating the nature of religious martyrdom (a theme touched upon more than once in the St Deiniol's conferences), this film ranks as one of the most challenging Christ films ever to have been made, and is a fitting one with which to end.

6. Conclusion

I began this chapter with the two faces of betrayal, those of Peter and Judas. I have attempted to show how, in the case of Peter, a pattern of betrayal followed by rehabilitation is a feature of his treatment in the New Testament and in subsequent history and tradition, art, literature and film. In the case of Judas, the pattern has been one of betrayal followed by vilification. It is nice to report, therefore, that Judas is the apostle who has come in from the cold, or in his case, the heat, and has finally been rehabilitated or redeemed, at least in film.

Notes

1 See, for example, B. Babington and P. W. Evans, *Biblical Epics. Sacred Narrative in the Hollywood Cinema,* Manchester: Manchester University Press, 1993; R. Kinnard and T. Davis, *Divine Images. A History of Jesus on the Screen,* New York: Citadel Press, 1992; R. C. Stern, C. N. Jefford and G. Debona, *Savior on the Silver Screen,* NY and Mahwah, NJ: Paulist, 1999; W. B. Tatum, *Jesus at the Movies: A Guide to the First Hundred Years,* Santa Rosa, CA: Polebridge, 1997.

2 See, for example, R. E. Brown, K. P. Donfried and J. Reumann, *Peter in the New Testament,* London: Geoffrey Chapman, 1973; O. Cullmann, *Peter. Disciple, Apostle, Martyr. A Historical and Theological Study,* The Library of History and Doctrine, London: SCM Press, 1953; W. Fenske and B. Martin, *Brauchte Gott der Verräter? Die Gestalt des Judas in Theologie. Unterricht und Gottesdienst,* Dienst am Wort, 85, Göttingen: Vandenhoeck & Ruprecht, 2000; L. Besserman, 'Judas Iscariot' and D. L. Jeffrey, 'Peter', in D. L. Jeffrey (ed.), *A Dictionary of Biblical Tradition in English Literature,* Grand Rapids, MI: Eerdmans, 1992, pp. 418–20, 603–8 resp.; W. Klassen, *Judas. Betrayer or Friend of Jesus?,* London: SCM Press, 1996; H. Maccoby, *Judas Iscariot and the Myth of Jewish Evil,* New York: Free Press, 1992; P. Perkins, *Peter. Apostle for the Whole Church,* Studies on Personalities of the New Testament, Edinburgh: T. & T. Clark, 2000.

3 M. Walsh, *An Illustrated History of the Popes. Saint Peter to John Paul II,* London: Marshall Cavendish, 1980, p. 11.

4 Cullmann, *Peter,* p. 157.

5 Brown, Donfried and Reumann, *Peter,* p. 166.

6 D. E. Hiebert, 'Peter' in J. D. Douglas and M. C. Tenney (eds), *The New International Dictionary of the Bible. Pictorial Edition,* Basingstoke: Marshall Pickering, 1987, p. 773.

7 R. P. Martin, 'Peter, Apostle', in W. Gentz (ed.), *The Dictionary of Bible and Religion,* Nashville, TN: Abingdon, 1986, p. 803.

8 G. W. Buchanan, 'Judas Iscariot', in G. W. Bromiley (ed.), *The International Standard Bible Encyclopedia,* Grand Rapids, MI: Eerdmans, 1982, p. 1151.

9 J. L. Houlden, 'Peter', in R. J. Coggins and J. L. Houlden (eds), *A Dictionary of Biblical Interpretation,* London: SCM and Philadelphia, PA: Trinity Press International, 1990, p. 534.

10 J. Hall (ed.), *Dictionary of Subjects and Symbols in Art*, London: John Murray, 1996, p. 243. 'The small church of S. Maria delle Piante on the Appian Way, commonly called *Domine Quo Vadis*, which was rebuilt early in the 17th cent., commemorates the incident' (F. L. Cross and E. A. Livingstone (eds), *The Oxford Dictionary of the Christian Church*, Oxford: Oxford University Press, 1997, p. 1359).

11 G. MacGregor (ed.), *The Everyman Dictionary of Religion and Philosophy*, London: Dent, 1990, p. 479.

12 Cf. e.g. 'Up in heaven, the pastor was shown his eternal reward. To his disappointment, he was only given a small shack. Down the street he saw a taxi driver being shown a lovely estate with gardens and pools. "I don't understand it," the pastor moaned. "I dedicated my whole life to serving God and this is all I get, yet a cabbie is awarded a mansion?" "It's quite simple," Saint Peter explained. "Our system is based on performance. When you preached people slept; when he drove, people prayed."' (J. Bergman, 'Laughter, the Best Medicine (St Peter joke)', *Reader's Digest* (April 2002), p. 92.

13 *Homily* on Ps. 108, cited in Besserman, 'Judas Iscariot', p. 418.

14 Besserman, 'Judas Iscariot', p. 418.

15 See H. Fisch, *The Dual Image. The Figure of the Jew in English and American Literature*, London: World Jewish Library, 1971, p. 15.

16 See Maccoby, *Judas*, pp. 108–9. Maccoby speculates that their mutual association with blood may account for this, Judas for accepting blood money (Mt. 26.14–16 and parallels) with which he purchased the 'field of blood' (Acts 1.18–19) and Herod for his massacre of the innocents (Mt. 2.16–18).

17 See MacGregor, *Dictionary of Religion and Philosophy*, p. 360.

18 See T. S. Kepler, 'Judas Iscariot', in F. C. Grant and H. H. Rowley (eds), *Dictionary of the Bible*, Edinburgh: T. & T. Clark, 1965, p. 536.

19 D. H. Farmer (ed.), *The Oxford Dictionary of Saints*, Oxford: Oxford University Press, 1987, p. 346.

20 N. Georges, 'Peter', in C. B. Pallen and J. J. Wynne (eds), *The New Catholic Dictionary*, New York: Universal Knowledge Foundation, 1929, p. 750.

21 Hall, *Subjects and Symbols*, p. 179.

22 J. C. J. Metford (ed.), *Dictionary of Christian Lore and Legend*, London: Thames & Hudson, 1983, p. 149.

23 Besserman, 'Judas Iscariot', p. 419.

24 Besserman, 'Judas Iscariot', p. 420.

25 See N. P. Hurley, 'Cinematic Transformations of Jesus', in J. R. May and M. S. Bird (eds), *Religion in Film*, Knoxville: University of Tennessee Press, 1982, p. 76; gratia C. Deacy, *Screen Christologies. Redemption and the Medium of Film*, Religion, Culture and Society, Cardiff: University of Wales Press, 2001, pp. 79–80 and 173.

26 One might also consider this comment from I. Butler: 'In the first of the four parts of Carl Dreyer's *Leaves from Satan's Book* (1922) the Devil disguises himself as the Pharisee who leads Judas to betray Christ, a curious example of the transference of guilt. The whole film has a similar form to Griffith's *Intolerance*, but with betrayal as the recurring theme. Halvard Hoff appears as Jesus' (I. Butler, *Religion in the Cinema*, The International Film Guide Series, New York: Barnes, 1969, p. 37).

27 See J. Walsh, *The Bones of St. Peter. The Fascinating Account of the Search for the Apostle's Body*, London: Victor Gollancz, 1983, pp. 1–2, 59–60, 107.

28 See Stern, Jefford and Debona, *Savior*, p. 38.

29 Kinnard and Davis, *Divine Images*, p. 74.

30 Kinnard and Davis, *Divine Images*, p. 132.

31 Babington and Evans, *Biblical Epics*, p. 129.

32 See, for example, Kinnard and Davis, *Divine Images*, pp. 15–16, 162–6 or O. Stack (ed.), *Pasolini on Pasolini: Interviews with Oswald Stack*, The Cinema One Series 11, London: Thames & Hudson, 1969, chap. 6.

33 Stern, Jefford and Debona, *Savior*, p. 170.

34 Tatum, *Jesus at the Movies*, p. 170.

Part 4

Religion in Film

14. Re-membering the American Radical Reformation in *The Apostle* and *O Brother Where Art Thou?*

JEFFREY F. KEUSS

1. Introduction: (Re)forming the Theological Frame through History and Imagination

This chapter is essentially an extended reflection on the question of film, theological poetics, and the 'Radical Reformation' in the American Church in the early nineteenth century. By way of operational definitions, I will be looking at the nature of film as a poetic frame that re-calls, re-frames and re-members aspects of popular culture that are often over-looked in high-minded cultural and theological reflection. In terms of film as a poetic framing, I will be using the notion of 'poetics' as that which cultural theorist Mieke Bal terms as 'a declaration of principle with regard to the ideas about literature [and film] that have been embodied in the events of a given text'.[1] Another way of saying this is to see poetics as those cultural products of intention, like works of art, music, or an unin-tentional by-product of cultural activity (responses to the disaster of September 11th) that exhibit a declaration of principle regarding lived practice and belief in common human experience. With this in mind, my discussion will seek the following: what declarations of principle(s) are being framed within the space and shape of a film such as *The Apostle* and *O Brother Where Art Thou?* given its relation to American Church history and, second, what released or veiled meaning – that is, what 'open secret' – are the viewers and film-makers sharing together? Often, the two lenses through which individuals frame meaning are those of history and imagination. As I will propose, the renewed interest in the rural common-place Christianity of the American South in such films as *The Apostle* and *O Brother Where Art Thou?* demonstrates a *re-membering* through the lens of history and imagination – a calling back together of members through an act of *poesis* – to some of the founding tenets of American Church history at the turn of the early nineteenth century that are germane to contemporary reflections on Christianity in the West.

To speak about film as poetics is to speak also about what a film as poetics is *framing*.[2] To make a declaration of principle is a means of delimiting what is important through controlling the gaze[3] (what Lacan termed *le regard*) of the individual so as to focus attention as an act of both framing *out* and framing *in* meaning. One way to address this is to look at a film as a composite of what Paul Tillich discusses in relation to religious and cultural products as bound in the dimensions of content, form and import.[4]

According to Tillich, a cultural formation such as a film in which form predominates over content and form is *autonomous* in meaning – shape that is not attached to the source of its shaping – while a cultural formation in which import predominates over form and content is *heteronomous* – something that has deep meaning yet cannot be grasped due to lack of definition such as a river without riverbanks. A film that strikes a synergistic balance of form, content and import is *theonomous*. *Theonomous* cultural forms are, for Tillich, explicitly open to and disclosive of the unconditioned depth of ultimate meaning. Here, the Gadamerian fusing of horizons allows for the eruption of meaning that is unfettered yet remains approachable – good but not tame – and known through knowing. Import as deep and abiding meaning cascades as overflowing abundance that continually shattering static form meant to contain it.[5] For Tillich, this overflowing and shattering of form by import is itself the pre-eminent aspect of religiously charged cultural products.[6] The Eucharist, A child's Easter poem, the Apostles' Creed, C. S. Lewis's *The Chronicles of Narnia*, and the rose window in York Minster are all possible *theonomous* forms. In our current cultural milieu, few genres succeed in this overflowing of import as the genre of film. The import in question in this discussion is that of American religious identity. In the wake of rapid expansion for nearly 200 years and the recent extreme downturn of numbers in mainline American denominations, there is a signalling to some that Christianity has lost its place altogether in the marketplace of American ideas. As these films and others continue to demonstrate, it is not the downturn of interest and import found in the Christian faith that is the question, rather the predominant form of the faith presumed to be efficacious. While some would view films like *The Apostle* and *O Brother Where Art Thou?* as characterizations of extreme factions within the American Christian tapestry, demographic responsiveness to these films and similar ones of the genre of films set in the American South show that what some critics view as fringe may in fact be the strong current of tradition that has been running strong albeit off the mainline churches' radar screen.

2. The Radical Reformation in America

As Christian traditions sought to be rooted in the American soil after the Revolutionary War in the late 1700s, questions with regard to the freedom to realize faith apart from the inherited traditions of the European Church came in the form of the Radical Reformers. Alexis de Tocqueville, in his classic 1835 reflections upon life in the early days of the USA entitled *Democracy in America*, wrote the following:

> Upon my arrival in the United States, the religious aspect of the country was the first thing that struck my attention; and the longer I stayed there the more did I perceive the great political consequences resulting from this state of things, to which I was unaccustomed. In France I had almost always seen the spirit of religion and the spirit of freedom pursuing courses diametrically opposed to each other; but in America I found that they were intimately united, and that they reigned in common over the same the country . . .
>
> Religion in America takes no direct part in the government of society, but nevertheless it must be regarded as the foremost of the political institutions of that country; for if it does not impart a taste for freedom, it facilitates the use of free institutions. Indeed, it is in this same point of view that the inhabitants of the United States themselves look upon religious belief. I do not know whether all the Americans have a sincere faith in their religion, for who can search the human heart? But I am certain that they hold it to be indispensable to the maintenance of republican institutions. This opinion is not peculiar to a class of citizen or to a party, but it belongs to the whole nation, and to every rank of society.[7]

Alexis de Tocqueville's assessment is representative of the incredible ferment of religious activity that took place just after the American Revolution amidst what I will term the 'American Radical Reformation' and has also been called the Second Great Evangelical Awakening – from 1799 to 1840. The Radical Reformation was a radicalizing of the Scottish and English Reformation impulse where new independent 'free churches' left the ranks of the first-generation mainline churches. This period of what American Church historian Sydney Ahlstrom called 'the revival of revivalism' was a rich period, with figures such as Francis Asbury, born in Birmingham, trained by John Wesley, and considered the father of American Methodism, and Peter Cartwright from Kentucky who along with other circuit riders travelled on horseback trails of 500-mile circuits through mining towns, logging camps and mountain outposts voicing a message to the religious affections of the frontier calling for a revival of deep faith. This was also the period of the Camp Meeting Movement founded by a Presbyterian minister named James McGready from Pennsylvania. In July 1800, McGready and his associates at Gasper River Church in Logan County, Kentucky devised 'a religious service of several days' length, held outdoors, for a group that was obliged to take shelter on the spot because of the distance from home'.[8] This camp meeting movement saw its zenith in the Cane Ridge Meetings of 6 August 1801 where Barton Warren Stone, another Presbyterian minister who founded the Disciples of Christ, drew between 10,000 and 25,000 clergy and laity to his revival meetings in Cane Ridge, Kentucky that lasted seven days. According to Stone, 'Many things transpired there, which were so much like miracles on infidels and unbelievers; for many of them by these were convinced that Jesus was the Christ, and bowed in submission to him.'[9]

Thomas Campbell, an Irish Presbyterian whose son Alexander trained in Divinity at Glasgow University and also became a key figure during this period, wrote the following regarding this period of revivalism and Radical Reformation in America:

> From the series of events which have taken place in the churches for many years past, especially in this Western country, as well as from what we know in general of the present state of things in the Christian world; we are persuaded that it is high time for us not only to think, but also to act for ourselves; to see with our own eyes, and to take all our measures directly and immediately from the Divine Standard ... We are also persuaded that as no man can be *judged* for his brother, so no man can *judge* for his brother: but that every man must be allowed to judge for himself, as every man must bear his own judgement ... We are also of opinion that as the divine word is equally binding upon all so all lie under an equal obligation to be bound by it, and it alone.[10]

In short, as documents such as Thomas Campbell's *Declaration and Address* display, the Radical Reformation was a period where the assumptions about the nature and form of the Church and the authority by which reformation continued to reform was challenged in colloquial language and affections.

3. Self Evident Faith – The Individual Set Apart from the Tradition as the Tradition

One of the key features of this period is the stress placed on the individual's right to think and act for himself or herself and to determine by way of one's own reading of Scripture that which is binding for the individual Christian. Often argued as a distinctive of the postmodern, tolerance for the individual's 'self-evident' right to interpret the Scriptures and their Christian faith was a hallmark of the Radical Reformation. The functions formerly relegated to the institutional Church and to its priests, bishops and theologians, became for Thomas Campbell, his son Alexander, and a number of his contemporary reformers, a responsibility of the laity. This was not so much an anti-clerical stance as some have argued, rather a *re-empowering of the laity* to become deeply concerned for their state before God. Theology is in line with politics in this regard as the emphasis on the equality of each individual as the basis for right of private judgement closely mirrors that of the Declaration of Independence: the 'self-evident' truth that all men are created equal and have a God-given right individually to seek truth and liberty for themselves.

4. 'You can't be here' – True Authority in *The Apostle*

This notion of self-evident faith is depicted in an early scene from Robert Duvall's 1997 film *The Apostle*. Set in the American South, Duvall plays Eulis 'Sonny' Dewey, a holiness preacher from Texas who we find out through a series of flashbacks was 'called to the ministry' at the age of 12 after a near-death experience. In this scene, Sonny is driving with his mother, 'Momma' Dewey (played by June Carter Cash, wife of singer Johnny Cash) when they happen upon an auto accident along the highway. Sonny crosses over the police tape and goes directly to the accident scene where a young couple is barely holding on to life. Sonny begins to speak to the young man in the driver's seat and asks him if he wants to 'come to Jesus' and find salvation. In a poignant scene, Sonny lays his leather Bible on the roof of the wrecked car and begins to pray for the couple's salvation. A police officer comes up to the scene and tells Sonny he needs to leave immediately – 'you can't be here' – and that he has no right to be there. Sonny continues to pray, ignoring the complaints of the police officer and eventually pushes the policeman away in order to finish his prayer.

This brief scene encapsulates much of the Radical Reformation: the question of authority and the question of the administering of sacraments such as unction and last rites in a means and form not found on either side of the reformation divide. The role of the democratic ideals seen in the grassroots movements that formed the Church of Christ, the Disciples, Church of the Nazarene, American Methodists and Baptists has become one of the continued dominant expressions of Christianity in America, at times both rivalling and eclipsing the more established Roman Catholic, Lutheran, Episcopalian and Presbyterian mainline denominations.[11] Peter Cartwright, one of the key Methodist circuit riders of this period, notes the difference between the more reserved mainline Presbyterians and the surging growth of the Radical Reformers:

> The Presbyterians, and other Calvinistic branches of the Protestant Church, used to contend for an educated ministry, for pews, for instrumental music, for a congregational or stated salaried ministry. The Methodists universally opposed these ideas; and the illiterate

Methodist preachers actually set the world on fire, (the American world at least,) while they [the others] were lighting their matches![12]

Cartwright's rather grand statement that the world was being set 'on fire' is not far from the truth given the exponential growth in converts to the Christian faith and the growth of preachers during this period. Between 1775 and 1845, the population of the United States grew from 2,500,000 to 20,000,000 – an increase due not to immigration but to high birth rates and the availability of land. Recorded numbers of preachers and ministers soared from 1,800 in 1775 to almost 40,000 by 1845 with the number of preachers *per capita* more than trebling from one minister per 1,500 inhabitants to one per 500.[13] This growth of American Christianity continued for the better part of the nineteenth century, and popular American Christianity has remained the dominant form of faith into the present day, steering away from high culture concerns found in large theological schools and gathering to its membership leaders and preachers from the ranks of the lower and middle classes. In this regard, the children of the American Radical Reformation are viewed, much to the consternation of the mainline theological institutions, as an 'untutored' or 'irregular' style of Christianity.[14] Statements like this one made by Peter Cartwright in his *Autobiography* represent the sentiments of many during the Radical Reformation: 'I have seen so many educated preachers who forcibly reminded me of lettuce growing under the shade of a peach-tree, or like a gosling that had got the straddles by wading in the dew, that I turn away sick and faint.'[15]

It is from this period that the face of American Christianity in its popular form continues to draw its identity. From the sawdust of the camp meetings and the passion of the revival circuit riders arose a number of American religious movements that preached an egalitarian, evangelical Christianity that spoke to the affections of a populace calling for freedom to try out new forms of Christianity as the truest form of the gospel.[16] As Nathan Hatch states in *The Democratization of American Christianity*, 'Christianity [in America] was effectively reshaped by common people who moulded it in their own image and who threw themselves into expanding its influence.'[17] As we saw earlier in Alexis de Tocqueville's reflections, it was not the form of Church governance that gave Christianity its democratic aspect, for power was often concentrated in a few leaders or a structured hierarchy, but the 'incarnation of the church into popular culture'.[18] This incarnation perhaps best expresses itself in these churches' disdain for regular clergy and the removal of any distinction between clergy and laity. By placing the common man in the pulpit, power was given to ordinary people to express and expound the truth of God, to develop their own forms, traditions and orthodoxies, and to employ the vernacular in sermon and song.[19]

5. 'Well, ain't it a small world, spiritually speakin'?' – Unity and Affiliation as Tradition in O *Brother Where Art Thou?*

Further democratic expression is found in the way various movements of the Radical Reformation allowed people to act on their own behalf in their practice of the teaching of Scripture rather than censuring their actions through the scrutiny of orthodoxy by the institutional Church and clergy. This freedom was seen as allowing space for the experience of the supernatural and the divine in the course of everyday life. The sanctioning of the dreams, ecstasies, and visions of ordinary people helped put them on an equal level.

In a scene 20 minutes into The Coen Brothers' 2000 release entitled *O Brother Where Art Thou?*, we see the fusing of realism and surrealism around a moment of baptism. Three escaped convicts – Ulysses Everett McGill (played by George Clooney), Pete (played by John Turturro) and Delmar (played by Tim Blake Nelson) – are on the run and in search of buried treasure when, in the middle of their brief meal of barbecued rodent, they are surrounded by the voices raised in song of white-robed penitents amidst the rite of baptism. Both Delmar and Pete hear the 'song of salvation' and are baptized. As they continue on their journey, the trio pick up a lone hitch-hiker standing at a dusty crossroads, named Tommy. Tommy claims to have had a meeting with the Devil where he sold his soul in order to be given the gift of playing blues guitar. Reflecting on being surrounded by the recently saved and the recently damned, George Clooney's Ulysses Everett McGill sums up the situation: 'Well, ain't it a small world, spiritually speaking ... I guess I'm the only one that remains unaffiliated!' The idea of affiliation is one of the key tenets of the Radical Reformation – unity and affiliation. In his *Declaration and Address*, Thomas Campbell expressed this notion beautifully by stating:

> That the church of Christ upon earth is essentially, intentionally, and constitutionally one; consisting of all those in every place that profess their faith in Christ and obedience to him in all things according to the scriptures, and that manifest the same by their tempers and conduct, and of none else as none else can be truly and properly christians.[20]

This quest for Christian unity arose out of a desire to do away with sectarianism and to simply be Christians – a simple faith and a simple message that went beyond the restrictions of denominationalism. Yet as demonstrated by Thomas Campbell serving as a minister for an Old Light, Anti-Burgher, Seceder Presbyterian Church, each phrase of the church name spelled out what the church was *against*, but no part of it said what it was *for*. It seemed to Thomas Campbell and the other leaders of the Radical Reformation movement that the Church had never been meant to be fractured as it was, and that unity was the chief need of the day. Figures like Wesley, Zinzendorf and Campbell had no initial intention of creating yet another denomination, rather they sought an ecumenicism worthy of many contemporary discussions. The high importance placed on finding the common thread – the connections that bind together – almost had a downside with the turning away from much of the theology and creeds of the previous 16 centuries of Christian thought and the promotion of a theological motto of 'No Creed but the Bible'. Their assumption was that if everyone came to the Bible and simply read it as if they had never seen it before, they would arrive at the same conclusions. In practice, this simply meant that everyone arrived, not at similar points of agreement, but each at their own conclusion. Further, in spite of their inclusive language, differing opinions were little tolerated (in fact, throughout the 200-year history of the Christians/Disciples, the question of just what was essential and what was opinion has been a great source of division among what is now three branches off the original tree). As Nathan Hatch points out, rather than 'erecting a primitive church free from theological tradition and authoritarian control, [the Radical Reformation] came to advocate their own sectarian theology and to defer to the influence and persuasion of a dominant few'.[21]

It was also in the unbounded hope that the various reformers of this period in America had for their chances of success that we see yet another democratic impulse. They felt that, through their efforts, a new age of religious and social harmony would be ushered in to replace the oppressive and sectarian forces at work.[22]

This 'radical reformation' of the social order was directed largely by the new breed of preachers that arose. Populist preachers, such as the preacher portrayed by Robert Duvall in *The Apostle* and the faceless Baptist in *O Brother Where Art Thou?* did much to accelerate both the rapid growth and the continual splintering of American Christianity into the various factions and denominations that exist today. As these preachers of the common man began to explain theological matters for themselves they arrived each at his/her own conclusion, differing from one another as easily as they differed from the established Churches. Religious options multiplied as each group taught its own particular brand of Christianity. Preachers tended to mingle diverse and often contradictory sources in order to make their points – whatever it took to sell the gospel was fair game. High and popular culture, supernaturalism and Enlightenment rationalism, mystical experience and biblical literalism were intermixed at will as preachers reversed the traditional religious authorities, promoting youth, free expression and emotional experiences over education, tradition and proper conduct.[23]

6. Unity in Diversity – Tent Meeting Form in *The Apostle*

There is a wonderful illustration of the different yet similar revivalist stylings of the Southern tent meetings about 16 minutes into *The Apostle*. Though their respective movements often held radically different beliefs from one another, the preachers and leaders from all groups shared several traits that contributed to the growth of each movement. Each group had a passion for reaching common people, through whatever means necessary, often in highly unorthodox manners. Each group recognized a need for the reformation of the Church as a response to the needs of the times and developed plans to accomplish that reformation.[24] Preachers actively sought out opportunities to preach and to spread their message. They did this in different ways, through revivalist camp meetings or circuit riding, in each case going to where the people were rather than waiting for people to come to them.[25] With little education or experience to inform their preaching, the popular sermon became something of a scandal among the educated clergy. The sermon's power and emphasis did not lie in doctrine and well-reasoned argument, but in 'daring pulpit storytelling, no-holds-barred appeals, overt humour, strident attack, graphic application, and intimate personal experience'.[26]

The Radical Reformation as a movement in American Church history was truly a *movement*. There was nothing static about this period. As Nathan Hatch notes in *The Democratization of American Christianity* these movements were:

> a new plateau of social possibility, based on self-confident leadership and widespread methods of internal communication, [which permitted] people to conceive of acting in self-generated democratic ways, to develop new ways of looking at things less clouded by inherited assumptions, and to defend themselves in the face of adverse interpretations from the orthodox culture.[27]

7. Common Media, Common Folks, Uncommon message

Part of what sustained and encouraged the numerous religious movements of this time was the loss of power and authority that had previously been centralized in the clergy, and more importantly, the explosion of religious communication through religious periodicals and pamphlets aimed at the common reader.[28] In this regard the Radical Reformation shares space with the multiplex cinemas of today – finding and using the media of the common person.

It was through the use of various print media that many of the obscure men who were to become the leaders of the disparate movements gained an equal footing with men such as Jonathan Edwards and Timothy

---

14.1 What is the American Restoration Movement?

The roots of the Restoration Movement extend backward to the period after the Revolutionary War in which several Americans with religious interests grew restless over autocratic structures, European control and theology, and denominational boundaries. These pressures revamped the mainline churches, but also resulted in independent movements springing up in various regions. Four such independent groups in (1) Virginia, (2) New England, (3) Kentucky and (4) Pennsylvania–West Virginia–Ohio, played a role in the crystallization of the Restoration Movement in the 1830s.

The two most important tributaries for the larger movement resulted from the work of Barton W. Stone (1772–1844) and the two Campbells, Thomas (1763–1854) and his son Alexander (1788–1866).

Early in the 1830s the churches from the Stone and Campbell groups began merging in Kentucky. The amalgamation expanded to churches in Pennsylvania, Ohio, Virginia, Tennessee, Indiana, Illinois and Missouri. Several churches from the New England Jones-Smith, and Virginia O'Kelly movements also became a part of the Stone–Campbell merger. After the Civil War the Christian Connexion churches that did not merge established headquarters in Dayton, Ohio. In 1931 they merged with the Congregational Church, then with the Evangelical and Reformed Church, to form in 1957 the United Church of Christ.

Dwight, many publishing more material and read by a wider audience than the foremost clergy of the day.[29] One chronicler of the period has estimated that of the 605 religious journals that could be found in the year 1830, only 14 of them had existed prior to 1790. Subscriptions skyrocketed from 5,000 at the turn of the century, to 400,000 by 1830. An 1823 editorial in the *Christian Herald*, argued for the inseparable connection of pulpit and press, one no less ordained by God than the other.[30] It was also through the use of the press and other methods of giving power to common people that they forever changed American life. Never again was a Jonathan Edwards to arise in the American cultural milieu – the authority of the man of ideas had been confined and authority was instead offered to the common man.[31]

Of all the religious movements of the days of the American ideal after the Revolutionary War, it was perhaps these Radical Reformers, second only to the Mormon Church, who took the ideologies of true theology as freedom for self-evident authority, equality and unalienable rights for all citizens, and the right of private judgement on scriptural matters to be at the forefront of their movement. As noted by Nathan Hatch, this fervour in the Radical Reformers was grounded in the 'self-evident [belief] that the priesthood of all believers meant just that – religion of, by, and for the people'.[32] The primary leaders of this movement, steeped in the common sense of the Scottish Enlightenment, all arrived independently at remarkably similar conclusions within the space of a few short years. They desired to throw off the messy confines of history and begin again as a Lockean *tabula rasa*. The way to accomplish this, they believed, was to form a Church based on democratic principles and return to the Bible as the only rule for faith and practice – a rule that not only allowed, but demanded that ordinary believers interpret the New Testament for themselves.[33]

8. Conclusion

I believe that what continues to captivate audiences and film-makers about these aspects of the 'Radical Reformation' is that it continues to be the 'open secret' of not only the American Christian landscape, but also the common human experience of Christendom worldwide. In an environment that has become so weary of postmodern rhetoric that circles and circles but never lands, there is the whisper of deep import that breaks forth in moments such as those portrayed in films such as *The Apostle* and *O Brother Where Art Thou?*. Not merely a nostalgia for a bygone time of simple truths prior to the Internet, junk bonds and September 11th, but a deeper and more abiding sense that in the affairs of the common human experience, there continues to be a hunger and thirst for meaning, community and creativity that is readily accessible and radically open to all. While factions of various Academic guilds may proclaim the final adieu to Christianity per se, darkened theatres continue to be a meeting place for viewers and film-makers who draw strange inspirations (particularly strange in the case of *O Brother Where Art Thou?*) from 'the age-old story'. Yet what is being portrayed on the flickering silver screen in films such as *The Apostle* and *O Brother Where Art Thou?* is a Christian faith that is something more than an aesthetic source or typology. There is a tendency for modern readers and viewers of the tent revivalists and Radical Reformers of this period not to take this movement seriously and merely typecast the 'Southern Tent Preacher' as comic, wicked or irrelevant. Like the Radical Reformers, what we see in these films is something that is alongside and yet somewhat apart from centre stage in the affairs of mainline Christendom proper. The depictions of Christian faith seen in these movies and others like them offer a threefold differential reading of American Church history:

1. a *nostalgic* retrieval of the tenets of this vital part of the Christian frontier history,
2. a *contemporary* framing of the content, form and import of the radical reformation tenets in a present and active way, and the use of an

imaginative medium in film where the viewer not only is asked to retrieve and enact the questions of the time, and

3. with the unspoken contract between viewer and film whereby the viewer engaged in what Samuel Taylor Coleridge termed a 'willing suspension of disbelief' as the *imaginative leap into the Possible*, the viewer is invited to recall and represent these possibilities into a re-imagined and re-membered Now.

But the words to the audience from the Blind Seer at the beginning of *O Brother Where Art Thou?* speak volumes:

> You seek a great fortune, you three who are now in chains. You will find a fortune, though it will not be the one you seek. But first . . . first you must travel a long and difficult road, a road fraught with peril. Mm-hmm. You shall see thangs, wonderful to tell. You shall see a . . . a cow . . . on the roof of a cottonhouse, ha. And, oh, so many startlements. I cannot tell you how long this road shall be, but fear not the obstacles in your path, for fate has vouchsafed your reward. Though the road may wind, yea, your hearts grow weary, still shall ye follow them, even unto your salvation.

Notes

1 Mieke Bal, *Narratology*, 2nd edition, Toronto: University of Toronto Press, 1997, p. 59. The use of the term 'poetics' throughout this paper will be in keeping with this operational definition.

2 With regard to 'framing', I refer to Jonathan Culler's assertion that 'since the phenomena criticism deals with are signs, forms with socially-constituted meanings, one might try to think not of context but of *the framing of signs*: how are signs constituted (*framed*) by various discursive practices, institutional arrangements, systems of value, semiotic mechanisms . . . The expression *framing the sign* has several advantages over context: it reminds us that framing is something we do; it hints of the framing up ('falsifying evidence beforehand in order to make someone appear guilty') . . . and it eludes the incipient positivism of 'context' by alluding to the semiotic function of framing in art, where the frame is determining, setting off the object or event as art, and yet the frame itself may be nothing tangible, pure articulation' (Jonathan Culler, *Framing the Sign: Criticism and Its Institutions*, Oxford: Blackwell, 1988, p. ix).

3 The notion of 'the gaze' (*le regard*) is explored in the twentieth century by Jacques Lacan. Lacan's use of *le regard* builds upon his reflections of Jean-Paul Sartre's phenomenological analysis of *le regard*. As noted by Sartre, what is 'seen' is not essentially grounded upon the physical act of sight: 'Of course what most often manifests a look is the convergence of two ocular globes in my direction. But the look (*le regard*) will be given just as well on occasion when there is a rustling of branches, or the sound of a footstep followed by silence, or the slight opening

of a shutter, or a light movement of a curtain.' See Jean-Paul Sartre, *Being and Nothingness: An Essay on Phenomenlogical Ontology*, trans. Hazel E. Barnes, London: Methuen, 1958, p. 257.

4 '*Substance or import* is something different from content. By content we mean something objective in its simple existence, which by form is raised up to the intellectual-cultural sphere. By substance or *import*, however, we understand the meaning, the spiritual substantiality, which alone gives *form* its significance. We can therefore say: *Substance or import is grasped by means of a form and given expression in a content*. Content is accidental, substance [or import] essential, and form is the mediating element. The form must be appropriate to the content; so there is no opposition between the cultivation of form and the cultivation of content; it is rather that these two represent one extreme, and the cultivation of substance [or import] represents the other' (Paul Tillich, 'On the Idea of a Theology of Culture,' in *What is Religion?*, trans. James L. Adams, New York: Harper and Row, 1969, pp. 165–6).

5 Jacques Derrida stated in an interview entitled 'This Strange Institution Called Literature' that authentic art is ultimately a 'fictive institution which in principle allows one to say everything'. The power of art is seen in its ability to 'break out of prohibitions in every field where law can lay down the law. The law of [art such as] literature tends, in principle, to defy or lift the law . . . It [in our case, film] is an institution which tends to overflow the institution.' This 'overflowing' that Derrida speaks of as the power found within the institution of true art often becomes dammed, blocked, and (with certain artists) constipated behind the structure or 'poetics' of a given text and how the poetics of a work is 'framed'. See Jacques Derrida, 'This Strange Institution Called Literature', in Derek Attridge (ed.), *Acts of Literature*, London: Routledge, 1992, p. 36ff.

6 See Paul Tillich, 'On the Idea of a Theology of Culture,' pp. 165ff.; 'The Nature of Religious Language', in *Theology of Culture*, Oxford: Oxford University Press, 1959, pp. 53ff.; and 'The Spiritual Presence and the Ambiguities of Culture' in *Systematic Theology Volume 3: Life and the Spirit; History and the Kingdom of God*, London: SCM Press, 1997, pp. 245–62.

7 Alexis de Tocqueville, *Democracy in America* (1835). Cited by Sydney E. Ahlstrom, *A Religious History of the American People*, New Haven: Yale University Press, 1972, p. 386.

8 Ahlstrom, *A Religious History of the American People*, p. 432.

9 Barton Warren Stone, 'A Short History of the Life of Barton W. Stone Written by Himself', in Rhodes Thompson (ed.), *Voices from Cane Ridge*, St Louis: Bethany Press, 1954, p. 68. Cited in Alhstrom, *A Religious History of the American People*, p. 433.

10 Thomas Campbell, *Declaration and Address of the Christian Association of Washington*, in Thomas H. Olbricht and Hans Rollmann (eds), *The Quest for Christian Unity, Peace, and Purity in Thomas Campbell's Declaration and Address: Text and Studies*, Lanham: Scarecrow, 2000, p. 5.

11 Nathan O. Hatch, *The Democratization of American Christianity*, New Haven: Yale University Press, 1989, p. 4.

12 Peter Cartwright, *Autobiography of Peter Cartwright*, ed. Charles Wallis reprint edn; London: Abingdon Press, 1986, p. 64. Cited in Ahlstrom, *A Religious History of the American People*, p. 438.

13 Nathan O. Hatch, *The Democratization of American Christianity*, p. 3.
14 Nathan O. Hatch, *The Democratization of American Christianity*, p. 5.
15 Peter Cartwright, *Autobiography of Peter Cartwright*, p. 64.
16 Peter Cartwright, *Autobiography of Peter Cartwright*, p. 7.
17 Peter Cartwright, *Autobiography of Peter Cartwright*, p. 9.
18 Peter Cartwright, *Autobiography of Peter Cartwright*, p. 9.
19 Peter Cartwright, *Autobiography of Peter Cartwright*, p. 9.
20 Thomas Campbell, *Declaration and Address*, p. 18.
21 Nathan O. Hatch, *The Democratization of American Christianity*, p. 80.
22 Nathan O. Hatch, *The Democratization of American Christianity*, p. 10ff.
23 Nathan O. Hatch, *The Democratization of American Christianity*, p. 35.
24 Nathan O. Hatch, *The Democratization of American Christianity*, p. 56.
25 Nathan O. Hatch, *The Democratization of American Christianity*, p. 55.
26 Nathan O. Hatch, *The Democratization of American Christianity*, p. 57
27 Nathan O. Hatch, *The Democratization of American Christianity*, p. 58.
28 Nathan O. Hatch, *The Democratization of American Christianity*, p. 126.
29 Nathan O. Hatch, *The Democratization of American Christianity*, p. 11.
30 Nathan O. Hatch, *The Democratization of American Christianity*, p. 142.
31 Nathan O. Hatch, *The Democratization of American Christianity*, p. 162.
32 Nathan O. Hatch, *The Democratization of American Christianity*, p. 69.
33 Nathan O. Hatch, *The Democratization of American Christianity*, p. 69.

15. Perversion and Fulfilment:

Revivalist Christianity in *The Night of the Hunter*

TOM AITKEN

To watch this film is, as they used to say in travelogues and documentaries, to journey through space and time to a distant land, far away and long ago. A rural land, where the faithful gather at the river to sing hymns and eat and drink in blameless sobriety. A land where economic depression is an overarching reality, informing every aspect of life. A land in which travelling evangelists of various sorts bring with them not merely their particular brand of salvation, but a whiff of an exotic otherwhere, of a wider world full of mysterious, sinister excitements.

As it happens this description fits not only the southern states of America in the 1930s, the setting for *The Night of the Hunter*, Charles Laughton's only film as director, but, *mutatis mutandis*, my youth in the town of Taumarunui, New Zealand, derisively known to sophisticates from other parts of the country as 'the dead centre of the North Island'. It was here, in the late 1950s, not too long after it was released, that I first saw *The Night of the Hunter*. No film I had seen previously portrayed a world of which I had first-hand experience and which I recognized effortlessly.

I had better add that none of the travelling evangelists who had come my way was a murderous exploiter of widows (for a summary of Revivalism, see Text Box 15.1). Nor, anywhere in New Zealand, had the depression of the Thirties continued into the 1950s. But my parents and uncles and aunts had all been at the sharp end of it. It had been the formative socio-economic experience of their lives. They were acquainted, if not with stomach-churning hunger, at least with living on short commons, the constant threat of unemployment and the need to make one penny do the work of two. In consequence, their ambition for their children was a secure, lifelong job – a concept which, 50-odd years on, seems as remote as other peculiarities of the period, such as unquestioning enlistment when required by King and Country, or going to school barefooted all summer long.

But, the wickedness of Harry Powell and the absence of actual as opposed to remembered economic depression aside, the world of Laughton's film was all there. We sang 'Leaning on the everlasting arms'

15.1 Revivalism

What is a 'Revival'?
• A time when believers are called to spiritual renewal and non-believers to faith.

What are the core beliefs of Revivalism?
• Everyone is a sinner, dependent upon repentance and conversion for eternal salvation.
• Preaching the gospel is the principal method of promoting revival.
• Belief is validated only through entire commitment of the believer's heart and life.

Where and when has Revivalism been practised?
• Revivalism is largely a Protestant evangelical phenomenon and in terms of sheer numbers, a largely North American one.
• In America there have been revivals, or 'great awakenings', since colonial times. At first they followed supposed evidence of God's anger in the form of natural disasters. Later they were associated with revivalist preachers, such as Charles Finney (1820s), Moody and Sankey (late nineteenth century), and, during the twentieth century, Billy Sunday, Aimee Semple McPherson and Billy Graham. Many such evangelists have preached throughout the world.
• Some Christian denominations have been, during their early history, almost entirely revivalist in their practice, including early Methodists, the Salvation Army, Baptists and others.
• Revivalism has traditionally been associated with rural or working-class industrial areas. The Alpha Course may be the most sophisticated and urbanized form of revivalism yet seen.
• Revivalism, usually in the form of parish missions conducted by members of religious orders, has also occurred in Catholicism. Such missions spread across Europe during the sixteenth and seventeenth centuries, following the Protestant Reformation, and, after declining in the eighteenth century, throughout the Catholic world during the nineteenth century. They declined again in the mid-twentieth century.

What faults have been ascribed to Revivalism?
• Emotionalism and enthusiasm may lower standards of theological precision and social decorum.
• Conversions arising from fear of hell-fire may be thought dubious.
• However obtained, conversions may prove superficial and temporary.
• Certain notorious revivalists have proved to be, like Harry Powell in *The Night of the Hunter*, financial exploiters and fraudsters, spiritual charlatans, philanderers and abusers.
• In the USA, in particular, 'televangelism' has generated large personal fortunes.

and 'Bringing in the sheaves'. We gathered each year at the riverside for the Sunday School picnic in an atmosphere of pious jollity very like that prevalent on the occasion at which Powell meets the hapless Willa. In Taumarunui, as in the film, evangelical Christians, with the best intentions but not always the best results, engaged in blatant matchmaking. And, outside the inner circle of the saved, there were one or two town drunks, casualties of economic change and domestic loss, like Uncle Birdie.

But it wasn't merely these day-by-day parallels that struck me; I also recognized a much deeper theme, that of a dichotomy within the sort of Christianity with which I was familiar, between, on the one hand, sensationalist preachers who were often in some way on the make – if not so vilely as Preacher Powell – and, on the other, people who possessed a serener, self-sacrificial, practical faith, like that of Rachel, the woman who looks after John and Pearl when they escape from Powell's clutches. But although Powell and Rachel are chalk and cheese, they nevertheless have revivalist Christianity in common, as is bizarrely demonstrated in the film during that last night when Powell is lurking outside Rachel's house, singing his theme song, 'Leaning on the everlasting arms', and Rachel joins in with a descant: 'Leaning on Jesus'. The same song: two entirely different takes on those everlasting arms. For Powell, the everlasting arms, one labelled love, one labelled hate, are those of a vengeful God who smites his opponents hip and thigh. For Rachel they are those of a comforting, merciful, benign saviour.

It is easy to conclude – and indeed it is the central plank of my platform, that Rachel's life is a fulfilment of Bible Belt revivalist Christianity and Powell's is a perversion of it. Nevertheless, I think we have to take Powell's religion as being, at least in part, more than just a ploy useful in the entrapment of widows in possession of money. He talks to God when there is no one present to hear him. An absolute hypocrite would not bother. The most perverted part of his religion, his loathing of sex, his uncontrollable, murderous misogyny, is itself a perverted version of a strand in historical Christianity, a kind of cracker-barrel version of the Manichaean heresy, according to which humans were formed by the rulers of darkness and procreation is demonic in origin. But his hatred of soft, frilly things and sexual allure also arises from his unconscious depths. He has looked in Christianity for something that appears to support his neurosis, and found it. Religion, for him, is not something handed down as a set of doctrines in which he has no say. In reply to John's father's enquiry as to what religion, exactly, he professes, he says it is one he and the Lord have worked out betwixt them. He is telling nothing more or less than the truth. This is a partial and egocentric version of a process many believers will recognize – of taking a faith on board in stages according to what aspects of it prove easiest to relate to. Many Catholic or Orthodox thinkers, however, would regard Powell's phrase

15.2 Are the Songs Sung by Harry Powell in *The Night of the Hunter* Genuine Revival Hymns?

'Leaning on the everlasting arms' was written in Alabama, in the southern states of America where *The Night of the Hunter* is set, by Anthony Showalter (1858–1924). In letters of condolence to two former pupils whose wives had died, he quoted Deuteronomy 33.27: 'Underneath are the everlasting arms' and was instantly inspired to compose, before finishing the letters, the words and music of a refrain on the theme. He sent this to Elisha A. Hoffman (1839–1929), who added the verses, beginning 'What a fellowship, what a joy divine'. The song was published in *The Glad Evangel, for Revival, Camp and Evangelistic Meetings* in 1887.

'Bringing in the sheaves' was first printed anonymously in *The Golden Gate for the Sunday School* in 1874. In 1877 it appeared in *The Morning Star, a New Collection of Sunday School Music,* attributed to Knowles Shaw (1834–78), who compiled both volumes.

Although the song is often sung at harvest festivals, it has a more general meaning, as the opening words of the first verse indicate: 'Sowing in the morning, sowing seeds of kindness . . .' picking up the metaphor found at Matthew 9.37 and Luke 10.2: 'The harvest is plentiful, but the labourers are few'. The sheaves are souls harvested for God.

as simply a working definition of Protestantism. But Powell has no yearning for the fullness of faith. He can relate to hatred and the notion of himself as the instrument of divine punishment. He has no idea of love, human or divine, despite the sermon he preaches on the subject.

Despite my possibly tendentious scriptural allusions (the God who smites his opponents hip and thigh as opposed to the merciful saviour), the different way in which Powell and Rachel understand the Bible-based revivalism they have in common is not traceable to the distinction between Old and New Testament ideas about God. It is, rather, that between contrasting – and, many would argue, both partial – forms of belief that have been found within Christianity throughout its history. Numerous revivalist movements during the last couple of centuries could, if they chose, trace their ancestry back to medieval heresies. Harry Powell would not have been altogether out of place preaching at the market cross in a medieval town. Nor is his religion of hatred and wrath so very remote, psychologically, from the terrifying Catholic hellfire sermons that render incandescent James Joyce's *Portrait of the Artist as a Young Man* and feature, more recently, in the film *Liam,* written by Jimmy McGovern and directed by Stephen Frears.

Turning to Rachel, we can see that her religion of love and sleeves-rolled-up practicality, of the sort once called 'muscular Christianity', is to be found in all manner of religious groupings, ranging from orders of monks and nuns to the Salvation Army in which I grew up.[1] Such people place the needs of humanity at the centre of their faith. It would be going much too far to say that Harry Powell, in contrast, exalts the demands of God above all other considerations, although he might appear to be doing so to anyone who failed to detect his self-serving hypocrisy.

Many of the early critics, who in all sorts of ways entirely missed the point of the film, assumed that Powell was simply mad. There is a sense in which this is obviously so, but another in which it demands careful examination. I have argued that his beliefs, such as they are, are genuine. But may we speculate that he may at one time have been a revivalist Christian in some more innocent sense? Why, after all, should he choose religion as the basis for his confidence trickery if it were not something to which he had once felt sincere attachment? Was it necessarily an easier option than dodgy insurance or bogus gold mines? Perhaps in the Bible Belt it was. But then, why does he murder his victims as well as fleece them? I think we must concede that Powell at least in part believes what he preaches, and sees himself in some way as an instrument of divine wrath.

This is madness enough, you may think, and in any case my questions (still more my conclusion) may seem to ignore the fact that this is a surrealist, not a naturalistic film. But I suggest that even in the context of a work that seeks to present vivid images of mental turmoil rather than to explain or analyse it, such points are worth raising.

Whatever his original vocation may have been, by the time we meet him it has rigidified into a technique for living off the gullible hero worship he can arouse in others and, especially, of exercising hostile, destructive power over women. His loathing for them, as I have already suggested, is the force that drives him, but as well as being his driving force it is also his downfall. Key moments in the film are the two occasions when he shouts abusively at Pearl. She has been his ally against her brother and has believed that he loves her. Now he has blown his cover.

These scenes are wonderfully played, not only by Mitchum, but by the young Sally Jane Bruce, and this is perhaps the moment to mention one of the odder ironies about this film and its making. To quote Laughton's biographer, Simon Callow:

As for the children, they too are perfect; which is something of a mystery, because Laughton kept as far away from them as possible. His special loathing was reserved for the little girl, Sally Bruce, but he didn't have much time either for Billy Chapin . . . after Mitchum had given Billy a note: 'Do you think John's frightened of the preacher?' 'Nope,' said Billy Chapin. 'Then you don't know the preacher and you don't know John.' 'Oh really?' said Billy. 'That's probably why I just won the New York Critics' Circle prize.' 'Get that child away from me,' roared

Laughton. Thereafter Mitchum directed the boy – with the most remarkable results. Odd paradox, that Laughton should have failed to create any rapport with the children, when it was his vision that the entire film should be a child's nightmare.[2]

But I digress. If Powell is a genuine believer who has slipped stage by stage into the role of a misogynist serial killer, perhaps he *is* mad. If, as seems more likely, he is a calculating, plausible villain who has made God in his own image, then surely he is less mad than wicked. This, however, I repeat, is not to say that he does not in some sense believe in the God he has created. His chats with him, for example when he salutes God for putting him in a cell with a convicted killer with $10,000 whose wife is a widow in the making, seem genuine enough, although we may note that Powell behaves as if he is virtually on more or less equal terms with the deity. He complains, for instance, of feeling tired and suggests that God neither understands nor extends sufficient sympathy to his problems. Then he moves to a point on which, he supposes, they are at one: women, those 'soft frilly things'.

That particular chat with God follows immediately after the scene in which Powell watches a stripper at work. This scene is interesting in various ways. It is one of the moments that early critics may have had in mind when they accused Mitchum of overacting. To my mind, however, his curious facial expressions and contortions express very aptly the inner turmoil of a man ill at ease with the strength of feeling that is aroused within him. But we should notice also the economy and tact with which the scene is shot. The bored dancer is not supposed to arouse the cinema audience; it is her effect on Powell which matters. That effect is conveyed by his face, then, as the camera pans down, his clenched left fist, its knuckles tattooed with the letters HATE. Then that hand goes into his pocket and we see the blade of his flick-knife rip through his black preacher's jacket. His eyes turn upwards and, in a further brief address to God, he regrets the fact that he cannot murder all of the world's harlots. Then the hand of a policeman falls on his shoulder and he is arrested as a car thief. All this happens in less time than it takes to tell it, and the swiftness of movement, coupled with the almost abstract, iconic nature of each of the images, is characteristic of Laughton's directorial method.

Much of what we are told about the making of the film makes it seem even more deplorable that its commercial failure brought Laughton's career as a director to a premature end. Although Laughton did not get on with his child actors, in most other respects he was a model of the collaborative leader. Lilian Gish, by 1955 a film acting veteran of more than 40 years' experience, wrote that

> I have to go back as far as D.W. Griffith to find a set so infused with purpose and harmony . . . there was not ever a moment's doubt as to

what we were doing. To please Charles Laughton was our aim. We believed in and respected him. Totally.[3]

Laughton, as it happens, had thought that Griffith's visual world was the appropriate one for his film and had looked at the senior director's work afresh. In fact it was watching *Birth of a Nation* that reminded him of the intense composure and inwardness of the work of Lilian Gish and led him to cast her as Rachel. If we recall the scene in Griffith's film in which Gish, as Elsie Stoneman, nurses the wounded, I think we can see the qualities of warmth and compassion that made Laughton want Gish to play Rachel. We can also see many of the devices that Laughton took over from Griffith. Short sequences of action and image build up into scenes; photographs inspire memories from the past; there are frequent frames within the frame; the titles introducing scenes have something of the sententious, quasi-proverbial nature of Rachel's utterances. And, of course, there is the luminosity of the black-and-white photography.

To reproduce that luminosity Laughton turned to Stanley Cortez, a dandyish, experimentally inclined cinematographer who had filmed *The Magnificent Ambersons* for Orson Welles. Cortez spent a deal of time explaining cameras and lenses to Laughton, finding after a while that in the matter of the poetic conception of a scene he had things to learn from his pupil. Between them they produced those stunning chiaroscuro effects, which, of course, are emblematic of light and dark, beauty and ugliness, good and evil.[4] This is particularly evident in the lyrical episode when John and Pearl, pursued on a stolen horse by Powell, escape down river in the skiff. Incidentally, the overhead shots of the children in the boat were filmed on location in Ohio, but the shots showing the river bank, with its screech-owl, turtle, frogs and rabbits were done in a studio. Most astonishing of all, the shot of Powell, a black silhouette riding across the skyline, singing, as ever, 'Leanin', leanin' . . .' while John and Pearl are hiding in the barn, was also filmed indoors, using, as Cortez tells us, 'a midget on a pony'.[5]

Not everything about the production was sweetness and light. Laughton entrusted the script to James Agee, much admired scriptwriter, critic and novelist, only to find himself confronted by a self-destructive drunk who eventually presented him with 350 pages of screenplay. This recreated Davis Grubb's rather floridly written – but at the time very popular – novel in extraordinary detail and demanded extensive sequences of newsreel footage that would have tied the story very firmly to the atmosphere and politics of the urban depression instead of letting it float free in a surreal Arcadia that had gone catastrophically wrong. Laughton himself set to to produce a workable script (for which he took no credit, leaving Agee's name on the film). Agee complained, but died before the film was released.[6]

Another source of minor friction was the fact that Mitchum deplored the casting of Shelley Winters as Willa, whom he thought fit only to end up in the river with her throat cut. Laughton, however, having been Winters's teacher, took no notice of Mitchum's curmudgeonly grumbling. In the event, whatever Mitchum thought, Winters brought both eroticism and innocence to the role. She thought this one of her best, most restrained performances. I would agree.

Mitchum also thought his performance in this film his best, and Laughton his best director. Surprisingly, the two men – macho boozer and bisexual teetotaller – got on well from the outset. Laughton said, 'I want you to play . . . a diabolical shit.' Mitchum's laconic reply was 'Present.' On some later occasion they were driving along the freeway when Laughton told Mitchum, 'I don't know if you know, and I don't know if you care, and I don't care if you know, but there is a strong streak of homosexuality in me.' 'No shit!' cried Mitchum. 'Stop the car!'[7]

To my mind, *Night of the Hunter* is one of the most genuinely frightening thrillers ever made. For most of the film this quality of fright derives from the relationship between Powell and the children. In thriller terms it is all very cunning. We know that the children are safe as long as Powell does not know where to find the money their father hid before he was arrested, but the fate of 25 dead widows reminds us that their lives will be at risk as soon as he has found out. The 'child's nightmare' that Laughton was set on making is principally John's nightmare and it is through his eyes that we see most of the action. Until his mother disappears and he and his sister go on the run, John is trebly burdened: first, by his promise to his father to tell nobody of the money's whereabouts; second, by his awareness that his mother – who believes that the money has been destroyed – would pass the news straight to Powell if she discovered otherwise; third, by Pearl's permanent eagerness to spill the beans because she loves Powell and does not understand the situation she and John are in. There is no one to whom John can talk, and Powell hounds him at every opportunity.

During the course of the film, John is deprived of or let down by a series of previously reassuring presences. His father is executed for murder, his mother murdered by Powell. When he goes on the run, dragging the reluctant Pearl, and turns for help to Uncle Birdie, the poor old soak proves quite useless, having seen Willa's body in the river and got into a state of moral and alcoholic collapse. Only at the very end of the story does John learn once again to trust an adult.

Two points I have raised in discussing *The Night of the Hunter* – whether or not Powell is mad, and John's successive loss of supportive figures – point forward rather interestingly to a later film by another director. When Alfred Hitchcock became interested in doing *Psycho* as a black-and-white, low budget thriller, *The Night of the Hunter* was one of the precedents for such an enterprise, albeit not an encouraging one, since it had been neither a critical nor a box office success. Stephen Rebello tells us that Hitchcock quizzed his colleagues about the profitability of Laughton's film as well as that of Howard Hawks' and Christian Nyby's *The Thing* (1951), a humorous sci-fi shocker, and Mervyn Leroy's *The Bad Seed* (1956), about a malicious child who causes several deaths.[8] This research does not of itself mean that he was artistically influenced by any of the three, but the two points I have just mentioned in *The Night of the Hunter* are interestingly echoed in *Psycho*. There is also a parallel in the later film to the stripping away of comforting presences that afflicts John in Laughton's piece, but as Kenneth Tynan pointed out, Hitchcock indulges his sadistic nature by inflicting this process of successive loss on the audience rather than on any of his characters. At the beginning of *Psycho*, we follow Marion, the absconding secretary; then she is murdered in the shower at a motel. The amiable, shambling investigator Arbogast sets out to find her. We follow him to the same motel, then up the hill to the Gothic pile behind it from which enigmatic conversations have been heard; he is last seen falling backwards down a flight of stairs, stabbed to death by, apparently, an old woman wielding a huge knife. We are now well over halfway through the film, still very much in the dark, and two people for whom we have developed affection and, in some sense, trust, have been taken from us. When Marion's sister Lila sets off in pursuit of Arbogast we are on the edge of panic. What will happen to her, and where will that leave us?

Then there is the question of the degree of insanity evident in Powell and in Norman Bates, the murderous motel-keeper in *Psycho*. When we see Norman having a long chat with Marion, in his office, we are made aware of his strangeness, but there are also many indications of self-awareness, in both speech and behaviour. Indeed, his repressed, allusive, stuttering nervousness is understandable enough in an isolated young man who finds himself talking to a cool, apparently self-possessed beauty like Marion. Given what we later learn about Norman, however, is his behaviour during this scene the play-acting of the deranged? Within moments of this conversation's conclusion, he is in drag, clutching his large knife, charging into Marion's shower, totally out of control. In *The Night of the Hunter*, by contrast, Powell seems very much in control almost throughout. There are some moments, however, when we are invited to suppose that he has lost that control: when he watches the stripper, when he appears upside down from his top bunk in prison; on the two occasions when he shouts abusively at Pearl; when he is stunned in the cellar and during the chase that follows before the children escape in the skiff; and when, again twice, he scuttles like a frightened rabbit from the gun toted by Rachel.[9]

This ambiguity over the degree and nature of the killer's supposed

madness is exploited powerfully but quite differently in the two films. In
Psycho a first time viewer might get almost to the end before realizing who
the villain – if that is the word – actually is. In *The Night of the Hunter,*
Powell's first appearance is heralded by the biblical text urging us to
beware false prophets: no ambiguity there.

There is a third similarity between the two films: *The Night of the
Hunter,* like *Psycho*, is a black comedy.

Whether or not Hitchcock was in fact 'influenced' by *The Night of
the Hunter*, the comparison between these two classic thrillers, which
appeared five years apart, in 1955 and 1960, makes clear the very special
quality of Laughton's film. In crude generic terms *Psycho* is a slasher
movie (although that is by no means all it is). *The Night of the Hunter* is
something quite different. Powell has a knife, it is true (a flick-knife,
which when closed looks like a stunted crucifix) but we do not see him kill
Willa with it, and since he does not find out where the money is until the
moment when the children finally elude him he can otherwise employ it
only as a threat. This means that our reactions, from the time he insinu-
ates himself into their home and starts hounding them, are governed by a
complex amalgam of pity and terror on their behalf; of disgust and horror
at his vicious pitilessness; and of powerful moral revulsion from the
thought that he might ever get his hands on the booty.

As I have mentioned, the film was neither a critical nor box office
success. Neither critics nor public seem to have understood it. One of the
reasons for this was the confusion over whether Powell is mad (which also
affected critical assessments of Mitchum's performance). The other, I
believe, was confusion over the nature of revivalist religion. Let us dip
into some of these critical assessments.[10]

Laughton's direction and the film in general were hammered: 'a hor-
rible yarn . . . [an] extremely morbid story . . . [a] repulsive picture',
'dismally arty . . . fearfully entangled with dreary allegory', 'so heavily
macabre that I found myself laughing in the wrong places'. Nor did the
child actors escape censure: they 'disappoint and fail to communicate
emotion'.[11] Only Lilian Gish attracted much praise.

But what of Robert Mitchum? 'Mitchum can't carry this story', thought
the *Evening Standard*, while the *Daily Mirror* considered that he over-
acted. *Variety* found intermittent depth in his performance, but barely
adequate conviction when he was lusting after the money. Dilys Powell
thought that Laughton should have taken the role himself. Some of these
critics seem to have wanted a more full-bloodedly melodramatic portrayal. Lillian Gish actually said to Laughton during shooting that she
wondered whether he was softening the role of Powell overmuch.
Laughton said, partly in jest, that he didn't want to ruin 'that young man's
career'.[12]

As I have already noted, however, Mitchum and, nowadays, many others regard this as his best performance ever. Those who complain that he was too restrained, perhaps fail to grasp that what is in question here is what Hannah Arendt, apropos Adolf Eichmann, called 'the banality of evil'. Although he towers over this film, Powell is really a small character, impressive only to those who want to be impressed. He can persuade Willa that she is a sinner needing redemption rather than a woman needing physical companionship, but John remains adamant that 'he's not my dad', and Rachel knows him for a fraud as soon as she claps eyes on him.

The critics' treatment of Shelley Winters and Willa will serve to introduce the second of my explanations for the initial failure of the film: neither critics nor audiences were closely or objectively enough aware of the nuances of revivalist Christianity to assess it with any great degree of perception. They provide evidence of the inadequacy of so-called sophisticated criticism. The *Daily Mail* was content to dismiss Willa unkindly as Powell's 'stupid wife', while the *Daily Herald* remarked of her death that 'since she has previously gone round saying things like my whole body is just a-quivering with cleanliness, I was rather glad.' A funny enough crack, of course, but disdainful of all the many, essentially innocent people who – however much we may disapprove – in real life have felt and spoken as she did.

Writing in 1976, the earlier of Laughton's two biographers, Charles Higham, describes the small community where the treasure is buried as 'gripped by religious hysteria'.[13] Even granted that many people are disposed to respond with this charge to any mention of personal faith, this assertion seems strange to me.[14] Icey and Ben Harper, the elderly couple who matchmake Willa into Powell's clutches still strike me, after many viewings of the film, as fairly run-of-the-mill small town believers, comic rather than sinister, their worst failing that they know not what they do. I accept that Higham's interpretation makes more convincing their metamorphosis, at the film's climax, into a lynch mob, but although this development is not unbelievable, Icey and Ben's abrupt change of personality strains at the limits of one's credulity. Ben, especially, who has always tried to put a brake on Icey's willingness to interfere in the lives of others, looks more than odd as he froths at the mouth with the worst of them. I've no doubt that high-minded Christians not revivalistically inclined might argue that the great weakness of revivalist Christianity is that it leaves its victims with no intellectual or spiritual bulwark against this kind of violent evolution from loving child of God into baying scourge of the guilty. Nonetheless, we see such howling mobs all over the place these days, and few of them have arrived where they are from the starting point of rural revivalism.

Perhaps even now most viewers of the film will not bother very much about taking on board the nuances of revivalist Christianity evident in Ben and Icey, Willa, Rachel and Powell, but at least now proper weight is given to the film's sensitivity; its imaginative and often poetic photography; its nerve-racking narrative power; its Mark Twain-like exteriors (idyllic riverside life) and expressionist interiors, full of moody night time shadows.

The star-lit moments which open and close the film are widely regarded as unfortunate intrusions of kitsch, and despite the almost angelic presence of Lilian Gish, I'm inclined to agree. Nonetheless, considering the film as a whole, I that that we can all salute a considerable miracle: that a bunch of (variously) agnostics, atheists and careless pagans, drunks and lechers, geniuses and fools, got together and against all the odds produced an overwhelmingly powerful parable of the perversion (in Powell) and fulfilment (in Rachel) of a variety of backwoods Christianity, which, however much it may be despised by irreligious people (even more, of course, by many other Christians) is, or was, the real world of the faith for millions of people during the decades between the Great Depression and the invention, as Philip Larkin expressed it, of sexual intercourse in 1963.

But the upward revision of critical estimation of *The Night of the Hunter* came too late for Laughton. There is a price to be paid for unrecognized miracles. As I have said, following the commercial and critical failure of his solitary masterpiece Laughton never worked as a director again.

Select Bibliography

Paul S. Boyer (ed.), *The Oxford Companion to United States History*, New York: Oxford University Press, 2001.

Simon Callow, *Charles Laughton: A Difficult Actor*, London: Methuen, 1987.

Lillian Gish, *The Movies, Mr Griffith and Me*, London: W. H. Allen, 1969.

Charles Higham, *Charles Laughton: An Intimate Biography*, London: W. H. Allen, 1976.

Stephen Rebello, *Alfred Hitchcock and the Making of Psycho*, London: Marion Boyars, 1990.

Gordon Taylor, *Companion to the Song Book of the Salvation Army*, London: International Headquarters of the Salvation Army, 1989.

Christopher Tookey, *The Critics' Film Guide*, London: Boxtree, 1994.

Notes

1 I should perhaps add that none of the evangelists more or less on the make to whom I referred earlier were Salvationists; when young I was often taken to hear peripatetic preachers.

2 Simon Callow, *Charles Laughton: A Difficult Actor*, London: Methuen, 1987, p. 233. During discussion following this paper, Dr Andrena Telford remarked that the film had put her in mind of many fairy stories, some of them

decidedly sinister, including *Cinderella, Snow White* and *Babes in the Wood.* The biblical text warning against wolves in sheep's clothing reminded her of *Little Red Riding Hood.* Charles Higham, *Charles Laughton: An Intimate Biography,* London: W. H. Allen, 1976, p. 193, suggests that Lillian Gish, as she opens and closes the film, is like Mother Goose.

3 Callow, *Charles Laughton,* p. 231.

4 Dr William R. Telford points out that Laughton's use of chiaroscuro may well have been influenced by David Lean's *Hobson's Choice,* in which Laughton had starred in 1954, the year before *The Night of the Hunter.*

5 Higham, *Charles Laughton,* pp. 191–2.

6 Higham, *Charles Laughton,* pp. 184–5.

7 Callow, *Charles Laughton,* pp. 229 and 232. Laughton's parents had been hotel-keepers and one of the legacies the experience left with him was a dislike of drunkenness. There was, however, a considerable amount of drinking during the filming of *The Night of the Hunter.* Mitchum said that a woman from the Welfare Department, 'used to hang around in a white hat and constantly threatened to report to the Welfare Department about the drinking and cursing on the set. Charles did not drink but Shelley and I always did, and so did the crew, when Charles wasn't looking. One day we caught the Welfare woman drinking beer behind a bush at Rowland V. Lee's ranch when we were shooting there. She gave up all thought of reporting us after that' (Higham, *Charles Laughton,* p. 192).

8 Stephen Rebello, *Alfred Hitchcock and the Making of Psycho,* London: Marion Boyars, 1990, p. 22.

9 In an all too characteristically American way, this film about redemption is finally resolved by a sweet old lady with a gun.

10 See Christopher Tookey, *The Critics' Film Guide,* London: Boxtree, 1994, pp. 585–6.

11 These hostile judgements are those of, respectively, Reg Whitley, John McCarten, *The Daily Herald* and *The Times.*

12 Lilian Gish, *The Movies, Mr Griffith and Me,* London: W. H. Allen, 1969, p. 364.

13 Higham, *Charles Laughton,* p. 193.

14 The scene in which, lit by flaming torches, Willa testifies that she drove a good man to murder, is certainly hysterical, but the excitement of the occasion need not be taken as evidence that all the townsfolk are 'gripped by religious hysteria' day-in, day-out.

16. 'His blood be upon us, and our children':

The Treatment of Jews and Judaism in the Christ Film

WILLIAM R. TELFORD

1. Introduction

The Aims of the Chapter

The title of this chapter is '"His blood be upon us, and our children": The Treatment of Jews and Judaism in the Christ Film'. The quotation is taken from Matthew 27.25, the notorious passage in which the first evangelist transfers responsibility to the Jews for the death of Jesus. Instrumental in fostering later antisemitism, this verse is an appropriate one to introduce the aims of this chapter, namely, an examination of the treatment of Jews and Judaism in the Christ film. What I wish to do in particular is to examine the depiction of Jews and Judaism in a selected number of biblical epics or Christ films stretching from the early silent movies to the late 1980s. After some preliminary remarks about methodology, I shall provide some background for our study, first, by giving a brief summary of the ways Jews and Judaism are treated in the New Testament (more particularly the Christian Gospels), and, second, by offering some general observations on Jews and Judaism in the cinema, and especially about the role of Jews in the film industry. Then we shall proceed to a discussion of six selected Christ films that, hopefully, will demonstrate some of the trends or strategies that can be observed in the treatment of Jews and Judaism therein. Text boxes will offer some background notes on the films selected, and the Notes at the end of the chapter will supply some select bibliography for further reading.

The term 'anti-Semitism', it should be said, was coined in the second half of the nineteenth century, and with predominantly political and racial connotations.[1] Some scholars regard it as anachronistic, therefore, to use it in connection with an ancient text like the New Testament, preferring instead the terms 'anti-Jewishness' or 'anti-Judaism'. While the term is relatively new, the phenomenon of hostility towards the Jews is an ancient one, and since this essay will also be more concerned with the effects of the New Testament texts than with their original context, I intend to follow common usage (and Wolfgang Benz) in employing the term to refer to 'all anti-Jewish statements, tendencies, resentments, attitudes, and actions, regardless of whether they are religiously, racially, socially, or otherwise motivated'.[2]

Approaching the Subject Critically

As in my previous chapter on the characterization of Peter and Judas, let me offer a brief word, if I may, on my methodological approach to the subject of this chapter. Here I refer the reader not only to the first chapter but also to that chapter. Since I shall, once again, be dealing with biblical epics or Christ films, one of my major concerns will be to examine them in relation to their New Testament sources and with respect to the question of how these sources have been used or treated. I shall be exploring them with regard to their intertextual references, therefore, looking at how film-makers have altered or adapted these texts in their filmic representations. Where aesthetics (camera-work, editing, *mise-en-scène*, visual quality, sets, lighting, music, etc.), as well as plot, settings and characterization, are relevant to our subject, I shall make appropriate comments. Films, as we have seen, are also interesting for their social context and ideology. They reflect the culture in which they were produced, and the audiences for which they were made, and it is this aspect, along with intertextuality, that will also occupy me.

The subject of 'Jews and Judaism in the Christ Film' relates to some very important concerns of our day. In general, it impinges upon the power of cinema to reflect and influence popular attitudes and values. It relates to the phenomenon of racial stereotyping in general, and antisemitism in particular. It touches upon the vexed question of the antisemitic nature of some aspects of Christianity's sacred text, the New Testament. As Margaret Davies points out in her article, 'Stereotyping the Other: The "Pharisees" in the Gospel According to Matthew':

> Stereotyping can be useful in learning to make initial distinctions and has always formed part of our didactic literature aimed at children. What is distinctive about our cultural individualism, however, is that we recognize this and guard against allowing these categories to become rigid. Our individualism gives us a sense that 'justice' requires a just appreciation of individual complexities, and has led to legislation that outlaws slandering and discriminating against ethnic and gender groups.[3]

In what follows, I shall attempt to demonstrate some of the complexities, as well as some of the ironies and conundrums, that are entailed in a study of the biblical epic or Christ film from a racial or ethnic perspective, and some of the strategies that have been used in dealing with the ethnically sensitive passages to be found in the New Testament Gospels. A major presupposition of this chapter is that, in making ourselves aware of these complexities, we can be more sensitive to the power of the filmic text, as well as the written one, to perpetuate damaging stereotypes.

2. Jews and Judaism in the New Testament

The first and major conundrum is this, and it faced me as I began this study: biblical epics were produced for mass audiences – the earlier ones for a predominantly Christian society – by largely Jewish directors and producers. Where the Christ film is concerned, this was based on the New Testament Gospels whose depiction of Jews and Judaism has in part been so derogatory that these sacred texts of Christianity have been used to justify the persecution of Jews down through the centuries. Why, then, did Jewish producers support the filming of these texts? How were the antisemitic elements in them treated? What compromises were made with Christianity's sacred texts? What compromises were made with Jews, Christians and mass audiences when they came to the cinema? It is this intriguing tension, then, between the Christian sacred text, the Jewish film producer and the exigencies of the market, shall we say, that I now want to explore.

Let me now fill out some of these points, and let us begin with a brief summary of the way Jews and Judaism are treated in the New Testament, with particular reference to the Gospels. The earliest Gospel was the Gospel of Mark, and this is where we find the mainspring of the New Testament's derogatory picture of Jews and Judaism. If any New Testament writing deserved to be described as antisemitic, Mark would be a good candidate. The Gospel's treatment of Jews and Judaism amounts, in the eyes of some scholars, to a pronounced campaign of vilification. Jewish religion is depicted in a poor light. Jewish lustration practice is disparaged, as are other Jewish practices (cf. Mk 7.1–23). Judaism is implied to be obsolescent (cf. Mk 2.21–22 – new wine is not be placed in old wineskins). The Markan Jesus himself is presented as more Gentile than Jewish.

The Jewish people, their leaders, and even his Jewish disciples and family fare no better. The Jewish authorities are depicted as hard of heart (cf. Mk 2.1 ff.; 3.5), as hypocrites (cf. Mk 7.6–7), as guilty of the unforgivable sin in questioning the source of the Markan Jesus's power (cf. Mk 3.28–30), and as wicked murderers for rejecting Jesus (the beloved Son of the vineyard owner) and the prophets before him (cf. Mk 12.1ff.). All the Jewish leadership groups are shown implausibly as plotting his death, with Jesus anticipating their culpability in the passion predictions (cf. Mk 8.31; 9.31; 10.33–34). They act with stealth and deviousness (cf. Mk

14.1–2), they are accused of acting out of envy (cf. Mk 15.10), and they are depicted as cruelly mocking Jesus on the cross (cf. Mk 15.31–32).

One New Testament scholar sums up Mark's treatment in this way:

> There can, accordingly, be traced throughout the Markan Gospel a consistent denigration of the Jewish leaders and people, and of the family of Jesus and his original Apostles, which adds up to a truly damning indictment of the Jews for their treatment of Jesus. The Jewish leaders and people are responsible for his death, his family regard him as insane, and his Apostles fail to understand him and finally desert him.[4]

Matthew, the most Jewish of the Gospels, draws on Mark, and introduces some new twists. It is Matthew who puts a powerful series of denunciations upon the lips of Jesus against the scribes and the Pharisees (Mt. 23). It is this evangelist who creates the famous passage quoted at the beginning of this chapter, where Pilate is made to wash his hands of responsibility for the death of Jesus, and who makes the Jewish crowd accept it, not only for themselves but for all subsequent generations of Jews, in the bloodcurdling words: 'His blood be on us, and on our children!' (Mt. 27.25).

Luke is generally regarded as being more benign toward Jews and Judaism. He it is who informs us that Jesus was circumcised as a Jew (Lk. 2.21) and purified in the Temple (2.22–32), and he it is who gives us the only childhood story of Jesus conversing with the learned doctors of the law in the Temple (Lk. 2.41–51). Nevertheless Luke includes, for example, the damning parable of the Pharisee and the tax collector, the former thankful that he is not like other men, the latter a paragon of humility (Lk. 18.9–14).

The Gospel of John is regarded as the most notoriously antisemitic of all. The Johannine Jesus is distanced from his Jewish roots, and speaks to his opponents, 'the Jews', as if they were a single hostile entity, and, in addressing them, uses terms such as 'your law', 'your fathers' (the patriarchs) or 'your father Abraham' as if they were not also his (e.g. Jn 8.17; 8.56). 'You are of your father the devil, and your will is to do your father's desires. He was a murderer from the beginning', he tells them (Jn 8.44).

All four Gospels have Jesus challenge Judaism's greatest institution, the Temple, in the famous 'Cleansing of the Temple' incident. All four Gospels, moreover, have Jesus judged and condemned not only by Pilate, but by the Jewish authorities themselves, under Caiaphas. All four Gospels make the Jews responsible, then, for the death of Jesus, and all have contributed, therefore, to the powerful image of Jews as Christ-killers. There have, of course, been scholarly attempts to soften this picture, and to claim in a number of ways that this was not the intention of the Gospel writers. For those of you interested in this discussion, a fuller summary of it (together with bibliography) is to be found in my book, *The Theology of the Gospel of Mark* (1999).[5] Nevertheless, it is not the *intention* here that counts, but the *effect*, and this effect has had disastrous consequences, as we know, for Jews through the centuries.

3. Jews and Judaism in the Cinema

Let me fill out the second half of the conundrum, namely, the fact that many of the biblical epics were produced and financed by Jews, or if they were not, they were produced in the context of a Hollywood that was dominated by Jews.

Jews have been associated with the cinema and the cinema industry from its very inception.[6] In their seminal essay exploring the dynamics of assimilation on the part of Jewish immigrants from Eastern Europe at the beginning of the twentieth century, Claire Pajaczkowska and Barry Curtis point out that Jews had played a prominent role (as performers and agents) in the theatre of the 1890s, that is, prior to the advent of cinema, and thereafter, with the arrival of the nickelodeons (the rough and ready motion picture theatres of the time) made eager audiences for the early films of the first decade of the new century.[7] Nickelodeons, as their name implies, charged only a nickel (five cents) for admission. They were particularly popular in the working class areas of major cities,[8] as well as among immigrant populations, and there is statistical evidence that they were exceptionally numerous in Jewish districts. Cheap and accessible, they not only offered appealing entertainment to poor, urban Jewish immigrants but also a visual route into American life and 'the American dream'.

Jews not only provided eager audiences for the infant film industry, but from the 1910s onwards, they also worked in Hollywood itself, where they founded many of the major film studios. The list is impressive, as Text Box 16.1 indicates, and you might like to research some of these names for yourself, with the aid of tools I have listed in the endnote.[9]

According to Claude Singer, '[a]lmost all the producers who managed to make their mark in the industry of the American Dream during the 1920s were Jewish'.[10] Many of these first cinema entrepreneurs came from humble origins, having made their money in the garment industry (or rag trade), as jewellers, or as the owners and managers of the nickelodeons. Pajaczkowska and Curtis cite a description of them as 'the old regime of fur peddlers, second hand jewellers and nickelodeon proprietors who started all the cinema companies . . .'.[11]

A second wave of Jewish émigrés arrived from Europe from the 1920s to the 1940s, some seeking to better themselves, others fleeing Nazi oppression. Some of these had had experience of the performing arts, or had worked in the European film industry, and they included directors

---

16.1 Jewish Producers and Directors

Harry Cohn
Samuel Goldwyn
Carl Laemmle
Fritz Lang
Ernst Lubitsch
Louis B. Mayer
Irving Thalberg
Harry Warner
Jack Warner
Billy Wilder
Adolph Zukor

---

such as Ernst Lubitsch, Billy Wilder or the half-Jewish Fritz Lang.[12] Many of the famous film studios, so familiar now to cinema audiences, were either founded by Jewish producers or bear their names: Columbia (Harry Cohn), Metro-Goldwyn-Mayer or MGM (Samuel Goldwyn, Louis B. Mayer and Irving Thalberg), Paramount (Adolph Zukor), Universal (Carl Laemmle), Warner Bros (Jack and Harry Warner). In an opinion that many would echo, A. Gordon considers that 'Louis B. Mayer of MGM was probably the most powerful, the most exemplary of the meddling, patriarchal style, and the one who best represents the complex mixture of showman-like *chutzpah* and subconscious abnegation of ethnic identity that so many of the others shared.'[13]

What is remarkable about the rise of these so-called Hollywood moguls, in the estimation of Pajaczkowska and Curtis, is 'the ease and rapidity with which they seemed to make the transition from the passivity of spectatorship to the activities of film exhibition, distribution, and production'. Their judgement is in fact worth quoting in full:

> The genius of the future Moguls was a complex one, partly sheer business ingenuity, partly ruthless risk taking and a kind of competitive solidarity; but perhaps its most interesting component was coherent with immigrant aspiration and Jewish prioritizing of 'culture'. They recognized that the potential of film and the basis for its future appeal lay in the compulsive attractions of narrative, star appeal, and the conspicuous glamor of *mise-en-scène* both on screen and in the theaters in which films were screened. Members of the audience had to be rescued from the crowd which they constituted, offered individualism and intimacy – respected and turned into individual spectators . . . In an important respect, men like Adolph Zukor, Carl Laemmle, Louis Meyer, Harry Cohn, and Jack and Harry Warner became conspicuous examples of the American dream.[14]

It was this connection with the American dream that explains one of the major paradoxes associated with the Hollywood moguls. This paradox is that, although they retained their Judaism, and they employed many Jewish associates, they tended not to promote Jews and Judaism within the context or content of the films that they produced. Claude Singer recounts the celebrated incident, which has been taken as indicative of the ethos then prevailing in the major studios:

> The story goes that a director employed by Columbia once asked his boss, Harry Cohn (1891–1958, known as King Kohn because of his legendary rages), to engage a certain actor for an important part. Cohn categorically refused to have the actor, who, he said, looked 'too Jewish'. In his studio, he pointed out, Jews only played Indians.[15]

L. Mulvey offers another insight into these complex individuals:

> The Jews who built Hollywood built it out of a double migration: that of their families to the United States and of their industry to California. California represented a new newness, in which the East Coast – its ghettos, ethnicities and traditions – could be left behind.[16]

The moguls were influenced, then, by the policy of assimilation, of America as the melting-pot of ethnic differences. 'The Hollywood cinema of the years between the wars', according to Singer, 'was not intended to promote the specific character of any minority group.'[17] The moguls wished to downplay racial differences, and to place emphasis on that which unites all upward-striving Americans in a common vision.

That vision was the American Dream, and indeed, there are those who would claim that it was Hollywood under the Jewish moguls who invented the American Dream itself. In the words of Pajaczkowska and Curtis: 'What is particularly interesting about the success of Hollywood is that the imaginings of the Jewish immigrant "arriviste" could become a format for widely shared representations of American life.'[18] According to another commentator: 'Hollywood – the American dream – is a Jewish idea in a sense, it's a Jewish revenge on America. It combines the Puritan ethic with baroque magnificence.'[19]

This is one reason why Hollywood took to the biblical epic because in its underlying mythology, concepts such as the exodus or the 'promised land' could be, and were, a vehicle for the promotion of American values, values such as liberation, freedom, justice and equality. There is a hint, too, that the Old Testament epic was embraced, especially in the 1950s, because it showed Israelite warriors and heroes vanquishing their enemies, a depiction that acted against the post-Holocaust criticism that Jews had done little to resist their Nazi oppressors.

Having said this, it is also important to point out that the Jews who ran the Hollywood establishment were also anxious to avoid perpetuating the age-old stereotypes of Jews. To cite Pajaczkowska and Curtis again:

> They were also subject and highly sensitive to successive waves of anti-Semitism, which found different forms of expression – panics about immigration and 'hyphenated Americans' in the 1920's [sic]; the omnipresence of Fascists in American public life; much publicized vilification by prominent figures like Henry Ford and Charles Lindbergh; various Christian fulminations opposed to the immoralities of Hollywood; attacks on the presumed link between Communism and Jews; and accusations of an inevitable 'racial feeling' among Hollywood Jews promoting war with Germany.[20]

It is these conflicting factors, then, that help account for some of the complexities and conundrums that we see in Jewish treatment of, and reactions to, the biblical epic, particularly the Christ film. And with these preliminary remarks, let us now turn to our selected films and clips.

4. Jews and Judaism in the Christ Film: Some Selected Films and Clips

In Text Box 16.2, you will find brief information about the six films selected.

With each of the films discussed, you will also find a selected sequence that you should watch (its approximate time location within the film is given in square brackets at the end of the subheading). Another text box (16.3) is supplied to enable you to make your own comments upon it. Further reading on each film is to be found in the endnotes. Our aim will be to observe how Jews and Judaism are depicted in our chosen films, and, in particular, to see how directors have dealt with the vexing passages, as well as the (so-called) 'notorious texts', in the Christian Gospels that portray Jewish complicity in the death of Jesus. Below you will find my remarks on each sequence, comprising an introduction to both the film and the sequence, followed by comments inspired in some cases by social context and ideology, in most cases by intertextual reflection. A summary of the trends or strategies observed is given at the end.

Intolerance *(1916): The Two Pharisees (the first cut to the Judaean story)* [00.07.21–00.10.13]

Our first film sequence is from D. W. Griffith's *Intolerance* (1916).[21] *Intolerance* is not strictly a biblical epic, since there are only two biblical

16.2 Notes on the Films Selected

Intolerance (D. W. Griffith, 1916)
Though not technically a biblical epic, since the biblical portions of this four-part treatment of hypocrisy and intolerance through the ages are confined to a Judaean story of the crucifixion of Jesus and a Babylonian story of the fall of the city of Babylon to Cyrus and the Persians, Griffith's silent epic, *Intolerance*, followed close on the heels of his famous and controversial *Birth of a Nation* in 1915.

The King of Kings (Cecil B. DeMille, 1927)
A major classic, this was the first full-length, silent Hollywood epic on the life of Jesus, as seen from the perspective of Mary Magdalene. It presents Mary as a rich courtesan with Judas as her lover. Its many memorable moments include Mary's riding off in her chariot to rescue her Judas from the clutches of the carpenter of Nazareth ('Harness my zebras – gift of the Nubian king!'), her subsequent exorcism by Jesus in a swirl of exiting demons, the moving giving of sight to a little blind girl and dramatic crucifixion and resurrection scenes.

King of Kings (Nicholas Ray, 1961)
A remake of the DeMille version in name only, this Sixties' Hollywood adaptation presents Judas and Barabbas as political revolutionaries, with Jesus as a reluctant pawn in their game. Criticized by the Catholic Legion of Decency as 'theologically, historically, and scripturally inaccurate' (R. Kinnard and T. Davis, *Divine Images. A History of Jesus on the Screen*, New York: Citadel Press, 1992, p. 132), the film is now viewed in retrospect as better than its critics made it out to be.

The Gospel according to St. Matthew (Pier Paolo Pasolini, 1964)
A low-budget, black-and-white, European film made by the Marxist director, Pier Paolo Pasolini and dedicated to Pope John XXIII, this unconventional adaptation of Matthew's Gospel in *cinéma verité* style had more impact on audiences than the traditional, glossy Hollywood epic, *The Greatest Story Ever Told*, which was to follow it a year later.

Jesus of Nazareth (Franco Zeffirelli, 1977)
With a screenplay by Anthony Burgess and others (later turned into a novel by William Barclay), this six-and-a-half-hour made-for-television movie (screened on ITV in 1977) was the result of a promise made by its producer Lew Grade to the Pope to do for Jesus what he had done for Moses.

The Last Temptation of Christ (Martin Scorsese, 1988)
Based on Kazantzakis's novel about 'the dual substance of Christ' and 'the incessant, merciless battle between the spirit and the flesh', and directed by one of Hollywood's most distinguished film-makers, this is one of the finest, most religious and yet most controversial Christ films ever made.

16.3 Comments on Films/Clips

Intolerance (D. W. Griffith, 1916): The Two Pharisees (the first cut to the Judaean story)

The King of Kings (Cecil B. DeMille, 1927): Jesus before the crowd

King of Kings (Nicholas Ray, 1961): Jesus before Pilate

The Gospel according to St. Matthew (Pier Paulo Pasolini, 1964): The Denunciation of the Pharisees

Jesus of Nazareth (Franco Zeffirelli, 1977): The Circumcision of Jesus

Jesus of Nazareth (Franco Zeffirelli, 1977): The Sanhedrin debates Jesus's Fate

The Last Temptation of Christ (Martin Scorsese, 1988): Jesus's Speech in the Temple

portions within what is a four-part treatment of hypocrisy and intolerance through the ages. These two biblical sections present a Judaean story
of the crucifixion of Jesus and a Babylonian story of the fall of the city of
Babylon to Cyrus and the Persians. The other two parts comprise a
modern story of a young man in the United States sentenced to die for
a murder he did not commit, and a French story of the St Bartholomew's
Day massacre of Huguenots by Catholics in 1572. The intercutting
between the biblical portions and the other stories, especially the modern
story, lend support for what W. Barnes Tatum describes as 'Griffith's
indictment of those social do-gooders (or "Uplifters," as he calls them in
the film) whose claim to know what was best for society often expressed
itself, in his eyes, as an intolerance toward others'.[22] The Judaean story is
told in seven individual cuts occupying in total (for reasons that will
shortly be explained) no more than twelve minutes of screen time. The
part you are asked to watch is the *first* cut to the Judean story, which
occurs after the opening sequence of the film that introduces the modern
story. The woman and the cradle, which is an image taken from lines in a
Walt Whitman poem in *Leaves of Grass* ('Out of the cradle endlessly
rocking'),[23] is the device he uses to mark the transition from one story to
another. You should watch out also for the tablets of stone in Hebrew,
which denote the biblical sections, and the intertitles characteristic of
these early silent films.

From an intertextual point of view, this sequence is interesting for a
number of reasons. One notes the incorrect reference to Bethlehem, not
Nazareth, as the place where Jesus was brought up. Visually, the depiction of the Jewish people in the streets owes much to the illustrated Bibles
of the period, especially those of Gustave Doré or James Tissot. One also
notes the madonna-like figure, with the child in her arms. The reference to
the party of the Pharisees and their identification with hypocrisy is particularly striking. Ethnic characteristics are clearly displayed, such as the
tefillah, or phylactery attached to the forehead of the Pharisee (cf. Exod.
13.1–10; 13.11–16; Deut. 6.4–9; 11.13–21). One notes the elaborate
bowing and scraping of the people, as well as the touch of humour, as one
man interrupts his eating while the Pharisees conduct their prayers in the
street. Interestingly, as Tatum observes, Griffith has here turned the parable of the Pharisee and the tax collector of Luke 18.9–14 (along with Mt.
6.5) into a narrative event.[24]

Griffith's silent epic, *Intolerance*, followed close on the heels of his
famous and controversial *Birth of a Nation* in 1915, and here an interpretative approach that emphasizes social context and ideology offers some
fascinating glimpses into the cultural processes behind the film. This is the
film that, on account of its glorification of the Klu Klux Klan, and its deni-
gration of blacks, was condemned by many as racist. Some have assumed
that Griffith made *Intolerance* as a way of making amends for the bigotry

deemed to have characterized that film. This is untrue, as Simon Louvish has pointed out,[25] and the following excerpt from the media journal, *Variety*, of Friday, 7 April 1916, cited in Louvish's perceptive article, makes this abundantly clear.

The headline of the article read: 'GRIFFITH FORCED TO RE-TAKE SCENES IN "MOTHER AND LAW"' (*The Mother and the Law*, as Louvish informs us, was Griffith's original title for *Intolerance*); and its caption: 'B'nai Brith Objected to Showing Saviour Being Nailed to Cross by Hebrews – Confront Producer with Proofs Backed by 48-Hour Ultimatum. Los Angeles, April 5'.

The article (which is worth quoting in full from Louvish's article) stated:

> David W. Griffith has about completed his latest 'masterpiece' entitled 'The Mother and the Law', dealing with the life of Christ. For the big crucifixion scene he repaired to the local ghetto and hired all the orthodox Hebrews with long whiskers he could secure.
>
> When the B'nai Brith (the most powerful Hebrew society in the United States) was apprised of it they requested Griffith to omit that portion of the picture, but he refused. They then brought pressure to bear upon him through his associates, but could not move him.
>
> A committee of three members of the society . . . brought the matter to the attention of Jacob H. Schiff, Joseph Brandeis, Louis Marshall and other prominent Hebrews. Armed with data gathered from colleges, professors and historians, the committee returned to Los Angeles and waited upon Griffith with so-called indisputable proofs that the Jews did not crucify the Saviour, showing that the orthodox method of killing in those days was strangulation and that the Romans believed in crucifixion. They supplemented the 'proofs' with a 48-hour ultimatum to destroy that portion of the 'masterpiece' negative on penalty of a concerted national campaign of blacklisting and other pressure which powerful financial and industrial interests might bring to bear, which included the assertion that censors, governors of states and even the President would do all in their power to prevent the showing of the picture with the objectionable scene.
>
> Confronted with such formidable antagonism Griffith burned the negative of the scene in the presence of the committee and has retaken it, showing Roman soldiers nailing Christ to the cross.

This is an astonishing episode, casting, as it does, a fascinating light into the ethnic tensions operating in the early cinema, and of the powerful forces operating on film-makers like Griffith in relation to their depictions of the life of Jesus on screen. It is a potent reminder, too, at the beginning of our study, of the issues involved in this subject, and of one of the more extreme courses of action taken by a film-maker when confronted with the problems of representing Jesus's death on screen. As an aside, too, it is one of the great ironies of film history that what enabled Louis B. Mayer, arguably, as we have seen, the greatest of the Jewish Hollywood moguls, to raise enough capital to found his own production company, was his acquisition of the north-east rights to Griffith's allegedly racist *Birth of the Nation* (1915)![26]

The King of Kings *(1927): Jesus before the crowd* [01.28.56–01.33.42]

We turn now to Cecil B. DeMille's *The King of Kings* (1927). Working in collaboration with his scriptwriter, Jeanie McPherson, and with religious consultants such as Bruce Barton, one of the founding figures of modern advertising, DeMille produced the first full-length, silent Hollywood epic on the life of Jesus, as seen from the perspective of Mary Magdalene. We had our first introduction to this film in chapter 13 ('The Two Faces of Betrayal: the Characterization of Peter and Judas in the Biblical Epic or Christ Film') to which you might like to refer, or to Text Box 16.2, which summarizes its plot. The sequence for viewing and comment is Jesus's appearance before Pilate, the High Priest and the Jewish crowd and his consequent condemnation to death. The source is Mk 15.1–15 and parallels. This is, therefore, one of the vexing passages I referred to earlier. It deals with the question of who was ultimately responsible for the death of Jesus, and it is interesting to observe how DeMille treats this issue.

The sequence begins after Jesus has been scourged by the Roman soldiers and mocked. He is brought before the crowd. Pilate releases Barabbas at the bequest of the crowd, and delivers Jesus for crucifixion. As we observe this sequence, we note the characteristic DeMille devices:

- the use of biblical captions;
- the little snatch of hymn music;
- the creative embellishment of the Gospel texts.

This last is seen, for example, in the various invented speeches, and in the treatment of Mary Magdalene. Here she is seen pleading for the crowd to call for Jesus's release, a role not found in the Gospels. In counterpoint to her role, one notes, is that given to the High Priest's henchmen in stirring up the crowd to demand Jesus's crucifixion. The crowd has been earlier bribed, on the High Priest's orders, and through these selfsame henchmen, to call for Jesus's condemnation. Also acting in counterpoint to each other are Pilate and the High Priest. Both appear together on the podium. Jesus has had a brief previous appearance before Caiaphas but in this film, as in so many of the Christ films that were to come later, there is no specific trial before the Sanhedrin.

Here DeMille plays up the individual characterization of the High Priest who appears like the devil at Pilate's shoulder. Most striking of all, the High Priest (contrary to the Gospels) takes sole responsibility for Jesus's death: 'If Thou, Imperial Pilate, wouldst wash thy hands of this Man's death, let it be upon me – and me alone.' The effect of these changes, then, is to remove culpability from the Jews as a people, and to place it firmly in the hands of one corrupt High Priest – and, as is stated earlier in the scene: 'The High Priest speaketh not for the people!' This point is later reinforced, in the crucifixion scene, when Caiaphas prays, 'Lord God, Jehovah, vent not thy wrath on thy people Israel – I alone am guilty.'

Bruce Babington and Peter Evans point out that, despite this alteration to the biblical text, in his autobiography DeMille complained about the 'organized opposition of certain Jewish groups to this filmed history of the greatest Jew who ever lived', claiming that 'we went to great lengths in *The King of Kings* to show that the Jewish people of Jesus's time followed and heard him gladly, that his death came at the hands of a few unrepresentative corrupt leaders and the cowardly and callous Roman government'. The opening title of the film was inserted in response to Jewish pressure, and it, too, implied that Caiaphas was unrepresentative of his people: 'The events portrayed in this picture occurred in Palestine nineteen centuries ago, when the Jews were under the complete subjection of Rome – even their own High Priest being appointed by the Roman procurator.'[27]

Like Griffith before him, and like the film-makers who were to succeed him, DeMille made use of Jewish advisors on his film, in order to anticipate and defuse Jewish sensitivities. Ironically, however, as Babington and Evans acutely observe:

Caiaphas, the Romans' Jew, asserted to be in no way representative of Jewry, is an anti-semite's dream caricature of wickedness: obese, cynical, rubbing his plump fingers together in gleeful anticipation of his plots, appearing like a well-fed devil at Pilate's side to whisper 'Crucify him!' So the scapegoat who apparently frees the Jews from blame is simultaneously the living epitome of ethnic guilt.[28]

King of Kings *(1961): Jesus before Pilate* [02.11.45–02.13.30]

Our next sequence is from Nicholas Ray's *King of Kings* (1961), a film also introduced and discussed in chapter 13.

The scene you should watch comes after Judas arrives with the soldiers, Jesus is taken away to Caiaphas and Peter denies Jesus before the retainers. It shows Jesus being tried before a brisk, quick-speaking and businesslike Pilate (played by Hurd Hatfield), with the omnipresent Lucius (played by Ron Randell) acting as his advocate. Lucius points out that the defendant has only spoken of the kingdom of God, and has said nothing about the kingdom of Judaea. The report of the Sermon on the Mount is discussed, and then Jesus is referred to the effete Herod Antipas who requests a miracle from him.

If Griffith's forced strategy in the face of Jewish opposition to his treatment of the Christ story was to burn the negative of an offending sequence, and DeMille's was to alter the biblical text so as to inculpate the Jewish High Priest only, the approach taken by Ray was simply to omit any public scene in which Jesus is condemned by either the Jewish crowd or the High Priest. Here one notes the entirely private nature of the proceedings. Brief reference is made to an interrogation before Caiaphas, but the audience is not presented with this scene, far less a full trial before the Jewish Sanhedrin. The charge against Jesus here is sedition, and the religious charge of blasphemy of which the Gospels speak (cf. Mk 14.53–65 and parallels) is simply set aside. The responsibility for condemning Jesus to death is taken by Pilate alone, and emphatically; indeed his words almost echo those of the High Priest in the DeMille version:

> You have just been interrogated by Caiaphas. They have adjudged you guilty on two counts, blasphemy and sedition. This court takes no cognizance of your blasphemy, but the charge of sedition is a major offence. The rules of Roman law will prevail. I, Pontius Pilate, the Procurator of Judea, by grace of the emperor, the divine Tiberius of Rome, will judge your case. No matter what you have done up until this moment, no matter what others have accused you of doing, I, and I alone, have the authority to sentence you to be crucified, or flogged, or to set you free. How you conduct yourself here and now, will determine your fate. Do you understand?

The Gospel according to St. Matthew *(1964): The Denunciation of the Pharisees* [01.28.40–1.30.09]

If Ray avoided the negative impact of the so-called antisemitic passages in the Gospels by simply omitting them, the same strategy could not be adopted by our next director, Pier Paolo Pasolini who made *The Gospel according to St. Matthew* in 1964.[29] By taking the words of the Gospel According to St Matthew as his primary textual source, Pasolini could hardly avoid the powerful anti-Jewish passages referred to in my introduction, passages that include the denunciation of the Pharisees (23.1–36), the trial before the Jewish Sanhedrin (26.57–67), the trial before Pilate and the condemnation of Jesus by the Jewish crowd (27.1–2, 11–26).

The sequence that we shall comment on is part of Jesus's denunciation of the Pharisees, a passage normally omitted or downplayed in the Christ film. It comes after the authorities try to trap Jesus by their questions only to be answered cunningly and confidently with teaching that ends with the famous love command ('Thou shalt love thy neighbour as thyself'). In the next scene, Jesus begins his denunciation of the Jewish leaders. The crowds are shown running to him, and he is seen from a distance addressing them with the words with which Mt. 23 begins: 'The scribes and Pharisees sit in the chair of Moses. Do what they tell you, observe what they tell you but do not imitate their actions, they do not practise what they preach. . . .' The people are shown reacting to his words. A shaky handheld camera then approaches Jesus through the crowd as he intones his denunciation. Choral music intensifies the effect of the scene, as does the total silence of the crowds.

In this scene, one should note, among other things, Pasolini's fondness for lingering facial close-ups, especially of Jesus whose animated persona is often in sharp contrast to the passive acting, silent stares and looks of awe from the supporting cast of unknown, untutored and unprofessional actors. The actor who played Jesus was likewise an unknown, a Spanish student, Enrique Irazoqui, who had never acted before. Pasolini also gives us a soundtrack throughout his film that draws upon the full range of the classical and Christian musical tradition: from Bach to Billie Holliday; from Prokofiev to the Congolese Missa Luba; from Mozart to Leadbelly; from the haunting sound of the flute to the world-weary sound of the negro spiritual 'Sometimes I feel like a motherless child'.

In this sequence, one particularly notes the savage condemnation of the scribes and Pharisees by Jesus, although no Jewish leaders are actually in attendance. One also observes the Southern Italian backdrop, and the Italian peasant audience. Accompanying the sequence, as we have observed, is the emotive choral background. The effect of all of this is to produce a solitary Jesus who denounces the religious establishment (and hence the Church) of the twentieth century and not the Judaism of the first.

W. Barnes Tatum observes something similar in the later appearance of Jesus before Caiaphas and the Sanhedrin.[30] Here what appears on screen closely follows what appears in the Matthean account. On the other hand, Jesus's appearance before Pilate has been considerably curtailed, when compared with the Gospel text. In contrast to what we find in Nicholas Ray's film, *King of Kings* (1961), he notes, Jesus is not presented as posing a *political* threat to the Roman state. Where Ray downplayed the charge of blasphemy, Pasolini plays it up, and has Jesus die ultimately on a *religious* charge, and at the instigation of the Jewish authorities, supported by the crowds. As he puts it: 'Ironically, Pasolini the Marxist has completely de-politicized the crucifixion.' At the same time, however, by abbreviating the trial before Pilate, Pasolini has eliminated those very elements, those 'notorious' texts, that have encouraged antisemitism. Pilate is not presented as washing his hands of responsibility for the death of Jesus, and the crowds are not depicted as asking that Jesus's blood be on them and on their children (Mt. 27.24–25).

Furthermore, opines Tatum, with the voicing of Isaiah 6.9–10 ('Hearing you will hear, but not understand and seeing you will see but not perceive, for the heart of this people has been hardened and with their ears they have been hard of hearing . . .'; cf. Mt. 13.14–15) at a key moment during the crucifixion, the implication is conveyed that responsibility for Jesus's death extends to everyone, and not just the religious authorities. This supports our reading of the sequence selected for discussion above, and leads us to concur with Tatum's overall conclusion:

> As Pasolini himself said, he was not trying to reconstruct the past but rather to find some equivalence between that past and his own present. This led him away from Palestine to Calabria in southern Italy as the site for filming. The logic of analogy draws an equivalence not between the Jewish leaders in first-century Palestine and twentieth-century Judaism, but between the religious establishment of ancient Palestine and the religious establishment of contemporary Italy – that is to say, the present-day church, specifically the Roman Catholic Church.

It is another of the ironies that surround this subject, however (as Tatum also notes) that if this were Pasolini's intention, then it failed, for the film was enthusiastically received by the Church, meriting among other things, an international Catholic film prize!

Jesus of Nazareth *(1977): The Circumcision of Jesus*
[Pt 1. 00.52.59–00.55.32]

If Christian religious authorities, the Church or religious hypocrisy in general are, in effect, the real targets in *The Gospel according to St. Matthew* (1964), and not the Jews and Judaism of Matthew's own day, then this is borne out by another observation that emerges from a close scrutiny of Pasolini's film. Pasolini's settings for the sayings and miracles of Jesus are striking, but despite the fact that Jesus's teaching and activity in the Gospel occurs within the vicinity of Jewish synagogues, no synagogue setting is ever provided for these by Pasolini in his film.[31] Like the Jewish authorities, the Matthean Jesus is likewise distanced from his Jewish roots and his Jewish community. Not so in the Christ films that emerged in the following years. One year after Pasolini issued his *Gospel according to St. Matthew*, the Roman Catholic Church, in the shape of Vatican Council II, issued its famous declaration on the Jews, *Nostra Aetate*. This statement emphasized the spiritual links between Christians and Jews, rejected the notion that all Jews indiscriminately were guilty of the death of Jesus, and condemned all forms of antisemitism.[32] It was this statement that led our next film-maker, Franco Zeffirelli to make *Jesus of Nazareth* in 1977, and it was this film that produced a very different image of Jews and Judaism. *Jesus of Nazareth* emphasized, perhaps more than any previous Christ film, the Jewishness of Jesus himself.

One of the two sequences that I have selected from the film is the circumcision of Jesus. It occurs in the film after the familiar story of Jesus's birth in the manger and the visit of the shepherds, and between the report to Herod of the coming of the magi and their eventual arrival. Jesus is circumcised with Simeon (played by Ralph Richardson) attending the service and celebrating the coming Messiah.

The story is found only in Luke's Gospel (2.21–40), but is considerably embellished. Here in this excerpt (as with Jesus's *bar mitzvah* which follows) all the elements of a Jewish origin and upbringing are signalled. One notes the synagogue location (and, by contrast, again, the lack of synagogues in Pasolini) rather than the Temple, which is the setting in Luke's account. Mary and Joseph approach the synagogue through a crowded marketplace. Joseph adjusts his prayer shawl before he enters. He is wearing ringlets. They are beckoned forward 'Come, come!' by the *huperetes*, the synagogue attendant. Joseph takes the infant Jesus to the table reserved for the circumcision, while Mary looks on. The rabbi is summoned, puts on his prayer shawl and intones over the infant Jesus 'And the Lord said to Abraham, "Keep my alliance and circumcise each child born unto Israel on the eighth day of his life".' 'Amen', the elders respond. 'This is the seal in the flesh of the covenant between the Lord and his people', says the rabbi. The circumcision is graphically depicted with a close-up of the circumcision knives, and a tiny whimper from Jesus when it is accomplished. 'The child shall be called?' asks the rabbi. Joseph looks at Mary, who nods. 'His name shall be called Jesus', says Joseph. A Christian overlay on this scene is provided, however, with the appearance of Simeon who points to Jesus's future destiny as '[a] light of revelation to the Gentiles, and the glory of thy people, Israel'.

Jesus of Nazareth (1977): The Sanhedrin debates Jesus's Fate
[Pts 3 & 4. 01.35.12–01.40.42]

If the biblical text is enlivened by Zeffirelli with such local colour, then a further striking example of a developed sensitivity to Judaism on the part of the film-maker is to be seen in our next sequence, the director's treatment of the Sanhedrin's debate over the fate of Jesus. The sequence occurs at the beginning of Part IV. The Sanhedrin deliberates over Jesus and the disturbance he is causing. Voices are raised both for and against him. Caiaphas (played by Anthony Quinn) listens to the debate in proud, uneasy silence before speaking. The crux of the matter, he says, is that Jesus declares himself to be the Son of God.

This scene is not found in the Gospels, since Jesus is not actually being arraigned in person before them at this point, but the influence of Jn 11.47–53 is clearly in view. What is significant about the sequence is that the Jewish Sanhedrin is treated with sympathy and respect by the film-maker. The debate is held in an imposing Hall. A genuine exchange of views is presented with people on either side of the debate. Jesus is defended here by Joseph of Arimathea (played by James Mason) and Nicodemus (played by Laurence Olivier). When a complaint is made that Jesus has interfered with the merchants in the Temple, and the Sanhedrin has not intervened, Joseph replies that the Sanhedrin itself has often protested at the presence of money-changers being allowed in the precincts of the Temple.

While not all Jews would accept Nicodemus's claim that '[t]he coming of the Messiah is the heart of our faith', Judaism is itself treated sympathetically, as can be seen in the case of the member of the Sanhedrin who, in answer to a disparaging comment about the plethora of visionaries and prophets, makes the following reply:

> That is the richness of our religion, that it is always being kept alive by new ideas ... What an incredible people we are! Thirsty for knowledge, but hypocrites afraid of change. We say that we want new ideas so our religion will speak to each generation, and yet when a prophet appears, burning with faith and fiery revelations, we stifle him. Shall we go down in history as a people who destroys its prophets?

Jesus's place within Judaism, therefore, is clearly established (Jesus is later described, too, as 'one of our brothers' by Joseph), but the Christian overlay, recognized in the circumcision sequence, is here summed up well by Caiaphas when he raises the crucial question of Christology, and the claim (ascribed here to Jesus himself) that Jesus is the Son of God. Belief in such a claim forms, of course, the essential dividing line between Jews and Christians, and so the debate reaches its climax with this fundamental point of difference.

The Last Temptation of Christ (1988): Jesus's Speech in the Temple [01.22.10–01.24.23]

Our final sequence, which deals with the action objected to by Zeffirelli's complainant, namely, the cleansing of the Temple, and which also presents in very sharp focus the Christological issue separating Jews and

Christians, is taken from Martin Scorsese's *The Last Temptation of Christ* (1988). The film was introduced and discussed in chapter 13. The sequence selected begins after Jesus has just overturned the tables of the money-changers, and consists of a direct exchange, this time, between him and the High Priest. A striking camera shot catches the coins as they ascend into the blue sky and descend – one of them to be picked up by the High Priest from a blood-spattered wall.

What impresses one about this scene is the clever, bold and lively script that was produced for Scorsese by ex-seminarian Paul Schrader. In the exchange, there is a striking restatement of the Gospels' Christology, which carries all the ambiguity of their confessional statements about Jesus, this 'saint of blasphemy'. 'When I say "I", Rabbi, I'm saying "God",' says Jesus. One also notes the use of the controversial 'I have not come to bring peace on earth, but a sword' saying of Matthew 10.34, here imported into a different but relevant context. One further observes Schrader's placing of Pauline teaching on Jesus's lips, with the echo of Romans 10.4: 'For Christ is the end of the law'. A sympathetic (and non-stereotyped) treatment, nevertheless, is offered of the High Priest (in contrast to that, for example, of DeMille in our second selected sequence). He is allowed to defend the Temple's practice regarding the Temple tax.

'You expect the people to pay the tax with Roman coins?' the High Priest asks (of Jesus).
'They have images of false gods on them!'
'You want pagan gods in the Temple?', he further protests.
'All foreign coins have to be exchanged for shekels. That is the Law!'

When Jesus says that he is 'throwing away the Law', and the High Priest asks, 'Has God changed his mind about the old law?', Jesus responds, not with a statement that implies the superiority of Christianity over Judaism, but with the delicate words: 'No, He just thinks our hearts are ready to hold more, that's all.'

Although Jesus is made to attack the Jewish doctrine of election, he does so by extending its scope, by emphasizing the principle of universality, by democratizing it, in a sense: 'God's an immortal spirit who belongs to everybody, to the whole world. You think you're special? God is not an Israelite!'

This representation of Jews and Judaism is in line with Scorsese's treatment elsewhere. In the Last Supper scene, as we shall see in chapter 17, the ethnic elements are profuse, with all the particularity of Judaism's customs and rituals being reflected, as in Zeffirelli's *Jesus of Nazareth* (1977). And when we look for Scorsese's treatment of the trial of Jesus before the Sanhedrin and his arraignment before the Jewish authorities on religious charges (Mk 14.53–65 and parallels), we seek for the scene in vain. As with Nicholas Ray's *King of Kings* (1961), it is absent from the film. Only Jesus's trial before Pilate is represented (Mk. 15.1ff. and parallels), but even here, when Jesus is put on public display, there is no sign of Barabbas, and Matthew's notorious 'his blood be upon us, and upon our children!' passage (27.25) is nowhere in evidence. Jesus is referred to as 'King of the Jews' or 'another Jewish politician' by Pilate, and the implication is that the charges against him, again as with Ray, are political, not religious.[33]

5. Conclusion

We began our discussion of our six selected films by noting the vigorous protest that Jewish groups made to D. W. Griffith's depiction of Jews in *Intolerance* (1916). Scorsese's more recent film, as is well known, attracted, on the other hand, a Christian fundamentalist crusade against it. The irony, then, is that, in this, our final film, 'instead of Jewish pressure groups objecting to representations of Jews, Christians accused Universal Studios of a Semitic plot against Christianity'.[34] In between we have seen a progressive sensitivity on the part of film-makers to the question of antisemitism, and a corresponding desire to promote fair and non-stereotypical images of Jews and Judaism in the biblical epic or Christ film.

We have observed various strategies at work in dealing with the awkward or vexing Gospel passages I summarized in my introduction:

- DeMille's attribution of sole culpability for the death of Jesus to a corrupt and venal High Priest;
- Ray's omission of the offending passages and his corresponding emphasis on the political dimension and Roman culpability;
- Pasolini's subtle alteration of the context so that the modern religious establishment, not ancient Judaism, is the target for Jesus's invective.

We have also seen Zeffirelli's attempt to root Jesus firmly within his Jewish context and community, and to represent Jews and Judaism with fairness and equity, albeit with a strong Christian conviction. And in the boldest Christ film of all, that of Scorsese, we have seen a deft combination of many of these strategies.

When I first gave this presentation at St Deiniol's Library in 2001, I ended by expressing the sentiment that such growing sensitivity boded well for the future of Jewish–Christian relations. In light of Mel Gibson's *The Passion of the Christ* (2004), and the discussion of its treatment of Jews and Judaism at the end of this book, the reader might wish to ponder whether that hope was justified.

Notes

1 See, for example, the article on 'Antisemitism' in R. J. Z. Werblowsky and G. Wigoder (eds), *The Oxford Dictionary of the Jewish Religion*, New York and Oxford: Oxford University Press, 1997, pp. 53–4; P. Pulzer, 'Antisemitism', in W. Laqueur (ed.), *The Holocaust Encyclopedia*, New Haven and London: Yale University Press, 2001, pp. 16–26; W. Benz, 'Anti-Semitism Research', in M. Goodman (ed.), *The Oxford Handbook of Jewish Studies*, Oxford: Oxford University Press, 2002, pp. 943–55.

2 Benz, 'Anti-Semitism Research', p. 943.

3 M. Davies, 'Stereotyping the Other: The "Pharisees" in the Gospel according to Matthew', in J. C. Exum and S. D. Moore (eds), *Biblical Studies/Cultural Studies. The Third Sheffield Colloquium*, Sheffield: Sheffield Academic Press, 1998, p. 430.

4 S. G. F. Brandon, *Jesus and the Zealots. A Study of the Political Factor in Primitive Christianity*, Manchester and New York: Manchester University Press; Scribner, 1967, p. 279.

5 W. R. Telford, *The Theology of the Gospel of Mark*, New Testament Theology, Cambridge, UK and New York: Cambridge University Press, 1999, pp. 234–41.

6 See, for example, P. Erens, *The Jew in American Cinema*, Bloomington, IN: Indiana University Press, 1984; N. Gabler, *An Empire of Their Own: How the Jews Invented Hollywood*, London: Allen, 1989; as well as L. D. Friedman, *Hollywood's Image of the Jew*, New York: Frederick Ungar, 1982, and his *The Jewish Image in American Film*, New Jersey, NJ: Citadel Press, 1987; M. J. Wright, 'Lights! Camera! Antisemitism? The Cinema and Jewish–Christian Relations', in E. E. Kessler and M. J. Wright (eds), *Themes in Jewish–Christian Relations*, Cambridge: Orchard Academic, 2004, pp. 171–200.

7 C. Pajaczkowska and B. Curtis, 'Assimilation, Entertainment, and the Hollywood Solution', in L. Nochlin and T. Garb (eds), *The Jew in the Text. Modernity and the Construction of Identity*, London: Thames & Hudson, 1995, pp. 238–52, and esp. p. 244.

8 See 'Nickelodeon' in E. Katz (ed.), *The Macmillan International Film Encyclopedia*, London: HarperCollins, 1994, p. 1013.

9 S. Hochman (ed.), *A Library of Film Criticism. American Film Directors. With Filmographies and Index of Critics and Films*, New York: Ungar, 1974; D. Quinlan, *The Illustrated Guide to Film Directors*, London: Batsford, 1983; D. Thomson, *A Biographical Dictionary of Film*, London: Deutsch, 1994; Katz, *Macmillan Encyclopedia*; J. Walker (ed.), *Halliwell's Who's Who in the Movies*, London: HarperCollins, 2001.

10 C. Singer, 'Films, US, Jews in', in G. Abramson (ed.), *The Blackwell Companion to Jewish Culture. From the Eighteenth Century to the Present*, Oxford: Blackwell, 1989, pp. 227–9, and esp. p. 227.

11 Pajaczkowska and Curtis, 'Assimilation', p. 244 and n. 19.

12 See A. Gordon, 'J for Jewish. Sight and Sound A-Z of Cinema', *Sight and Sound*, 7,3 (1997): 28–32, and esp. p. 30.

13 Gordon, 'J for Jewish', p. 30.

14 Pajaczkowska and Curtis, 'Assimilation', pp. 244, 245.

15 Singer, 'Films, US, Jews in', p. 229.

16 L. Mulvey, 'The Innovators 1920–1930: Now you has Jazz', *Sight and Sound*, 9,5 (1999): 18.

17 Singer, 'Films, US, Jews in', pp. 227–8.

18 Pajaczkowska and Curtis, 'Assimilation', p. 240.

19 Jill Robinson in Studs Terkel, 'American Dreams Lost and Found', cited in Friedman, *Jewish Image*; *gratia* Pajaczkowska and Curtis, 'Assimilation', p. 238 and n. 3.

20 Pajaczkowska and Curtis, 'Assimilation', pp. 245–6.

21 For useful discussion on this film see W. B. Tatum, *Jesus at the Movies: A Guide to the First Hundred Years*, Santa Rosa, CA: Polebridge, 1997, pp. 33–43.

22 Tatum, *Jesus at the Movies*, p. 34.

23 *Gratia* Tatum, *Jesus at the Movies*, p. 35.

24 Tatum, *Jesus at the Movies*, p. 37.

25 S. Louvish, 'Burning Crosses', *Sight and Sound*, 10,9 (2000): 12–13.

26 Gordon, 'J for Jewish', p. 30.

27 B. Babington and P. W. Evans, *Biblical Epics. Sacred Narrative in the Hollywood Cinema*, Manchester: Manchester University Press, 1993, p. 121.

28 Babington and Evans, *Biblical Epics*, p. 122.

29 See chapter 13 on 'The Two Faces of Betrayal: the Characterization of Peter and Judas in the Biblical Epic or Christ Film' for information and discussion on this film (cf. Text Box 16.2).

30 Tatum, *Jesus at the Movies*, pp. 111–12.

31 This point is made, for example, by R. C. Stern, C. N. Jefford and G. Debona (eds), *Savior on the Silver Screen*, New York: Paulist, 1999, p. 107.

32 See Tatum, *Jesus at the Movies*, p. 133.

33 See Tatum, *Jesus at the Movies*, p. 170.

34 Babington and Evans, *Biblical Epics*, p. 107.

17. Ritual Recast and Revisioned:

Hollywood Remembers the First Passover and the Last Supper

WILLIAM R. TELFORD

1. Introduction

The Aims of the Chapter

The title of this chapter is 'Ritual Recast and Revisioned: Hollywood Remembers the First Passover and the Last Supper'. My general aim will be to examine two of the most important religious rituals within the Jewish and Christian traditions, the Passover Meal, or Pesah Seder, as Jews refer to it, and the Last Supper – or what is variously termed by Christians 'the Lord's Supper', the 'Eucharist' or simply 'communion'. I wish to conduct this examination by observing the narrative reconstruction of these rituals within film, and I want to direct your attention to sequences from seven biblical epics or Christ films in which the Pesah Seder and the Last Supper have found cinematic expression. By way of background, let me say that the genesis of this presentation was an international conference to which I was invited in May 1999, at the Hebrew University in Jerusalem on the subject of ritual, or more precisely, 'Narratives of Rituals: Reconstruction in Religious Studies'. This interdisciplinary conference drew together a number of scholars in a variety of fields (anthropology, religious studies, ancient history, etc.) and I was asked if I might do something on the subject of ritual from the perspective of a New Testament scholar interested in film. A developed form of the paper was subsequently given in April 2000, at the St Deiniol's Theology and Film conference.

This essay operates from the assumption that film is an important reflector of our cultural values, ideologies and traditions, that it is a legitimate medium for scholarly analysis, and that it offers valuable insights into the way societies understand and configure their religious traditions. Furthermore, in making my selections from the biblical epic, I do so with little apology. In the face of the disparagement often directed at this particular genre, but in line with recent scholarly rehabilitation of it, as in B. Babington and P. W. Evans, *Biblical Epics. Sacred Narrative in the*

Hollywood Cinema (1993),[1] I intend to treat the biblical epic, for the most part, with some seriousness.

Approaching the Subject Critically

First of all, let me offer a brief word, as usual, on the subject of criticism. Discussion of film criticism and film theory has a long academic history, and a distinguished pedigree, as was pointed out in chapter 1. The inter-disciplinary study of religion and film, by comparison, is still in its infancy. In my 1995 article, 'The New Testament in Fiction and Film: A Biblical Scholar's Perspective',[2] I charted some of the developments in this field, and suggested some ways in which films might by approached by biblical scholars, like myself, with no proper grounding in film theory or criticism, yet with a love for film, with other legitimate perspectives, and with the conviction that the critical study of films as cultural products should not be left simply to experts in film studies with their differing concerns.

Since 1995, a number of books have appeared on the subject, particularly on methodology, and you are referred again to chapter 1 for a review of these. One written from the perspective of religious studies, and worth recalling, in particular, is J. W. Martin and C. E. Ostwalt (eds), *Screening the Sacred. Religion, Myth, and Ideology in Popular American Film* (1995).[3] In line with the experience of Martin and Ostwalt, I have worked for a number of years in a department of religious studies in Newcastle (although I am currently now in the Department of Theology and Religion in Durham). There I have taught biblical studies, and hence my approach to film has been influenced by the perspectives appropriate to these two interrelated disciplines. In approaching the Passover and the Last Supper in film, therefore, and following a similar procedure to that in previous chapters, I shall be sensitive to intertextuality, to the various ways that the biblical sources have been used, to the creative power of the cinematic imagination in bring these sources to visual expression, and to the influence of ideology and social context as a factor in interpreting them. A prominent concern will also be the relation of the filmic Last Supper accounts to the Pesah Seder meal, and the degree to which our film-makers have represented the Judaism of the period, the Jewishness of Jesus and his disciples, and the Jewish features of his last meal with them.

2. The Passover and the Last Supper in the Bible

Where the biblical texts are concerned, Exodus 12.1—13.16 is the major source dealing with the Passover and the Feast of Unleavened Bread.[4] There is no space to outline the main features of the ritual, but you might care to consult Text Box 17.1 in which I have included a brief section from my old teacher and mentor, Professor William Barclay's book on *The Last Supper* (1967),[5] which gives an admirable outline of the Passover Meal ritual.

Barclay describes the six main things necessary in the preparation of the ritual (highlighted in the text), namely, the lamb, the unleavened bread, the bowl of salt water, the collection of bitter herbs, the paste of fruit and nuts (or *charosheth*), and the four cups of wine.

He also summarizes the meal itself with its various elements: the first cup, or cup of the Kiddush or consecration, the first handwashing by the celebrant (*u'rechatz*), the eating of the lettuce or parsley after it has been dipped in the salt water (*karpas*), the first breaking of the unleavened bread (*yachatz*), the paterfamilias' explanation to his son of the meaning of the Passover (the proclaiming) (*maggid*), the singing of the first two psalms of the Hallel (Psalms 113—118), the drinking of the second cup (of the proclaiming), the normal ceremonial handwashing (*rachtzah*), the grace (*motzie matzah*), the eating of more bitter herbs (*maror*), the dipping of the sop and the eating of bitter herbs and *charoseth* (*korech*), the meal proper (*shulchan orekh*), the conclusion of the meal with the ceremonial handwashing, the eating of the remainder of the Passover bread (*afikoman/tzafun*), the thanksgiving, the drinking of the third cup (of thanksgiving) (*barekh*), including a libation for Elijah and the coming Messiah, and the conclusion of the ritual with the drinking of the fourth cup (*nirtzah*), the singing of the remainder of the Hallel, and the final prayers, shout and prayer of praise to God.

I myself have never attended a modern Pesah Seder (although I have celebrated Shabbat in Jerusalem, courtesy of my good friend and colleague, Professor Ithamar Gruenwald) and for the text of the Seder I am grateful not only to a former colleague in Newcastle, Rabbi Moshe Yehudai-Rimmer, but also to Jonathan Sacks's *The Chief Rabbi's Haggadah* (2003).[6]

Turning now to the Last Supper in the New Testament, let me make a few brief comments. The New Testament Last Supper narratives are found in Mark 14, Matthew 26, Luke 22 and 1 Corinthians 11. The Fourth Gospel, it should be noted, offers no account of the institution by Jesus of the Christian ritual we now know as the Lord's Supper, or the Eucharist, a fact, as we shall see, that has not proved a deterrent to film-makers in their cinematic reconstructions.

A number of questions and problems confront the New Testament scholar, with regard to the Last Supper accounts, and there are four in particular. First, what was the origin of the meal? Did Jesus himself institute the rite and mean it to be celebrated regularly by successive generations of disciples as a sacrament? Film representations never question this.

Second, what was the nature of the original meal? Was it in fact a Passover meal or some other kind of meal, a Kiddush, that is, a meal held

17.1 Passover Meal and Last Supper in the Biblical Epic: An Outline of the Passover Ritual

There were **six things necessary for the Passover** and which had to be prepared in advance.

1. There was **the lamb** to remind them of the lamb with whose blood the lintel and the door posts of their houses in Egypt had been smeared, so that the angel of death would pass over them in the night of the slaying of the Egyptian firstborn (Exodus 12.21–23). It had to be cooked in a special way. It must not be boiled or stewed; nothing must touch it, not even water, not even the sides of a pot. It had to be fixed on a spit which went through it from mouth to vent, and then roasted, entire with head and legs and tail, over an open fire. The minimum number who could constitute a Passover company was twelve, and the lamb had to be eaten entire and nothing left.

2. There was **the unleavened bread.** Unleavened bread is not like bread at all, but like a water biscuit. It was unleavened bread that the Israelites made on the night of their escape, because there was not time to make leavened bread in the haste of their way-going (Exodus 12.33f.).

3. There was a **bowl of salt water**, partly to remind them of the tears they had shed in their wretchedness in Egypt, and partly to remind them of the waters of the Red Sea through which they had been brought in miraculous safety.

4. There was a collection of **bitter herbs**, such as horse-radish, chicory, endive, lettuce, horehound, once again to remind them of the bitterness they had endured as slaves. All through this meal there runs the observance of the more than once repeated saying of God to the people: 'You shall remember that you were a slave in the land of Egypt, and the Lord your God redeemed you' (Deuteronomy 15.15).

5. There was a paste called *Charosheth*. It was made of apples, dates, pomegranates, and nuts, and through it there ran sticks of cinnamon. The paste was to remind them of the clay with which they had made bricks in Egypt, and the cinnamon was to remind them of the straw which was necessary to make the bricks, and which the Egyptians had withheld from them (Exodus 5.7–9).

6. Lastly, and very important, there were **four cups of wine** each containing one-sixteenth of a *hin*, that is, a little more than half a pint of wine, diluted in the proportion of two parts of wine to three of water. They were so important that the poorest must have them, even if he had to be helped from the poor-box to buy them, and even if, as the Talmud says, a man had to pawn his coat, or hire himself out to get them. The four cups of wine were drunk at different points in the meal, and stood for the four promises of Exodus 6.6f.:

I am the Lord, and I will bring you out from under the burdens of the Egyptians, and I will deliver you from their bondage, and I will redeem you with an outstretched arm and with great acts of judgment, and I will take you for my people, and I will be your God.

One thing is absolutely clear from beginning to end – the Passover meal was a commemoration of deliverance, of rescue and of redemption. We now turn to **the meal itself.**

1. It began with the **first cup, the cup of the Kiddush, or the consecration.** Certainly in later times, most likely even in the time of Jesus, the cup was accompanied with a prayer, thanking God for this memorial of redemption, and for taking Israel to himself as his own people.

2. There followed **the first handwashing,** in which only the person to preside ceremonially three times cleansed his hands.

3. Next **a piece of lettuce or parsley was taken**; it was then **dipped into the salt water, and eaten.** The lettuce or parsley stands for the hyssop which was dipped in the blood of the Passover lamb, and with which the lintel and the doorposts were smeared (Exodus 12.22), and the salt water stands, as we have seen, for either the tears of Egypt or the waters of the Red Sea.

4. Next there came **the first breaking of bread.** Three unleavened cakes of bread were in front of the host. The larger part was to be eaten later, but at this point he took the centre one, and broke it into little pieces.

The broken bread was to remind them of the bread of affliction which they ate in Egypt and it was broken into little pieces to remind them that a slave never had a whole loaf, but only fragments to eat. In the full ritual of the Passover the host then says:

> This is the bread of affliction which our forefathers ate in the land of Egypt. Whosoever is hungry, let him come and eat; whosoever is in need, let him come and eat the Passover with us.

It was, and is, at this point that the Jews of the Dispersion say: 'This year we eat it here, next year in Jerusalem.'

5. Next there came **the proclaiming.** It was the duty of the father to explain to his son what the Passover meal meant.

'And you shall tell your son on that day, It is because of what the Lord did for me when I came out of Egypt' (Exodus 13.8). In the full order for the Passover, here the youngest person present is to ask:

> Why is this night different from other nights? For on all other nights we eat leavened or unleavened bread, but on this night only unleavened bread. On all other nights we eat any kind of herbs, but on this night only bitter herbs. On all other nights we eat meat roasted, stewed or boiled, but on this night only roasted.

In reply the father must begin at the saying in Deuteronomy 26.5: 'A wandering Aramaean was my father', and, beginning with Abraham, he must tell the story down to the deliverance of the Passover.

6. For the Jew, one of the most sacred parts of scripture, a part to be memorized in youth and never forgotten, is **the Hallel**. Hallel means 'Praise God', and the Hallel consists of Psalms 113—118, which are praising psalms. At this point the first two psalms of the Hallel, Psalms 113 and 114 are sung.

7. At this point **the second cup** is drunk. It is called the cup of the proclaiming, because it followed the proclaiming of the hand of God in Israel's history.

8. At this point all who were to participate cleansed their hands. This is the **normal ceremonial handwashing** before a meal, for now the meal proper was to begin.

9. First, **grace** was said, and small pieces of the unleavened bread were distributed to the company. The Passover grace is:

> Blessed art thou, o Lord our God, who bringest forth fruit from the earth. Blessed art thou who hast sanctified us with thy commandment, and enjoined us to eat unleavened cakes.

10. Some more of the **bitter herbs** were then eaten, once again to waken the memory of their bitterness and of God's redemption from it.

11. There followed what was known as **the sop**. Some of the bitter herbs were placed between two pieces of Passover bread, dipped in the *charosheth* and eaten. Still again, memory is awakened.

It is here that the narrative of the Fourth Gospel takes a Passover turn, for it is there said that Jesus dipped the morsel in the dish and gave it to Judas (John 13.26f.). This looks like the taking and the giving of the sop.

12. Then **the meal proper** began. It was a meal of hungry men for the rule was that no food might be eaten after the sacrifice of the lamb in the Temple, until the Passover meal itself, and the sacrifice could be as early as midday. As we have already noted, the whole lamb had to be eaten. Anything that remained had to be burned, for it could not be used for any ordinary purpose.

13. At the **conclusion** of the meal the **hands** were again **ceremonially cleansed**.

14. The **remainder of the Passover bread** was brought out and eaten.

15. There followed a long **thanksgiving** for the meal, which to this day contains a petition for the coming of Elijah as the herald of the Messiah.

16. After the thanksgiving prayer, **the third cup**, which was called the cup of thanksgiving, was drunk, with this prayer:

> Blessed art thou, O Lord our God, King of the universe, who hast created the fruit of the vine.

17. The **cup** was **filled for the fourth and last time**. The second part of the Hallel, Psalms 115—118, was sung, and then the Great Hallel, Psalm 136 with its ever-recurring refrain:

> O give thanks to the Lord, for he is good, for his steadfast love endures for ever.

After that the fourth cup was drunk.

18. There follow **two prayers**. In the full ritual, the second of them runs as follows:

> The breath of all that lives shall praise thy name, O Lord, our God. And the spirit of all flesh shall continually glorify and exalt thy memorial, O God, our King. For from everlasting to everlasting thou art God, and beside thee we have no king, redeemer, or saviour.

And so the **Passover ends** with a shout and a prayer of praise to God. (W. Barclay, *The Lord's Supper*, London: SCM Press, 1967, pp. 20–4).

before the Sabbath in order to set it apart, or a Chaburah meal, a fellowship meal? That these questions arise at all stems from a discrepancy in the accounts given respectively by the Synoptic Gospels and the Gospel of John.

Third, what were the original words of Jesus at that meal? The precise wording of the accounts differs, suggesting that in early Christian practice there were at least two streams of tradition in connection with the words of institution. The first is represented by Mark and followed by Matthew, the second by Paul and Luke.[7] While Mark/Matthew, for example, have 'This is my body', Luke has 'This is my body, which is given for you' and Paul 'This is my body, which is for you' (Some MSS have 'broken' or 'crushed' or 'given' or 'which I have delivered for you'). Where the cup is concerned, Mark has 'This is my blood of the covenant, which is poured out for many' and Matthew 'This is my blood of the covenant, which is poured out for many, for the forgiveness of sins.' Luke, on the other hand has 'This cup, which is poured out for you, is the new covenant in my blood' and Paul, likewise, 'This cup is the new covenant in my blood'.

Luke's text of the words of institution has come down to us, moreover, in two forms, a longer and a shorter text (Lk. 22.15–19a/22.15–20). Some authorities, in other words, in whole or in part, omit Luke 22.19b–20: '["This is my body] which is given for you. Do this in remembrance of me". And likewise the cup after supper, saying, "This cup which is poured out for you is the new covenant in my blood".' Furthermore, the words, 'Do this in remembrance of me' appear in Luke once (in the longer text) and in Paul twice, but not in Matthew and Mark.

Finally, there is the interpretation of the words themselves. Even if we could reconstruct the original words from these variant versions, the New Testament scholar would have to ask what these words actually meant.

3. The Passover and Last Supper in Film: Some Selected Clips

None of these problems are of particular concern for the holistic reconstructions of the cinema. The meal is usually a Passover meal, although its relation to the Pesah Seder, as Jews practise it, varies, as we shall see. Filmic versions of the Last Supper are given to conflation of all the accounts, incorporating into them elements from the separate Johannine discourses. Their interest, as we shall see, lies, for the most part, in the dramatic elements of these accounts (the betrayal by Judas, the prediction of the disciples' desertion and Peter's denial). Their particular focus is on the figure of Jesus who is almost invariably treated in a conservative way, that is, as the Christian Christ of faith and not the Jewish Jesus of history.

In approaching these filmic texts, we need, moreover, to be sensitive to three factors in particular which govern their production:

- Their religious/ecclesiastical context;
- Their contemporary context;
- The fact that they were produced for mass audiences.

With these preliminary remarks, let us now turn to the films themselves. Text Box 17.2 offers some brief information on the films selected (in some cases, where the films overlap with information given in previous chapters, the information has been repeated).[8] Further reading is to be found in the Notes. I shall give a brief general introduction to each sequence (whose approximate time location in the film is given in square brackets), and then make some comments on its depiction of either the Passover meal or the Last Supper. When you yourself view the sequences, you may wish to note down your own observations and comments on them, and for this purpose a further text box (17.3) is provided.

17.2 Notes on the Films Selected

The Ten Commandments (Cecil B. DeMille, 1923/1956)
For sheer pageantry and spectacle, few motion pictures can claim to equal the splendour of C. B. DeMille's 1956 remake of his epic *The Ten Commandments* (1923). Filmed in Egypt and the Sinai with one of the biggest sets ever constructed for a motion picture, this version tells the story of the life of Moses (Charlton Heston), once favoured in the Pharaoh's (Yul Brynner) household, who turned his back on a privileged life to lead his people to freedom.

The King of Kings (Cecil B. DeMille, 1927)

A major classic, this was the first full-length, silent Hollywood epic on the life of Jesus, as seen from the perspective of Mary Magdalene. It presents Mary as a rich courtesan with Judas as her lover. Its many memorable moments include Mary's riding off in her chariot to rescue her Judas from the clutches of the carpenter of Nazareth ('Harness my zebras – gift of the Nubian king!'), her subsequent exorcism by Jesus in a swirl of exiting demons, the moving giving of sight to a little blind girl and dramatic crucifixion and resurrection scenes.

King of Kings (Nicholas Ray, 1961)

A remake of the DeMille version in name only, this Sixties' Hollywood adaptation presents Judas and Barabbas as political revolutionaries, with Jesus as a reluctant pawn in their game. Criticized by the Catholic Legion of Decency as 'theologically, historically, and scripturally inaccurate' (R. Kinnard and T. Davis, *Divine Images. A History of Jesus on the Screen*, New York: Citadel Press, 1992, p. 132), the film is now viewed in retrospect as better than its critics made it out to be.

The Greatest Story Ever Told (George Stevens, 1965)

Perfectionism in pursuit of the Perfect, George Stevens's Christ film was the most expensive ever made. Though luminescent with its galaxy of stars, and presenting some memorable sequences (such as the raising of Lazarus as well as the crucifixion), this was a commercial failure that set the Christ film back where Hollywood was concerned.

Jesus Christ, Superstar (Norman Jewison, 1973)

Filmed in Israel, where young tourists re-enact episodes of the life of Christ, this vibrant movie, which was based on the successful rock opera by Tim Rice and Andrew Lloyd-Webber (with a screenplay by Norman Jewison and Melvyn Bragg, and musical direction by André Previn) mixes the historical and the contemporary to good effect.

Jesus of Nazareth (Franco Zeffirelli, 1977)

With a screenplay by Anthony Burgess and others (later turned into a novel by William Barclay), this six-and-a-half-hour made-for-television movie (screened on ITV in 1977) was the result of a promise made by its producer Lew Grade to the Pope to do for Jesus what he had done for Moses.

The Last Temptation of Christ (Martin Scorsese, 1988)

Based on Kazantzakis's novel about 'the dual substance of Christ' and 'the incessant, merciless battle between the spirit and the flesh', and directed by one of Hollywood's most distinguished film-makers, this is one of the finest, most religious and yet most controversial Christ films ever made.

17.3 Comments on Films/Clips

The Ten Commandments (Cecil B. DeMille, 1923/1956): The First Passover

The King of Kings (Cecil B. DeMille, 1927): The Classic Last Supper

King of Kings (Nicholas Ray, 1961): The Y-shaped Last Supper

The Greatest Story Ever Told (George Stevens, 1965): The Greatest Supper Ever Eaten

Jesus Christ, Superstar (Norman Jewison, 1973): The Last Picnic

Jesus of Nazareth (Franco Zeffirelli, 1977): The Supper That Lasts

The Last Temptation of Christ (Martin Scorsese, 1988): The Last Last Supper

The Ten Commandments *(1956): The First Passover* [2.47.49–2.53.04]

For sheer pageantry and spectacle, few motion pictures can claim to equal the splendour of C. B. DeMille's 1956 remake of his epic *The Ten Commandments* (1923). Filmed in Egypt and the Sinai with one of the biggest sets ever constructed for a motion picture, this version tells the story of the life of Moses, once favoured in the Pharaoh's household, who turned his back on a privileged life to lead his people to freedom. The part of Moses was played by Charlton Heston, that of Aaron by John Carradine, and that of the Egyptian princess, who brought Moses up, and who appears in the sequence under review, by Nina Foch (cf. 1 Chron. 4.17 'the daughter of Pharaoh whom Mered married'). Of his casting for this part, Heston writes (facetiously) in his autobiography:

> The embodiment of the most important role I got through the nose (as it were) is on permanent display in the Chapel of San Pietro in Vincoli, in Rome. Michelangelo's marble figure of *Moses* is one of the greatest statues in the world, certainly the finest representation of the prophet. It also looks a lot like me, particularly the nose. The overall likeness is startling. Someone pointed this out to C. B. DeMille early in his deliberations on casting the part for *The Ten Commandments*. I think he never could get it out of his mind.[9]

With these few frivolous words of introduction, let us now turn to *the* classic cinematic presentation of the Pesah Seder meal.

The Passover in *The Ten Commandments* (1956) is eaten in a dramatic setting, as God wreaks his vengeance on the Egyptians for refusing to let his people go. In depicting the Pesah Seder, DeMille, a practising Christian but with part-Jewish origins,[10] has captured certain characteristic elements. The meal begins with the pouring of wine. There are bowls of bitter herbs on the table, as well as lamps. A space is provided around the table for a stranger (here the Egyptian princess, Bithia). There is even one cup that appears not to belong to anyone (is it the prefiguration of the cup reserved for Elijah?). In the background there is the intoning of scriptural references by one of the characters, in the manner of a cantor, and there are refrains from the others. Moses himself is, in this case, the paterfamilias. Following the Pesah Seder ritual, he blesses the bread with the prayer 'Blessed art thou, O Lord our God, who bringest forth bread from the earth'. A prayer is offered by John Carradine's Aaron. A junior, here Eliezer, Moses' nephew, questions the paterfamilias: 'Why is this night different from all others?' 'Why do we eat unleavened bread, and bitter herbs, my uncle?' he then asks. The bitter herbs are explained first, and then the unleavened bread. Unleavened bread is passed around. The wine is drunk from individual cups. The narration of the story of salvation is understandably brief, as the tenth plague (represented by a green slime) is here enacted rather than recounted, with the viewer being given a glimpse of the blood on the lintels of the door, which protects the Israelites.

There are also some differences. Apart from the fact that, in a number of places, Moses' words are freely adapted from the Pesah Seder, certain elements are missing. There is no removal of leaven. There is no washing of the hands (*u'rechatz*) or eating of salted vegetable (*karpas*). There is no highlighting of the four specific cups of wine consumed at the Pesah Seder. There is no breaking of the middle matzah (*yachatz*) or eating of the afikoman (*tzafun*). The junior's question 'Why do we eat unleavened bread, and bitter herbs, my uncle?' usually precedes rather than follows, the preliminary blessing over the food in the Pesah Seder.[11] The bitter herbs are explained first, and then the unleavened bread, where the reverse order is followed in the Pesah Seder.[12] Overall, the ritual aspects of the meal itself are overshadowed by the action (the death of Egypt's first-born, the arrival of Bithia, the arrival of Joshua played by John Derek).

These differences and omissions are all consistent not only with the biblical epic's emphasis on dramatic action and spectacle but also with the genre's de-emphasis of particularity or what we might call ethnic elements, and its championing of universal values.[13] For his audiences, whether Jewish, Christian, Muslim or secular, DeMille distils the essence of the Passover meal and interprets it as a ritual statement about freedom or liberty. 'This night the Lord will deliver us from the bondage of Egypt', says Moses. 'Tomorrow the light of freedom will shine as we go forth from Egypt', he later declaims. When Bithia asks if her Nubian slaves can be included in the exodus, Moses replies, 'All who thirst for freedom may come with us.' According to Exodus 12.44, however, slaves who participated in the Passover needed first to be circumcised.

Universality is the keynote here, therefore, and another core value enacted is that of inclusivism. Inclusivism is represented by Bithia's journey with the Israelites, and DeMille's elaboration of the 'stranger' motif. When Bithia arrives, she asks: 'May a stranger enter?' 'There are no strangers among those who seek God's mercy,' says Moses. Bithia is conducted to the table where a space is provided for her. According to the Exodus account (12.43) no foreigner or sojourner was allowed to participate in the passover meal unless they, too, were circumcised. This inclusivism in DeMille's version is, surprisingly, even made to extend to all of the Egytians. 'They are my people!' says Bithia (as Egyptian screams are heard in the background). 'All are God's people' is the response (although a somewhat ironic one, given the circumstances!).

But deeper mythic elements also inform the narrative, and carry it away from the emphasis on ethnicity and particularity that characterize, by contrast, the biblical accounts. The film's social context and its ideology, in reality, inform its presentation. DeMille's film was made in the 1950s at the height of the Cold War, and when America was also grappling with racial issues. Here Babington and Evans (in speaking of the epic genre, in general, and DeMille's prologues to his films in particular) perceptively capture the ideological essence:

> De Mille's prologues to *Samson and Delilah* and *The Ten Command-ments* clearly articulate the allegory of America: Democracy; Russia: Slavery, for all that the enemy is never named. This, the most constant motif across the genre, disappears only in the 1980s where its polarities have begun to feel simplistic . . . The presence of blacks in the film [*The Ten Commandments*] (for instance the King of Ethiopia; Bithia's Nubians), while alluding to racial questions in America, also signifies America's concern about the Third World beginning to fall under Soviet influence. In the Statue of Liberty allusion at the end of the film where Moses stands holding the torch of freedom, his rhetoric looks forward to the triumph of democracy, expressed not so much in the maternal, intaking words on the original statue ('Give me your tired, your poor,' etc.) as in the expansionist direction of 'Proclaim Liberty throughout all the lands! Unto all the inhabitants thereof!'[14]

The King of Kings *(1927): The Classic Last Supper* [01.01.18–01.09.06]

We turn now to the first major representation of the Christian Last Supper in the biblical epic, that in Cecil B. DeMille's *The King of Kings* (1927). As mentioned in chapters 13 and 16, this major classic was the first full-length, silent Hollywood epic on the life of Jesus, as seen from the per-spective of Mary Magdalene. The film presents itself to us as if it were an illustrated Bible story book. This is no accident since DeMille drew upon not only the religious art and paintings of the Renaissance (including, as here, Leonardo da Vinci's *Last Supper*), but also on the Bible illustrations of the Victorian period based upon it, in particular those of the painter James Tissot and the engraver Gustave Doré. In viewing the sequence, you should also note the music. When the film was reissued in 1931 with synchronized music and sound effects, DeMille made effective use of traditional Christian hymns played at strategic moments (in this excerpt you will recognize, for example, 'Abide with Me'). A third feature is the intimate use of the camera, with medium, close-up and point-of-view shots that do much to humanize the biblical characters. The stylized religious expressionism, however, a static camera, and special effects such as the radiance around Jesus as well as the stunning finale to this sequence preserve the image of an objective Christ, whose divinity is

clearly recognizable. The actor chosen by DeMille to portray Jesus was
the distinguished British actor H. B. Warner. Judas (at Jesus's left) in the
sequence is represented as a gigolo. Peter, the big fisherman, is the one
hugging the cup to his breast. Mary, the mother of Jesus, appears at the
end of the sequence.

A noticeable feature of DeMille's *The King of Kings* (1927) is the selec-
tion of biblical quotations from the Authorized Version (some wrested
from their original context) that are presented as captions, and act as an
unspoken commentary on the action. The rise of fundamentalism would
have made the King James Bible familiar to the audiences of this period.
Where the film's treatment of its biblical sources is concerned, you might
also note the conflation that has occurred with respect to the Gospel texts.
In the words of the institution, the Longer Version of Luke 22.19(ab) is
quoted: 'Take, eat – this is My body which is given for you. This do in
remembrance of Me'. Sayings from the Fourth Gospel are included, however, despite the absence of the institution of the Last Supper in that
Gospel: 'Little children, yet a little while I am with you. A new commandment I give unto you – that ye love one another, as I have loved you' (Jn
13.33–34). Another verse from Luke is also given: 'Behold, the hand of
him that betrayeth Me – is with Me on the table!' (Lk. 22.21), and Judas
is despatched by Jesus with a verse from the Fourth Gospel: 'That which
thou doest – do quickly!' (Jn 13.27). As Judas creeps out – the order is
reversed from the Matthean text where Judas is still present at this point
– the other disciples remonstrate in words drawn from Matthew (Mt.
26.22): 'Lord, is it I?' Jesus then delivers another utterance from one of the
Johannine discourses (Jn 16.33): 'My peace I give unto you. In the world
ye shall have tribulation, but be of good cheer – I have overcome the
world!' He ends with a Matthean passage ('The Son of man came not
to be ministered unto, but to minister, and to give His life a ransom
for many!' Mt. 20.28) which, though it, too, is taken out of context,
effectively captures the essence of the meaning of the Last Supper for
Christians.

In addition to these textual conflations, DeMille, or his scriptwriter,
Jeanie McPherson, has also taken artistic liberties with the Last Supper
account. Jesus, it should be noted, embraces his mother (who is dressed in
wimpled and nun-like fashion) at the end. She, of course, does not appear
in the Gospel Last Supper narratives. Here she is given an invented speech:
'O my beloved Son – wilt Thou not return to Nazareth with me? Here I
fear Thine enemies!' The whole sequence ends stunningly with the empty
Passover meal table and the symbolic imagery of the 'holy grail'[15] and the
dove, the former so increasingly incandescent as to call to mind the 'burning bush' of the Hebrew Bible (Ex. 3.2).

In relation to the Pesah Seder meal, and where the ritual aspects are
concerned, the meal is clearly overshadowed by the dramatic action (the

betrayal of Judas, the responses of the disciples and, in the closing sequence, Jesus's relationship with his mother). For purely dramatic effect, for example, Judas is made to decline the bread by dropping it surreptitiously. His discomfiture at receiving the cup is emphasized, and he treats it as if it were a poisoned chalice. The breaking of the bread by Jesus comes first, it should be observed, rather than the blessing over the first cup as in the Pesah Seder. Jesus next takes the cup, the caption reading: 'This is My blood of the new testament – which is shed for many unto the remission of sins. Drink ye all of it' (Mt. 26.27–28). The wine too, as in traditional Christian iconography, is drunk from a common cup. In short, there are few elements that draw on the Pesah Seder meal, and the Jewish features are subordinated to Christian piety or mythology.

King of Kings *(1961): The Y-shaped Last Supper*
[01.58.56–02.04.30]

Not so with our next film, Nicholas Ray's *King of Kings* (1961), for which I supplied an introduction in chapter 13 ('The Two Faces of Betrayal: the Characterization of Peter and Judas in the Biblical Epic or Christ Film'). The first thing to note about Ray's version of the Last Supper is the curious Y-shaped table arrangement that characterizes the scene, with Jesus (Jeffrey Hunter) at the centre of the Y. Jesus is dressed in white, and his disciples (in keeping with the style of the film) in garments with solid blocks of colours (brown, grey, dark red, dark blue) or stripes.

Ray's version is clearly a Passover meal. The voice-over at the beginning announces its Passover/Feast of Unleavened Bread setting. The table has a bowl of bitter herbs, and lighted lamps. The meal is preceded by a ritual handwashing. Jesus begins with the prayer, 'Blessed are you, O Lord our God, King of the Universe, who bids us eat bitter herbs', an invocation associated (albeit in slightly different form) with the Seder.[16] They all eat the bitter herbs. The first cup (of the Pesah Seder) is not drunk, however, and there are no preliminary blessings over the food at this point (but see below). A second prayer is given by Jesus: 'Blessed are you, O Lord our God, King of the Universe, who brings forth bread from the earth', a prayer which in the Pesah Seder is included with the preliminary blessings over the food.[17] Jesus next intones, 'Blessed are you, O Lord our God, King of the Universe, who creates the fruit of the vine' which in the Pesah Seder meal represents the first cup (the cup of sanctification – kiddush – at the beginning of the Pesah Seder before the handwashing).[18] All of these elements, it is to be emphasized, are absent from the Gospel texts, or merely adumbrated there. It is clear, therefore, that a special effort has been made to give a 'ritual visualization' to the Gospel text by conforming it to the Pesah Seder.

So much for the ritual setting, and the sequence's relation to the Seder, but what about the plot and characterization, and the sequence's relation to the Gospel narratives? Here the film follows its genric predecessors, its action centring on the betrayal by Judas who shortly departs. Jesus's words thereafter to his disciples are a freer rendition of the Gospel texts, yet they are still formal and stylized. Hunter's lines are in modern English (Revised Standard Version style) but are delivered in a traditional way, at a formal, measured pace, and in a smooth, mellifluous, controlled voice. They include material from the Johannine discourses (Jesus's words about his departure, and the love commandment, for example) and from the Synoptics (the prophecy of the desertion of the disciples, for example) and Peter's denial). Jesus's words 'Take . . . Eat . . . For this is my body. Do this in remembrance of me' conflate the shorter Markan version with the Lukan 'Do this in remembrance of me', and the word over the cup comes from Matthew's version (Mt. 26.28). The scene, in short, is decidedly Christian, and more than a touch ecclesiastical, with its choral background, with Jesus as the solemn celebrant, with the disciples each in turn taking the single cup and sipping from it in silence. The Y-shaped table arrangement, with the prominent display of wood, even gives a certain suggestion of church pews!

The Greatest Story Ever Told *(1965): The Greatest Supper Ever Eaten* [02.18.32–02.25.37]

Perfectionism in pursuit of the Perfect, our next film, George Stevens's *The Greatest Story Ever Told* (1965) was the most expensive ever made. Though luminescent with its galaxy of stars, and presenting some memorable sequences (such as the raising of Lazarus as well as the crucifixion), this was a commercial failure that set the Christ film back where Hollywood was concerned. The part of Jesus is played by Max von Sydow. Although a distinguished actor, von Sydow was little known at the time outside of Europe, where he had acted in a number of Ingmar Bergman films such as *The Seventh Seal* (1957). With his straight, black hair and beard, and Swedish accent, his Byzantine Jesus conveys a spiritual and unearthly quality. Jesus's nobility of character, firmness of purpose, certainty of mind, and sadness of spirit are conveyed well by him. The pace, as elsewhere throughout the film, is slow, even stately, with frequent close-ups of Jesus and the disciples' faces. The musical accompaniment by Alfred Newman is subdued, unobtrusive but effective.

The Last Supper in *The Greatest Story Ever Told* (1965) takes place with Jesus and the disciples seated at a long table. As with other directors before him, Stevens immersed himself in centuries of Christian art, using Leonardo da Vinci's famous painting as his model for the Last Supper.

Unlike the other characters, Jesus's language, as also that of Charlton Heston's John the Baptist, is largely inspired by the King James Version of the Gospels. The American poet and historian Carl Sandburg was involved, among others, in the writing of the script and, while this is at times banal (one notes here, for example, Jesus's address to his disciples as those 'who have walked with me down all those dusty roads'), it is also frequently beautiful, poetic and subtly nuanced. The words of institution are conflated from both the Markan/Matthean and Lukan/Pauline traditions. Again, as in most of the Christ films, the Synoptic Last Supper accounts are supplemented by the Johannine discourses ('In my Father's house . . .' Jn 14.2; 'I am the Way . . .' Jn 14.6; the new commandment of love, Jn 13.34, etc.), as elsewhere throughout the film. The scene ends climactically with Jesus's solemn words 'Now is the Son of Man glorified' (Jn 13.31).

What is noteworthy in this sequence is that, although all the disciples are in white, appropriately for a Passover meal, there is little reference, in contrast to Ray's *King of Kings* (1961) to the Jewish aspects of the Passover meal. The focus in this presentation of the Last Supper is Christological rather than ritualistic. It focuses on Jesus himself, rather than on the notion of a communal meal celebrating the Passover. Once again, too, the ritual aspect of the meal is overshadowed by the dramatic elements, especially the betrayal of Judas, and the prediction of Peter's denial. Jesus is a Christian priest officiating at a future Christian Eucharist, not a Jew celebrating the Passover with his disciples.

Jesus Christ, Superstar *(1973): The Last Picnic* [00.53.22– 00.59.32]

Our next sequence, from Norman Jewison's *Jesus Christ Superstar* (1973), offers an entirely different re-enactment of the Last Supper. An introduction and comment was given to this film in chapter 13 and this (or Text Box 17.2) should be consulted.

What strikes us about this version of the Last Supper, in contradistinction to the last one, is its vitality rather than its spirituality. Here we have the Last Supper as a picnic. 'Forget all my trials and tribulations . . . they'll still sing about us when we die' sing the disciples in the opening number, which is staged in an olive grove, and leads on to the Last Supper celebrated alfresco. In keeping with the Gospel accounts, Jesus predicts the denial and betrayal of his disciples. The audience is offered in particular a dramatization of the conflict between Jesus and Judas. 'You think I once admired you, now I despise you', sings Judas. 'You made me do it', he cries. 'For all you care, this wine could be my blood/this bread could be my body', sings Jesus, rebuking his disciples but raising thoughts in the mind of the audience of the relationship between the bread and the wine and the body and blood in the Christian Eucharist.

Where the Passover meal is concerned, there is the absence of the usual Passover setting, but the sequence, one notes, is framed by the image of the shepherd and the sheep, recalling perhaps the origins of the Passover as a nomadic shepherds' rite,[19] or perhaps evoking the Paschal lamb of the Fourth Gospel (cf. e.g. Jn 1.36 or 10.1–3). There is a handwashing at the start, and wine is drunk first here, before the bread.

In terms of its ideology and social context, however, it is noticeable that where Cecil B. DeMille's *The Ten Commandments* (1956) is permeated with the ethos of the 1950s, all the characters of Norman Jewison's *Jesus Christ Superstar* can clearly be seen to be rehearsing the rhetoric and counter-rhetoric of the youth revolution of the late 1960s and early 1970s.

Jesus of Nazareth (1977): *The Supper that Lasts* [01.48.05/ 01.53.30–01.59.15]

The complete Last Supper sequence in our next Christ film, Franco Zeffirelli's *Jesus of Nazareth* (1977) is almost 11 minutes long – hence my description of it not as the Last Supper but as the Supper that lasts. It is worth looking at in full, but a shortened, alternative, five-minute segment of it is included in the time location information. With a screenplay by Anthony Burgess and others (later turned into a novel by William Barclay), this six-and-a-half-hour made-for-television movie (screened on ITV in 1977) was the result of a promise made by its producer Lew Grade to the Pope to do for Jesus what he had done for Moses. The part of Jesus is played by the British actor Robert Powell, although Al Pacino and Dustin Hoffman were also considered for the role.

In its depiction of the Last Supper, the usual conventions are followed. The scene focuses on such basic elements as the prediction of Peter's denial, and the betrayal of Judas, and draws liberally on the Johannine discourses. The words pertaining to Jesus's departure are cited, as well as the new/love commandment (Jn 13.34), the Johannine Jesus's invocation to 'glorify the son' and his so-called high priestly prayer (Jn 17). The Christological declaration 'I am the way, the truth and the life' is the saying chosen to end the scene (Jn 14.6).

Some liberty is taken with the words of the institution. The Synoptic words of institution are given interpretative embellishments, as when Jesus intones: 'From now on, this cup will not only be a memorial and sacrament to the covenant God made with our fathers on Mount Sinai. This is the blood of the new covenant which is poured out for the many.' In some cases, the words are invented, but with Johannine overtones.

'From now on this will no longer be the bread of the passage of our fathers from bondage to freedom,' says Jesus. 'This Passover is for you today the passage from the bondage of death to the freedom of life.' In other cases, Johannine passages are freely adapted. 'This is the bread of life' intones Jesus. 'Whoever eats of this bread shall have eternal life' (cf. the 'bread of life' discourse of Jn 6.25–71).

Some care has been taken, therefore, at a theological level, to relate the Christian Last Supper to the Pesah Seder. And this care also reveals itself in the setting, which offers the audience some of the particularity, or ethnic elements often lacking in the biblical epic or Christ film. The Last Supper takes place in a low-ceilinged, mud-walled room. There is music, dancing and singing at the beginning (in the longer version of this sequence). Jesus leans against a wall, the others sit around, cross-legged, in an arc, on the floor. There is a genuine sense of a shared celebration of the Passover on the part of Jesus and his disciples. The participants drink wine from individual cups, or bowls.

The Last Temptation of Christ (1988): *The Last Last Supper* [01.40.10–01.44.30]

Our final sequence, and our last Last Supper, is taken from Martin Scorsese's *The Last Temptation of Christ* (1988), a film commented upon in previous chapters. What one notes here is that Scorsese's version is at last a genuine Passover meal. The ethnic elements are profuse. Oriental music is heard throughout in the atmospheric 'world music' soundtrack by Peter Gabriel. The Passover begins with the blowing of the *sophar*, the long horn with the turned-up end, used to summon people on a religious occasion. In keeping with the Passover feast, there is chanting to the accompaniment of timbrels (cf. Ex. 15.20). A Passover lamb is shown slaughtered, its blood being caught in a bowl. Blood is shown being thrown over an altar. Pilgrims entering Jerusalem are dressed in white, and carrying torches. Ritual ablutions are taking place. A seven-branched candlestick or *menora* is shown at the start of the Last Supper scene itself. Jesus meets with his disciple in a canopied area. The women are bringing the items needed for the meal (wine). Jesus is sitting cross-legged, and his disciples reclining. The unleavened bread is passed around in a circle.

In his treatment of the words of institution, Scorsese has brilliantly solved the problem of previous enactments of the Last Supper. Here the words of the institution are minimal: 'Take this bread. Share it together. This bread is my body . . . Now drink this wine. Pass the cup. This wine is my blood. Do this to remember me.' 'All of you. I want to tell you something', says Jesus and the scene ends. Thus there are no laboured or artificial borrowings from the Johannine discourses, or no climactic saying chosen by the scriptwriter from the Gospels and wrested from its context for dramatic effect.

Scorsese's Last Supper is distinctive in other ways too. Reflecting the 1980s, for example, is its inclusion of women in the circle receiving the bread and the wine (Mary Magdalene included). What is truly remarkable about this re-enactment is that it is truly visual and truly cinematic. This is a film drawing on visual imagery rather than words to make its point. Here cinema becomes the counterpart to myth and ritual, with its offering of visual images and ritual actions in place of a superfluity of words to represent the transcendent. Peter removes a mouthful of wine between thumb and forefinger, and we are shown it as a trickle of blood in his upturned palm. Judas (who actually drinks of the cup, one observes, in contrast to the Judas of DeMille's *The King of Kings* who lets it pass) looks on. The wine/blood is poured over the unleavened bread. Judas departs without a word. The economy demonstrated in this scene is impressive. As with the finale to DeMille's *The King of Kings*, striking visual imagery and symbolism is used to good effect, obviating the need to repeat the now familiar elements of the Last Supper to audiences.

Notes

1 B. Babington and P. W. Evans, *Biblical Epics. Sacred Narrative in the Hollywood Cinema,* Manchester: Manchester University Press, 1993.

2 W. R. Telford, 'The New Testament in Fiction and Film: A Biblical Scholar's Perspective', in J. G. Davies, G. Harvey and W. Watson (eds), *Words Remembered, Texts Renewed. Essays in Honour of J. F. A. Sawyer*, Sheffield: Sheffield Academic Press, 1995, pp. 360–94.

3 J. W. Martin and C. E. Ostwalt (eds), *Screening the Sacred. Religion, Myth, and Ideology in Popular American Film*, Boulder, CO: Westview, 1995.

4 See, for example, J. C. Rylaarsdam, 'Passover and Feast of Unleavened Bread' in G. A. Buttrick (ed.), *The Interpreter's Dictionary of the Bible*, New York and Nashville: Abingdon, 1962, pp. 663–8; D. L. Jeffrey, 'Passover', in D. L. Jeffrey (ed.), *A Dictionary of Biblical Tradition in English Literature*, Grand Rapids, MI: Eerdmans, 1992, p. 587; J. Jeremias, 'pasca', in G. Kittel (ed.), *Theological Dictionary of the New Testament*, Grand Rapids, MI: Eerdmans, 1967, pp. 896–904.

5 W. Barclay, *The Lord's Supper,* London: SCM Press, 1967.

6 J. Sacks, *The Chief Rabbi's Haggadah*, London: HarperCollins, 2003.

7 D. L. Jeffrey and I. H. Marshall, 'Eucharist', in Jeffrey (ed.), *Dictionary of Biblical Tradition in English Literature*, pp. 243–50, and esp. p. 244. See also J. Jeremias, *The Eucharistic Words of Jesus*, Oxford: Blackwell, 1955; M. H. Shepherd, 'Lord's Supper', in Buttrick (ed.), *The Interpreter's Dictionary of the Bible*, pp. 158–62.

8 For more information on these films, see, for example, R. Kinnard and T. Davis, *Divine Images. A History of Jesus on the Screen*, New York: Citadel

Press, 1992; L. J. Kreitzer, *The Old Testament in Fiction and Film. On Reversing the Hermeneutical Flow,* The Biblical Seminar 24, Sheffield: Sheffield University Press, 1994, pp. 21–7 (on DeMille's *The Ten Commandments,* 1923/1956); W. R. Telford, 'Jesus Christ Movie-Star: The Depiction of Jesus in the Cinema', in C. Marsh and G. Ortiz (eds), *Explorations in Theology and Film. Movies and Meaning,* Oxford: Blackwell, 1997, pp. 115–39.

9 C. Heston, *In the Arena. The Autobiography,* London: HarperCollins, 1995, p. 126.

10 Babington and Evans, *Biblical Epics,* pp. 34–5.

11 See Sacks's description of the fifteen stages of the Seder in Sacks, *Haggadah,* pp. 2–3.

12 See Sacks, *Haggadah, ad loc.*

13 Babington and Evans, *Biblical Epics,* pp. 34–6.

14 Babington and Evans, *Biblical Epics,* pp. 54, 55.

15 The cup is in the form of a traditional chalice, and hence evocative of all the imagery surrounding the 'holy grail'.

16 See the Eating of the Bitter Herb (*maror*): 'Blessed are You, O God our Lord, King of the world, who made us holy with His commandments, and instructed us to eat the bitter herbs', Sacks, *Haggadah,* p. 55.

17 See the Blessing and Eating of the Matzah (*motzie matzah*): 'Blessed are you, O God our Lord, King of the world, who brings bread out of the earth', Sacks, *Haggadah,* p. 53.

18 See the recitation of Kiddush (*kaddesh*): 'Blessed are you, O God our Lord, King of the world, Creator of the fruit of the vine', Sacks, *Haggadah,* p. 7.

19 See Rylaarsdam, 'Passover', p. 664.

Epilogue
Table Talk:

Reflections on *The Passion of The Christ* (Mel Gibson, 2004)

Tom Aitken (TA), Eric S. Christianson (EC), Peter Francis (PF), Jeffrey F. Keuss (JK), Robert Pope (RP), William R. Telford (WRT), Melanie Wright (MW)

As this book was in preparation, Mel Gibson's *The Passion of The Christ* was released. As contributors, we wanted to offer some response to the film. In the summer of 2004, most of the contributors to this volume gathered at St Deiniol's Library to reflect on the film. This is an edited version of a long afternoon of discussion.

The discussion focused on the film as the latest in the genre of Christ films and went on to consider it as a 'Mel Gibson' film, exploring common traits and themes. We were all numbed by the relentless violence of the film and the discussion pondered the point and purpose of depicting such excessive violence. The claims of 'realistic' violence led us into a discussion of the film's claim to authenticity, which in turn led us to discuss the antisemitism and possible homophobia of the film. We all noted that Gibson was trying to make a film with a clear theological message; some of us more cynically thought that the theological stance of the film was part of a deliberate marketing strategy. However, before embarking on these critical reflections, we'll start with what we liked about the film.

1. The Opportunity for Debate

PF: Whether you love it or loathe it, *The Passion of The Christ* was arguably the most talked about religious film of all time. It is not everyday that such blatant theology storms the box office and we must be grateful for the opportunity it gives us to debate and discuss the Gospels and in particular the death of Christ. We have all been involved in debates, public and private, about the film. Shouldn't we trust the audience to make up their own mind?

EC: It is a deeply personal film. I want to applaud the fact that he has made, in an age when film-makers are not necessarily making 'position' films, a film with a distinct theology and spirituality.

TA: Some of the worst effects of the film will be absorbed by the fact that a lot of people who go and see it will already have a Christian belief and they will back off in certain parts of this film. They will like parts and they will think parts are over the top.

MW: For some inter-faith professionals, who ostensibly see the film as problematic, it is frankly the best thing that has happened to them for years. It offers free publicity for organizations, brings issues into the open. And the direct threat of the film is really small: research suggests that watching a film is unlikely to make one adopt (or reject) antisemitic or other prejudices.

2. The Horror of Crucifixion

TA: The main thing that is an advance on previous Jesus biopics is the scene of the crucifixion itself. No one will ever produce a movie with Robert Powell, beautifully composed, not looking all that uncomfortable. It won't be possible to have that kind of crucifixion scene again.

PF: No more looking on the bright side of life.

3. Cinematography

TA: The acting was competent but didn't really require great skill or range. But it was a tremendous film to look at when you weren't busy thinking 'I really don't want to see the result of seven hours of make-up again and again please.'

WRT: Critics have actually spoken quite well of the cinematography. The film was photographed by Caleb Deschanel who did the *Black Stallion*, *The Right Stuff* and Gibson's *The Patriot*. Richard Corliss, for example, in *Time Magazine*,[1] describes the film as 'an attractive clash of eerie blues in the outdoor night scenes, burnished umbers in the trial scenes, and blistering whites and yellows on the road to Calvary'.

MW: You can locate this film vis-à-vis other dark epics: for example, the film stock, tones, etc., evoke *Gladiator* and *Lord of The Rings*. The opening images of the moon in a dark smoky sky, the menacing demonic children are evidence that several production crew members cut their teeth in the horror genre.

WRT: Caleb Deschanel gives us a very objective camera with very few point-of-view shots. The only significant ones that I could spot were in connection with the scourging, the road to the cross, the crucifixion and its dramatic outcome. When Jesus was being scourged, you get the point-of-view of Jesus as he is being dragged away. The camera turns upside down and you see things from the victim's point of view. Then at various points on the Via Dolorosa, you get a point-of-view shot from Jesus's perspective. There are two other notable shots: God looking down on the crucifixion scene with the fall of the raindrop/teardrop expressing his sadness or judgement; and following the earthquake and before the deposition, a similar heaven-to-earth view of Satan being condemned, again conveying the divine perspective on the triumph of Jesus.

JK: Caleb Deschanel's camera fulfils Gibson's hallmark as director and producer of a controlling gaze that is very particular and akin to the name of his production company Icon Entertainment, always bent on trans-fixing the viewer – at times in a voyeuristic and pornographic sense – to that which lies beyond, beneath and behind the flickering images on the screen.

EC: The camera objectifies the whole experience. We identify with the perpetrators of violence and the spectators and not with Jesus.

PF: In that respect, Deschanel and Gibson have been uncomfortably successful.

4. Atonement Theology

RP: One of the things that strikes me is that if you take the story of Jesus in Christian theology as being redemptive, then virtually all Jesus films are intensely dissatisfying. When it comes down to it you are still left wondering why it is that the crucifixion of one man has drawn this theological significance. Now this film attempts from the start to address that. None of the Jesus films are able to explain the meaning of this atoning death. Gibson at least prefaces his film with the quotation from Isaiah showing his intention to offer an explanation.

PF: It does have a definite theological slant compared to the other Jesus films. The devil frames the whole film, the film presents a cosmic battle beginning with the devil in Gethsemane and ending with the devil being cast down and defeated.

WRT: Well, it's interesting that *Time* magazine ran a cover story entitled 'Why did Jesus die?'[2] It is extraordinary to have theology on the front page of an international news magazine, and the claim was made in the article that, throughout America now, atonement theory is back on the agenda, and people are discussing it. Gibson's film dramatizes two of the classic atonement theories: first, Anselm's idea of substitutionary atonement: the notion that payment is made to God on behalf of humankind by Jesus's vicarious death; and second, the interpretation that Gustav Aulén calls the classic theory in his book *Christus Victor*.[3] In this theory, Jesus's sacrifice is seen to be directed not towards God but against the devil, who is defeated by a display of superior power (or even by divine subterfuge). Gibson's film can be seen to exemplify the classic theory in that Satan appears in all the key scenes, and is shown being finally overcome.

PF: Atonement debate hasn't been central in theology for a long time. Contemporary theology seems more interested in the life, ministry and mission of Jesus rather than his atoning death. Perhaps Gibson's film is a corrective to this trend. It certainly serves to make us reflect on the current enthusiasm for Jesus's life and ministry. Gibson ignores Abelard's theory of Jesus's death as a supreme example of self-giving love, a theory that honours his life and ministry to a much greater extent.

RP: The film has a serious theological intent in contrast to the other Jesus biopics.

5. Intertextuality

PF: Eric and Bill, as biblical scholars, was there anything you particularly admired about the film?

EC: Gibson does show a little bit of flair with intertextuality, for example, with the Genesis reference in Gethsemane, crushing the serpent's head. Though the example I found most interesting was the reference to the Jewish liturgy of Passover. Jesus is starting to undergo his torture, Mary wakes up from sleep realizing that something is wrong with her son. We see a light under the door and you have the Passover citation about this night being different from all other nights (cf. Exod. 12.26–27; 13.14). The citation fails, however, as the door bursts open – in other words, the angel of death *will* visit this night. For me, this Passover reference was the most creative moment of the film.

WRT: The use of the New Testament is all fairly conventional, with very little evidence of creative invention. Very few sayings on the lips of Jesus tease the mind. Except in one flashback, where Jesus is a child, he falls, and his mother runs to him. She reaches him, with the help of the beloved disciple, through the back alleys and rushes to pick him up. He rises to his feet and at that point he turns to her and says 'Mother, I make all things new.' Now suddenly we have a quotation from the book of Revelation (a quotation from its penultimate chapter),[4] which is found on the lips of God Almighty himself. I wondered why Gibson had chosen to put this saying on the lips of Jesus at that point in the film having hitherto given us a series of standard Gospel sayings.

6. *The Passion of The Christ* as a Jesus Biopic

PF: That's what we like about the film. It is time now to consider Gibson's film *The Passion of The Christ* as the latest in a long line of films that try to put on screen the life of Christ, Jesus biopics as we might call them. It belongs to the group that I often refer to as 'reverential re-tellings'[5] as opposed to the 'imaginative re-tellings'.[6] These reverential retellings, attempt to be standard biopics of Jesus's life. Gibson's film shares many of the faults of these films, and it fits within the conventions of this genre of Jesus biopics.

TA: As far as genre is concerned it's intensely old-fashioned. The actual structure of the script is identical in principle and practice with all of the other big action, pious spectacles. They have taken a bit out of this Gospel, a bit out of that Gospel, the occasional pious legends (Veronica with her veil, etc.).

WRT: When I looked at the film in relation to other Jesus films, I was looking for general borrowings from the genre. I was also looking out for the presence of the conventional scenes that we see time and time again in Jesus films. One example of a borrowing from the genre would be the scene in the first flashback, in which Jesus makes a table and when he's alone with his mother at home. That scene made me think very much of Nicholas Ray's *King of Kings*, 1961 film, in which a very similar scene is shown.

PF: It is also reminiscent of the carpentry shop scenes in Scorsese's *Last Temptation of Christ*.

WRT: There were a whole series of conventional borrowings: the Sermon on the Mount, the woman taken in adultery, the entry into Jerusalem, the cleansing of the Temple, the Last Supper, the resurrection. These are scenes that appear in virtually all Jesus films.

TA: But I defy anybody who doesn't know the Gospels quite well to understand those flashbacks. The triumphal entry is flashed on screen when Jesus is halfway up the Via Dolorosa. Unless you know what it is, you won't have the least idea.

PF: I was struck by the brief Sermon on the Mount scene. It was straight out of Monty Python's spoof version. I wanted to add their caption, 'Saturday. Tea Time. About 4:00 p.m.' It presented the same kind of image that the Pythons ridicule so well of Christ on the mountain top instructing the masses who wouldn't hear a word. Gibson also borrows from Jewison's *Jesus Christ Superstar* with its camp miracle-demanding Herod. He borrows the devilish figure from George Stevens's *Greatest Story Ever Told*, where Donald Pleasance plays the ever-lurking devil figure. Like all the other reverential re-tellings the film is very painterly in tone.

MW: Yes, the classic *pietà* pose when Jesus is taken down from the cross.

PF: It borrows its iconography from great Renaissance paintings (Piero della Francesca, Mantegna) and especially from Caravaggio. Gibson constructs carefully composed scenes that are *tableaux vivants* based on these great masters (just like Stevens, de Mille and Zeffirelli have done before him).

EC: It's as if those painterly scenes and borrowings are a kind of structural reassurance. Gibson is taking us into new territory in the violence. We are being reassured with the nice comfortable genre conventions of the Jesus biopics.

TA: The problem with filming the life of Jesus is that there is very little biographical colouring in the Gospels. What can we know of Jesus the human being? Who does he love? Everybody. Who does he hate? No one. What makes him laugh? We don't know. What are his flaws and shortcomings? He has none.

PF: All the Jesus biopics fail in that respect. We get very little impression of why Jesus is so charismatic. There's no bio!

TA: The film leaves out any sort of context. Other Jesus biopics give us context. Ray's *King of Kings* paints a careful picture of the political situation, for example. In Gibson's film we have no context. What is going on in Jerusalem? In reality nobody cared about Jesus's fate, nothing out of the ordinary was going on. But in Gibson's film the whole world is watching Jesus. I think in reality people were enjoying the preparations for the Passover festival and carrying on as usual. There is no sign of that in this film. There is no real mention of the fact that Passover is going on. He doesn't stress that this was a very tense time and the Romans and Jews had ways of trying to deal with it and instead of abusing each other, Caiaphas and Pilate would have been at their closest. Other films in the genre give us a lot of context.

7. A 'Gibson' Film

PF: OK, it shares a lot in common with other Jesus biopics, except for its failure to supply a context for the violence, but is it recognizably a 'Mel Gibson' film?

MW: It is identifiably a Gibson film in the sense that it fetishizes violence and constructs the roles of masculine and feminine genders conservatively. Gibson is a heavy-handed director and to borrow a phrase from *Spinal Tap*, in *The Passion* he gives us the crucifixion 'turned up to 11'.

WRT: In *The Patriot, Lethal Weapon, The Year of Living Dangerously, Mad Max, Mad Max 2, Signs, Conspiracy Theory, We were Soldiers*, you have this character (Gibson) who can take a lot of punishment but also acts in a kind of redemptive way. Mad Max is an apocalyptic hero but, at the same time, someone receiving violence as well as perpetrating it. In *Braveheart*, William Wallace is almost a Christ-figure at the end, even adopting the cruciform position as he is tortured.

PF: Of course, *Braveheart* whipped up a great deal of anti-English feeling in Scotland when it was released as well as anti-WASP feeling in USA. *The Passion* whipped up a good deal of antisemitic feeling when it was released. Like *The Passion, Braveheart* was not at all nuanced in its characterization, with very clear distinctions between the good and the bad. If you heighten the cruelty and humiliation done to the good by the bad and link it to emotive subjects like national independence or religion, the result is bound to be explosive. Neither of these two films is easy to have a calm rational conversation about; they both instil outrage.

JK: One thing that is clear throughout Mel Gibson's filmic history (going back to *Mad Max* in fact) is a central theme that cultures, nationalism and even religion will perish but what remains is the call of the family. The plot of *Mad Max, Braveheart, The Patriot* and *The Passion of The Christ* are all cut from the same Shroud of Turin. If the storylines of these films are based on a good sense of the market, then it appears that today's audiences can't imagine any cause that could justify political violence other than injury to a child or wife (your own, not your neighbour's – that's *their* problem). What Gibson has picked up on is that the back story of global apocalypse (*Mad Max*), the parochial patriotism of colonial elites (*The Patriot*), the genocide of a people and their way of life (*Braveheart*) and extreme religious intolerance (*The Passion of The Christ*) are incomprehensible to today's audiences – all that matters to those sitting in the multiplex cinema is 'kin'.

WRT: There is this strong notion of the primal unit, the family in Gibson's films. In *The Passion,* the family is, in fact, a threesome that you see at various important points in the film. And the threesome is Mary, the mother of Jesus, Mary Magdalene and the conflated figure of John/ the beloved disciple. They, in a sense, are almost humanizing elements. When Jesus is being constantly harassed by his enemies, the camera often goes to this threesome who shadow him at every point, lending him succour. The sense of Jesus as the embattled man but, nevertheless, surrounded by a supportive family is so distinctive in this film. There is, of course, no trace of the tension between Jesus and his mother that you find in the Gospels.

JK: The '*pietà* on the move' in the form of Maia Morgenstern's Mary and Monica Bellucci's Magdalene are the only consistent people who follow Jim Caviezel's Jesus through the trial, up the *Via Dolorosa,* and wait oh-so-patiently at the foot of the cross. As a reward for patient attention to the torture, Jesus bestows not salvation per se but the blessing of family – 'Son, behold your mother/Mother, behold your son.' The fact that Gibson is drawing this from the Gospel of John account (Jn 19.26) is not what is significant – it is the fact that Gibson frames this scene so distinctly and gives as much screen time to it where other Jesus films give little or no time. All other things will perish – but family will remain.

WRT: In this scene lifted from John's Gospel, where Jesus is on the cross and his mother is at the foot of the cross with the beloved disciple, the biblical text says 'woman' ('Woman, behold your son!') using the same pejorative term that you find also in John 2, at the marriage in Cana. In the version that we see in this film Jesus doesn't address her as 'woman'; he says 'mother' ('Mother, behold your son!') and then when the beloved disciple is addressed, there is no 'son' in John's text ('Behold, your mother!'), but Gibson's version puts in the word 'son' ('Son, behold your mother!'). So mother/son is reinforced in the dialogue of the film in a way that is not in the biblical text.

Gibson gives us a diabolic family running through the film as well as the holy threesome, who represent the holy family. I see one explanation for this in the convention that one finds sometimes in apocalyptic literature, that there will always be a diabolic equivalent to God. The devil mimics God and, therefore, what you are seeing (with Satan and his offspring) is the family theme again – only this is the diabolic equivalent of the Holy Family. This is the diabolic family here: Satan, the father/mother, with his demonic brood who hound Judas, for example, or evil's alternative 'virgin and child', the androgynous figure carrying his grotesque, dwarf-like, superannuated child through the Roman soldiers.

MW: I think the film doubles Mary with the devil. Despite the dubbing of a male voice for this androgynous character, I think we are meant to see these figures as a pair. For example, in the scourging scene, the devil and Mary are clothed alike, the devil is seen suckling a diabolic child.

RP: You know, what we've just discussed about the family is good old American Republicanism. The family unit is where you find security and safety and all that and you've got to watch the people in government because they can look like they are flogging you to death.

8. A Violent Film

PF: My overriding memory of the film is the relentless violence.

TA: I know I was totally benumbed by the violence, I mean I'd been benumbed since about 20 minutes after the beginning of the film. I think many people would argue that realism is the only possible excuse for that level of violence.

EC: Are we going to talk about the realism of the violence? That's interesting. People have noted that Jesus bleeds in impossible ways.

WRT: One reviewer has challenged the view that 'blood plus dead language equals reality'.[7] The violence is such that a number of critics, as well as audience, have noted its artificiality. There's a splendid quotation from the same reviewer who says of the film: 'an incredibly obtuse piece of macho-masochism, overlooking Jesus's message of love and his human complexity in favour of a bizarre make-up bloodbath, turning his body into a gory lattice of latex weals, cosmetic stripes and prosthetic wounds which proclaim their lurid and ridiculous fakeness to the very heavens'.

EC: What strikes me, the more I think about *The Passion*, is that it's as if Gibson is wanting you to reflect on the perpetrators of the violence and their sadism rather than the victim. It'd be interesting to ask that of the other Gibson films, whether our attention is drawn to the perpetrators. It seems to me, after seeing the violence perpetrated on Jesus, that after an hour it had no impact. Jesus became simply a cipher of abuse. We are completely desensitized and our focus is on the sadism, the pleasure, the voyeurism.

JK: That's Gibson's gaze.

TA: What I want to say is that when you compare the violence inflicted on individual people in the last 160 or so years, who can say that the comparatively short suffering Jesus underwent is comparable. There are stories from many situations that show awful long-term suffering compared to Jesus's last 24 hours. I think that, perhaps unconsciously, the film-makers wanted to make the violence comparable to the deliberate, sadistic and sustained violence that millions of people suffered during the twentieth century.

RP: There are theological reasons for the death of Jesus and there are the actual mechanics of the death. The film does try to give theological reasons. What it fails to do is convincingly portray the mechanics of his death in a historically accurate manner. Nobody could have that done to them and then stand up and ask for more, and that's what led me to read the film as iconic rather than realistic. If it was intended to be iconic, then it takes us into the kind of mentality that asks how many stripes you would have to have in order for the world to be healed.

WRT: When Isaiah 53 says 'by his stripes we are healed,' then the more stripes the better, and the more healed we are going to be!

RP: The violence is also tied to his literal understanding of Anselm and penance. It is almost as though he believes that one stroke of the whip would be ten sins, therefore, dying for the sins of the world would mean so much pain. Stroke after stroke of the whip.

WRT: Anselm belongs to the early medieval world and Gibson presents us, in fact, with a medieval Christ. The film has a fascination for medieval passion iconography and theology. We are back in the period of the Black Death where whole populations were decimated and people saw in the suffering Christ a figure to whom they could relate. Traditional passion/atonement theology became enshrined in Catholic doctrine, and Mel Gibson taps into this whole medieval world-view.[8]

PF: Medieval? Maybe, but is it a film for our times? There is the uncomfortable parallel of the stories of the torturing of Iraqi prisoners during the film's theatrical release. A priest from London told me of a group of Pakistani Christians in his parish who had suffered a great deal of violence in Pakistan, who felt that the film showed Jesus suffering like them, with them even. We live in violent times and this is a violent film.

TA: I think you have to take on board the fact that there are large parts of the world where people won't find this quite so astonishing and awfully violent as we do.

MW: The film is highly resonant. It speaks to (certain) American audiences with their post-September 11th sense of embattlement – physically (war, terrorism) and spiritually (some see conflict with terrorism as a religious war). Conservative Christianity also feels itself to be under 'attack' from liberalism. Gibson's film offers a muscular Jesus who is also embattled but wins through. The final scene reminded me of *The Terminator*. It promises much for the audience in terms of confrontation leading to victory.

9. Authenticity

PF: Gibson's and Benedict Fitzgerald's text, although delivered in Latin and Aramaic, is a compilation from all four Gospels as have been nearly all the screenplays of Jesus biopics. Its claim to authenticity is, of course, complete nonsense. Gibson's film is pre-critical, taking no account of modern biblical scholarship. George Stevens in the 1960s went to great pains to use biblical scholarship to emphasize that the Jews were not to blame for the death of Jesus. Zeffirelli, Scorsese, Pasolini and Nicholas Ray all used mainstream biblical scholars in an effort to 'get it right' and to offend nobody. Even DeMille and D. W. Griffith in the silent era posted footnotes in their captions to give historical and theological insight. Gibson eschews all this and that in itself is a theological choice. For Gibson, the Gospel account and Catholic tradition is more authentic than any historical knowledge about Pilate, for instance, or about the trial process in Roman Palestine. He takes little or no account of what archaeology now tells us about the manner of crucifixion. All of this is Gibson's deliberate choice. Nothing is really authentic, not the violence, nor, indeed, the dead languages.

WRT: Romans in Roman Judaea would not have spoken Latin. They would have spoken Greek and there is some historical evidence that Jesus too may possibly have spoken Greek. Once you start using the original biblical languages in a Jesus film, then you make yourself a hostage to foreign fortune because then the scholar in the audience notes that Pilate, for example, is speaking Aramaic to the Jewish authorities – and one wonders if the historical Pilate would have had a command of Aramaic! Jesus speaks Aramaic to his disciples but he then moves into Latin with Pilate. From a historical point of view, it doesn't smack of reality at all.

TA: If you have done 12 years of research (as Gibson claims), you may have been expected to get that right.

EC: The authenticity of the language doesn't matter for what Gibson is trying to achieve. This is an element of the film that really worked for me. It makes strange something that is familiar to us. I thought it successfully achieved that and it made the phrases that we hear so much in Christ films in English, new and fresh. It gave us that sense of encountering an ancient culture.

WRT: I agree with you, if Gibson's purpose was an aesthetic one of that kind, but in fact that's not what he claimed. Gibson makes the claim that everything you see on screen is taken from the Gospels and is, therefore, historically true. Any biblical scholar would dispute that claim. First of all, even if something is in the Gospels, it may not necessarily be historically true. You have to look, moreover, at the question of authenticity from different angles. You have to look, for example, at whether the film presents a genuine historical *context* and explains that *context* to the viewer. The film lacked, in my view, a proper political and religious context for the presentation of its material. The one area where Gibson could have done this was in the flashbacks, but instead of using the flashbacks to convey an overall historical context you get intra-New Testament Gospel passages conveying all the regular things: the triumphal entry into Jerusalem, the Last Supper, etc. The treatment of Pilate jarred with the kind of presentation of Pilate we find in Josephus. There is no attempt by Gibson to address the problems highlighted by biblical scholarship with regard to the trial narratives and the evangelists' historical depiction of contemporary Jewish legal procedures. In the crucifixion scene, there is no attempt at historical reconstruction. Gibson has nails through the victim's hands rather than his wrists, shows Jesus on a high cross and the two malefactors on lower crosses, etc. and so privileges traditional Christian iconography over historical authenticity.

TA: I think that, in all of these senses, it's inauthentic and it has some other really crazy things in it as well. I mean the Roman soldiers. They beat Jesus all the way up the Via Dolorosa. You know they've seen crucifixions before. Don't they want to get the job over and get back to barracks and get on with playing cards and whatever? It seemed to me that there was absolutely no reason for what they were doing there except that, as I've indicated, Gibson wants to show all of us being responsible for Jesus's death.

WRT: One further thing about authenticity. Mel Gibson uses post-biblical traditions: the tradition of Veronica, the tradition of the good and bad thieves, the stations of the cross, the sorrowful mysteries of the rosary. But in addition, a major part of the film and the ostensibly invented scenes are drawn from the mystic visions of Anne Catherine Emmerich's *The Dolorous Passion of Our Lord Jesus Christ.*[9]

PF: It is from Emmerich's visions that much of Gibson's material about the agony in Gethsemane, the scourging, the crucifixion, the farewell to the Virgin Mary, Pilate's crisis of conscience all come.

WRT: This introduces a whole new dimension to this film that's never appeared in any other Jesus film. Gibson seems to be making the claim that one of his historical sources is this late eighteenth/early nineteenth-century German Catholic visionary, thereby presupposing that visionary experiences are giving us historical knowledge about Jesus's life. It is an approach that obviously has to be questioned.

PF: Just before we finish this section, I would like to say that I don't think the screenplay and the actors help us feel that it is authentic or real in any sense. There is no characterization.

TA: The actors do not play characters, they all play icons. They don't behave anything like people. Jesus is not given a chance to behave anything like a person except in an odd little moment, Mary is an icon of suffering and love, Caiaphas is an icon of utter filthiness, the soldiers are icons of sadism. And I'm afraid Pilate is an icon of a decent, liberal man, trapped in an awkward situation.

EC: All of them are limited by flat characterization. The women cannot be developed as characters because they are not in a dialectical relationship with Jesus. This is what makes them come alive in the Gospels, Jesus speaking with them and transgressing social barriers. There is no opportunity for that in the film. You just see them again almost objectively because they are not in a relationship with Jesus, so it's very difficult to talk about any of these characters because we do not know them.

PF: What about constructions of masculinity and femininity in the film?

WRT: Mary is one of those characters who is 'knowing', who recognizes what is really going on behind the scenes and who suffers along with the central character. There's this tremendous empathy, and when you look at the other women, they are all presented in the same way; they lament, they weep, they show anguish. The women are the ones who encourage Simon of Cyrene to come to Jesus's assistance. They are constantly present as a group offering succour. In some ways, that's a fairly stereotypical construction of femininity in Jesus films. They also look like nuns.

TA: The men are almost without exception sadists, creeps and conspirators.

WRT: Well, we see them through Catholic eyes. We see Pilate's wife, for example, not simply through Matthew's eyes (the only Gospel in which she appears, although she remains unnamed). We see her through the lens of Catholic tradition where she has been turned into a prototypical Christian. Gibson gives her a name, Claudia Procles, a version of her name in the Roman calendar of saints. Like Mary, we see her as a comforter who is prayerfully watching and concerned, and we see her bringing Mary the scarf to mop up Jesus's blood. All of this is part and parcel of this whole characterization of the woman (in the Jesus film) as the saintly figure.

RP: The women exude a kind of empathy, it is often quite moving, like a traditional Renaissance painting.

EC: But we do not learn anything about them.

WRT: There were also some male characters that had more characterization; for example, Abenader, the commanding officer. One senses that he has some sympathy for Jesus. He's the one who stops the soldiers from exceeding orders. And Pilate, too, is depicted as a questioning individual, reflecting upon his actions, and concerned about his moral responsibility. Historically, in fact, we learn from Josephus that he was a brutal tyrant.

PF: But Gibson prefers Emmerich to Josephus, visionary imagining to historical scholarship.

WRT: If we are looking for other characters that run counter to the predominantly hard, harsh, and brutal construction of masculinity in the film, then there is the black figure at the court of Herod who is presented, like the women, as a 'knowing' character. He comprehends the theology of suffering here and the heroic victim who is subject to it.

RP: And again it's because he's black isn't it? He, like the women, understands what suffering is.

PF: But it is so fleeting as to be tokenistic.

TA: Smacks of a brainstorming session to me.

10. Antisemitism/Anti-Judaism/Homophobia

MW: The film is clearly supersessionist. However, it is hard to see how one would make a dramatically compelling Jesus film, recognizable to popular audiences, that avoids this pitfall. But as we consider the charge of antisemitism, it is important to distinguish anti-Judaism from antisemitism. Both are offensive to Jews and to some non-Jews who work in inter-faith relations and who believe that Judaism can be a valid means to a relationship with God. Conflating the two is unhelpful generally and especially in relation to this film. Teasing them apart helps us to understand the reception of the film. Antisemitism is defined to mean negative prejudice against Jews grounded in incorrect identification of Jews as a race, a genetically distinct group.

PF: Is the film antisemitic?

MW: Antisemitism does not *motivate* Gibson's film. However, the film does project a racialized Jewish identity. It also plays on themes in modern antisemitic discourse. We first see the priests discussing money: modern anti-Jewish prejudice is inserted into the story of Christian beginnings.

For the most part, the film approach coheres with the once mainstream Christian anti-Judaism. It certainly contains within it the potential to feed the 'teaching of contempt' and retains the Gospels' move to attribute more blame to the Jews than the Romans for the death of Christ. It offers a sympathetic portrait of Pilate.

EC: Our focus is on violence as applied by Jews and soldiers. In contrast Pilate is always shot in white, with this kind of aura of sensibility and peace (Feng Shui almost). The Jews are shot, particularly at night, in this pale, sickly amber light. The most disturbing thing is the none too subtle association of sadism and voyeuristic violence with Jewish spectators.

TA: That relates very much to the treatment of Caiaphas, which is extremely implausible. Gibson has him present at the crucifixion, which wouldn't have happened. He's present at the trial before Herod, which wouldn't have happened. He demands freedom for Barabbas, which wouldn't have happened. He witnesses the scourging, he starts the yell of 'crucify' – all of this is nonsense. What is happening here is not mob rule, but the boss man, Caiaphas, making it official policy.

WRT: Yes, that's right. Caiaphas is even present at the foot of the cross in Gibson's film. It's only in John's Gospel that we have someone present at the foot of the cross and that's the mother of Jesus together with the beloved disciple.

PF: There's a very interesting difference from the biblical account. 'Father forgive them for they know not what they do' is said in the Gospel of Luke to the soldiers. In the film it appears to be said to Caiaphas.

WRT: It's highlighted by the thief, who then repeats it for the sake of the audience, saying to Caiaphas at the foot of the cross, 'He is praying for you.'

PF: It is a hugely irresponsible time to paint the Jews in such unpleasant tones because it will play very well in some parts of the world.

RP: I didn't feel it was antisemitic or anti-Jewish when I first watched it. It does present a clear-cut distinction between goodies and baddies, but some of the goodies are Jews.

PF: I'm not sure the goodies are Jews, I think the goodies are Catholics and nuns.

EC: My concerns about the film aren't that people will go out to inflict violence on Jews or burn synagogues but that it will subtly influence how people think about Judaism and how they approach the Gospel text. The film does reinforce a way of thinking and an approach that is closed. I don't think that the one-dimensional presentation has raised as much concern as it should.

WRT: The fact that a film presents Christian propaganda in this biased one-dimensional way should worry all of us, shouldn't it? What you get is a sustained negative portrayal of Jews and Jewish leaders. This comes out in the absence of the kind of devices that other directors have used to mitigate this effect. For example, if you want to humanize the Jewish authorities, you put in dissenting voices. I noted only a very few dissenting voices on the Jewish side within the film. You get some leaders, for example, averting their eyes when Jesus is flogged and in the trial scene you get someone pointing out the illegality of the proceedings. What you do not get (as you got, for example, in Zeffirelli's *Jesus of Nazareth*) is an intelligent and plausible apologetic coming from the dissenters, explaining their position so that the audience is presented with the other side.

EC: There was a very interesting moment of historical authenticity when the Sanhedrin meets at night and one of the objectors highlights the illegality of the meeting. I thought: this will be interesting; Gibson's actually making an attempt to engage with authenticity. Then it becomes apparent that the only reason he is doing it is to exaggerate the group's resistance to that allegation, so it makes their barbarism even clearer.

I think it might have been Gibson's naivety and that it was not intentionally anti-Jewish or antisemitic. It is mainly due to very poor storytelling. It could also account for the failure to flesh out the characters or
present their views. The only possible exceptions are Pilate and the visual
representation of the Jews. Pilate is given two distinct extra-biblical scenes
to establish his reasonableness and his inner struggle, which is only vaguely hinted at in the Gospels, if at all. Compare the visual and narrative representation of the Jews with extra scenes devoted to demonstrating their
hatred.

WRT: Gibson says that he's not an antisemite. He claims that he has presented a film in which we should recognize that we are all more or less
equally to blame for Christ's death. My point of view would be that if you
are going to present that kind of theology, then you use your artistry to
work it into the film. When I've seen defences on the part of Gibson and
his crew against the charge of antisemitism, three things are pointed out:
one, they removed the subtitle for 'his blood be upon us and our children'.
Two, when the nails are put into Jesus' hands, the first nail is hammered
in by Mel Gibson himself. Three, Maia Morgenstern, who plays Mary,
mother of Jesus, has Jewish roots. It is a terribly flimsy defence, since it
depends, among other things, on the audience's extrinsic knowledge of
these facts! You need something much more powerful in a film than what
is being presented here if you are going to present a theology of universal
responsibility.

MW: There's a racializing discourse at play here: Morgenstern's Jewish
family become important in the marketing; Caviezel is given a prosthetic
nose. The foregrounding of certain casting details in the film's publicity
suggests a racializing construction of Jewish identity.

PF: And that would be classed as antisemitic presumably.
  To change tack (or at least prejudices), what about the criticism of the
film as homophobic? The criticism centres around the androgynous devil
figure.

EC: Gibson said in an interview that 'His face is symmetric and beautiful
in a certain sense, but not completely, and then we shot her almost in
slow motion so you don't see her blink. We dubbed in a man's voice,
even though the actor was a woman. That's what evil was about, taking
something that's good and twisting it a little bit.'

PF: That's the way many conservative evangelicals and traditionalist
Catholics would describe homosexuality.

EC: Yes, I agree.

11. The Purpose of The Film: Theology and Pedagogy

WRT: The pedagogical purpose of the film is reinforced by his statement that he's going to try to release it every year at Easter time.

PF: I do think he believes that he is presenting the Truth. Of course, for us, it is one-dimensional propaganda; but for him, it is the Truth. We might applaud his courage in putting theology on the screen, his attempt to dramatize the atonement. We all seem to recognize that the film has a more serious theological intent than all the other reverential retellings of the Gospel story, but we dislike his theology. The film is out there on release and we are free to debate it.

EC: The key to the problem that we are having with the film is that Christian theology, as we understand it, is aware it is doing theology. Gibson doesn't seem to have been aware that he's doing theology.

PF: His theology is powerful stuff. He is quite deliberately going back to a time before critical theology started to undermine the tradition and suggest diverse theologies and alternate readings. Gibson's is a pre-critical theology, isn't it? It is as though Vatican II and twentieth-century critical insights have vanished. I'm struck that two people have come to my study after watching the film and talked to me about the film. They hadn't been aware of the depth of their sin and hadn't realized that they had done all of that to Christ by their sin. They felt their sin had flayed Christ's flesh and nailed him to the cross. They felt personally responsible. It strikes me that it's deliberate and that was exactly the reaction Gibson wanted. It is an evangelical tool with traditional Catholic trappings and copious eucharistic references. The whole film is shot through with a Tridentine, sacrificial understanding of the Mass. The film appeals not only to those who have a very clear substitutionary atonement theology but also to those who have a pre-Vatican II understanding of the Mass.

12. The Purpose of The Film: Making Money

PF: It is a distinct possibility that what this film is doing is simply trying to make money. There is money to be made in producing a Jesus biopic. Gibson for instance has shrewdly played to American traditional Catholics (25% of US Christians are Catholic) and American evangelicals (60%).

At the time of writing, this film is the twenty-fourth most popular film of all time. No other recent mainstream film has had so many column inches devoted to it.

MW: The film has become an event in the USA. One in ten have seen the film. In April, I discussed the film with a range of Catholic, Protestant and Historic Peace Church members across Ohio and Indiana. For many, viewing the film was a marker of Christian identity. I suspect this may have been the case in some UK Christian churches too, but things tend to play out in more muted ways here.

WRT: Mel Gibson has found a very important audience. We have to consider the fact that there are 159 million Christians in America. His film, untainted by biblical criticism, particularly appeals to an audience of evangelical Christians in America. They have been given a film that does not come with all the cynicism of the Hollywood production machine. It's a film for them, and allied with this group is the smaller but nevertheless influential group of pre-Vatican II Catholic traditionalists. These two markets are symbolized in the two great referees for it. Billy Graham on the one hand has come out and said that at the screening he wept. He said that here in this film is a lifetime of sermons in one movie. And then at the same time you have the Pope, claiming initially that this film was authentic.

PF: 'It is as it was.' The apparent papal endorsement, which was later denied, although it had already been widely used in interviews and publicity.

I think we are being naive. The film comes with a very shrewd Hollywood marketing strategy. Like George Stevens before him, Gibson's film was flagged up as a very personal project, something he felt he had to do. Both men had to invest their own capital in their projects. It is quite possible that Stevens' and Gibson's much vaunted costly commitment to their projects is PR spin to show their religious and spiritual commitment and, of course, their sincerity.

TA: I think it was a personal project. He made it for himself and people like him. It does seem to be the case that he was going to make the film come what may. Peter Malone, who thinks far better of the film than I do, says it's a religious home movie. This is the equivalent in a way of the Passion play, of the thing that happens in certain Italian villages on Good Friday night. Everybody gets together and they make a procession with icons and statues and so on, which gives the essence of what they think of as a Christian faith. Often, in those circumstances, it's full of semi-pagan influences, just as Gibson's is full of Hollywood influences.

EC: I found this statement from Icon's press release of the film, 2003: 'The partnership combines the expertise of Icon, the company formed by Mel Gibson, and Bruce Deady, which has launched a grassroots, faith-based marketing effort.'

PF: The effort was a phenomenal success.

WRT: Film is a medium that should be respectful of its audience. This is a film that is disrespectful to its *Jewish* audience, that is disrespectful to its *secular* audience – because it doesn't allow us to identify with any secular perspective – and that is also disrespectful to its mainstream *Christian* audience because it addresses the kind of concerns and theological perspectives of conservative evangelicals and traditionalist Catholics.

EC: It's the degree to which it is propaganda without the film-maker being aware of it that is disturbing to me. Watching *Triumph of the Will* recently I was reminded that Leni Riefenstahl, to her dying day, claimed it was a historical depiction of events 'as they were', when in fact it is a highly rhetorical, ideologically driven Nazi propaganda film that conveys a very unpleasant ideology. The same kind of historiographical naivety plagues Gibson's *The Passion of The Christ*.

Notes

1 Richard Corliss, 'The Goriest Story Ever Told', *Time* (1 March 2004), p. 68.

2 D. Van Biema, 'Why Did Jesus Die?', *Time* (12 April 2004), pp. 48–55.

3 Gustav Aulén, *Christus Victor*, London: SPCK, 1931.

4 Rev. 21.5; cf. Isa. 43.19.

5 *Intolerance* (D. W. Griffith, 1916), *King of Kings* (Cecil B. DeMille, 1927), *King of Kings* (Nicholas Ray, 1961), *Greatest Story Ever Told* (George Stevens, 1965), *Gospel according to St. Matthew* (Pier Paolo Pasolini, 1966), *Jesus of Nazareth* (Franco Zeffirelli, 1977), *Jesus Christ Superstar* (Norman Jewison, 1973), *Godspell* (David Greene, 1973), *Gospel of John* (Philip Saville, 2004).

6 *Celui Qui Doit Mourir* (Jules Dassin, 1956), *Monty Python's Life of Brian* (Terry Jones, 1979), *Je Vous Salue Marie* (Jean-Luc Godard, 1985), *Last Temptation of Christ* (Martin Scorsese, 1988), *Jesus of Montreal* (Denys Arcand, 1989).

7 Peter Bradshaw, 'Review of *The Passion of The Christ*', *The Guardian* (26 March 2004). See http://film.guardian.co.uk/

8 See D. Van Biema, 'Why It's So Bloody', *Time* (1 March 2004), p. 70.

9 Anne Catherine Emmerich, *The Dolorous Passion of Our Lord Jesus Christ*, London: Burns, Oates and Washbourne, 1923.

Bibliography

Aaron, David H., *Biblical Ambiguities: Metaphor, Semantics and Divine Imagery*, Leiden: Brill, 2001.

Aaron, Michelle, *The Body's Perilous Pleasures: Dangerous Desires and Contemporary Culture*, Edinburgh: Edinburgh University Press, 1999.

Ahlstrom, Sydney E., *A Religious History of the American People*, New Haven: Yale University Press, 1972.

Aichele, G., and T. Pippin (eds), *The Monstrous and the Unspeakable. The Bible as Fantastic Literature*, Playing the Texts, 1, Sheffield: Sheffield Academic Press, 1997.

— (eds), *Violence, Utopia, and the Kingdom of God*, London: Routledge, 1998.

Aichele, G., and R. Walsh (eds), *Screening Scripture: Intertextual Connections Between Scripture and Film*, Harrisburg, PA: Trinity Press International, 2002.

Alsford, M., *What If? Religious Themes in Science Fiction*, London: Darton, Longman & Todd, 2000.

Alter, R., *The Art of Biblical Narrative*, London: George Allen & Unwin, 1981.

Ambler, Eric, *Here Lies*, London: Weidenfeld and Nicholson, 1985.

Ambler, Eric, *The Mask of Dimitrios*, London: Macmillan, 1999.

Amit, Yairah, *The Book of Judges: The Art of Editing*, BIS, 38; Leiden: Brill, 1999.

Attridge, Derek (ed.), *Acts of Literature*, London: Routledge, 1992.

Augustine, *Confessions*, tr. Henry Chadwick, Oxford: OUP, 1991.

Aulén, G., *Christus Victor*, London: SPCK, 1931.

Babington, B., and P. W. Evans, *Biblical Epics. Sacred Narrative in the Hollywood Cinema*, Manchester: Manchester University Press, 1993.

Bal, Mieke, *Narratology*, 2nd edition, Toronto: University of Toronto Press, 1997.

Barclay, W., *The Lord's Supper,* London: SCM Press, 1967.

Barker, Martin, *From Antz to Titanic: Reinventing film analysis*, London: Pluto, 2000.

Barthes, Roland, *The Rustle of Language*, tr. Richard Howard, Berkeley and Los Angeles: University of California Press, 1986.

Baudrillard, Jean, *Simulacra and Simulation,* tr. Sheila Faria Glaser, Ann Arbor: University of Michigan Press, 1994.

Baugh, Lloyd (ed.), *Imaging the Divine: Jesus and Christ Figures in Films*, Kansas City: Sheed and Ward, 1997.

Baxter, John, *Buñuel*, London: Fourth Estate, 1994.

Benz, W., 'Anti-Semitism Research', in M. Goodman (ed.), *The Oxford Handbook of Jewish Studies*, Oxford: Oxford University Press, 2002, pp. 943–55.

Bergesen, Albert J., and Andrew M. Greeley, *God in the Movies: A Sociological Investigation*, London: Transaction, 2000.

Bergman, J., 'Laughter, the Best Medicine (St Peter joke)', *Reader's Digest*, April 2002.

Besserman, L., 'Judas Iscariot', in D. L. Jeffrey (ed.), *A Dictionary of Biblical Tradition in English Literature*, Grand Rapids, MI: Eerdmans, 1992, pp. 418–20.

Blake, R., *Afterimage: The Indelible Catholic Imagination of Six American Filmmakers*, Chicago: Loyola, 2000.

Boer, Roland, 'Non-Sense: *Total Recall*, Paul and the Possibility of Psychosis,' in G. Aichele and R. Walsh (eds), *Screening Scripture: Intertextual Connections Between Scripture and Film*, Harrisburg, PA: Trinity Press International, 2002, pp. 120–54.

Bolin, R., *Judges: A New Translation with Introduction and Commentary*, Anchor Bible, 6A, New York: Doubleday, 1975.

Borde, Raymond, and Étienne Chaumeton, 'Towards a Definition of *Film Noir*', in A. Silver and J. Ursini (eds), *Film Noir Reader*, New York: Limelight Editions, 1996, pp. 17–25.

Bordwell, David, *The Films of Carl-Theodor Dreyer*, Berkeley: University of California Press, 1981.

Bordwell, David, and Kristin Thompson, *Film Art: An Introduction*, 7th International edn, New York: McGraw-Hill, 2003.

Bowman, Richard G., 'Narrative Criticism: Human Purpose in Conflict with Divine Presence', in Gale A. Yee, *Judges and Method: New Approaches in Biblical Studies*, Minneapolis, MN: Fortress Press, 1995, pp. 17–44.

Boyer, Paul S. (ed.), *The Oxford Companion to United States History*, New York: Oxford University Press, 2001.

Bradshaw, P., Review of *The Passion of The Christ*, *Guardian* (26 March 2004). See http://film.guardian.co.uk.

Brandon, S. G. F., *Jesus and the Zealots. A Study of the Political Factor in Primitive Christianity*, Manchester and New York: Manchester University Press; Scribner, 1967.

Brettler, Marc, 'Never the Twain Shall Meet? The Ehud Story as History and Literature', *Hebrew Union College Annual* 42 (1991): 285–304.

Brown, R. E., K. P. Donfried and J. Reumann, *Peter in the New Testament*, London: Geoffrey Chapman, 1973.

Browne, D., 'Film, Movies, Meanings', in C. Marsh and G. W. Ortiz (eds), *Explorations in Theology and Film. Movies and Meaning*, Oxford: Blackwell, 1997, pp. 9–19.

Browne, Nick, 'Fearful A-Symmetries: Violence as History in *The Godfather* Films', in Nick Browne (ed.), *The Godfather Trilogy*, Cambridge Film Handbooks; Cambridge: Cambridge University Press, 2000, pp. 1–22.

Buchanan, G. W., 'Judas Iscariot', in G. W. Bromiley (ed.), *The International Standard Bible Encyclopedia*, Grand Rapids, MI: Eerdmans, 1982, pp. 1151–3.

Buhle, P., and Dave Wagner, *A Very Dangerous Citizen: Abraham Lincoln Polonsky and the Hollywood Left*, Berkeley: University of California Press, 2001.

Bukatman, Scott, *Blade Runner*, London: British Film Institute, 1997.

—*Matters of Gravity: Special Effects and Supermen in the 20th Century*, Durham, NC: Duke University Press, 2003.

Buñuel, Luis, *My Last Breath*, tr. Abigail Israel, London: Vintage, 1994.

Butler, I., *Religion in the Cinema*, The International Film Guide Series, New York: Barnes, 1969.

Callow, Simon, *Charles Laughton: A Difficult Actor*, London: Methuen, 1987.

Camon, Alessandro, '*The Godfather* and the Mythology of Mafia', in N. Browne (ed.), *The Godfather Trilogy*, Cambridge Film Handbooks; Cambridge: Cambridge University Press, 2000, pp. 57–75.

Campbell, Joseph S., *The Hero with a Thousand Faces*, New York: Meridian, 1956.

Campbell, Thomas, '*Declaration and Address of the Christian Association of Washington*', in Thomas H. Olbricht and Hans Rollmann (eds), *The Quest for Christian Unity, Peace, and Purity in Thomas Campbell's Declaration and Address: Text and Studies*, Lanham: Scarecrow, 2000.

Carr, Raymond (ed.), *Spain, A History*, Oxford: Oxford University Press, 2000.

Cawelti, John G., *The Six-Gun Mystique*, Bowling Green, OH: Bowling Green University Popular Press, 1973.

Chion, Michel, *Kubrick's Cinema Odyssey*, London: British Film Institute, 2001.

Christianson, Eric S., *A Time to Tell: Narrative Strategies in Ecclesiastes*, Sheffield: Sheffield Academic Press, 1998.

— 'A Fistful of Shekels: Scrutinizing Ehud's Entertaining Violence (Judges 3:12–30)', *Biblical Interpretation* 11.1 (2003): 53–78.

Cohan, Steven, and Ina Rae Hark (eds), *Screening the Male: Exploring Masculinities in Hollywood Cinema*, London and New York: Routledge, 1993.

Cohan, Steven, and Ina Rae Hark (eds), *Masked Men: Masculinity and the Movies in the Fifties*, Bloomington and Indianapolis: Indiana University Press, 1997.

Cook, Pam, and Mieke Bernink (eds), *The Cinema Book*, London: British Film Institute, 1999.

Corliss, R., 'The Goriest Story Ever Told', *Time* (1 March 2004), pp. 68–9.

Corrigan, T., *A Short Guide to Writing about Film*, The Short Guide Series, New York: HarperCollins College, 1994.

Cowie, Peter, *The Godfather Book*, Faber and Faber, 1997.

Cross, F. L., and E. A. Livingstone (eds), *The Oxford Dictionary of the Christian Church*, 3rd edn, Oxford: Oxford University Press, 1997.

Crossan, John Dominic, 'Hymn to a Savage God', in Kathleen E. Corley and Robert L. Webb (eds), *Jesus and Mel Gibson's* The Passion of The Christ: *The Film, the Gospels and the Claims of History*, London: Continuum, 2004, pp. 8–27.

Culler, Jonathan, *Framing the Sign: Criticism and Its Institutions*, Oxford: Blackwell, 1988.

Cullmann, O., *Peter. Disciple, Apostle, Martyr. A Historical and Theological Study*, The Library of History and Doctrine, London: SCM Press, 1953.

Cupitt, Don, *After God: The Future of Religion*, London: Weidenfeld & Nicolson, 1997.

Davies, M., 'Stereotyping the Other: The "Pharisees" in the Gospel according to Matthew', in J. C. Exum and S. D. Moore (eds), *Biblical Studies/Cultural*

Studies. The Third Sheffield Colloquium, Sheffield: Sheffield Academic Press, 1948, pp. 234–41.

Deacy, Christopher, *Screen Christologies. Redemption and the Medium of Film*, Cardiff: University of Wales Press, 2001.

De Concini, Barbara, 'Seduction by Visual Image', *The Journal of Religion and Film*, 2.3 (December 1998): Section 1.

Deleuze, Gilles, *The Logic of Sense*, tr. Mark Lester and Charles Stivale, New York: Columbia University Press, 1990.

— *Cinema 1: The Movement Image*, London: The Athlone Press, 1992.

Denby, David, 'The Two Godfathers' in N. Browne (ed.), *The Godfather Trilogy*, Cambridge Film Handbooks; Cambridge: Cambridge University Press, 2000, pp. 173–80.

Derrida, Jacques, 'This Strange Institution Called Literature', in Derek Attridge (ed.), *Acts of Literature*, London: Routledge, 1992.

Desjardins, Michel, 'Retrofitting Gnosticism: Philip K. Dick and Christian Origins', in G. Aichele and T. Pippin (eds), *Violence, Utopia, and the Kingdom of God*, London: Routledge, 1998, pp. 122–33.

Detweiler, R., 'Christ and the Christ Figure in American Fiction', in M. E. Marty and D. G. Peerman (eds), *New Theology No. 2*, New York: Macmillan, 1965, pp. 297–316.

Diaz-Plaja, Fernando, *The Spaniard and the Seven Deadly Sins*, London: Victor Gollancz, 1968.

Dick, Philip K., *Blade Runner*, New York: Ballantine Books, 1982. (Originally published in 1968 as *Do Androids Dream of Electronic Sheep?*)

Dika, Vera, 'The Representation of Ethnicity in *The Godfather*', in N. Browne (ed.), *The Godfather Trilogy*, Cambridge Film Handbooks; Cambridge: Cambridge University Press, 2000, pp. 76–108.

Dixon, Paul B., *Reversible Readings: Ambiguity in Four Modern Latin American Novels*, Tuscaloosa: University of Alabama Press, 1985.

Douglas, Mary, *Implicit Meanings*, London: Routledge and Kegan Paul, 1975.

Drazin, Charles, *In Search of The Third Man*, London: Methuen, 1999.

Dyer, Richard, 'Resistance through Charisma: Rita Hayworth and *Gilda*', in E. Ann Kaplan (ed.), *Women in Film Noir*, new edn; London: British Film Institute, 1998, pp. 115–29.

Dyer, Richard, *Stars*, London: British Film Institute, 1998.

Ebert, Roger, 'The Godfather', *The Chicago Sun Times*, 1999, *http://www.sun times.com/ebert/ebert_reviews/1999/10/god1028.html*.

Eichenberger, A., 'Approaches to Film Criticism' in J. R. May (ed.), *New Image of Religious Film*, Kansas City, MO: Sheed & Ward, 1997, pp. 3–16.

Eliade, Mircea, *The Sacred and the Profane: The Nature of Religion*, New York: Harcourt Brace Jovanovich, 1959.

Emmerich, Anne Catherine, *The Dolorous Passion of Our Lord Jesus Christ*, London: Burns, Oates and Washbourne, 1923.

Evens, P., *The Jew in American Cinema*, Bloomington, IN: Indiana University Press, 1984.

Exum, J. Cheryl, 'The Centre Cannot Hold: Thematic and Textual Instabilities in Judges', *Catholic Biblical Quarterly* 52.3 (1990): 410–31.
—*Plotted, Shot and Painted: Cultural Representations of Biblical Women*, Sheffield: Sheffield Academic Press, 1996.
Exum, J. Cheryl, and S. D. Moore (eds), *Biblical Studies/Cultural Studies. The Third Sheffield Colloquium*, Journal for the Study of the Old Testament Supplement Series 266, Gender, Culture, Theory 7; Sheffield: Sheffield Academic Press, 1998.

Fabry, H.-J., and M. Weinfeld, 'מִנְחָה *minḥâ*', *Theological Dictionary of the Old Testament*, VIII, pp. 407–21.
Falk, Quentin, *Travels in Greeneland*, 3rd edn, London: Reynolds & Hearn Ltd., 2000.
Farmer, D. H. (ed.), *The Oxford Dictionary of Saints*, Oxford: Oxford University Press, 1987.
Fenske, W., and B. Martin, *Brauchte Gott der Verräter? Die Gestalt des Judas in Theologie. Unterricht und Gottesdienst*, Dienst am Wort, 85, Göttingen: Vandenhoeck & Ruprecht, 2000.
Fernandez, Eleazar S., *Towards a Theology of Struggle*, Maryknoll: Orbis, 1994.
Finke, Laurie, 'Mystical Bodies and the Dialogics of Vision', in Ulrike Wiethaus (ed.), *Maps of Flesh and Light*, New York: Syracuse University Press, 1993.
Fisch, H., *The Dual Image. The Figure of the Jew in English and American Literature*, London: World Jewish Library, 1971.
Ford, David, *Self and Salvation*, Cambridge: Cambridge University Press, 1999.
Foucault, Michel, *Language, Counter-Memory, Practice*, tr. Donald F. Bouchard and Sherry Simon, Ithaca, NY: Cornell University Press, 1977.
Frank, Nino, 'A New Kind of Police Drama: The Criminal Adventure' (tr. A. Silver) in A. Silver and J. Ursini (eds), *Film Noir Reader 2*, New York: Limelight Editions, 1999, pp. 15–19.
Fraser, Ian, *Study Encounter No 39*, Geneva: World Council of Churches, 1975.
Fraser, P., *Images of the Passion. The Sacramental Mode in Film*, Trowbridge, Wilts: Flicks Books, 1998.
Fraser, P., N. Fraser, and V. Edwin, *ReViewing the Movies. A Christian Response to Contemporary Film*, Wheaton: Crossway Books, 2000.
Frayling, Christopher, *Sergio Leone*, London: Faber and Faber, 2000.
—*Spaghetti Westerns: Cowboys and Europeans from Karl May to Sergio Leone*, London: I.B. Tauris, rev. edn, 2000 [1981].
French, Philip, *Westerns: Aspects of a Movie Genre*, London: Secker and Warburg/British Film Institute, 1973.
—Review of a re-release of *The Third Man*, London: *The Observer*, 18 July 1999.
Friedman, L. D., *Hollywood's Image of the Jew*, New York: Frederick Ungar, 1982.
—*The Jewish Image in American Film*, New Jersey, NJ: Citadel Press, 1987.

Gabler, N., *An Empire of their Own: How the Jews Invented Hollywood*, London: Allen, 1989.
Garcia Mainar, Luis, *Narrative and Stylistic Patterns in the Films of Stanley Kubrick*, London: Camden House, 1999.

Gardner, Jared, 'Covered Wagons and Decalogues: Paramount's Myth of Origins,' *Yale Journal of Criticism*, 13.2 (Fall 2000): 361–89.

Garrett, G., 'The American West and the American Western: Printing the Legend', *Journal of American Culture*, 14 (1991): 99–105.

Geertz, Clifford, *The Interpretation of Cultures*, New York: Basic Books, 1973.

Gellrich, Michelle, *Tragedy and Theory: The Problem of Conflict Since Aristotle*, Princeton: Princeton University Press, 1988.

Georges, N., 'Peter', in C. B. Pallen and J. J. Wynne (eds), *The New Catholic Dictionary*, New York: Universal Knowledge Foundation, 1929, pp. 749–50.

Giannetti, Louis, *Understanding Movies*, New Jersey: Prentice Hall, 2004.

Gish, Lillian, *The Movies, Mr Griffith and Me*, London: W. H. Allen, 1969.

Gledhill, Christine, and Linda Williams (eds), *Reinventing Film Studies*, London: Arnold, 2000.

Godawa, B., *Hollywood Worldviews. Watching Films with Wisdom and Discernment*, Downers Grove, IL: InterVarsity, 2002.

Gordon, A., 'J is for Jewish. Sight and Sound A–Z of Cinema', *Sight and Sound*, 7 (1997), pp. 28–32.

Graham, D. J., 'The Uses of Film in Theology', in Clive Marsh and Gaye Ortiz, (eds) *Explorations in Theology and Film. Movies and Meaning*, Oxford: Blackwell, 1997, pp. 35–43.

Greeley, A. M., 'Babette's Feast of Love: Symbols Subtle but Patent', in A. Bergesen and A. M. Greeley (eds), *God in the Movies: A Sociological Investigation*, New Brunswick, NJ: Transaction Publishers, 2000, pp. 49–53.

Greene, Graham, *Collected Essays*, London: Penguin Books, 1970.

— *A Sort of Life*, London: Bodley Head, 1971.

— *The Third Man* and *The Fallen Idol*, Harmondsworth: Penguin Books, 1975.

— *Ways of Escape*, Bodley Head: London, 1980.

Greene, Graham and Carol Reed, *The Third Man: A Film by Graham Greene and Carol Reed*, London: Lorrimer, 1969.

Gunning, Tom, ' "Animated Pictures": tales of cinema's forgotten future, after 100 years of film', in Christine Gledhill and Linda Williams (eds) *Reinventing Film Studies*, London: Arnold, 2000, pp. 316–31.

Hall, J. (ed.), *Dictionary of Subjects and Symbols in Art*, London: John Murray, 1996.

Hall, Mordaunt, 'Poignant French Film – Maria Falconetti Gives Unequaled Performance as Jeanne d'Arc', *New York Times*, 31 March 1929, s.8, p. 7.

Halpern, B., *The First Historians: The Hebrew Bible and History*, University Park, PA: Pennsylvania State University Press, 1996 [1988].

Hamlin, E.J., *Judges: At Risk in the Promised Land*, ITC; Grand Rapids, MI: Eerdmans, 1990.

Hanna, Martha, 'Iconology and Ideology: Images of Joan of Arc in the Idiom of the *Action française*, 1908–1931', *French Historical Studies*, 14.2 (1985): 215–39.

Harrison, Peter, *Religion and the Religions of the English Enlightenment*, Cambridge: Cambridge University Press, 1990.

Hatch, Nathan O., *The Democratization of American Christianity*, New Haven: Yale University Press, 1989.

Hayles, N. Katherine, *How We Became Posthuman: Virtual Bodies in Cybernetics, Literature, and Informatics*, Chicago: University of Chicago Press, 1999.

Heston, C., *In the Arena. The Autobiography*, London: HarperCollins, 1995.

Hiebert, D. E., 'Peter', in J. D. Douglas and M. C. Tenney (eds), *The New International Dictionary of the Bible. Pictorial Edition*, Basingstoke: Marshall Pickering, 1987, pp. 771–3.

Higashi, Sumiko, *Cecil B. DeMille and American Culture: The Silent Era*, Berkeley, Los Angeles and London: University of California Press, 1994.

Higham, Charles, *Charles Laughton: An Intimate Biography*, London: W. H. Allen, 1976.

Hochman, S. (ed.), *A Library of Film Criticism. American Film Directors. With Filmographies and Index of Critics and Films*, New York: Ungar, 1974.

Houlden, J. L., 'Peter', in R. J. Coggins and J. L. Houlden (eds), *A Dictionary of Biblical Interpretation*, London: SCM Press and Philadelphia, PA: Trinity Press International, 1990, pp. 532–4.

Hurley, N. P., 'Cinematic Transformations of Jesus', in J. R. May and M. S. Bird (eds), *Religion in Film*, Knoxville: University of Tennessee Press, 1982, pp. 61–78.

Hyman, Gavin, 'The Study of Religion and the Return of Theology', *Journal of the American Academy of Religion* 72/1 (2004): 195–219.

Jackson, Kevin (ed.), *Schrader on Schrader and Other Writings*, rev. edn, London: Faber and Faber, 2004 [1990].

James, Nick, 'Hell in Jerusalem', *Sight & Sound* 14/4 (April 2004): 62–3.

Jameson, Fredric, *Postmodernism, or the Cultural Logic of Late Capitalism*, Durham, NC: Duke University Press, 1991.

Jasper, David, 'On Systematizing the Unsystematic', in C. Marsh and G. W. Ortiz (eds), *Explorations in Theology and Film: Movies and Meaning*, Oxford: Blackwell, 1997, pp. 235–44.

Jeffrey, D. L., 'Passover', in D. L. Jeffrey (ed.), *A Dictionary of Biblical Tradition in English Literature*, Grand Rapids, MI: Eerdmans, 1992, p. 587.

—'Peter', in D. L. Jeffrey (ed.), *A Dictionary of Biblical Tradition in English Literature*, Grand Rapids, MI: Eerdmans, 1992, pp. 603–8.

Jeffrey, D. L., and I. H. Marshall, 'Eucharist', in D. L. Jeffrey (ed.), *A Dictionary of Biblical Tradition in English Literature*, Grand Rapids, MI: Eerdmans, 1992, pp. 243–50.

Jeremias, J., *The Eucharistic Words of Jesus*, Oxford: Blackwell, 1955.

—'pasca', in G. Kittel (ed.), *Theological Dictionary of the New Testament*, Grand Rapids, MI: Eerdmans, 1967, pp. 896–904.

Jewett, R., *Saint Paul at the Movies. The Apostle's Dialogue with American Culture*, Louisville, KY: Westminster John Knox, 1993.

—*St Paul Returns To The Movies. Triumph over Shame*, Grand Rapids, MI: Eerdmans, 1999.

Johnson, Vida T., and Graham Petrie, *The Films of Andrei Tarkovsky: A Visual Fugue*, Bloomington, IN: Indiana University Press, 1994.

Johnston, Robert K., *Reel Spirituality: Theology and Film in Dialogue*, Grand Rapids: Baker Academic, 2000.

Jull, Tom A., 'מקרה in Judges 3: A Scatological Reading', *Journal for the Study of the Old Testament*, 81 (1998): 63–75.

Katz, E., 'Theory, Film', in Ephraim Katz (ed.), *The Macmillan International Film Encyclopedia*, London: HarperCollins, 1994, pp. 1348–9.

— 'Nickelodeon', in Ephraim Katz (ed.), *The Macmillan International Film Encyclopedia*, London: HarperCollins, 1994, p. 1013.

Katz, Ephraim (ed.), *The Macmillan International Film Encyclopedia*, 2nd edn, London: HarperCollins, 1994.

Kelly, Richard, *The Name of this Book is Dogme 95*, London: Faber & Faber, 2000.

Kepler, T. S., 'Judas Iscariot', in F. C. Grant and H. H. Rowley (eds), *Dictionary of the Bible*, Edinburgh: T. & T. Clark, 1965, pp. 535–6.

Kerman, Judith B. (ed.), *Retrofitting Blade Runner*, Bowling Green, OH: Bowling Green State University Popular Press, 1991.

Kermode, Mark, 'Drenched in the Blood of Christ', *The Observer*, 29 February 2004.

— *The Exorcist*, London: British Film Institute, 1998 [1997].

King, Geoff, *New Hollywood Cinema: An Introduction*, London: I.B. Tauris, 2002.

Kinnard, R. and Davis, T., *Divine Images. A History of Jesus on the Screen*, New York: Citadel Press, 1992.

Kirgo, Julie and A. Silver, 'In a Lonely Place (1950)', in A. Silver and E. Ward (eds), *Film Noir: An Encyclopedic Reference to the American Style*, rev. 3rd edn; Woodstock, NY: The Overlook Press, 1992, pp. 144–46.

Kitzberger, I. R. (ed.), *Transformative Encounters. Jesus and Women Reviewed*, Leiden: Brill, 2000.

Klassen, W., *Judas. Betrayer or Friend of Jesus?*, London: SCM Press, 1996.

Klein, Lillian R., *The Triumph of Irony in the Book of Judges*, JSOTSup, 68; Sheffield: Almond Press, 1988.

Koosed, J. L., and T. Linafelt, ' "How the West Was Not One": Delilah Deconstructs the Western', *Semeia*, 74 (1996): 167–81.

Kort, Wesley, *Narrative Elements and Religious Meaning*, Philadelphia: Fortress Press.

Kraeling, E. G., 'Difficulties in the Story of Ehud', *Journal of Biblical Literature*, 54 (1935): 205–10.

Kreitzer, L. J., *The New Testament in Fiction and Film. On Reversing the Hermeneutical Flow*, The Biblical Seminar, 17, Sheffield: Sheffield Academic Press, 1993.

— *The Old Testament in Fiction and Film. On Reversing the Hermeneutical Flow*, The Biblical Seminar 24, Sheffield: Sheffield University Press, 1994.

— *Pauline Images in Fiction and Film. On Reversing the Hermeneutical Flow*, The Biblical Seminar, 61, Sheffield: Sheffield Academic Press, 1999.

— *Gospel Images in Fiction and Film. On Reversing the Hermeneutical Flow*, The Biblical Seminar, 84, Sheffield: Sheffield Academic Press, 2002.

Kuhn Annette (ed.), *Alien Zone II: The Spaces of Science Fiction Cinema*, London: Routledge, 2000.

Kutsko, J., 'Eglon', in *Anchor Bible Dictionary* (CD-ROM edition).

Landon, Brooks, 'Diegetic or Digital? The Convergence of Science Fiction literature and Science-fiction film in Hypermedia', in Annette Kuhn (ed.), *Alien Zone II: The Spaces of Science Fiction Cinema,* London: Routledge, 2000, pp. 31–49.

Landres, J. Shawn, and Michael Berenbaum (eds), *After the Passion is Gone: American Religious Consequences,* Lanham, MD: Alta Mira Press, 2004.

Lash, Nicholas, *Holiness, Speech and Silence: Reflections on the Question of God,* Aldershot: Ashgate, 2004.

Lawrence, John Shelton and Jewett Robert, *The Myth of the American Superhero,* Grand Rapids: Eerdmans, 2003.

Le Fanu, Mark 'Bewitched,' *Sight and Sound* 13.7 (2003): 30–322.

Lenihan, John H., *Showdown: Confronting Modern America in the Western Film,* Chicago, IL: University of Illinois Press, 1980.

Levine, Donald N., *The Flight from Ambiguity: Essays in Social and Cultural Theory,* Chicago: University of Chicago Press, 1985.

Lindvall, Terry, 'Religion and Film Part 1: History and Cinema', *Communication Research Trends* 23/4 (2004): 1–44.

Lothe, J., *Narrative in Fiction and Film. An Introduction,* Oxford: Oxford University Press, 2000.

Loughlin, Gerard, *Alien Sex: The Body and Desire in Cinema and Theology,* Oxford: Blackwell, 2004.

— 'Looking: The Ethics of Seeing in Church and Cinema', in M. K. Nation and S. Wells (eds), *Faithfulness and Fortitude: In Conversation with the Theological Ethics of Stanley Hauerwas,* Edinburgh: T & T Clark, 2000, pp. 257–85.

— 'The University Without Question: John Henry Newman and Jacques Derrida on Faith in the University', in Jeff Astley, Peter Francis, John Sullivan and Andrew Walker (eds), *The Idea of a Christian University: Essays in Theology and Higher Education,* Carlisle: Paternoster Press, 2005.

Louvish, S., 'Burning Crosses', *Sight and Sound,* 10 (2000), pp. 12–13.

Lyons, Arthur, *Death on the Cheap: The Lost B Movies of Film Noir,* New York: Da Capo Press, 2000.

Lyotard, Jean-François, *The Postmodern Condition: A Report on Knowledge,* tr. Geoff Bennington and Brian Massumi, Minneapolis: University of Minnesota Press, 1984.

Maccoby, H., *Judas Iscariot and the Myth of Jewish Evil,* New York: Free Press, 1992.

MacDonald, Paul, *The Star System,* London: Wallflower, 2000.

MacGregor, G. (ed.), *The Everyman Dictionary of Religion and Philosophy,* London: Dent, 1990.

MacIntyre, A., 'Existentialism', in P. Edwards (ed.), *The Encyclopedia of Philosophy,* Macmillan, 1967, pp. 147–59.

MacKinnon, Kenneth, 'After Mulvey: Male Erotic Objectification', in Michelle Aaron (ed.), *The Body's Perilous Pleasures: Dangerous Desires and Contemporary Culture,* Edinburgh: Edinburgh University Press, 1999, pp. 13–29.

Maher, I., *Faith and Film. Close Encounters of an Evangelistic Kind,* Cambridge: Grove Books Ltd, 2002.

Mainar, Luis Garcia, *Narrative and Stylistic Patterns in the Films of Stanley Kubrick,* London: Camden House, 1999.

Maisto, M. C., 'Cinematic Communion? *Babette's Feast*, Transcendental Style, and Interdisciplinarity', in S. B. Plate and D. Jasper (eds), *Imag(in)ing Otherness. Filmic Visions of Living Together*, Atlanta, GA: Scholars Press, 1999, pp. 83–98.

Malone, P., *Movie Christs and Antichrists*, New York: Crossroad, 1990.

—'Jesus on our Screens', in J. R. May (ed.), *New Image of Religious Film*, Kansas City, MO: Sheed & Ward, 1997, pp. 57–71.

—'*Edward Scissorhands*: Christology from a Suburban Fairy-tale', in C. Marsh and G. W. Ortiz (eds), *Explorations in Theology in Film*, Oxford: Blackwell, 1997, pp. 73–86.

Malpezzi, Frances M. and William M. Clements, 'The Passion of Joan of Arc (La Passion de Jeanne d'Arc)', in Frank N. Magill (ed.), *Magill's Survey of Cinema: Silent Films Volume 2*, Epping: Bowker Publishing Company, 1982, pp. 854–7.

Maltby, Richard, 'The Spectacle of Criminality', in J. David Slocum (ed.), *Violence and American Cinema*, AFI Film Readers, Routledge, 2001, pp. 117–52.

Man, Glenn, 'Ideology and Genre in *The Godfather* Films', in N. Browne (ed.), *The Godfather Trilogy*, Cambridge Film Handbooks; Cambridge: Cambridge University Press, 2000, pp. 109–32.

Margolis, Nadia, 'Trial by Passion: Philology, Film and Ideology in the Portrayal of Joan of Arc (1900–1930)', *Journal of Medieval and Early Modern Studies*, 27.3 (1997): 445–93.

Marsh, Clive, 'Films and Theologies of Culture', in C. Marsh and G. W. Ortiz (eds), *Explorations in Theology and Film*, Oxford: Blackwell, 1997, pp. 21–34.

—'Did You Say "Grace"?: Eating in Community in *Babette's Feast*', in C. Marsh and G. W. Ortiz (eds), *Explorations in Theology and Film. Movies and Meaning*, Oxford: Blackwell, 1997, pp. 207–18.

—*Cinema and Sentiment: Film's Challenge to Theology*, Carlisle: Paternoster, 2004.

Marsh, Clive and Gaye Ortiz (eds), *Explorations in Theology and Film*, Oxford: Blackwell, 1997.

Martin, Joel W., and Conrad E. Ostwalt Jnr (eds), *Screening the Sacred: Religion, Myth and Ideology in Popular American Film*, Oxford: Westview Press, 1995.

Martin, R. P., 'Peter, Apostle', in W. Gentz (ed.), *The Dictionary of Bible and Religion*, Nashville, TN: Abingdon, 1986, pp. 803–5.

Martin, T. M., *Images and the Imageless. A Study in Religious Consciousness and Film*, Lewisburg, London and Toronto: Bucknell University Press; Associated University Presses, 1991.

Marty, Joseph, 'Toward a theological interpretation and reading of film: incarnation of the Word of God – relation, image, word', in John R. May (ed.), *New Image of Religious Film*, Kansas City: Sheed and Ward, 1997, pp. 141ff.

Matter, E. Ann, 'Internal Maps of an Eternal External', in Ulrike Wiethaus (ed.), *Maps of Flesh and Light*, New York: Syracuse University Press, 1993.

May, J. R. (ed.), *Image and Likeness: Religious Visions in American Film Classics*, Isaac Hecker Studies in Religion and American Culture; New York: Paulist, 1992.

—*New Image of Religious Film*, Kansas City: Sheed and Ward, 1997.

McBrien, Richard P. (ed.), *The HarperCollins Encyclopedia of Catholicism*, New York: HarperCollins, 1995.

McCaffery, Larry (ed.), *Storming the Reality Studio*, Durham, NC: Duke University Press, 1991.

McGilliagan, Patrick, *Clint – The Life and Legend*, London: Harper Collins 1999.

McLuhan, Marshall (with Quentin Fiore), *The Medium is the Massage*, New York: Bantam, 1967.

McKenzie, J. L., *The World of the Judges*, London: Geoffrey Chapman, 1967.

McNulty, E., *Praying the Movies. Daily Meditations from Classic Films*, Louisville, KY: Geneva, 2001.

Metford, J. C. J. (ed.), *Dictionary of Christian Lore and Legend*, London: Thames & Hudson, 1983.

Metz, Christopher, *Film Language: A Semiotics of the Cinema*, reprint edn; Chicago: University of Chicago Press, 1990.

Miles, M. R., *Seeing and Believing. Religion and Values in the Movies*, Boston, MA: Beacon, 1996.

Mills, Michael, 'Narrative Innovations in Film Noir', (http://www.modern times.com/palace/inv_noir.htm).

— 'Two from Siodmak: The Killers, Criss Cross' (http://www.moderntimes.com/palace/kc.htm).

Milne, Tom, 'Darkness and Light: Carl Theodor Dreyer', *Sight and Sound*, 34.4 (1965): pp. 167–72.

Mitchell, Lee Clark, *Westerns – Making the Man in Fiction and Film*, Chicago: University of Chicago Press, 1996.

— 'Violence in the Film Western', in J. David Slocum (ed.), *Violence and American Cinema*, AFI Film Readers; New York: Routledge, 2001, pp. 176–91.

Monaco, James, *How to Read a Film*, 3rd edn, Oxford and New York: Oxford University Press, 2000 [1981].

Mulvey, Laura, 'Visual Pleasure and Narrative Cinema', *Screen*, 16.3 (1975): 6–18; reprinted in Mandy Merck (ed.), *The Sexual Subject: A Screen Reader in Sexuality*, London and New York: Routledge, 1992, pp. 22–34.

— 'The Innovators 1920–30: Now you has Jazz', *Sight and Sound*, 9 (1999): 16–18.

Nadel, Alan, 'God's Law and the Widescreen: *The Ten Commandments* as Cold War Epic,' *Proceedings of the Modern Language Association*, 108.3 (May 1993): 415–30.

Naremore, James, *More Than Night: Film Noir in Its Contexts*, Berkeley: University of California Press, 1998.

Nash, Mark, *Dreyer*, London: British Film Institute, 1977.

— 'Joan Complete: A Dreyer Discovery', *Sight and Sound*, 54.3 (1985): 157–8.

Neale, Steve, 'Masculinity as Spectacle: reflections on men and mainstream cinema', *Screen* 24, 6 (1983); reprinted in Steven Cohan and Ina Rae Hark (eds), *Screening the Male: Exploring Masculinities in Hollywood Cinema*, London and New York: Routledge, 1993, pp. 9–20.

— *Genre and Hollywood*, London: Routledge, 2000.

Nelson, Thomas Allen, *Kubrick: Inside a Film Artist's Maze*, Bloomington: Indiana University Press, 1982.

Newsom, C., 'Women and the Discourse of Patriarchal Wisdom: A Study of

Proverbs 1—9', in P. L. Day (ed.), *Gender and Difference in Ancient Israel*, Fortress Press, 1989, pp. 142–60.

Niditch, Susan, *War in the Hebrew Bible: A Study in the Ethics of Violence*, Oxford: Oxford University Press, 1993.

Niebuhr, H. Richard, *Christ and Culture*, London: Faber and Faber, 1952.

Nietzsche, Friedrich, *The Gay Science*, tr. Walter Kaufmann, New York: Random House, 1974.

Northcott, Michael, 'Spirituality in the Media Context', in Derek C. Weber (ed.), *Discerning Images: The Media and Theological Education*, Edinburgh: University of Edinburgh Press, 1991.

Olbricht, Thomas H. and Hans Rollmann (eds), *The Quest for Christian Unity, Peace, and Purity in Thomas Campbell's Declaration and Address: Text and Studies*, Lanham: Scarecrow, 2000.

Ostwalt, C. E., 'Hollywood and Armageddon: Apocalyptic Themes in Recent Cinematic Presentation', in J. W. Martin and C. E. Ostwalt (eds), *Screening the Sacred. Religion, Myth, and Ideology in Popular American Film*, Oxford: Westview Press, 1997, pp. 55–71.

Otto, Rudolph, *The Idea of the Holy: An Inquiry into the Non-Rational Factor in the Idea of the Divine and Its Relation to the Rational*, London: Oxford University Press, 1950.

Pajaczkowska, C., and B. Curtis, 'Assimilation, Entertainment and the Hollywood Solution', in L. Nochlin and T. Garb (eds), *The Jew in the Text. Modernity and the Construction of Identity*, London: Thames & Hudson, 1995, pp. 238–52.

Pattie, D., 'Mobbed Up: The Sopranos and the Modern Gangster Film', in D. Lavery (ed.), *This Thing of Ours: Investigating The Sopranos*, New York: Columbia University Press, 2002, pp. 135–45.

Peoples, David Webb, *Unforgiven – Screenplay*. www.man-with-no-name.com.

Perkins, P., *Peter. Apostle for the Whole Church*, Studies on Personalities of the New Testament, Edinburgh: T. & T. Clark, 2000.

Phillips, Gene D., *Stanley Kubrick: A Film Odyssey*, London: Popular Library, 1977.

Pinsky, Mark I., *The Gospel According to the Simpsons: The Spiritual Life of the World's Most Animated Family*, Louisville: Westminster John Knox, 2001.

Pipolo, Tony, 'The spectre of Joan of Arc: Textual Variations in the Key Prints of Carl Dreyer's Film', *Film History*, 2.4 (1988): 301–24.

Pippin, T., 'Of Gods and Demons. Blood Sacrifice and Eternal Life in *Dracula* and the Apocalypse of John', in G. Aichele and R. Walsh (eds), *Screening Scripture. Intertextual Connections Between Scripture and Film*, Harrisburg, PA: Trinity Press International, 2002, pp. 24–41.

Plate, S. B. and D. Jasper, (eds), *Imag(in)ing Otherness. Filmic Visions of Living Together*, American Academy of Religion Cultural Criticism Series, 7; Atlanta, GA: Scholars Press, 1999.

Porfirio, Robert, '*The Killers*: Expressiveness of Sound and Image in *Film Noir*', in A. Silver and J. Ursini (eds), *Film Noir Reader 2*, New York: Limelight Editions, 1999, pp. 177–87.

Porfirio, Robert, 'No Way Out: Existential Motifs in the *Film Noir*', in A. Silver and J. Ursini (eds), *Film Noir Reader*, New York: Limelight Editions, 1996, pp. 77–93.

Postman, Neil, *Amusing Ourselves to Death*, London: Methuen, 1985.

Potter, Philip, *Life in All Its Fullness*, Geneva: World Council of Churches, 1981.

Prince, S., 'Tom Horn: Dialectics of Power and Violence in the Old West', *Journal of Popular Culture* 22 (1988): 119–29.

— *Classical Film Violence: Designing and Regulating Brutality in Hollywood Cinema, 1930–1968*, New Jersey: Rutgers University Press, 2003.

Pulzer, P., 'Antisemitism', in W. Laqueur (ed.), *The Holocaust Encyclopedia*, New Haven and London: Yale University Press, 2001, pp. 16–26.

Quinlan, D., *The Illustrated Guide to Film Directors*, London: Batsford, 1983.

Rebello, Stephen, *Alfred Hitchcock and the Making of Psycho*, London: Marion Boyars, 1990.

Richter, Philip, and Leslie J. Francis, *Gone But Not Forgotten*, London: Darton, Longman & Todd, 1998.

Roncace, M., 'Paradoxical Protagonists: *Sling Blade*'s Karl and Jesus Christ', in Aichele and Walsh (eds), *Screening Scripture: Intertextual Connections Between Scripture and Film*, Harrisburg, PA: Trinity Press International, 2002, pp. 279–300.

Rylaarsdam, J. C., 'Passover and Feast of Unleavened Bread', in G. A. Buttrick (ed.), *The Interpreter's Dictionary of the Bible*, New York and Nashville: Abingdon, 1962, pp. 663–8.

Sacks, J., *The Chief Rabbi's Haggadah*, London: HarperCollins. 2003.

Sammon, Paul M., *Future Noir: The Making of* Blade Runner, New York: Harper Collins, 1996.

Sanders, T., *Celluloid Saints. Images of Sanctity in Film*, Macon, GA: Mercer University Press, 2002.

Saunders, John, *The Western Genre*, London: Wallflower, 2001.

Sartre, Jean-Paul, *Being and Nothingness: An Essay on Phenomenlogical Ontology*, tr. Hazel E. Barnes, London: Methuen, 1958.

— *Nausea*, tr. Lloyd Alexander, New York: New Directions, 1964.

Schrader, Paul, *Transcendental Style in Film: Ozu, Bresson, and Dreyer*, Berkeley: University of California Press, 1972.

— 'Notes on *Film Noir*', in A. Silver and J. Ursini (eds), *Film Noir Reader*, New York: Limelight Editions, 1996, pp. 53–63.

Schwarz, C., G. Davidson, A. Seaton, and V. Tebbit (eds), *Chambers English Dictionary*, Cambridge: Chambers, 1988.

Scorsese, Martin, and Michael Henry Wilson, *A Personal Journey with Martin Scorsese Through American Movies*, London: Faber and Faber, 1997.

Scott, B. B., *Hollywood Dreams and Biblical Stories*, Minneapolis, MN: Augsburg Fortress, 1994.

Sheen, Erica '*The Ten Commandments* Meets *The Prince of Egypt*: Biblical Adaptations and Global Politics in the 1990s', *Polygraph* 12 (2000): 85–99.

Shelden, Michael, *Graham Greene: The Man Within*, London: William Heinemann, 1994.

Shepherd, M. H., 'Lord's Supper', in G. A. Buttrick (ed.), *The Interpreter's Dictionary of the Bible*, New York and Nashville: Abingdon Press, 1962, pp. 158–62.

Singer, C., 'Films, US, Jews in', in G. Abramson (ed.), *The Blackwell Companion to Jewish Culture. From the Eighteenth Century to the Present*, Oxford: Blackwell, 1989, pp. 227–90.

Skoller, Donald (ed.), *Dreyer in Double Reflection. Translation of Carl Th. Dreyer's Writings about the Film*, New York: E. P. Dutton and Co., 1973.

Smith, Henry Nash, *Virgin Land: The American West as Symbol and Myth*, Cambridge: Harvard University Press, 1950.

Smith, Jeff, 'Careening Through Kubrick's Space', *Chicago Review*, 33.1 (Summer 1981): 62–73.

Smith, Wilfred Cantwell, *The Meaning and End of Religion*, London: SPCK, 1978.

Soggin, J. A., *Judges: A Commentary*, OTL; SCM Press, 2nd edn, 1987.

Spicer, Andrew, *Film Noir*, Inside Film; Harlow: Longman, 2002.

Stack, O. (ed.), *Pasolini on Pasolini: Interviews with Oswald Stack*, The Cinema One Series 11, London: Thames & Hudson, 1969.

Stam, R., *Film Theory. An Introduction*, Oxford: Blackwell, 2000.

Steiner, Rudolf, *Mysticism at the Dawn of the Modern Age*, New York: Garber Communications, 1996.

Stern, R. C., C. N. Jefford, and G. Debona, *Savior on the Silver Screen*, New York and Mahwah, NJ: Paulist, 1999.

Sternberg, Meir, *The Poetics of Biblical Narrative: Ideological Literature and the Drama of Reading*, Bloomington, IN: Indiana University Press, 1987.

Stone, B. P., *Faith and Film. Theological Themes at the Cinema*, St Louis, MI: Chalice, 2000.

Stone, Barton Warren, 'A Short History of the Life of Barton W. Stone Written by Himself', in Rhodes Thompson (ed.), *Voices from Cane Ridge*, St Louis: Bethany Press, 1954.

Sweetman, Will, '"Hinduism" and the History of "Religion": Protestant Presuppositions in the Critique of the Concept of Hinduism', *Method and Theory in the Study of Religion* 15 (2003): 329–53.

Tatum, W. B., *Jesus at the Movies: A Guide to the First Hundred Years*, Santa Rosa, CA: Polebridge, 1997.

Tarkovsky, Andrei, *Sculpting in Time: Reflections on the Cinema*, tr. Kitty Hunter-Blair, Austin, TX: University of Texas Press, 1996 [1986].

Taylor, Gordon *Companion to the Song Book of the Salvation Army*, London: International Headquarters of the Salvation Army, 1989.

Telford, W. R., *The Theology of the Gospel of Mark*, New Testament Theology; Cambridge, UK and New York: Cambridge University Press, 1999.

— 'The New Testament in Fiction and Film: A Biblical Scholar's Perspective', in J. G. Davies, G. Harvey and W. Watson (eds), *Words Remembered, Texts Renewed. Essays in Honour of J. F. A. Sawyer*, Sheffield: Sheffield Academic Press, 1995, pp. 360–94.

— 'Jesus Christ Movie-Star: The Depiction of Jesus in the Cinema', in C. Marsh and G. Ortiz (eds), *Explorations in Theology and Film. Movies and Meaning*, Oxford: Blackwell, 1997, pp. 115–39.

— 'Jesus and Women in Fiction and Film', in I. R. Kitzberger (ed.), *Transformative Encounters. Jesus and Women Reviewed*, Leiden: Brill, 2000, pp. 353–91.

— 'Religion, the Bible and Theology in Recent Films (1993–99)', *Epworth Review*, 27 (2000), pp. 31–40.

— 'Searching for Jesus: Recognizing or Imagining Christ-Figures in the Movies' (unpublished paper given at the St Deiniol's Theology and Film conference, April, 2004).

Thomas, Hugh, *The Spanish Civil War*, Harmondsworth: Penguin Books, 1977.

Thomson, D., *A Biographical Dictionary of Film*, London: Deutsch, 1994.

Tillich, Paul, *The Shaking of the Foundations*, New York: Charles Scribner's, 1948.

— 'The Nature of Religious Language', in *Theology of Culture*, Oxford: Oxford University Press, 1959.

— 'On the Idea of a Theology of Culture', in *What is Religion?* tr. James L. Adams, New York: Harper and Row, 1969.

— *Systematic Theology 3: Life and the Spirit; History and the Kingdom of God*, London: SCM Press, 1997.

Tinkcomm, Matthew, and Amy Villarejo, 'Introduction', in Matthew Tinkcomm and Amy Villarejo (eds), *Keyframes: Popular Cinema and Cultural Studies*, London: Routledge, 2001, pp. 1–29.

Tompkins, J., 'Language and Landscape: An Ontology for the Western', *Art Forum* 28 (1990): 94–9.

— *West of Everything: The Inner Life of Westerns*, Oxford: Oxford University Press, 1992.

Tookey, Christopher, *The Critics' Film Guide*, London: Boxtree, 1994.

Tooze, Andrew G. 'Moses and Reel exodus,' *Journal of Religion and Film*, 7.1 (April 2003), 51 pars; http://avalon.unomaha.edu/jrf/Vol7No1/MosesExodus. htm, paragraph 58.

Turner, Frederick Jackson, *The Frontier in American History*, New York: Dover, 1996.

Tuska, Jon, *The Filming of the West*, Garden City, NY: Doubleday and Company, 1976.

Tybjerg, Casper, 'Dreyer and the National Film in Denmark', *Film History*, 13.1 (2001): 23–36.

Tyler, Parker, *Classics of the Foreign Film*, London: Spring Books, 1966.

Van Biema, D., 'Why Did Jesus Die?', *Time* (12 April 2004), pp. 48–55.

— 'Why It's So Bloody', *Time* (1 March 2004), p. 70.

Vernet, Marc, 'Wings of the Desert; or, The Invisible Superimpositions', *Velvet Light Trap*, 28 (Fall 1991): 65–72.

Walker, J. (ed.), *Halliwell's Film and Video Guide*, London: HarperCollins, 2000.

— (ed.), *Halliwell's Who's Who in the Movies*, London: HarperCollins, 2001.

Walsh, J., *The Bones of St. Peter. The Fascinating Account of the Search for the Apostle's Body*, London: Victor Gollancz, 1983.

Walsh, M., *An Illustrated History of the Popes. Saint Peter to John Paul II*, London: Marshall Cavendish, 1980.

Ward, Philip (ed.), *The Oxford Companion to Spanish Literature*, Oxford: Clarendon Press, 1978.

Warner, Marina, *Joan of Arc: The Image of Female Heroism*, London: Vintage, 1991.

Webb, Robert L., 'The Passion and the Influence of Emmerich's *The Dolorous Passion of Our Lord Jesus Christ*', in Kathleen E. Corley and Robert L. Webb (eds), *Jesus and Mel Gibson's* The Passion of the Christ: *The Film, the Gospels and the Claims of History*, London: Continuum, 2004, pp. 160–72.

Weber, Derek C. (ed.), *Discerning Images: The Media and Theological Education*, Edinburgh: University of Edinburgh Press, 1991.

Weil, Simone, *Gravity and Grace*, New York, G. P. Putnam & Sons, 1952.

Wills, Gary, *John Wayne's America: The Politics of Celebrity*, New York: Simon and Schuster, 1997.

Wolfe, G., 'Screening Mystery. The Religious Imagination in Contemporary Film', *Image. A Journal of the Arts & Religion*, 20 (1998).

Wright, Will, *Six Guns and Society: A Structural Study of the Western*, Berkeley, CA: University of California Press, 1975.

Wright, M. J., *Moses in America. The Cultural Uses of Biblical Narrative*, AAR Cultural Criticism Series, Oxford: Oxford University Press, 2002.

— 'Lights! Camera! Antisemitism? The Cinema and Jewish–Christian Relations', in E. E. Kessler and M. J. Wright (eds), *Themes in Jewish–Christian Relations*, Cambridge: Orchard Academic, 2004, pp. 171–200.

Yee, Gale A., *Judges and Method: New Approaches in Biblical Studies*, Minneapolis, MN: Fortress Press, 1995.

Ziolkowski, T., *Fictional Transfigurations of Jesus*, Princeton, NJ: Princeton University Press, 1972.

Unattributed articles
'St. Joan', *The Times*, 27 April 1929, 10.
'Joan of Arc. Celebrations in France', *The Times*, 27 April 1929, 13–14.
'Joan of Arc. Celebrations at Chinon', *The Times*, 29 April 1929, 14.
'Film Society: The Passion of Joan of Arc', *The Times*, 17 November 1930, 10.
'Antisemitism', in R. J. Z. Werblowsky and G. Widoger (eds), *The Oxford Dictionary of the Jewish Religion*, New York and Oxford: Oxford University Press, 2001, pp. 16–26.

Appendix 1
Religion, Theology and the Bible in Recent Films (1993–2004)

The cinema has recently presented us with a very rich harvest of films that engage to a greater or lesser extent with religion, theology and the Bible, or which offer scope for religious, biblical, or theological study. The list below is based on an exploration of such films that William Telford presented in a paper at the second St Deiniol's Theology and Film conference (16–18 April 1999) and that was subsequently published in a popular form as an article, 'Religion, the Bible and Theology in Recent Films (1993–99)', *Epworth Review*, 27 (2000): 31–40. The original list (arranged chronologically) contained some 134 films up until 1999, but this has now been updated to December, 2004.

The paper/article subdivided the films into seven categories, reflecting everything from a slight to a major degree of engagement with religion, theology or the Bible. The reader is referred to the article for details. In brief, attention was drawn to the following:

1. At the most basic level, the number of recent films which have made use of a religious, biblical or theological theme or motif in their titles, or as a 'macguffin';
2. The interest in or use made either of the supernatural or the occult, or of myths or stories drawn from religion in general or the Bible in particular;
3. The way in which a number of recent films have used religion as the background, setting or social context for their stories (whether Buddhism, Sufism, Judaism, Islam or Christianity);
4. Their use of religion or the Bible for character definition (Bible-quoting characters, religious characters in general, clergy/holy men);
5. The number and nature of those films which borrow or present treatments, directly or indirectly, of religious or biblical figures (David and Goliath, Moses, Christ-figures, God, the Devil, angels) or which offer imaginative representations of familiar religious or biblical 'locations' like heaven and hell;
6. Their use of religion as a focus for a character's 'journey', development or personal growth (e.g. by means of a conversion, or some kind of transformative encounter or experience);

7. The many films which engage with or otherwise treat religious, biblical or theological themes or concerns, or those which address moral issues or values (e.g. creation, human nature, good and evil, innocence, love, sin, hypocrisy, repentance, confession, forgiveness, acceptance, regeneration, transcendence, suffering, sacrifice, redemption, damnation, death, grief, the afterlife, apocalyptic, etc).

Fearless (Peter Weir, 1993)
In the Name of the Father (Jim Sheridan, 1993)
In weiter Ferne, so nah! (*Faraway, So Close*) (Wim Wenders, 1993)
Little Buddha (Bernardo Bertolucci, 1993)
My Life (Bruce Joel Rubin, 1993)
Philadelphia (Jonathan Demme, 1993)
Schindler's List (Steven Spielberg, 1993)
Shadowlands (Richard Attenborough, 1993)
Tombstone (George P. Cosmatos, 1993)

Butterfly Kiss (Michael Winterbottom, 1994)
Death and the Maiden (Roman Polanski, 1994)
Forrest Gump (Robert Zemeckis, 1994)
Holy Matrimony (Leonard Nemoy, 1994)
Interview with a Vampire. The Vampire Chronicles (Neil Jordan, 1994)
Natural Born Killers (Oliver Stone, 1994)
Nell (Michael Apted, 1994)
Priest (Antonia Bird, 1994)
Pulp Fiction (Quentin Tarantino, 1994)
Sirens (John Duigan, 1994)
Stargate (Roland Emmerich, 1994)
The Addiction (Abel Ferrara, 1994)
The Client (Joel Schumacher, 1994)
The Shawshank Redemption (Frank Darabont, 1994)
Tom and Viv (Brian Gilbert, 1994)

Angels (William Dear, 1995)
Antonia's Line (Marleen Gorris, 1995)
Big Night (Stanley Tucci, Campbell Scott, 1995)
Casino (Martin Scorsese, 1995)
Dead Man Walking (Tim Robbins, 1995)
Eye for an Eye (John Schlesinger, 1995)
La Haine (Matthieu Kassovitz, 1995)
Land and Freedom (Ken Loach, 1995)
Leaving Las Vegas (Mike Figgis, 1995)
Moonlight and Valentino (David Anspaugh, 1995)
Mr Holland's Opus (Stephen Herek, 1995)
Nixon (Oliver Stone, 1995)
Secrets and Lies (Mike Leigh, 1995)
Seven (David Fincher, 1995)
Strange Days (Kathryn Bigelow, 1995)
The Brothers McMullen (Edward Burns, 1995)
The Confessional (Robert Lepage, 1995)
The Crossing Guard (Sean Penn, 1995)
The Last Supper (Cynthia Roberts, 1995)
The Last Supper (Stacy Title, 1995)
The Neon Bible (Terence Davies, 1995)
The Scarlett Letter (Roland Joffé, 1995)
Things to Do in Denver When You're Dead (Gary Fleder, 1995)

A Time to Kill (Joel Schumacher, 1996)

Appendix 1   **349**

Before and After (Barbet Schroeder, 1996)

Box of Moon Light (Tom DiCillo, 1996)

Breaking the Waves (Lars von Trier, 1996)

Carla's Song (Ken Loach, 1996)

Entertaining Angels The Dorothy Day Story (Michael Ray Rhodes, 1996)

Ghosts from the Past (Rob Reiner, 1996)

In Love and War (Richard Attenborough, 1996)

Kissed (Lynn Stopkewich, 1996)

Kolya (Jan Sverák, 1996)

La Vie de Jésus/The Life of Jesus (Bruno Dumont, 1996)

Mary Reilly (Stephen Frears, 1996)

Michael (Nora Ephron, 1996)

Phenomenon (Jon Turteltaub, 1996)

Ponette (Jacques Doillon, 1996)

Shine (Scott Hicks, 1996)

Sleepers (Barry Levinson, 1996)

Some Mother's Son (Terry George, 1996)

The Crucible (Nicholas Hytner, 1996)

The Day of the Beast/El día de la bestia (Alex de la Iglesia, 1996)

The Funeral (Abel Ferrara, 1996)

The Myth of Fingerprints (Bart Freundlich, 1996)

The People vs. Larry Flynt (Milos Forman, 1996)

The Preacher's Wife (Penny Marshall, 1996)

The Winter Guest (Alan Rickman, 1996)

Touch (Paul Schrader, 1996)

A Life Less Ordinary (Danny Boyle, 1997)

A Price above Rubies (Boaz Yakin, 1997)

Affliction (Paul Schrader, 1997)

Alien Resurrection (Jean-Pierre Jeunet, 1997)

Amistad (Steven Spielberg, 1997)

Contact (Robert Zemeckis, 1997)

Devil's Advocate (Taylor Hackford, 1997)

Fairytale A True Story (Charles Sturridge, 1997)

Going All the Way (Mark Pellington, 1997)

Heart (Charles McDougall, 1997)

Kundun (Martin Scorsese, 1997)

L'Arche du desert (Mohamed Chouikh, 1997)

Lawn Dogs (John Duigan, 1997)

Life is Beautiful/La vita è bella (Roberto Benigni, 1997)

Monk Dawson (Tom Waller, 1997)

Mother and Son/Mat I syn/Mutter und Sohn (Aleksandr Sokurov, 1997)

Mrs Brown (John Madden, 1997)

Oscar and Lucinda (Gillian Armstrong, 1997)

Paradise Road (Bruce Beresford, 1997)

π (Darren Aronofsky, 1997)

Photographing Fairies (Nick Willing, 1997)

Regeneration (Gillies MacKinnon, 1997)

Savior (Peter Antonijevic, 1997)

Seven Years in Tibet (Jean-Jacques Annaud, 1997)

Something to Believe In (John Hough, 1997)

The Apostle (Robert Duvall, 1997)

The Blackout (Abel Ferrara, 1997)

The Butcher Boy (Neil Jordan, 1997)

The Fifth Element/La Cinquièm Elément (Luc Besson, 1997)

The Full Monty (Peter Cattaneo, 1997)

The Game (David Fincher, 1997)

The Governess (Sandra Goldbacher, 1997)

The Kingdom [series II]/Riget II (Lars von Trier, 1997)

The Peacemaker (Mimi Leder, 1997)

The Sweet Hereafter (Atom Egoyan, 1997)

Turbulence (Robert Butler, 1997)

Under the Skin (Carine Adler, 1997)

A Civil Action (Steven Zaillian, 1998)
After Life (Hirokazu Koreeda, 1998)
Armageddon (Michael Bay, 1998)
Beloved (Jonathan Demme, 1998)
Blast from the Past (Hugh Wilson, 1998)
Central Station (Walter Salles, 1998)
City of Angels (Brad Silberling, 1998)
Deep Impact (Mimi Leder, 1998)
Eternity and a Day (Theo Angelopoulos, 1998)
Fallen (Gregory Hoblit, 1998)
Hands/Ladoni (Artur Aristakisyan, 1998)
Hideous Kinky (Gillies MacKinnon, 1998)
Holy Man (Stephen Herek, 1998)
Jack Frost (Troy Miller, 1998)
Les Misérables (Bille August, 1998)
Love is the Devil (John Maybury, 1998)
Meet Joe Black (Martin Brest, 1998)
Mercury Rising (Harold Becker, 1998)
My Name is Joe (Ken Loach, 1998)
Pleasantville (Gary Ross, 1998)
Pourquoi pas Moi? (Stéphanie Giusti, 1998)
Prometheus (Tony Harrison, 1998)
Simon Birch (Mark Stephen Johnson, 1998)
Solomon and Gaenor (Paul Morrison, 1998)
Stepmom (Chris Columbus, 1998)
The Acid House (Paul McGuigan, 1998)
The Horse Whisperer (Robert Redford, 1998)
The Loss of Sexual Innocence (Mike Figgis, 1998)
The Prince of Egypt (Brenda Chapman, Steven Hickner, Simon Wells, 1998)
The Thin Red Line (Terrence Malick, 1998)
The Truman Show (Peter Weir, 1998)
What Dreams May Come (Vincent Ward, 1998)

Bicentennial Man (Chris Columbus, 1999)
Boys Don't Cry (Kimberly Peirce, 1999)
Bringing Out the Dead (Martin Scorsese, 1999)
Broken Vessels (Scott Ziehl, 1999)
Dogma (Kevin Smith, 1999)
El Mar (Agustí Villaronga, 1999)
End of Days (Peter Hyams, 1999)
Holy Smoke (Jane Campion, 1999)
Joan of Arc (Luc Besson, 1999)
Kadosh (Amos Gitai, 1999)
Liberty Heights (Barry Levinson, 1999)
Magnolia (Paul Thomas Anderson, 1999)
Play It to the Bone (Ron Shelton, 1999)
Sacred Flesh (Nigel Wingrove, 1999)
Simon Magus (Ben Hopkins, 1999)
Star Wars Episode I The Phantom Menace (George Lucas, 1999)
Stigmata (Rupert Wainwright, 1999)
Sunshine (István Szabó, 1999)
The Big Kahuna (John Swanbeck, 1999)
The Cup (Kyentse Norbu, 1999)
The Darkest Light (Simon Beaufoy and Bille Eltringham, 1999)
The End of the Affair (Neil Jordan, 1999)
The Green Mile (Frank Darabont, 1999)
The Matrix (Andy and Larry Wachowski, 1999)
The Miracle Maker (Derek Hayes, 1999)
The Nine Lives of Tomas Katz (Ben Hopkins, 1999)
The Ninth Gate (Roman Polanski, 1999)
Three Kings (David O. Russell, 1999)

Apocalypse Now Redux (Francis Ford Coppola, 2000)
Bedazzled (Harold Ramis, 2000)
Bless the Child (Chuck Russell, 2000)

Cast Away (Robert Zemeckis, 2000)
Chocolat (Lasse Hallström, 2000)
Divided We Fall (Jan Hrebejk, 2000)
Dracula 2001 (Patrick Lussier, 2000)
Finding Forrester (Gus Van Sant, 2000)
Gladiator (Ridley Scott, 2000)
Keeping the Faith (Edward Norton, 2000)
Liam (Stephen Frears, 2000)
Little Nicky (Steven Brill, 2000)
Lost Souls (Janusz Kaminski, 2000)
O Brother, Where Art Thou? (Joel Coen, 2000)
Offending Angels (Andrew Rajan, 2000)
Original Sin (Michael Cristofer, 2000)
Pay It Forward (Mimi Leder, 2000)
Songs from the Second Floor (Roy Andersson, 2000)
The Body (Jonas McCord, 2000)
The House of Mirth (Terence Davies, 2000)
The Man Who Cried (Sally Potter, 2000)
The Pledge (Sean Penn, 2000)
Time of Favor (Joseph Cedar, 2000)
Unbreakable (M. Knight Shyamalan, 2000)
Under the Sand (François Ozon, 2000)
Very Annie-Mary (Sara Sugarman, 2000)
What Women Want (Nancy Meyers, 2000)

40 Days and 40 Nights (Michael Lehmann, 2001)
A Beautiful Mind (Ron Howard, 2001)
A.I. Artificial Intelligence (Steven Spielberg, 2001)
Amélie (Jean-Pierre Jeunet, 2001)
Ash Wednesday (Edward Burns, 2001)
Asoka (Santosh Sivan, 2001)
Brotherhood of the Wolf (Christophe Gans, 2001)

Donnie Darko (Richard Kelly, 2001)
Dust (Milcho Manchevski, 2001)
Hannibal (Ridley Scott, 2001)
Heaven (Tom Tykwer, 2001)
Kandahar (Mohsen Makhmalbaf, 2001)
K-PAX (Iain Softley, 2001)
Late Marriage (Dover Kosashivili, 2001)
Monster's Ball (Marc Forster, 2001)
Revelation (Stuart Urban, 2001)
The Believer (Henry Bean, 2001)
The Devil's Backbone (Guillermo del Toro, 2001)
The Last Castle (Rod Lurie, 2001)
The Lord of the Rings: The Fellowship of the Ring (Peter Jackson, 2001)
The Man Who Sued God (Mark Joffe, 2001)
The Others (Alejandro Amenábar, 2001)
The Son's Room (Nanni Moretti, 2001)
Twenty-Four Hour Party People (Michael Winterbottom, 2001)
What Time is It There? (Tsai Ming-Liang, 2001)

Amen (Costa-Gavras, 2002)
City of God (Fernando Meirelles, 2002)
Dragonfly (Tom Shadyac, 2002)
Far from Heaven (Todd Haynes, 2002)
Northfork (Michael Polish, 2002)
Road to Perdition (Sam Mendes, 2002)
Signs (M. Knight Shyamalan, 2002)
Solaris (Steven Soderbergh, 2002)
Star Wars Episode II Attack of the Clones (George Lucas, 2002)
The Crime of Padre Amaro (Carlos Carrera, 2002)
The Hours (Stephen Daldry, 2002)
The Lord of the Rings: The Two Towers (Peter Jackson, 2002)
The Magdalene Sisters (Peter Mullan, 2002)

The Pianist (Roman Polanski, 2002)
The Three Marias (Aluizio Abranches, 2002)
Whale Rider (Niki Caro, 2002)
Windtalkers (John Woo, 2002)

21 Grams (Alejandro González Iñárritu, 2003)
A Thousand Months (Faouzi Bensaïdi, 2003)
Bruce Almighty (Tom Shadyac, 2003)
Dogville (Lars von Trier, 2003)
House of Fog and Sand (Vadim Perelman, 2003)
Man Dancin' (Norman Stone, 2003)
Osama (Siddiq Barmak, 2003)
Spring, Summer, Autumn, Winter ... and Spring (Kim Ki-Duk, 2003)
Terminator 3 Rise of the Machines (Jonathan Mostow, 2003)

The Barbarian Invasions (Denys Arcand, 2003)
The Lord of the Rings: The Return of the King (Peter Jackson, 2003)
The Matrix Reloaded (Andy and Larry Wachowski, 2003)
The Matrix Revolutions (Andy and Larry Wachowski, 2003)
The Missing (Ron Howard, 2003)
The Sin Eater (Brian Helgeland, 2003)

Ae Fond Kiss (Ken Loach, 2004)
Bad Education (Pedro Almodóvar, 2004)
Exorcist The Beginning (Renny Harlin, 2004)
My Summer of Love (Pawel Pawlikowski, 2004)
Saved! (Brian Dannelly, 2004)
The Passion of the Christ (Mel Gibson, 2004)

Appendix 2
Christ-Figures in Film

In a recent paper (as yet unpublished) for the St Deiniol's Theology and Film conference (16–18 April, 2004), entitled 'Searching for Jesus: Recognizing or Imagining Christ-Figures in the Movies', William Telford reviewed the Christ-figures claimed to have been recognized in films and explored the question of what constitutes genuine 'recognition' and what constitutes mere 'imagination' in the alleged detection of such figures. Below is a filmography incorporating a list of suggested Christ-figures from recent literature. For further reading, the following will be found useful:

Baugh, L., *Imaging the Divine. Jesus and Christ-Figures in Film*, Kansas City, MO: Sheed and Ward, 1997.

Detweiler, R., 'Christ and the Christ Figure in American Fiction' in M. E. Marty and D. G. Peerman (eds), *New Theology No. 2*, New York: Macmillan, 1965, pp. 297–316.

Fraser, P., *Images of the Passion. The Sacramental Mode in Film*, Trowbridge, Wilts: Flicks Books, 1998.

Hurley, N. P., 'Cinematic Transformations of Jesus' in J. R. May and M. S. Bird (eds), *Religion in Film*, Knoxville: University of Tennessee Press, 1982, pp. 61–78.

Malone, P., *Movie Christs and Antichrists*, New York: Crossroad, 1990.

Malone, P., 'Jesus on our Screens' in J. R. May (ed.), *New Image of Religious Film*, Kansas City, MO: Sheed and Ward, 1997, pp. 57–71.

Tatum, W. B., *Jesus at the Movies: A Guide to the First Hundred Years*, Santa Rosa, CA: Polebridge, 1997, Appendix.

Ziolkowski, T., *Fictional Transfigurations of Jesus*, Princeton, NJ: Princeton University Press, 1972.

Accattone (Pier Paolo Pasolini, 1961) {Accattone}

Alien Resurrection (Jean-Pierre Jeunet, 1997) {Ripley}

Antonia's Line (Marleen Gorris, 1995) {Antonia}

Au hasard, Balthazar (Robert Bresson, 1966) {Balthazar}

Babette's Feast (Gabriel Axel, 1987) {Babette Hersant}

Being There (Hal Ashby, 1979) {Chauncey Gardener/Chance}

Ben Hur (William Wyler, 1959) {Ben Hur}

Box of Moon Light (Tom DiCillo, 1996) {the Kid}

Bram Stoker's Dracula (Francis Ford Coppola, 1992) {Vlad/Dracula}

Braveheart (Mel Gibson, 1995) {Willam Wallace}

Breaking the Waves (Lars von Trier, 1996) {Bess}
Cape Fear (Martin Scorsese, 1991) {Max Cady}
City Lights (Charles Chaplin, 1931) {The Tramp}
Cool-Hand Luke (Stuart Rosenberg, 1967) {Luke}
Cries and Whispers (Ingmar Bergman, 1972) {Agnes}
Dead Man Walking (Tim Robbins, 1995) {Sister Helen Prejean}
Dead Poet's Society (Peter Weir, 1989) {John Keating}
Destination Unknown (Tay Garnett, 1933) {the Stranger}
Diary of a Country Priest (Robert Bresson, 1950) {the Priest}
Die Hard (John McTiernan, 1988) {John McClane}
Edward Scissorhands (Tim Burton, 1990) {Edward Scissorhands}
The Elephant Man (David Lynch, 1980) {John Merrick}
End of Days (Peter Hyams, 1999) {Jericho Cane}
ET-the Extra-Terrestrial (Steven Spielberg, 1982) {E.T.}
The Face (Ingmar Bergman, 1958) {the Mesmerist}
Fearless (Peter Weir, 1993) {Max Klein}
The Fifth Element (La Cinquième Elément) (Luc Besson, 1997) {Leeloo}
The Fugitive (John Ford, 1947) {the Priest}
The Full Monty (Peter Cattaneo, 1997) {Gaz, the Robert Carlyle character}
The Good, the Bad and the Ugly (Sergio Leone, 1966) {the Clint Eastwood character}
The Green Mile (Frank Darabont, 1999) {John Coffey}
Hannibal (2001) {Hannibal Lecter}
He Who Must Die (Jules Dassin, 1956) {Manolis}

High Noon (Fred Zinnemann, 1952) {Will Kane}
The Hunchback of Notre Dame (William Dieterle, 1939) {the deformed bellringer}
Interview with a Vampire (Neil Jordan, 1994) {Louis, the Brad Pitt character}
In the Name of the Father (Jim Sheridan, 1993) {Guiseppe Conlon}
Jesus of Montreal (Denys Arcand, 1989) {Daniel Colombe}
Kolya (Jan Sverák, 1996) {the child, Kolya}
La Strada (Federico Fellini, 1954) {Gelsomina}
Lawn Dogs (John Duigan, 1997) {Trent Burns}
Lethal Weapon (Richard Donner, 1987) {Martin Riggs}
Magnolia (Paul Thomas Anderson, 1999) {Frank Mackey}
Man Facing Southeast (Eliseo Subiela, 1986) {Rantes}
The Man Who Fell to Earth (Nicholas Roeg, 1976) {Newton}
The Mask of Zorro (Martin Campbell, 1998) {Zorro}
The Matrix (Andy & Larry Wachowski, 1999) {Neo Anderson}
Monty Python's Life of Brian (Terry Jones, 1979) {Brian}
Nell (Michael Apted, 1994) {Jerry Lovell}
Nights of Cabiria (Federico Fellini, 1957) {Cabiria}
One Flew over the Cuckoo's Nest (Milos Forman, 1975) {Randle P. McMurphy}
On the Waterfront (Elia Kazan, 1954) {Terry Malloy}
Ordet (The Word) (Carl Dreyer, 1957) {Johannes}
The Outlaw Josey Wales (Clint Eastwood, 1976) {Josey Wales}
Out of Rosenheim (Bagdad Cafe) (Percy Adlon, 1988) {Jasmin Münchgstettner}

Pale Rider (Clint Eastwood, 1985)
{Preacher}

The Passing of the Third Floor Back
(Berthold Biertel, 1935) {the
Stranger}

Patch Adams (Tom Shadyac, 1998)
{Patch Adams}

Phenomenon (John Turteltaub, 1996)
{George Malley}

Platoon (Oliver Stone, 1986)
{Chris}

Powder (Victor Salva, 1995)
{Jeremy Reed/Powder}

Pulp Fiction (Quentin Tarantino,
1994) {Jules Winnfield}

Raging Bull (Martin Scorsese, 1980)
{Jake La Motta}

Raiders of the Lost Ark (Steven
Spielberg, 1981) {Indiana Jones}

Rocky (John G. Avildsen, 1976)
{Rocky Balboa}

Romero (John Duigan, 1989)
{Archbishop Oscar Arnulfo
Romero}

The Ruling Class (Peter Medak, 1972)
{Jack, 14th Earl of Gurney}

The Saint of Fort Washington (Tim
Hunter, 1994) {Matthew}

Schindler's List (Steven Spielberg,
1993) {Oskar Schindler}

Serpico (Sidney Lumet, 1973) {Frank
Serpico}

The Seventh Sign (Carl Schultz, 1988)
{David}

Shane (George Stevens, 1953) {Shane}

The Shawshank Redemption (Frank
Darabont, 1994) {Andy Dufresne}

A Short Film about Love (Krzysztof
Kieslowski, 1988) {Tomek}

The Sixth Sense (M. Night Shyamalan,
2000) {Cole}

Sling Blade (Billy Bob Thornton,
1996) {Karl Childers}

Some Mother's Son (Terry George,
1996) {Bobby Sands}

Spartacus (Stanley Kubrick, 1960)
{Spartacus}

The Spitfire Grill (Lee David Zlotoff,
1996) {Percy Talbott}

Star Wars (George Lucas, 1977) {Obi-
Wan Kenobi}

Strange Cargo (Frank Borzage, 1942)
{Cambreau}

Superman (Richard Donner, 1978)
{Clark Kent/Superman}

Taxi Driver (Martin Scorsese, 1976)
{Travis Bickle}

The Truman Show (Peter Weir, 1998)
{Truman}

The Year of Living Dangerously
(Peter Weir, 1982) {Billy Kwan}

Whistle down the Wind (Bryan
Forbes, 1961) {Arthur Blakey/
The Man}

Index of Names: Actors, Authors and Directors

Index of Subjects

Abelard 314
Action Française 72
ambiguity 69, 112, 118, 121,
    143, 151, 152–3, 155, 157,
    162–6, 164, 208, 261–2, 285,
    309–10
American church history 239,
    241, 247–8, 249–50
American dream 155, 160, 162,
    270, 271–2
American monomyth 192, 196,
    197
American Restoration Movement
    249,
    see also Radical Reformation
American west 185–6, 196–7, 199,
    see also westerns
androids 139–40, 141, 142, 144
animation 171–3, 178
Anselm 314, 320
anti-heroes 187, 188, 199
anti-Judaism *see* antisemitism
antisemitism 133, 134, 219,
    266–7, 273, 282, 283, 286, 312,
    325–7
apocalypse 92, 137, 138, 143,
    144, 318
atheism 102, 107, 137
auteur theory 20, 22, 28, 37,
    45–6, 57, 82
authenticity 66, 321–4, 326

Basement Room, The 127
belief 137, 145–7
betrayal 124–8, 129, 131,

see also Judas, Peter
biblical epics 214–215, 272–3
biblical studies approach 29
'Bishop Bloughman's Apology'
    132
Blade Runner (novel) 139, 140–1,
    143
blasphemy 101, 102, 104
body, the 138, 143
    female 49–50, 51
    male 50–1
Breen, Joseph 155, 156
Brighton Rock 127, 132
Buñuel and Christianity 94, 98–9,
    104, 105–8
Burnt Out Case, A 132

camera angle of vision 84–5, 87,
    see also lenses of film reading,
    camera shots; Steadicam
Capone, Al 113
Catholic Church 71, 74, 282
Catholic Legion of Decency 223,
    228, 274, 297
Catholic technical terms 102
Catholicism 125, 131, 132
    in Franco's Spain 106
chaos 90
chiaroscuro 153, 154, 259
childhood 124–5
Christ 169, 189, 190, 296, 301–2,
    see also Christ-figures, Christology
Christ-figures 31, 34, 174, 192,
    317,
    see also American monomyth

regard, la see gaze
rehabilitation 216, 217, 219
religion 90, 140–1, 143, 179,
  255, 256–7
religious art 45, 72, 301, 316,
  see also *Last Supper* (da Vinci);
  *The Twelve Year Old Jesus in
  the Temple*
religious context 72–3, 322
religious studies approach 27–9
repentance 143–4, 145, 146, 147
revivalism 254, 255, 256, 257,
  263
Romano-Christian epics 226
Rosza, Miklos 228

sacramental approach 33–4
sacrilege 101, 102
salvation 185
Sandburg, Carl 305
Satan 6, 134, 135, 142, 217, 313,
  314, 318
satire 98, 100, 102, 209, 310
semiotics 22, 146
simulacrum 137, 138, 143, 144,
  145, 147
Smolka, Peter 130, 131
Smollett, Peter see Smolka, Peter
social context 209, 210, 246, 267,
  300–1, 306
social science approach 72
Société Général des Films 65, 73
sociology and ethnography 23
son of man 145, 147, 302, 305
Sopranos, The 112
Spain 94, 98–9, 105, 106,
  see also Catholicism

spectacle 52–5, 57
spectatorship 23–4, 46–7, 49
spiritual approach 33, 47
Steadicam 87–8
stereotyping 50, 189, 191, 219,
  267, 273, 285, 323
surrealism 94, 102, 103, 145, 257
synchronic approach 20–1

text-based theories 20
textual analysis 21
thematic criticism 22, 68, 69–71
theological approaches 27, 32–4,
  168–71, 182
theology 15, 26, 168–9, 246, 311
  atonement 313–14, 320
  and film 27, 169
  and *Passion of The Christ, The*
  328
  practical 182
transcendence 28, 168, 169, 170,
  171, 308
*Twelve Year Old Jesus in the
  Temple, The* 101

Vatican II 328, 329
Via Vecchia 115, 116, 117
Vienna, post-war 131
violence 110, 194, 199, 206,
  207–8, 209, 319–21
Viper of Milan, The 124
voyeurism 23, 49, 86,
  see also gaze

Wallace, William 317
westerns 183–97, 199–210
  motifs 202, 203
World Council of Churches 185

Index of Films: Title, Director and Year